GREATER TUNIS
AND CAP BON

GREATER TUNIS
AND CAP BON
PENINSULA
Pages 90–121

THE SAHEL
Pages 144–173

JERBA AND THE
MEDENINE
AREA
Pages 174–189

EYEWITNESS TRAVEL GUIDES

TUNISIA

ELŻBIETA AND ANDRZEJ LISOWSCY

DK

916.1105
WS

DK

LONDON, NEW YORK,
MELBOURNE, MUNICH AND DELHI
www.dk.com

Produced by Wydawnictwo Wiedza i Życie, Warsaw

SENIOR GRAPHIC DESIGNER Paweł Pasternak
EDITORS Robert G. Pasieczny,
Joanna Egert-Romanowska, Agnieszka Majle
AUTHORS Andrzej and Elżbieta Lisowscy
GRAPHIC DESIGN Paweł Kamiński, Piotr Kiedrowski

CARTOGRAPHERS Magdalena Polak, Olaf Rodowald
PHOTOGRAPHERS Artur Pawłowski,
Nicolas Fauque, Krzysztof Kur
ILLUSTRATORS Bohdan Wróblewski,
Michał Burkiewicz, Paweł Marczak
CONTRIBUTORS MaDar sc
and Sabina Kocieszczenko

For Dorling Kindersley

TRANSLATOR Magda Hannay
EDITOR Matthew Tanner
SENIOR DTP DESIGNER Jason Little
PRODUCTION CONTROLLER Rita Sinha

Reproduced by Colourscan, Singapore
Printed and bound in by L-Rex Printing Company Ltd., China

First American Edition, 2005
05 06 07 08 10 9 8 7 6 5 4 3 2 1

Published in the United States by DK Publishing, Inc.,
375 Hudson Street, New York, New York 10014

Copyright 2005 © Dorling Kindersley Limited, London

Published in Great Britain by Dorling Kindersley Limited.

ISSN 1542-1554

ISBN 0-7566-0912-7

**The information in this
Dorling Kindersley Travel Guide is checked regularly.**
Every effort has been made to ensure that this book is as up-to-date
as possible at the time of going to press. Some details, however,
such as telephone numbers, opening hours, prices, gallery hanging
arrangements and travel information are liable to change. The publishers
cannot accept responsibility for any consequences arising from the
use of this book, nor for any material on third party websites,
and cannot guarantee that any website address in this book
will be a suitable source of travel information. We value the views and
suggestions of our readers very highly. Please write to:
Publisher, DK Eyewitness Travel Guides
Dorling Kindersley, 80 Strand, London WC2R 0RL, Great Britain

◁ **Mosque in Chenini – a town built on rocky terraces**

CONTENTS

HOW TO USE
THIS GUIDE *6*

**Ruins of a Roman temple on the
capitol hill in Dougga**

INTRODUCING
TUNISIA

PUTTING TUNISIA ON
THE MAP *10*

A PORTRAIT OF TUNISIA
12

TUNISIA THROUGH
THE YEAR *38*

**Comfortable tents for visitors in
Ksar Ghilane**

Tourist centre in Port el-Kantaoui

SURVIVAL GUIDE

PRACTICAL
INFORMATION *310*

TRAVEL INFORMATION
320

GENERAL INDEX *328*

ACKNOWLEDGMENTS
348

GLOSSARY *350*

THE HISTORY OF
TUNISIA *44*

**TUNISIA REGION
BY REGION**

TUNISIA AT A GLANCE
62

**TRAVELLERS'
NEEDS**

WHERE TO STAY *244*

WHERE TO EAT *266*

SHOPPING IN TUNISIA
290

ENTERTAINMENT IN
TUNISIA *298*

SPORT IN TUNISIA *302*

ACTIVITIES FOR
VISITORS *304*

Vegetable stall at Menzel
Temime market

ROAD MAP OF TUNISIA
Inside back cover

Seafood – a mainstay of Tunisian
cuisine

TUNIS *64*

GREATER TUNIS AND
CAP BON PENINSULA *90*

NORTHERN TUNISIA *122*

THE SAHEL *144*

JERBA AND THE
MEDENINE AREA *174*

SOUTHERN TUNISIA *190*

CENTRAL TUNISIA *212*

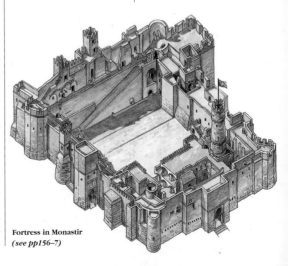
Fortress in Monastir
(see pp156–7)

HOW TO USE THIS GUIDE

THIS GUIDE WILL HELP you to make the most of your visit to Tunisia. The first section, *Introducing Tunisia*, locates the country geographically and gives an outline of its history and culture. The following sections are devoted to the country's capital and various regions, and include the major towns, sights and attractions. Information on accommodation, restaurants, shopping, entertainment and activities can be found in the *Travellers' Needs* section, while the *Survival Guide* provides practical tips on everything you need to know, from money and language to getting around and seeking medical care.

TUNIS
The country's capital has its own section. All the sights are located and numbered on the area map. The main streets, bus stations and railway stations, car parks and tourist offices are also shown.

Sights at a Glance lists the sights in an area, in alphabetical order.

Visitors' Checklist provides practical information to help you plan your visit.

1 Town Map
For easy reference the major sights are numbered and located on the town map.

Suggested route for a walk is marked with a red dotted line.

2 Street-by-Street Map
Shows the location of the main museums and sights within the town centre including mosques and historic buildings.

3 Detailed Information
All the major sights in Tunis have a separate entry that includes details of addresses, opening hours and any admission charges.

1 Introduction
This section provides a brief overview of each region, describing its history, geographical features and cultural characteristics as well as its main attractions.

TUNISIA REGION BY REGION
In this guide Tunisia is divided into six regions, each of which has its own section. The most important cities, towns and villages, as well as other major attractions, are marked on the Area Map.

2 Area Map
The map shows the main road network and the overall topography of the region. All sights are numbered, and there is also information on public transport.

Colour coding, explained on the inside front cover, makes it easy to locate each region.

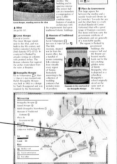

3 Regional Information
Towns, villages and tourist attractions are listed in numerical order, corresponding with the Area Map. Each entry contains information on important sights. Major towns are given at least two pages.

Detailed plans give a bird's-eye view of an interesting sightseeing area described in this section.

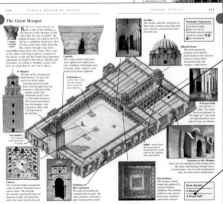

4 Star Sights
At least two pages are devoted to each major sight. Historic buildings are dissected to reveal their interiors.

Star Attractions suggest some main points of interest that no visitor should miss.

Introducing Tunisia

Putting Tunisia on the Map 10-11
A Portrait of Tunisia 12-37
Tunisia Through the Year 38-43
The History of Tunisia 44-59

Putting Tunisia on the Map

Mediterranean Sea

THE NORTHERNMOST POINT of the African continent, Tunisia is sandwiched between Algeria to the west and Libya to the east. Some 1,300 km (800 miles) of Mediterranean coastline mark the country's eastern and northern boundaries. Covering an area of 163,610 sq km (63,170 sq miles), Tunisia measures 150 km (93 miles) from east to west. It has a wide diversity of landscapes, ranging from its northern mountainous region to the fertile Medjerda Valley and, in the south, a region of desert.

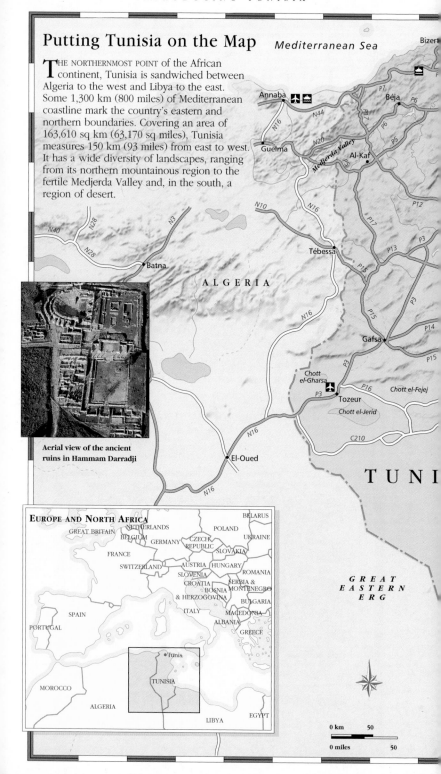

Aerial view of the ancient ruins in Hammam Darradji

Bizert

Annaba

Béja

P7

P6

Guelma

N44

N20

Al-Kaf

Medjerda Valley

N16

N10

N16

N16

N40

N28

N28

N3

P5

P12

P17

Batna

Tébessa

P13

P3

ALGERIA

P15

N16

P15

P3

Gafsa

P14

P15

Chott el-Gharsa

P3

P16

Chott el-Fejej

Tozeur

Chott el-Jerid

N16

C210

El-Oued

N16

T U N I

EUROPE AND NORTH AFRICA

GREAT BRITAIN

NETHERLANDS
BELGIUM
GERMANY
CZECH REPUBLIC

POLAND

BELARUS

UKRAINE

FRANCE

SWITZERLAND

SLOVAKIA

AUSTRIA HUNGARY

SLOVENIA
CROATIA
BOSNIA
& HERZOGOVINA

ROMANIA

SERBIA & MONTENEGRO

BULGARIA

SPAIN

ITALY

MACEDONIA

ALBANIA

GREECE

PORTUGAL

Tunis

TUNISIA

MOROCCO

ALGERIA

LIBYA

EGYPT

G R E A T
E A S T E R N
E R G

0 km   50

0 miles   50

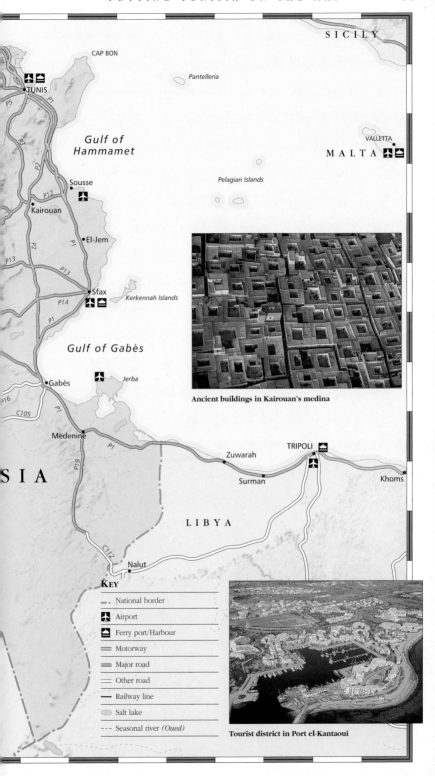

SICILY

CAP BON

Pantelleria

TUNIS

Gulf of Hammamet

Sousse

Kairouan

El-Jem

Pelagian Islands

VALLETTA

MALTA

Sfax

Kerkennah Islands

Gulf of Gabès

Gabès

Jerba

Medenine

Ancient buildings in Kairouan's medina

Zuwarah

TRIPOLI

Surman

Khoms

SIA

LIBYA

Nalut

KEY

- National border
- Airport
- Ferry port/Harbour
- Motorway
- Major road
- Other road
- Railway line
- Salt lake
- Seasonal river *(Oued)*

Tourist district in Port el-Kantaoui

A PORTRAIT OF TUNISIA

O F ALL THE NORTH AFRICAN COUNTRIES, *Tunisia is the most visitor-friendly. Its attractions include the walled medinas of Tunis and Sousse, historic remains at Bulla Regia and Dougga, and Jerba's glorious beaches. For the more adventurous, there is much to explore including ancient troglodyte villages, the glimmering Chott el-Jerid salt flats and the vast expanse of the Sahara Desert.*

The history of Tunisia has been shaped by the Phoenicians, Romans, Turks, Berbers and – above all – the Arabs. The mountainous north acts as the country's garden, providing cereals, vegetables and fruit. This area has many Phoenician and Roman remains, and includes the once-mighty Carthage. In contrast to the fertile north, the yellow-red desert in the south is almost completely deprived of rain. Here, Tozeur and Nefta are fascinating towns that have grown up around desert oases. Nefta, surrounded by desert sands, once provided a refuge for Muslim mystics, and now produces the best dates in

A tombstone from Carthage

Tunisia. Even further south there is nothing but desert – an endless sea of hot sand. Many visitors flock to "blue" Tunisia, to enjoy the warm waters and beaches of Hammamet, Sousse and Jerba, but the country has much more to offer.

Tunisia's colourful past has left it rich in historical remains. These include the sites of Phoenician and Roman Carthage, the ruins of the Punic town of Kerkouane, the Roman remains at Dougga, the amphitheatre at El-Jem, the holy city of Kairouan and the magnificent medinas of Tunis and Sousse where Islamic architecture dating back more than 1,000 years can be seen.

Green fields and olive groves around Testour

◁ **Women walking by the medina wall in Kairouan**

Cobbler in a souk in Tozeur

SOCIETY

Tunisia has a population of almost 10 million and the vast majority of the country's inhabitants, some 98 per cent, is of Arab stock. Nearly all are Muslim, though there is a tiny percentage of Jews and Christians. The original Berbers make up a small part of the population and are found mainly in the south of the country.

Tunisian society is young; the average age is 26 and slightly over one quarter of the population is under the age of 15. A family planning policy introduced in the 1960s has brought about a steady fall in the birth rate and the model of the Tunisian family has gradually changed since independence. It is now becoming common for Tunisian

An indoor vegetable stall

women to go out to work. As a result of factors such as these, families living in the major towns and cities are generally smaller in size than those in the villages.

Tunisia has a modern and well-developed education system; primary education is compulsory and a great deal of importance is attached to learning foreign languages in school. Nearly three-quarters of the population is literate.

CULTURE AND TRADITIONS

Tunisia's busy tourist areas show many signs of western influence, including fast food, modern pop music and the latest fashions. Elsewhere, traditional life has developed at a gentler pace and the mosque and bathhouse (hammam) are still important parts of everyday life. Tunisian culture has evolved over the generations through an intermingling of strands from both European and Arab traditions. Successive cultures, rather than simply supplanting their predecessors, blended with them to produce a wonderfully diverse social and cultural melting pot. This blend is most clearly manifested in Tunisian music, which displays Berber and Andalusian influences (these also have echoes in modern Tunisian pop music).

Berber dressed in traditional *djellaba* and turban

Tunisian literature is mainly associated with Arabic writing (*see pp32–3*). In its early days, it consisted primarily of theological and historic works. The 20th century saw an increase in the popularity of Tunisian writers expressing themselves in French. The most famous modern Tunisian writer is Abu el-Kacem el-Chabbi (1909–34), a native of Tozeur, whose poem "Will to Live" is taught to schoolchildren throughout the Arab world.

Though open to foreign ideas, Tunisian society is very protective of its traditions. The *hijab* (veil or headscarf) is often seen on the streets of Tunisia, though it is more common in rural areas. Muslim festivals are celebrated with due ceremony in Tunisia,

Modern Tunisian painting by Ali ben Salem

particularly two feasts known as Aïd el-Adha and Aïd el-Fitr *(see p39).* Ramadan – the month of fasting from sunrise to sunset – is strictly observed. As with most Islamic countries, family is particularly important in Tunisian society and relatives are expected to celebrate festivities together, as well as help one another.

An Early Christian relief

THE ARTS

Pottery and ceramic arts have flourished since Roman times and have been enriched by Andalusian and Italian influences. Ancient Tunisian mosaics are justly famous and a great many have been found, some of which date back to

the 2nd century AD. Most places of any size in 3rd-century Tunisia had a mosaic workshop producing wonderfully colourful designs with a distinctive African influence including scenes of hunting and wildlife, which were used mainly as floor decorations. From these early beginnings, mosaics have become one of the main decorative elements of Tunisian architecture.

Many public buildings, including hammams, kasbahs and, above all, mosques are works of art in their own right. All are based on Islamic styles and motifs and include elaborately decorated doorways, bright colours and striking minarets.

Influenced by the French and Italians, painting has become a popular art form in Tunisia. The year 1949 marked the birth of the most famous Tunisian school of painting – the École de Tunis. Its pioneers combined new trends in art with scenes from everyday life, and introduced modern art to Tunisia. Yahia Turki, an early member of this school, is considered by

Stonemason at work

many to be the father of modern Tunisian painting. The traditional Arab-style music that visitors are likely to hear is *malouf* (which means "normal"). It was first introduced in the 15th century by refugees from Andalusia. Using a mixture of western and Arab instruments, it is a lively blend of Hispanic and Arabic folk music.

Equestrian statue of Bourguiba

by a democratic vote. The government and the prime minister are responsible to the country's elected president. Tunisia's presidential role carries supreme executive power and has overall command of the armed forces.

Despite making a number of major reforms, Habib Bourguiba eventually lost touch with his people and the Arab world in general and in 1987 he was replaced by his Interior Minister Zine el-Abidine ben Ali. This change marked a turning point in the history of modern Tunisia. Ben Ali abolished life presidencies and introduced a multi-party system. At present there are seven political parties in Tunisia. The most powerful of these is the ruling party, the Democratic-Constitutional Assembly (RCD), which is still led by Ben Ali. A number of other parties also enjoy popular support including the Democratic-Socialist Movement (MDS) and the Communist Party.

MODERN-DAY POLITICS

Tunisia is a constitutional republic and won its independence from France on 20 March 1956 with Habib Bourguiba, a French-educated lawyer, as its first president. Three years later, Tunisia's assembly passed a constitution that put a lot of power in the hands of the president and gave the country a legal system based on a mixture of French civil law and Islamic law. Under this constitution, which has undergone a series of reforms over the years, the members of the National Assembly are elected for five-year terms

Posters of President Ben Ali, on the streets of Nabeul

Women on the beach in La Goulette

WOMEN IN TUNISIA

Thanks in large part to the influence of Tunisia's former president, Habib Bourguiba, the freedom allowed to Tunisian women is greater than in most Muslim countries. In 1956 he outlawed such practices as polygamy and divorce by renunciation and banned the *hijab* (veil) from schools as part of an (unsuccessful) campaign to phase it out altogether.

Islamic groups have been eliminated from the political life of the country. The law disallows registration of any party whose manifesto is based on religious or ethnic principles.

Tunisia has played an important role in North African affairs, as well as mediating in the Israeli-Palestinian conflict. It has also exerted a major influence in promoting regional economic co-operation.

During the 1990 Gulf War public opinion in Tunisia was strongly behind the former Iraqi leader Saddam Hussein. Ben Ali condemned Iraq for its invasion of Kuwait but felt unable to fully support the United States' action. Tunisia also withheld its support during the most recent Iraq conflict. However, Ben Ali has long strived to maintain cordial relations with the West and his party continues to have a broadly pro-Western policy. In 1995, Ben Ali signed up to an agreement with the European Union (EU) which agreed to respect the principles of human rights and democracy.

Women in Tunisia have far more opportunities to work than in many Muslim countries and these days it is not unusual for women to be doctors, lawyers and airline pilots. Since 1961, as a result of the family planning policy, pharmacies have begun to sell methods of contraception. The signing of further conventions during the 1980s ensured women's rights to education, and to equal pay. What this adds up to is that the problems faced by Tunisian women are not so different from those faced by women in the West.

Berber woman in traditional attire

In the villages, however, where many traditional norms still apply, the situation can be somewhat different. If in work, it is not unusual for women to hand over all of their pay directly to their husbands or (if unmarried) save their wages towards a dowry. And even though many women can be seen socializing in some of the European-style cafés, they are a

The old and new: women in the street in Bizerte

less common sight in traditional Tunisian cafés, which are normally occupied by pipe-smoking, card-playing men. But overall, the situation of women has improved vastly since the country gained independence.

ECONOMY

Tunisia's economy is based on agriculture, power generation, tourism and the service industry. Tunisia is the world's largest producer of dates (a fact not reflected in its export figures) and the fourth largest producer of olive oil. Mining also plays an important part in the country's economy and Tunisia is among the world's leading producers of phosphates.

Agricultural land occupies nearly half of the country's total area. The main crops include cereals, olives,

Tunisian craftsmen, important contributors to the economy

tomatoes, oranges, dates, pomegranates, grapes and sugar cane. The agricultural sector has declined in the last few years, however, and Tunisia now imports 40 per cent of its food.

The country's natural resources include phosphate rock, oil and natural gas (in the south), as well as iron, lead and zinc ores.

The processing of olive oil, petro-chemicals and ceramics account for a significant portion of the country's economy, as does the production of handicrafts (including carpets, jewellery and tourist souvenirs). Fishing brings in additional income and is based mainly on tuna, sardines and mackerel.

By far the largest share of Tunisia's national revenue comes from the textile industry with most exports going to France, the USA, Italy and Germany. In 1995 Tunisia signed an agreement with the EU that opened up new markets. Under this agreement, trade tariffs should one day be dropped, leading to free trade between Tunisia and the EU. The current Tunisian government is hoping that this move might eventually encourage some much needed foreign investment in the country.

An oil well, producing one of Tunisia's natural resources

TOURISM

Tourism is a major source of the country's income. Since 1998, Tunisia has allocated over 300 million dinars a year to developing its tourism infrastructure. The country now attracts some five million visitors annually. This number of visitors generates nearly $2 billion a year for the economy. The

A covered souk in Tunis – popular with both locals and tourists

700 or so hotels, major international airports and passenger ports connecting Tunisia to Europe (and to the USA via Casablanca) mean that demand can be met.

The country's 1,300 km (800 miles) of coastline and the coral reef around Tabarka makes Tunisia a good destination for those who want a beach holiday. The many historic sites are also a big draw, of course, especially for holidaymakers interested in ancient history. For sports lovers, there are the championship-quality golf courses, and the many opportunities for hiking, horse riding, camel-trekking, fishing and diving.

A decorated jar from Nabeul

To cope with the demand, tourist zones *(zones touristiques)* have been created to give visitors an added feeling of safety and comfort within holiday villages. These offer a high standard of accommodation, lush surroundings, easy access to the beaches, large swimming pool complexes, an easy-going atmosphere and lively entertainment. Their major disadvantage, however, is that they offer little of the culture and everyday life of Tunisia.

Tourism has also been boosted by the many film-makers who have used the country's stunning landscape and architecture in the making of films such as *Star Wars (see pp34–5)*.

A popular beach in the tourist resort of Tabarka

Tunisia's Landscape and Wildlife

SEEN FROM THE AIR, Tunisia appears as a golden-brown land interwoven with green and blue. The mountainous north is overgrown with oak forests and heather. The Medjerda Valley, irrigated by Tunisia's largest permanent river, is used for growing corn and is one of Tunisia's most fertile regions. The craggy northern coast is extraordinarily picturesque, while the eastern shores, with their sandy beaches, are home to most of Tunisia's hotels and coastal resorts. In contrast to the fertile north, Tunisia's flat, southern desert region is almost totally devoid of rain.

Desert area, sparsely covered with palms, at the foot of the mountains near Toujane

SAHARA DESERT

Tunisia's desert covers the southern tip of the country. A sea of sand *(erg)*, it is formed of the eastern extremity of the Great Eastern Erg (or "Grand Erg Oriental") which extends over a large part of eastern Algeria. This inhospitable area is more commonly known as the Sahara Desert. Parts of it can go for years without rain and the rainfall in this region never exceeds 50 mm (1.96 inches) per year.

The fennec, a desert fox with large ears, is regarded as the most voracious predatory mammal of the Sahara. It hunts at night, feeding on beetles, rodents and birds' eggs. During the day it hides in cool burrows.

Rocky desert occupies the large central region of the country. It is overgrown with spiky esparto grass, which is used in the production of high-quality paper.

Sahara in the classic Arabic language means "empty area". Later, it also began to mean an area devoid of water – a desert. You can drive for many miles here and not see a single plant.

Chott el-Jerid – this dry salty lake bed can turn into a boggy morass covered by shallow pools of water that take on a variety of bright colours.

OUED

A *oued* (pronounced "wed") is a riverbed. Parched during the dry season, it fills with water with the arrival of the rains. Often with craggy banks, it can run for many miles. The waters may swell suddenly – a single downpour is enough to flood a *oued* in a flash, with the turbulent flow gouging out the valley and altering the shape of the bed. Following rain, the banks of the *oued* burst forth with vegetation.

Roman bridge over a *oued*, near Sbeïtla

THE COAST

Tunisia has two types of coastline: rocky in the north and, in the east, sandy shores that gently descend towards the Mediterranean Sea. The country's long stretch of coast is extended by marshland and seasonal lakes that adjoin the sea. Tunisia has plenty of sandy beaches. These are found mainly on the east coast, in the regions of Hammamet, Gabès, Jerba, and on the Kerkennah Islands, as well as in the northeast – along the Gulf of Tunis and between Bizerte and El-Haouaria. The extraordinarily picturesque north coast, stretching from Bizerte into Algeria, has high rugged cliffs. Coral reefs, rich in marine life, can be found here that are unique to this part of the Mediterranean.

Sandy beaches, used mainly by visitors, are found to the east. Here there are tourist zones (zones touristiques), which have facilities and entertainment laid on. The beaches on Tunisia's north coast around Tabarka are far less frequently visited.

The craggy coastline around El-Haouaria dropping steeply into the sea creates small picturesque coves.

Oyster-catchers are one of many species of wading bird found along the sandy regions of the coast.

Rocks in Tabarka display some of the most striking geological formations found along the north coast.

CENTRAL REGIONS

The landscape of the interior is somewhat harsh, its colours faded. To the north is the Tell region, separated from the Tunisian Atlas range of mountains by the Medjerda River. Tell forms the western end of the Atlas range that runs east from Morocco. Its western section comprises agricultural land. The southern part of the central region has two salt lakes – Chott el-Jerid and Chott el-Gharsa – which are dry for much of the year.

Mountain oases and palm oases are features of the Tunisian landscape. The roads leading to them are often extremely picturesque and wind among volcanic rocks.

The northwestern and western regions are among the greenest corners of Tunisia, with extensive fields and wooded hills.

Prickly pear, cultivated in the western region of Tunisia, iss also a popular hedge plant. It can grow to a height of 7 m (23 ft) and forms an impenetrable barrier.

Olive groves are found in the eastern parts of the central region and on the coast. Olives, planted here in even rows, are an important part of Tunisia's economy.

Tunisian Architecture

A LONGSIDE THE OBVIOUS PRESENCE of Islam, Tunisian architecture includes a variety of influences. The earliest of these can be seen in the Roman and Punic remains that are scattered throughout the northern regions and along the coast. Much later, the colonial era brought with it new civic styles including the French Ville Nouvelle with wide streets, public parks and houses with elaborate street-facing façades. Ancient Berber architecture is most common in the south of the country where the troglodyte pit houses and *ksour* (fortified granaries) reveal a way of life that has changed little over the centuries.

Makthar – the remains of one of many Roman towns in Tunisia

SOUTHERN ARCHITECTURE

Some Berbers of southern Tunisia lived partly underground. Their ancient homes, dug down into circular pits, maintained the same temperature of about 17° C (63° F) throughout the year. This building tradition goes back many hundreds of years, but the most famous homes of this type, found in Matmata, date from the 19th century. A "pit house" was inhabited by just one family, with the number of rooms being appropriate to the family's size and wealth.

The courtyard (houch) *in the shape of a giant well is accessed through a descending tunnel. The living quarters, well away from the sun's rays, are dug into its walls, on one or two levels.*

The entrance *and inner walls are white. Simple rooms have recesses and dug-out shelves for storing everyday items.*

PUNIC ARCHITECTURE

Punic architecture is associated mainly with Carthage, which was founded in 813 BC. Its most obvious feature is a distinct town layout, with houses built on slopes around a square. Another hallmark of this style is the horizontal and vertical arrangement of building stones, known as *opus africanum*. Coastal towns often had two harbours, northern and southern, which were used depending on the wind direction. The temples were built in the mountains, close to springs, trees and stones, which were seen as sacred.

Carthage *has many remains of Punic architecture, although they can be hard to spot amid the Roman ruins.*

Capitals *and other architectural details bear witness to the architectural skills of the Carthaginians.*

The Antonine Baths *is one of Carthage's most important Roman sites. What little remains gives visitors some idea of their sheer scale.*

ROMAN ARCHITECTURE

A typical Roman town was constructed on a chequered layout. At its heart was the forum, which was dominated by a temple (capitol) devoted to various deities. Everyday life concentrated around the market square. Entertainment was provided by the theatre, and the baths were used for relaxation and hygiene.

The Capitol in Dougga was built to stand on the town's highest point.

The theatre was of equal importance as the capitol. Some could accommodate an audience of several thousand people.

THE COLONIAL ERA

With the advent of the French protectorate in 1881, Tunisian towns acquired straight avenues, flanked by public buildings. The style of the day combined European and Islamic elements. European design incorporated arcades and horseshoe arches and the façades of elegant villas were further embellished with loggias and balconies adorned with beautiful wrought-iron grilles.

Tunis's Cathedral, with its eclectic mix of forms and styles, is one of the few remaining churches from the colonial era.

Buildings in towns such as Tunis and Bizerte were designed in contemporary styles. Multi-storey hotels and apartment blocks often bore the signs of Modernism and Art Nouveau.

Villa in Hammamet, an early 20th-century Modernist house owned by George Sebastian.

MODERN ARCHITECTURE

Initially, 20th-century Tunisian architecture was under the influence of Art Nouveau. The Art Deco style arrived during the 1920s and 30s, bringing with it more geometric ornamental patterns. The late 1990s marked a return to simpler, traditional forms.

Contemporary offices in Tunisia can be an interesting blend of modern materials, such as smoked glass, and Islamic influences.

The Hotel du Lac in Tunis, built in the shape of an upturned pyramid, is one of the most interesting examples of modern architecture.

Tourist zones, seeking to amuse, often feature fairytale designs. Some hotels are built to resemble ancient palaces or Tunisian ksour (age-old Berber strongholds).

Islamic Architecture

T UNISIA HAS BEEN UNDER THE INFLUENCE of Islam since the 7th century and this is apparent in its architecture. The most striking example of this influence is the large number of mosques, with their distinctive minarets. Other Islamic buildings include medersas, *zaouias* (tombs) and the humble hammam or bathhouse. Islamic architecture is the result of many cultures and includes Roman, Moorish and Persian elements. However, from grand Aghlabid buildings to domestic courtyards, a number of common features run through it. These include the horseshoe arch, richly-coloured tiles forming swirling Arabesques and the frequent use of carved plaster as a decorative element.

Elaborate doorways, a typical feature of Islamic architecture

MINARETS

Minarets (from the Arabic for lighthouse) are found at one corner of a mosque. According to tradition, the Prophet Mohammed intended to use a trumpet (as did the Jews) or a rattle to call the faithful to prayer but one of his disciples saw a mysterious apparition that revealed to him the words of a prayer. Mohammed instructed the Bilal (the first muezzin), endowed with a powerful voice, to learn the words. Since then, five times a day, the muezzin's chant cuts through the daily bustle of Muslim towns and villages. There are two main styles of minarets found in Tunisia; the older one has a rectangular base, while the ones built on an octagonal plan were popularized by the Turks.

Dome on top of the minaret

Gallery, from which the muezzin calls the faithful to prayer

The minaret in Kairouan dates from AD 730, and is older than most of the mosque it serves.

The decorations of some Tunisian mosques are very ornate; others are more austere.

Octagonal minarets are based on Turkish towers. Many Tunisian minarets are square all the way up.

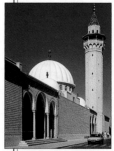

Bourguiba Mosque in Monastir is a modern building but has some traditional features.

MOSQUES

The mosque or *masjid* ("a place of worship") is one of the main forms of Islamic architecture. The basic elements include a courtyard surrounded by columns, and a prayer hall. The design is thought to be based on the house that belonged to Mohammed in Medina which had an oblong courtyard with huts. This courtyard has become the prayer hall which faces toward Mecca. The hall is separated from the rest of the mosque by a step or balustrade.

Mosques were often surrounded by zaouias (tombs). These were used as burial grounds for Islamic holy men (marabouts) and serve as destinations for pilgrimages. One such complex can be found in Le Kef.

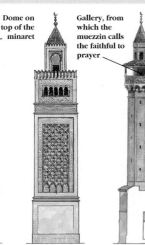

ZAOUIAS

Zaouias are humble resting places for people who have dedicated their lives to Islam. Simple in design, they are usually whitewashed and less grand than mausoleums, and can be found dotted around the towns and villages of Tunisia. Initially the name was given to an isolated part of a mosque that was used as a gathering place for Muslim mystics, mainly ascetic Sufis. Following the death of its master, a *zaouia* often became a sanctuary that attracted pilgrims.

Zaouia *in Mahdia, situated outside the town beside a cemetery. The site is conducive to meditation. Zaouias are not only used as places of pilgrimage but often have a social function as well. They may be used to hold a weekly market, for instance.*

MEDERSAS

In the Middle Ages, a medersa was a law school, a type of Muslim university, and the main centre for promoting Sunni orthodoxy, Muslim law and theology. They generally included lecture halls and, as students traditionally lived there, boarding rooms. Designed along the same lines as a mosque, medersas have an inner courtyard beyond the main entrance and also a prayer hall. The classrooms are generally located to the side of the courtyard. Most often found in the medina of large towns and cities, medersas can have incredibly elaborate decoration.

The courtyard of a medersa *is surrounded by arcades, much like a mosque. The shaded arcades sheltered visitors and provided a place for quiet contemplation.*

BAB

A *bab* is a door or gate that not only leads into a town but is also used to divide a town's areas into smaller quarters, creating a feeling of security, and guarding against unwelcome visitors. In the 20th century many of the gates disappeared, turning the private areas into public ones. But even now in Tunis or Kairouan, there are still gates that are centuries-old leading to private homes.

Bab Diwan *is one of the gates leading to the medina in Sfax.*

Medinas *were always surrounded by high walls. Entry was through a number of gates guarded by fortified towers or bastions.*

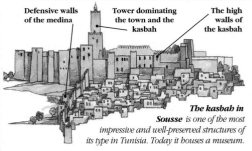

Defensive walls of the medina

Tower dominating the town and the kasbah

The high walls of the kasbah

The kasbah in Sousse *is one of the most impressive and well-preserved structures of its type in Tunisia. Today it houses a museum.*

KASBAH

The kasbah is a specific type of fortress palace. It was normally the residence of the local ruler but it also provided shelter for the local population. Kasbahs (or citadels) were generally built on hilltops, mountain slopes or near harbours. Their distinctive features include high walls and small windows. Some of the most beautiful examples have survived in Sousse, Le Kef and Tunis.

Islam in Tunisia

Decorative minaret

ISLAM REACHED TUNISIA in the wake of the Arab conquest and began to spread as early as the second half of the 7th century. It rapidly became the dominant religion and, despite a period of colonial rule, remains so today. Islam is the state religion, though Tunisia's system of government is largely secular. Islamic customs play a major role in people's lives and over 98 per cent of Tunisians profess adherence to the practices of Sunni Islam.

Wells are used for ritual ablutions and are found in many mosques. For Muslims, prayers should be said in a state of cleanliness achieved through ritual cleansing.

Before entering the prayer hall it is obligatory for the faithful to remove their shoes. Similar to the practice of ritual washing, the aim is to ensure spiritual cleanliness.

Pages of the religious books produced for many wealthy Muslims were often richly ornamented.

Koranic verses are written in a decorative script and are believed to be the literal word of God.

Mosques are decorated with geometric patterns, plant motifs and verses from the Koran.

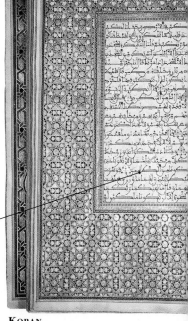

Ceramic tiles are a popular decorative element and often adorn mosques or other religious buildings such as tombs and medersas. Intricate designs can also often be seen in wealthy Tunisian homes.

KORAN

The Koran, or Quran, is the holy book of Islam and was revealed by God to Mohammed with the angel Gabriel acting as an intermediary. Mohammed is believed to have been illiterate, and the first written texts of the Koran were compiled after the Prophet's death. The Koran consists of 114 *suras* (chapters), starting with the longest and finishing with the shortest. The first *sura* revealed to Mohammed is thought to be number 96. The Koran is in verse and every Muslim is expected to learn it by heart.

A Muslim is a person who "submits to the will of God" (Islam means submission). Pious Muslims spend long hours studying the Koran, placing the book on a special folding support.

Prayer brings together crowds of the faithful, who gather in the mosque and courtyard. The women are required to stand in an area separated by a screen or curtain.

The chapters, or *suras*, of the Koran are separated by elaborate circular illuminations.

THE FIVE PILLARS

The Muslim religion rests on five principles – the "Five Pillars" of faith. They are:
1. *shahada* – an avowal of Allah as the only God
2. *salat* – the obligation to pray five times a day, facing Mecca
3. *zakat* – the giving of alms to the poor
4. *sawm* – fasting during the month of Ramadan, between the hours of sunrise and sunset
5. *hadj* – pilgrimage to Mecca.

A mosque is a place of communal worship for Muslims. Separated from the outside world by high walls, a mosque's most distinctive feature is its minaret.

Al-Kabah in Mecca is the main destination of Muslim pilgrimages

Tunisian Traditions

TUNISIAN SOCIETY ATTACHES great importance to its own traditions. These include religious festivals, rituals associated with religious practices and customs that predate Muslim times including the "night of henna", which takes place before weddings. Circumcision for boys is commonplace. Ramadan (the month in which devout Muslims fast between sunrise and sunset) is celebrated with great ceremony. In the provinces it is customary for people to visit public baths, wear jewellery with magic talismans, and make pilgrimages to the tombs of Muslim holy men. The family is held in high esteem throughout the country, with frequent gatherings of its members and communal meals.

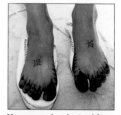

Henna – *a dye obtained from ground privet leaves. The painted patterns are believed to protect and purify.*

Tunisian women *are supposed to cover their heads. The traditional veil* (hijab) *is found in various forms all over the Muslim world. The* sifsari *(above) is mainly worn in Tunis.*

The souk *or market has been the centre of town social life for hundreds of years. They are run according to strict principles, with every product having its own permanently allocated space according to how close it is to the mosque: religious items and books are top of the list while household goods have a low status.*

Wedding jewellery of gold and silver, decorated with precious stones and magic symbols, is intended to bestow beauty, ensure fertility and bring wealth and happiness.

WEDDINGS

During the pre-Islamic era, the Arabs practised polygamy. The Koran maintained this tradition, but limited the number of wives to four. In Tunisia polygamy was outlawed in 1956. As in most cultures, a wedding is an important public occasion, attended by the entire family. The bride's feet and palms are covered in henna tattoos. Though dancing forms part of the festivity, Western-style discos and mixed dancing are far less common.

The custom of circumcision involves the removal of a boy's foreskin and is practised by Jews and Muslims. Though the Koran does not pronouce on the subject, the authority for Muslim circumcision probably derives from the example of the Prophet who is believed to be descended from Kedar, a descendant of Abraham's eldest son.

CHECHIAS

In modern-day Tunisia *chechias* are worn mainly by older men

A red cap with a silk tassel, similar to a fez, was once regarded as a vital element of a man's attire, and during the colonial era it became almost a national symbol. The *chechia* originates from Central Asia. Initially it was taller and took on its present shape around 1850. The tassel has also had many transformations – first changing its colour from blue to black and then, around 1930, vanishing altogether. *Chechias* remain popular to this day and the craftsmen who produce them are held in high regard.

Wedding costumes are rich in adornments. The fabrics and designs are reminiscent of traditional Tunisian costumes.

Games *are popular in Tunisia and men can often be seen in cafés playing dominoes, dice and cards. Dry dates or stones may sometimes serve as pawns in a game of chess.*

Chichas *– hookahs – are popular throughout Tunisia and are used to smoke tobacco in cafés. Solitary smoking is rare; normally one is ordered for a party of people. Many men still smoke* chichas *and the pipes are generally provided free (smokers need pay only for the tobacco).*

The Berbers

BERBERS ARE THE INDIGENOUS (non-Arab) people of North Africa. Their name probably originates from the Greek word "barbaroi", which was a description attached to anyone who did not speak Greek. The Berbers inhabited the region from around 4000 BC, and survived as nomads. During the 4th and 5th centuries many Berbers converted to Christianity. Until AD 700 they resisted the Arab invasion. Despite having much in common with the Arabs (their nomadic lifestyle, individualism and tribal solidarity) and despite having quickly embraced Islam, the Berbers have continued to maintain their own ethnic and linguistic identity.

Berber women *decorate their faces and hands with henna patterns in order to protect themselves from evil spirits.*

The International Sahara Festival, *held in November or December, attracts many visitors. The event includes expert displays of horsemanship and recreations of nomadic ceremonies such as weddings and caravan departures.*

BERBER WOMEN

Women are the custodians of the ancient Berber traditions. Their clothes differ considerably from those seen in the towns. Their typical garment – the *hauli* – is a draped piece of material held with a belt and fastened with clasps *(hela)* at the shoulders. To this is often added a shawl. Women often weave cloth for their dresses at home. The colours most often worn are deep red, purple and indigo. The designs consist mainly of colourful stripes.

Berber ceramics *are easily recognizable by their pure abstract designs that are reminiscent of tattoos. The most popular colours include beige, red ochre and black. Here, the geometric design is first drawn in raw clay then the grooves are filled with black resin.*

A fortified Berber village is known as a ksar. Ksour *(the plural of* ksar*) were originally granaries with* ghorfas *(rooms) situated around an inner courtyard and reached by a concealed entrance. After some time, people began to live in* ksour *and some are still inhabited today.*

The Berber social system is based on a tribal structure. Berber women perform most of the domestic duties, such as washing, but have maintained an independent status.

Highly ornamental gold jewellery

Colourful costumes worn all year round

Traditional Berber clasp (hela) *combines practicality with decorative and even protective roles. Made of silver, it is often covered with designs that are believed to ensure fertility, guard against the "evil eye" and bestow beauty on the wearer.*

Agriculture and stock keeping are the main occupations of the Berbers. There are some 50,000–90,000 currently living in Tunisia. Most of them inhabit mountain oases. Some villages are becoming short of men, who move to towns in search of work. It is therefore left to the women to cultivate the land.

Tunisian Literature and Music

ALTHOUGH IT WAS THE PHOENICIANS who introduced the alphabet to the Mediterranean region, few of their writings have survived, except for some inscriptions dating from the Punic era. Any survey of Tunisian literature, therefore, must start with the Roman and Byzantine periods. The most outstanding writer who worked in the area of present-day Tunisia was St Augustine. Later, the widespread reading of the Koran played an enormous role in the development of Arab literature. The ranks of prominent Arab writers include the 8th–9th-century Al-Jahiz. Tunisian literature is little known beyond its borders.

St Augustine, the best-known writer of the Roman era in Tunisia

ROMAN WRITERS

THE MOST FAMOUS author to live in the area of present-day Tunisia was St Augustine (354–430). Born in Tagaste (in what is now Souk Ahras in Algeria), Augustine studied philosophy in Carthage. He was at first attracted to the philosophy of Plato but a study of St Paul's writings induced him to become baptised as a Christian. He recorded his thoughts in numerous writings, including the *Treatise on the Holy Trinity*, and a dissertation entitled *On the Divine State*. His most accessible work, however, is the *Confessions*, which combines theological and philosophical meditations with insightful personal and semi-autobiographical writings.

Another influential Christian writer and theologian was Tertullian, who wrote in Latin, and lived at the beginning of the 3rd century. Tertullian was a Carthaginian lawyer who converted to Christianity in Rome after being deeply moved by the attitude of the Christian martyrs. One interesting document from this period is the anonymously written *Martyrdom of St Perpetua and St Felicity* in which the heroism of these two young women is graphically described. Tertullian became a priest and the first Christian writer to work in Latin. His numerous works, produced in Carthage, gave western Christianity its Latin foundations.

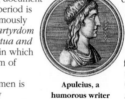

Apuleius, a humorous writer

One other Roman writer associated with Tunisia is Apuleius who was born in AD 123 and taught philosophy in Carthage. His famous comedy *Metamorphoses* is still studied today.

ARAB LITERATURE

THE BEGINNINGS OF Arabic literature go back to the 6th century and pre-Islamic times. The legacy of this early period consists mainly of Bedouin writings. Many of these were poems and were preserved in oral traditions. The most famous authors to have survived from this time are the writers of the *al-Mu'allaqat (The Seven Odes)*. Most notable among these are Antarah, Tarafah and Imru'al-qays who, along with others, produced a wide-ranging collection of poems covering everything from court life to love and adventure.

Court poetry flourished during the Ummayad rule (7th–8th century AD). During this time love poetry became the vogue. The most famous of these recounts the plight of Qays who is driven mad by his love for Layla and is afterwards known as Majnun (the demented one).

Arabic manuscript from the National Library in Tunis

The period of the Aghlabid dynasty was a golden age of Arabic literature and saw the birth of literary prose. The best-known writer from this period is Abu Nuwas who died in the 9th century. Much of his life was spent in the pursuit of pleasure and his witty poems are drawn from urban life. One of his famous lines is "Accumulate as many sins as you can".

Agar – a novel written in French by Albert Memmi

TUNISIAN LITERATURE

MANY EARLY writings produced in Ifriqiyya (the Arab province of North Africa that included Tunisia) were associated with Muslim theology. The 9th-century collection of *hadiths* by Sahnoun ibn Sa'id is devoted to the life and teachings of the Prophet. However, the most famous writer born in Tunisia is Ibn Khaldoun (1332–1406), an outstanding historian who is regarded as the founding father of sociology and political science. He compiled his studies and thoughts in a grand work on world history, *Kitab al-Ibar (The Book of Experience)*. More famous than the main text, however, is the *Muqaddimah*, or foreword, in which he summarises the state of contemporary knowledge, and attempts to explain social and economic processes.

Many of Abu Nuwas's themes were continued by Mohammed an-Nafzawi in the 14th century, the author of the erotic *Perfumed Garden*. Then, following a period of stagnation, Tunisian literature blossomed once again at the end of the 19th century with writers such as Abu el-Kacem el-Chabbi (1909–1934), who gave Arabic literature a fresh lease of life.

The most famous living Tunisian writer is Albert Memmi (*b.* 1920), who lives in France and writes in French. His best-known novel, *The Pillar of Salt*, was written in 1953.

A performance by traditional musicians

MUSIC IN TUNISIA

ISLAMIC MUSIC springs from a number of cultures. The kind of music that is most frequently heard is *malouf*. This traditional folk music typically features a solo vocalist. *Malouf* music lacks the polyphony that typifies European music and can sound repetitive to some western ears. Another form of traditional music is *mouashahat dawa*, which originates from Syria and Egypt. An important element of this is the *qasida* – a type of poetry popular in pre-Islamic Arabia, and later at the courts of the caliphs and provincial rulers.

Traditional small drum

The skill involved in this type of music lies in the interpretation of the sung version of *qasida*. The piece begins with a motif that returns repeatedly, in a strict order. Many musicians practise both styles of music. Traditional music has a broad appeal in Tunisia among all ages, and one of the most popular groups is the all-female *El-Azifet*. The ranks of famous musicians who play traditional music with Mediterranean overtones include Anur Brahem (lute).

MALOUF

Arabic music from Andalusia arrived in North Africa in the late 15th century. In Tunisia the word *malouf* became synonymous with music. The *malouf* ensemble consists of a lute, a sitar, a violin-type instrument called a *rbab* and a variety of percussion instruments (a tambourine and a small drum). The music shows clear Berber influences, particularly in its rhythm.

Man playing *malouf* on a lute

Film-makers in Tunisia

GREEN HILLS AND PALM OASES surrounded by a sea of sand; ancient medinas and troglodyte homes; Oriental bazaars and coastal scenery; Roman and Muslim relics – all add up to a fascinating variety of images. For the film director, Tunisia offers rich pickings which is why over 130 world film productions have been carried out under Tunisian skies. It was here that George Lucas shot *Star Wars* and Steven Spielberg filmed *Raiders of the Lost Ark*. The Monty Python group chose it as the location for *Life of Brian*, and Roman Polanski came here to make *Pirates*. *The English Patient* – winner of nine Oscars – was also shot in Tunisia.

Poster for a contemporary Tunisian film, *Une Odyssée*

Rex Ingram, an early film-maker in Tunisia

technicians, art directors and extras. Some Tunisian directors achieved a reputation that was not limited to Arab countries. In 1994, Moufida Tlatli's film *The Silences of the Palace* won a prize at the Cannes Film Festival. Tunisians are proud of the fact that the chief art director of *Star Wars* was a fellow countryman – Taieb Jallouli.

Tunisia took advantage not only of its diverse landscape and the enthusiasm of local artists and technicians, but also its natural links – both with the Maghreb countries and with France. Tunisian cinema became a bridge between Arab and European cultures. The attraction of Tunisian locations and the achievements of Tunisian cinema contributed even further to the development of mass tourism.

THE ADVENT OF CINEMA

LOCAL FILM-MAKERS claim that well-kept roads lead to such romantic places as the "Jewel of Jerid" – Nefta, the "Garden of Henna" – Gabès, the "Gates of the Desert" – Kebili and Douz and the "Desert Rose" – Gafsa. It was these locations, combined with the great diversity of the landscape and the French cultural influence that brought about the rise of Tunisia's film industry, as early as the 1920s. This coincided with the arrival of foreign film-makers; Rex Ingram was one of the first.

TUNISIAN CINEMA

TUNISIA SWIFTLY became a magnet for big-budget film productions (Tozeur in particular), and this soon began to affect the domestic film scene. The epic productions created a group of local, world-class

STAR WARS

YOU DON'T HAVE to search for it in a distant galaxy or in Hollywood: Tatooine – the mythical planet of Luke Skywalker, hero of *Star Wars*, can be found in southern Tunisia. Located south of Medenine, it is full of craters cut into the soft rock. George Lucas also used nearby Ksar Haddada for the filming of the slave quarters in *The Phantom Menace*. However, most of the scenes from *Star Wars* were shot in Matmata, 43 km (27 miles) south of Gabès. The local troglodyte houses are still inhabited; they also house shops, hotels and restaurants. The Sidi Driss hotel was the set for the interior shots of Luke Skywalker's home. There are some 700 of these cave dwellings, half of them inhabited. Some locals earn a living by showing their homes to tourists, many of whom are

Remains of scenery from *Star Wars*, in Matmata

fans of the movie. There are even some specialized travel agencies offering overnight accommodation to lovers of the science fiction epic. There is also no shortage of road signs pointing to *Star Wars*.

It is to the creator of *Star Wars* that Tunisia owes its cinematic fame. Lucas arrived here for the first time in the 1970s. He was captivated not only by the scenery and the extraordinary light, but also by the welcome he received. The co-operation brought benefits to both sides and part of the revenue obtained from ticket sales for the original *Star Wars* movie was set aside to help the poorest regions of Tunisia.

Scene from the epic film *Quo Vadis* shot near El-Haouaria

Oscar Winners

Tunisia also provided about 80 per cent of the locations for *The English Patient*, which scooped an impressive nine Oscars at the 1997 Academy Awards.

The film's director, Anthony Minghella, set up camp on the banks of Chott el-Jerid, a vast dry salt lake about 45 km (28 miles) from Tozeur. Cairo has changed too much over the years for a period drama, so the city scenes set in the 1930s were shot in the medinas of Tunis and Mahdia. In other scenes, Sfax stands in for Tobruk. The most important location of all, however, was the desert. The film's creators decided that the sand in Morocco was too similar to the American desert, and so

***The English Patient* with Ralph Fiennes and Kristin Scott Thomas**

Tunisia's Saharan sand proved to be ideal.

Aficionados of the film can follow in the footsteps of *The English Patient*'s director by travelling on an early 20th-century train to the Seldja Gorge *(see p216)*, or alternatively by driving a jeep to the mountain oases of Chebika and Tamerza.

Tunisian Locations

Taieb Jallouli, the art director on *Star Wars*, claims that it is the diversity of Tunisia's scenery, within a relatively small area, that attracts film-makers. Northern Tunisia has even stood in for Japan in Frédéric Mitterrand's *Madame Butterfly*, while other regions of the country – squeezed

between Libya, Algeria and the Mediterranean Sea, have been used as the Holy Land for Franco Zeffirelli's *Jesus of Nazareth*. In the early 1950s, Tunisia proved the ideal location for the Hollywood adaptations of Nobel Prize winner Henryk Sienkiewicz's novels including *Quo Vadis*. Steven Spielberg also used it to shoot many of the scenes for *Raiders of the Lost Ark*, while the medina in Monastir featured in *Monty Python's Life of Brian*.

It was no accident that the majority of scenes for Roman Polanski's *Pirates* were shot on the Sahel coast, a dozen or so kilometres north of Sousse. Tunisia was once a jumping-off point for Mediterranean corsairs and the base of the famous Red Beard (Barbarossa). Today, Port el-Kantaoui, packed with luxury yachts, is a place where visitors can eat the best fish in Tunisia, and also set sail on board one of the caravels from Polanski's film. Although the original vessels were bought by a Frenchman immediately after filming was completed, their replicas provide an exciting chance to "swashbuckle", particularly for younger would-be pirates!

Polanski shooting *Pirates* on Tunisia's coast

Handicrafts in Tunisia

T UNISIAN HANDICRAFTS GET SUPPORT from the government and provide employment for over 120,000 people. Each region has its own speciality: Kairouan is famous for its carpets; Nabeul and Jerba for their ceramics; Sidi Bou Saïd for its birdcages; Douz and Tozeur for shoes. It tends to be women who produce the carpets, decorate pottery, and weave baskets and mats while the men attend to carpentry, metalwork and, above all, selling.

Ornate "Hand of Fatima"

Carpet from Kairouan, with traditional Berber patterns

Potter at work at a wheel

CERAMICS

T HE TWO MAIN centres of ceramics in Tunisia are Nabeul on the Cap Bon peninsula and Guellala on the island of Jerba. Nabeul is known for its brightly coloured, glazed pottery. Much of this is produced solely for visitors and it can be very good quality. The inhabitants of Guellala cater more for the home market and their workshops offer every type of utility ware – from items used for cooling water and storing food, to enamelled products and "Ali Baba" jars. The northern town of Sejnane and some of the surrounding villages are famous for a primitive Berber pottery that still employs techniques used in Neolithic times. All three styles are available throughout Tunisia.

CARPETS

T UNISIAN CARPETS are mainly produced in Kairouan and Jerid. All are handmade but there are two basic types, those that are knotted and those that are woven. The knotted variety cost more and have up to 160,000 knots per square metre. Most of the designs tend to be based on a central diamond shape that is thought to derive from the lamp in the Great Mosque in Kairouan. Knotted carpets come in two main types: *Alloucha* and *Zarbia. Zarbia* carpets use reds, greens and blues while the *Alloucha* carpets are produced in beiges, browns and whites. Woven or *Mergoum* carpets are cheaper to buy and have Berber origins.

COPPER AND BRASS PRODUCTS

I N SMALL WORKSHOPS, tucked away in the narrow streets of most medinas, men can be seen bent over hammers and copper sheets, which they shape into bowls, trays and garden ornaments. Bronze is used for making jewellery boxes and jugs with distinctive narrow necks. Intricate birdcages are also plentiful and typically Tunisian; their shapes resemble small mausoleums and their patterns are borrowed from the *moucharaby* – the lattice-work window or screen seen in traditional Arab houses. Gleaming copper and brass plates are also plentiful and come in a wide variety of sizes – some are bigger than dustbin lids!

Craftsman decorating brass and copper plates in a souk workshop

WOODWORK

POPULAR WOODEN items on sale in Tunisia include salad bowls and containers for salad dressing, and wooden dolls dressed in colourful clothes. While strolling through the streets of medinas or exploring a market it is worth stepping into a carpenter's workshop to see how they make cupboards, trunks and traditional Tunisian doors. The material used in the north of the country is mainly olive-tree wood – suitable for making bowls and oil containers. In the south, palm wood is the most popular material.

Making shoes at a workshop in Kairouan

LEATHER GOODS

TUNISIANS WERE ONCE famous for producing saddles though sadly these skills have all but died out. Instead, they produce ottomans and furniture upholstery. Other common products include travel bags, wallets, leather jackets, handbags and a variety of souvenirs. Look out for the *babouche* slippers, with flattened heels, which are worn mainly in the south of the country.

Try to do some shopping in a craft shop run by ONAT (Organization Nationale de l'Artisanat). These, and the SOCOPA shops, which are gradually replacing them, sell quality Tunisian items at reasonable prices *(see p292).*

Traditional fabrics woven on looms in a workshop

MOSAICS

MOSAIC WORK IN Tunisia dates back to Punic times but flourished with the Roman occupation. When artists first began to produce intricate patterns using *tesserae* – finely polished pieces of brick, glass and marble – the workshops could not keep up with demand. Mosaics were used everywhere – from the floors in public baths, to the domes and the walls of public buildings. After the 3rd century, they also began to be used in private homes which led to a distinctive naturalistic Tunisian style.

Modern mosaic from El-Jem

OTHER HANDICRAFT PRODUCTS

JEWELLERY IS popular in Tunisia. It is produced from silver, gold and other metals, with precious and semi-precious stones used in traditional designs. The largest jewellery centres include Tunis, Sfax and Jerba. Tabarka produces lovely coral and amber items. Another typically Tunisian product is

the *chechia* – a distinctive red woollen cap. It was originally worn under the turban, but with time it became an item of headgear and a symbol of Tunisian national identity. The production of mats, baskets and fans is also widespread. These are woven using grass and date palm leaves. In recent years increasing numbers of artists have returned to the tradition of painting on glass, an art form inspired by Egyptian and Syrian examples. Items to look out for include beautiful mirrors and intricately-decorated glass perfume jars.

The Cap Bon peninsula is known for the production of perfumes and essences; orange blossom, rose and jasmine essences are particularly highly valued in Tunisia.

Making sieves in a souk workshop

TUNISIA THROUGH THE YEAR

ONE OF THE most pleasant times to visit Tunisia is in spring when flowers are in full bloom and the temperature has not yet reached its summer peak. During summer, the most comfortable place to be is on the coast where sea breezes cool the air. By autumn the temperature is starting to lower, making the all-important work of harvesting olives a

Desert rose – a symbol of Tunisia

little more bearable. The Tunisian winter can get very cold, especially high up in the mountains, while on the coast the weather can be damp and rather dreary. Public holidays in Tunisia are mostly bound up with Islam and take place according to the Islamic calendar *(see opposite)*. Visitors should get specific details of festivals and events when they are in the country.

A profusion of spring flowers flourish amid olive trees

SPRING

SPRING IS TUNISIA'S most colourful season with many flowers in bloom at this time. March and April are ideal for exploring the country. The heat is not oppressive, yet daytime temperatures rise above 20° C (68° F). Rains can be heavy but usually come in the form of brief showers. The first half of March is the final opportunity to embark on a camel trek across the desert; April brings sandstorms; May is filled with the scent of jasmine and the warming seas herald the arrival of summer.

MARCH

Independence Day
(20 Mar). National holiday that is celebrated on the anniversary of the country's independence, which was

declared in 1956 by the then president Habib Bourguiba.
Orange Blossom Festival
(late Mar–early Apr), celebrated in Menzel Bou Zelfa, Nabeul and Hammamet. A traditional festival with competitions for the best bouquet.
Octopus Festival, Kerkennah Islands. A fisherman's festival that involves locals dressing up in octopus costumes and plenty to eat.
Spring Festival, Sousse. This international arts festival includes traditional concerts, shows and theatre.

APRIL

Festival of the Mountain Oases *(late Apr)*, Midès, Tamezret. A grand display of Berber culture, including a Berber wedding ceremony, body painting with henna, performances of traditional music and horse shows.

Ksour Festival, Tataouine. Celebrates the life and customs of the *ksar* dwellers, including reconstructions of a Berber wedding and scenes from everyday life with music and camel races.
Folk Art Festival, Tataouine. This annual festival includes exhibitions of local handicrafts, folk music, dancing and displays of local costumes.

MAY

The Jerid festival, Nefta and other towns of the region. Festival of traditional art including concerts, music and dance performances.
Music Festival, Sfax. Arab music concerts including both classical and pop.
Passover Festival, El-Ghriba Synagogue, Jerba. A big event in the Jewish calender, attracting pilgrims from all over North Africa.

Independence Day as celebrated in Tataouine

THE ISLAMIC CALENDAR

Muslim religious festivals are celebrated in accordance with the lunar calendar, with each year composed of 12 months and each month of 29 or 30 days. The Muslim year is 11 days shorter than the Gregorian (Western) year. The dates of festivals depend upon the sighting of the new moon for the start of a new month. Ramadan – the month of fasting – is solemnly celebrated. Friday is held as a holy day; however, unlike the majority of Arab countries, it is not regarded as a public holiday in Tunisia.

Al-Hijra
The first day of the Muslim year, this marks the anniversary of the Hijra *(the name given to the Prophet Mohammed's migration from Mecca to Medina).*

Aïd el-Adha ("the day of offering")
This is one of the most important dates in the Muslim calendar. It marks the day when, by divine order, Abraham prepared to sacrifice his son before Allah interceded by providing a ram in place of the child.

Aïd el-Fitr ("the small festival")
This festival marks the end of the month of Ramadan, and begins on the evening of the last day of the 30-day fast. Custom decrees that on this day entirely new clothes, from headscarf to socks are put on, and that money is given to children and people in need.

Mouloud
This is the anniversary of the Prophet Mohammed's birth and is celebrated on the twelfth day of rabi al-aoual, *the third month of the Muslim calendar. For the majority of the population, it is an occasion for family gatherings and festivities.*

Ramadan
is the Muslim holy month when the faithful renew their covenant with Allah through fasting during the hours of daylight. It is only after the sun has set, following communal prayers, that Muslims are allowed to eat meals and special sweets.

Wide, sandy beaches attract many visitors during the summer

SUMMER

SUMMER TEMPERATURES on the coast can reach 40° C (104° F) but the sea breezes temper the heat. The south of the country is hotter still, and even the nights don't bring relief. Market stalls fill with every variety of melon and other fruit and vegetables. Summer in Tunisia is the traditional season for weddings; it is also a time when most people visit, filling the hotels and beaches. Many of the concerts and festivals are staged throughout the country at this time of year.

JUNE

Falconry Festival *(2nd half of Jun)*, El-Haouaria. Flying displays are accompanied by a traditional falcon hunt for partridges.
Jazz Festival *(late Jun)*, Tabarka. One of the most important events in the Tunisian cultural calendar, featuring artistes from all over the world.
Arab Horse Festival, Sidi Bou Saïd. Horse shows, races, displays of riding prowess and music concerts.
International Malouf Music Festival, Testour. Concerts of Arab-Andalusian *malouf* given by artists from Arab countries and Spain.

Kharja Festival, Sidi Bou Saïd. This religious festival is devoted to Sidi Bou Saïd, a 13th-century Islamic Sufi and teacher after whom the town is named.

JULY

Ulysses Festival *(1–25 Jul)*, Houmt Souk. Festival with singing and dancing that incorporates historic and mythological themes.
International Festival of Classical Theatre, Dougga. Theatre festival held at the site of these monumental Roman excavations.

Falcon from El-Haouaria

Plastic Arts Festival *(22 Jul–6 Aug)*, Mahrès (Sfax). Exhibitions in art galleries showing mainly young Tunisian artists.

Mermaid Festival, Kerkennah Islands. This lively festival includes music concerts and other performances by traditional Tunisian and Arab artistes.
Nights of La Marsa, La Marsa. Cultural festival which includes music concerts, live theatre and performances of ballet.
International Festival of Symphonic Music, El-Jem. Concerts are held in the amphitheatre, by candlelight. One of Tunisia's most interesting cultural events.
Republic Day *(25 July)*. The day commemorating the proclamation of the Tunisian Republic in 1956, celebrated throughout the country.

AUGUST

Amateur Theatre Festival *(late Jul-early Aug)*, Korba (Cap Bon). Presentation of new works by talented amateur Arab playwrights.
Women's Day *(13 Aug)*. The Citizens' Rights Code was proclaimed on this day in 1956, granting, among other things, equal rights for men and women.
Jasmin Road, Bizerte. Festive end of Toulon-Bizerte yacht race, accompanied by fireworks and lively stage shows.
Sponge Festival, Zarzis. Marine festival, a day of sponge diving, accompanied by folklore shows.
Festival of Diving *(late Aug)*, Tabarka. Diving displays and competitions, music concerts.

Traditional music, a common element of Tunisian festivals

AUTUMN

September can still be baking hot, especially in the south, but by October the coastal temperature is beginning to lower to a comfortable average of around 20° C (68° F). October is a good time to visit Tunisia as the water is still warm enough for swimming and the resorts are far quieter. Autumn is harvest time and the market stalls bend under the weight of fresh fruit and vegetables, while the dates are ripening in Kebili, Tozeur and Nefta.

September, marking the start of the grape harvest

SEPTEMBER

Coralis *(6–9 Sep)*, Tabarka. Festival of diving and underwater photography aimed at promoting the local coral trade.
Wine Festival *(late Sep)*, Grombalia. The end of the grape harvest in the heart of Tunisia's wine growing region gives the locals an opportunity to celebrate.
Wheat Festival *(late Sep)*, Béja. Colourful harvest festival that is celebrated in one of the most fertile regions of the country.

OCTOBER

Medina Festival *(Ramadan)*, Tunis. A major festival in the capital that includes numerous pop and traditional music concerts, dance, poetry, Koran-reciting competitions and religious processions.

International Film Festival *(every other year)*, Carthage. Tunisia's most important film festival. Presented works come from all over the world, but mainly from Arab countries. Theatre performances are also featured. On alternate years, this event is organized in Burkina Faso.
Evacuation Day *(15 Oct)*. Nationwide celebrations are held on the anniversary of the day when the last French troops pulled out of Bizerte in 1963. The celebrations are particularly festive in Bizerte itself, which hosts its own Festival d'Evacuation de Bizerte including street decorations and parades.

NOVEMBER

New Era Day *(7 Nov)*. Celebrated throughout the country to commemorate the day on which President Ben Ali assumed power in 1987 and mapped out a new direction and ethos for Tunisia's development.
Festival of Ksour, Ksar Ouled Soltane. One of a handful of festivals held in

The International Festival of the Sahara

this region, presenting the culture and traditions of the Berbers. It is accompanied by dancing and displays of traditional customs.
Date Harvest Festival, Kebili. The end of the date harvest is celebrated with shows, local music and fairs.
International Oases Festival, Tozeur. Celebration devoted to the Saharan way of life that is timed to coincide with the date harvest in this region. The special events include displays of some of the local rituals and ceremonies.

International Festival of Symphonic Music at El-Jem

WINTER

WINTER WEATHER is the most unsettled of all. There are days when the midday temperature on the coast and inland rises above 24° C (75° F); but when the winds blow, the chill can be felt not only on Cap Bon, but also way down in the south. These conditions discourage many visitors, and some hotels and restaurants in tourist resorts are closed. The end of winter is usually very sunny, but the winter sun gives little in the way of warmth.

The advent of winter is marked in many regions by festivals celebrating the end of the olive and date harvests. These are fairly low profile events, and apart from the Douz and Dakar Rally, are unlikely to draw large crowds of visitors.

Camel market during the International Festival of the Sahara

DECEMBER

Olive Festivals, Jerba, Mahdia, Kairouan, Kalaa Kebira. The production of olives is an important part of Tunisia's economy and the end of the olive harvest, also celebrated in other towns, is a big event and always accompanied by a lot of fun.

Harvesting olives in December

Because of the heavy work involved in the harvest, this is a popular festival.
International Festival of the Sahara *(early Dec)*, Douz. This is the most famous of all Tunisian festivals. It provides an opportunity to see many local practices and traditions including the preparation of Bedouin meals, camel races and wedding ceremonies. Tents are pitched in the desert and lit by torches at night to create a scene that could have come from the *Arabian Nights*.

JANUARY

New Year *(1 Jan)*. The European New Year is celebrated by many Tunisians within their family circle. Celebration of the Muslim New Year is equally quiet and occurs later.
The Dakar Rally. This major endurance race draws many big-name teams and thousands of motoring fans to Tunisia. For a few days the normally quiet roads fill with off-road cars, motorcycles and trucks. The rally route changes each year so that it can pass through different sections of the Sahara Desert.

FEBRUARY

Aïd el-Adha. This is a major feast in the Tunisian calendar. It takes place 68 days after the end of Ramadan and marks the day when Abraham, under divine orders, prepared to sacrifice his son. The day is celebrated throughout the Arab world and families who can afford it sacrifice an animal as Abraham is believed to have done as a substitute for his son. According to tradition, one third of the meat is distributed to the poor while the remainder is consumed within the family circle to mark the festival.

PUBLIC HOLIDAYS

New Year
(1 Jan)
Independence Day
(20 Mar)
Youth Day
(21 Mar)
Martyrs' Day
(9 Apr)
Labour Day
(1 May)
Republic Day
(25 Jul)
National Day
(3 Aug)
Women's Day
(13 Aug), Celebrates the Citizens' Rights Code.
Evacuation Day
(15 Oct), Marks French evacuation of Bizerte.
New Era Day
(7 Nov), Anniversary of Ben Ali's succession

The Tunisian Climate

Tunisia lies within the mediterranean subtropical zone. Its hot dry summer lasts from May until October. The southern regions of the country have only two seasons: a long summer and a short, rainy season. The remaining regions also have a spring and autumn – although much shorter than those in Europe. The sweltering summer heat is felt throughout the entire country, but particularly in the mountain valleys, caused by the sirocco wind. The Sahel's climate is tempered by the sea breeze. In late autumn, cold currents from the Atlantic bring wind and rain.

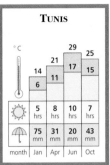

TUNIS

month	Jan	Apr	Jun	Oct
°C max	14	21	29	25
°C min	6	11	17	15
hrs	5	8	10	7
mm	75	31	20	43

TUNIS

AREA AROUND TUNIS AND CAP BON

NORTHERN TUNISIA

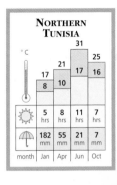

NORTHERN TUNISIA

month	Jan	Apr	Jun	Oct
°C max	17	21	31	25
°C min	8	10	17	16
hrs	5	8	11	7
mm	182	55	21	7

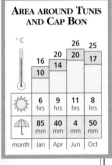

AREA AROUND TUNIS AND CAP BON

month	Jan	Apr	Jun	Oct
°C max	16	20	26	25
°C min	10	14	20	17
hrs	6	9	11	8
mm	85	40	4	50

CENTRAL TUNISIA

THE SAHEL

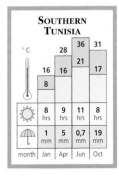

CENTRAL TUNISIA

month	Jan	Apr	Jun	Oct
°C max	17	25	36	28
°C min	8	13	13	16
hrs	6	9	10	7
mm	14	20,1	2	20,2

JERBA AND THE MEDENINE AREA

THE SAHEL

month	Jan	Apr	Jun	Oct
°C max	17	23	31	26
°C min	9	14	23	20
hrs	6	8	11	7
mm	38	21	3	47

SOUTHERN TUNISIA

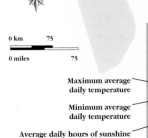

SOUTHERN TUNISIA

month	Jan	Apr	Jun	Oct
°C max	16	28	36	31
°C min	8	16	21	17
hrs	8	9	11	8
mm	1	5	0,7	19

0 km   75
0 miles   75

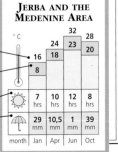

JERBA AND THE MEDENINE AREA

month	Jan	Apr	Jun	Oct
°C max	16	24	32	28
°C min	8	18	23	20
hrs	7	10	12	8
mm	29	10,5	1	39

Maximum average daily temperature

Minimum average daily temperature

Average daily hours of sunshine

Average monthly rainfall

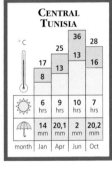

THE HISTORY OF TUNISIA

THE RICH CULTURAL AND SOCIAL HERITAGE *that can be found in modern-day Tunisia is largely due to the major powers that have inhabited this area including the Phoenicians, the Romans, the Vandals, the Arabs and the French. Tunisia is one of the oldest countries in Africa and the name given to it by the Romans – Ifriqiyya – came to designate the entire continent.*

The earliest prehistoric humans most probably appeared here during the early Palaeolithic era, and primitive stone tools discovered near Kebili in the south date this early activity to about 200,000 years ago. At this time the climate was very different and the area that is now called the Sahara had regular rainfall and may well have been covered in forest. From these early

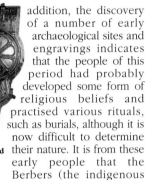

Breast-plate with head of Minerva

beginnings evolved the Aterians, who were able to make and use specialized tools. The Aterians were followed, about 10,000 years ago, by fair-skinned tribes from western Asia who brought with them the ability to make flint tools. These Capsian people, named after archaeological finds near Gafsa (which was earlier known as Capsa), settled in southern Tunisia and developed a sophisticated culture with a language and early forms of art. They lived here until about 4500 BC and, as well as being hunter-gatherers, began to develop forms of agriculture, domesticating several species of animals. In

addition, the discovery of a number of early archaeological sites and engravings indicates that the people of this period had probably developed some form of religious beliefs and practised various rituals, such as burials, although it is now difficult to determine their nature. It is from these early people that the Berbers (the indigenous non-Arab North Africans) are probably descended.

The information about Berber culture and religious beliefs prior to the arrival of the Phoenicians in 1100 BC is scarce. Their name derives from the Greek word "barbaroi" – meaning anyone who could not speak Greek. The majority of Berbers lived in family-based tribal societies, were nomadic and spoke a language that belongs to the Hamitic group of languages. Roman expansion impinged on their freedom and, because of their intense spirit of independence, the Berbers have often found themselves in conflict with the dominant power throughout Tunisia's history.

TIMELINE

150,000 BC	50,000 BC	10,000 BC	5000 BC	2500 BC	1100 BC

100,000–40,000 BC Neanderthal man appears in Tunisia

9000–4000 BC Capsian civilization arrives in North Africa. Named after implements discovered near Gafsa, Capsian man is distinguished by the use of sophisticated flint tools and early forms of art

10,000–8000 BC *Homo sapiens* appear in the region of Gabès and on the northern edges of the Tell

1100 BC Phoenician sailors establish trading outposts in Tunisia

Flint arrowheads

◁ **Picture of Hannibal fighting a Roman legion in the Alps**

Phoenician traders sailing around the Mediterranean Sea

THE PHOENICIANS

The so-called Punic period (the name given to 128 years of war between the Phoenicians and the emerging Roman empire) began about 814 BC with the founding of Carthage. The Phoenicians were supreme sailors and colonized many islands and coastal regions, which they established as trading posts. They built new towns, mostly on craggy headlands, with two harbours – to the north and south, so that they could be used regardless of the wind direction and the season of the year. As the compass had not yet been invented, they had to navigate by the stars – mainly by *Ursa Minor*, the Little Bear. Their longest sea voyage was the circumnavigation of Africa, which was accomplished on the orders of the Egyptian pharaoh Nechon, in 600 BC. An account of this historic voyage can be found in the writings of Herodotus.

CARTHAGE

The foundation of Carthage is linked to Dido, Princess of Tyre. Persecuted by her brother, Pygmalion, who murdered her husband, she fled her homeland. Having arrived at what is now Tunisia, she pleaded with the local chieftain, Labus, to give her a piece of land big enough to cover the hide of a bull. Dido cut the hide into narrow strips and used them to encircle the area that later became the site of Carthage's fortress – Byrsa.

Despite such legends, the history behind this city is more prosaic. The Phoenicians, wanting secure staging posts along the trade route between Tyre (in modern-day Lebanon) and silver mines

Phoenician terracotta mask

in southern Spain, needed a presence on the Tunisian coast. The outpost soon grew into a powerful state that took control of the trading posts, which were remote and scattered over a large area. In the 7th century BC, the Carthaginians were strong enough to take control of Tyre in the west and began establishing colonies for themselves. By the 4th century BC, Carthage had become an independent state. Carthage's wealth grew

Numidian mausoleum
in Dougga

TIMELINE

814 BC Punic era – founding of Carthage by the Phoenicians. Development of new towns; major centres include Acholla, necropolis in Mahdia, Hadrumètum (Sousse), Kerkouane, Hippo Diarrhytus (Bizerte). Tanit and Baal Hammon are the most popular deities in Carthage

1100 BC	1000 BC	900 BC	800 BC	700 BC
1000–1100 BC Earliest Phoenician settlements	**975–942 BC.** Phoenician economy flourishes under the rule of Hiram I, King of Tyre	**1000–900 BC** The oldest examples of Phoenician writing		**654 BC** First Punic colony established on Ibiza (Balearic Islands)

Sphinx-shaped vase

and its culture flourished and at its peak this important Phoenician metropolis had a population of about 500,000.

The Phoenician colonization was purely commercial and did not involve any military conquests but the success of Carthage, which had a strong navy and a firm grip on trade throughout the 5th and 4th century, inevitably threatened to eclipse other powers, especially Rome.

Dido Building Carthage by J.M.W. Turner

The first Punic War began in 263 BC when Rome embarked on a campaign to take control of Sicily, 80 km (50 miles) northeast of Carthage. These two major powers fought each other for the next 20 years until Rome managed to destroy the Carthaginian fleet off Trapani (western Sicily) and forced Carthage to surrender.

The second Punic War began in 218 BC. This time it was Carthage that went on the offensive. With Rome for the time being busy with its new conquests, Carthage had turned its attention to its position in Africa. In an attempt to force Rome's hand, the Carthaginian general Hannibal had earlier captured a region of Spain. Then, in 218, he crossed the Alps with a 90,000-strong army and 37 elephants and launched what would turn out to be an unsuccessful assault on Rome.

The third Punic War began in 149 BC when the Romans landed in Utica and laid siege to Carthage. The mighty city fell three years later and was destroyed. The Romans took possession and the former territory of Carthage became the Roman province of Africa.

Reconstruction of ancient Carthage, from the Phoenician period

) BC Phoenicians circumnavigate Africa the orders of the Egyptian pharaoh, Nechon

Stone tablet with Phoenician writing

111–106 BC Romans wage war against the Numidian King Jugurtha

300 BC Carthage takes control of Numidia

) BC	**500 BC**	**400 BC**	**300 BC**	**200 BC**	**100 BC**

263–241 BC First Punic War

149–146 BC Third Punic War, ending with the destruction of Carthage

146 BC Founding of the first Roman colony – Africa, with its centre in Utica. Agriculture and architecture flourish

500–400 BC Carthage becomes an dependent state

218–202 BC Second Punic War. Hannibal crosses the Alps with elephants. Carthaginians are finally defeated in Africa

THE ROMANS

The destruction of Carthage in 146 BC was followed by the foundation of the Roman province of Africa, with its capital in Utica – a former Punic colony. This was the first Roman colony outside Italy and covered the territory of northeastern Tunisia. The land captured from Carthage became *ager publicus* – state-owned land on which a tribute was levied. Only the towns that had surrendered to the Romans during the war were exempt. In 44 BC, the "infernal land", now dedicated to the goddess Juno, became the site of Julia Carthage. The former city was resurrected and became the capital of this part of the world for several centuries. In 27 BC, a new consular province was created – *Africa Proconsularis* – with a resident proconsul in Carthage. It covered the area from Cyrta in the west to Cyrenaica in the east. After the years of wars, the reign of Octavian Augustus brought with it stability and created a new climate for economic development.

Roman triumph following the defeat of Hannibal

A marble bust from the Roman era

During the period of the Flavian dynasty (AD 69–96), Rome continued with its southerly expansion. The building and maintenance of roads assisted with the development of trade and communication.

Agriculture became increasingly important to the area and the Romans turned the wheat-growing plains of the Medjerda Valley into a "breadbasket" with the region supplying some 60 per cent of the Empire's requirements for grain. This produced a golden age for the African economy. Its wealth was based on the cultivation of corn and olives, and also on its vineyards. Many locals, including the Berbers, prospered under the new regime and a number of colonies sprang up on the Tunisian coastline that provided holiday and retirement homes for wealthy Romans. With so much Roman influence this part of Africa underwent a gradual process of Romanization. Roman towns sprang up everywhere. Religious buildings were erected to honour gods such as Juno and Minerva. Nearly one sixth of Roman senators were of African origin at this time. Africa even provided an Emperor, the Libyan-born Septimius Severus.

The smooth running of the African economy was briefly upset in 238 when Gordian, the proconsul of Africa, proclaimed himself emperor

Roman amphitheatre at El-Jem

TIMELINE

27 BC Founding of *Africa Proconsularis*, covering most of modern day Tunisia, up to Chott el-Jerid (not including the Sahara)

69–96 Flavian dynasty – the country flourishes

238 Revolt in Africa Proconsularis, led by the Gordians (father and son)

100 BC	AD 1	100	200

Relief from Chemtou region

96 Beginning of Antonine dynasty – a golden age for the African economy

193–235 Peak of the territorial expansion under the Severan dynasty. Strengthening of borders and building of defensive walls around many cities

284 Emperor Diocletian carri out reform plans Africa becom *Dioecesis Afric*

Ruins of the forum in Sufetula

in a gesture of defiance against the heavy taxes imposed by Rome. Gordian sent his son, Gordian II, into battle against Capellianus, the governor of Numidia, who was loyal to Rome. Gordian II was killed on the battlefield and, on hearing of his death the father killed himself. He had ruled for just 21 days.

THE VANDALS

One of Rome's biggest challenges during the 4th and 5th centuries was the Vandals, a fierce tribe of Aryan barbarians who had been slowly but surely working their way through Spain and into Africa. In AD 429

Byzantine-style column decoration

the Vandals arrived in Africa and began demolishing much of what the Romans had built. In 439, they seized Carthage, which became the capital of a new state that covered the area of present-day Tunisia. Its founder, Genseric, ruled for half a century (428–477) building the Vandal empire and expanding it further into Sicily, Sardinia and Italy. He also had the audacity to

carry out one of the most daring deeds imaginable at that time: the plunder of Rome in 455.

BYZANTIUM

The political makeup of the Roman Empire was changed forever with the adoption of Christianity by Constantine the Great in 312. Much of Rome's power was transferred to Byzantium (Istanbul), which was to control the eastern portion of the Roman Empire.

In 533 the Byzantine Emperor Justinian, who dreamt of reasserting Roman authority, sent his general Belisarius to attack the Vandals at the Battle of Ad Decinum, near present-day Tunis. Belisarius had a swift and decisive victory and on 15 September 533 he entered Carthage.

The next century of Byzantine rule was not so easy. Despite building heavy fortifications, constant Berber resistance and insurrection in the army meant that the Byzantine hold on Tunisia was weak.

A mosaic from the Byzantine period

439 Carthage conquered by the Vandals

Belisarius – commander of Emperor Justinian's army

698 Carthage taken over by Arab forces

| 300 | 400 | 500 | 600 | 700 |

533 Carthage occupied by Byzantine army

647 Beginning of the Muslim era. Byzantine army defeated at Sufetula

670 Founding of Kairouan by Oqba ibn Nafi

A stele with an image of Baal-Saturn

Christian Tunisia

CHRISTIANITY ARRIVED IN AFRICA from Rome and was taken up by many people in Tunisia, including some of the Berber tribes. Thousands of Christian converts were martyred during the third century, including St Perpetua who was thrown to the animals in Carthage. A split in the church occurred in the 4th century when Donatus, the Bishop of Carthage, refused to recognize the authority of church leaders who had failed to stand up to Rome. These "Donatists" built their own churches and many Roman sites in Tunisia have two churches for this reason.

Christian monogram
This was created by combining the letters X and P. It was used following the Tolerance Edict (4th century).

St Augustine
Augustine (AD 354–430) spent his youth in Carthage and later returned there as a priest and bishop. He also participated in synods.

The apse of a forum basilica was used to seat the officials; the emperor sat in the imperial basilica.

The door of every Christian church has a symbolic meaning.

Christian tombstones
Tombstones were usually in the form of inscribed tablets. Tombstones that bear images of the deceased are quite rare.

MOSAICS

This unique mosaic kept in the Bardo Museum, Tunis, shows a Christian church. It gives some idea of the original appearance of the early churches whose ruins can be seen in many of Tunisia's oldest towns.

The Greek language
Early Christians used the Greek language in their liturgy and writing. The first Christian text in Latin was written in AD 180 in Africa.

Ruins of Basilicas
Many Tunisian towns contain the ruins of Christian basilicas that were built in the town centres or on the outskirts, often on the sites of earlier sacred buildings.

Floor mosaics in basilicas included rich animal and floral motifs.

Inscriptions were often incorporated into the mosaics.

Baptistry
Pools decorated with mosaics were used by Christians in their baptisms.

Inscriptions
Many of the surviving Christian inscriptions are on tombstones that bear only the name of the deceased and the simplest of ornamentation.

A peacock featured in Christian tomb mosaics symbolized resurrection.

The Good Shepherd
By the 2nd century AD Christianity was already widespread in North Africa. The image of the Good Shepherd was among the most popular motifs in Christian art.

Catacombs
A well-preserved underground resting-place can be seen in Sousse.

ARAB RULE

One hundred years after the death of Mohammed (632), the Muslim Empire stretched from Spain to India. The first strong resistance encountered by the Muslim army was in the area of present-day Tunisia. The attacks on Ifriqiyya (Tunisia and parts of Libya) started immediately after the conquest of Egypt (640–43); nevertheless it took more than 20 years to win control over it. This was finally achieved by Oqba ibn Nafi after he defeated the Byzantine army in 647. In 670, he founded the city of Kairouan, which

Muslim cemetery outside the medina walls, Kairouan

A page from the Koran (1202)

became the most important town in North Africa and an excellent base for military operations against the Berber tribes. Oqba, who according to a legend went forward until the Atlantic waves stopped his horse, was killed in 683 at the battle of Basra in Iraq. After his death, the Muslim army was forced to leave Ifriqiyya and it was only during 693–700 that the governor Hassan ibn Nooman (founder of Arab Tunis)

quashed the Berbers' resistance and confirmed Arab rule. The work of Ibn Nooman was continued by Musa ibn Nusair. Under his rule, Kairouan gained independence from Egypt and was controlled directly by Damascus. Having conquered the coast of North Africa, Ibn Nusair opened the gateway to Europe. In 800, power in Ifriqiyya passed to the hands of the independent deputies of the Abassid Caliphs – the Aghlabids. The founder of this dynasty was Ibrahim ibn al-Aghlab who made Kairouan the capital of a region that covered western Algeria, Tunisia and part of Libya. The resulting dynasty proved to be successful and during its reign

Courtyard of the 11th-century Sidi Driss Mosque, Gabès

TIMELINE

Doorway to the Great Mosque's minaret in Kairouan

800–909 Expansion of Islam. Founding of the Aghlabid dynasty, which rules the country from its capital in Kairouan

921 Founding of Mahdia, which becomes the country's capital

700	800	900	1000	1100

Golden coin, from the Aghlabid period

909–972 The Fatimids assume power and rule for a period before moving to Egypt

972–1152 Founding of the Zirid dynasty and their assumption of power. Raid by the Banu Hilal tribe

1056–1147 Period of rule by the Almoravid dynasty

THE HISTORY OF TUNISIA

the country that had until now written in Latin and professed Christianity became an Arabic-speaking Muslim state.

FATIMIDS

Towards the end of the 9th century, the main threat to the Aghlabids came from

Marble relief from Mahdia depicting a king and a musician

the increasingly strong opposition movements centring around the Shiite groups. One of the leaders of this movement was Abu Abdullah who claimed descent from the Prophet's daughter, Fatima. Abu Abdullah was a gifted commander and in 909 the Aghlabids were defeated. A little later he conquered Alexandria. The Fatimids constructed a new capital, Mahdia, and set about making plans to capture Egypt.

Abu Abdullah's successors continued this policy of expansion. Having conquered Egypt, they handed control of Ifriqiyya to their Berber nominee. In 972, he founded the Zirid dynasty (972–1152), which withdrew allegiance from the Fatimids in 1041. There followed a period of great instability. The Zirids were overthrown by the Almoravids, who ruled the Maghreb and Spain from 1056 until 1147. They were followed by the Almohads, who in their turn, were replaced by the Hafsid dynasty.

HAFSIDS

The Hafsids (1228–1574) introduced wide-ranging changes beneficial to the economy of present-day Tunisia. Their great political skill enabled them to play the Tunisian tribes off against one another. This, and a reputation

for military skill, which was partly earned when they defeated a crusade led by Louis IX of France, led to a time of stability. Tunis was made the capital and did well under the new regime, enjoying a new-found wealth. Separate districts were allocated to Muslim refugees from Spain, European diplomats and merchants. The Great Mosque (Jemaa el-Zitouna) acquired a medersa and a minaret, and a palace was built on the site of the present Bardo Museum. At the same time, the Great Mosque in Kairouan was restored.

OTTOMAN RULE

It was the arrival of the Ottoman Turks that spelt the end for the Hafsid dynasty. The Ottomans had fought wars with Byzantine Rome, which they finally defeated, taking Constantinople in 1453.

Death of Louis IX during a plague epidemic in Tunisia, in 1270, after his unsuccessful crusade

---

1159–1230 The Almohads unite the Maghreb countries	1240 The first medersa (Islamic school) established in Tunis	1574 Spanish withdraw from Tunisia. Tunis is partially destroyed in the course of fighting. Tunisia is seized by the Ottoman Turks	

1200	1300	1400	1500	1600

1228–1574 Tunis is ruled by the Hafsid dynasty. Art and architecture flourish	1270 Crusade by Louis IX	1574 Rise of the corsairs: with the assistance of the Barbary pirates, Aruj and Khair ed-Din Barbarossa, Tunisia falls under the control of the Ottoman Empire. Turkish becomes the official language

King Louis IX

Genoese fort guarding the entrance to Tabarka harbour

Turkey. Until 1574, the Spanish kings tried to establish a protectorate over Tunisia, but were defeated by the Turks, on land and at sea.

Tunisia became a province of the Ottoman Empire and was ruled over by an elaborate hierarchy which included the Pasha (the sultan's representative) and an elite of Ottoman high-ranking army officials including a civil administrator (bey), and a military administrator (dey). Such a complex sharing of power did not result in a stable government and rebellions and struggles for control weakened the state. Central rule was restored by the Muradids (1628–1702), the first line of hereditary beys, who brought about the country's revival. They also enriched its art with Ottoman influences and popularized the habit of coffee drinking.

During the 16th century, the dynasty ruled over a powerful empire that included the Balkans and Arab countries. The golden era of the Ottoman Empire coincided with the rule of Suleyman the Magnificent (1520–66). During that time the Ottomans also took control of Tunisia with the help of mercenaries. In the 16th century the corsairs, sailing under the Ottoman flag, won control of the entire Maghreb coast. Assisted by the Barbary pirates – Aruj and Khair ed-Din Barbarossa – Tunisia was taken. In the later stages of the Hafsids' rule, the country, ruined by numerous dynastic squabbles, had become the object of a dispute between Spain and

Ottoman-style finial of a minaret

HUSAYNIDS

The Muradid line was replaced by the Husaynids in the early part of the 18th century when Husayn bin Ali took control of the country and established a new dynasty that would rule until 1957. Having no sons, Bin Ali at

Ceramic decoration with a plant motif

TIMELINE

1606 Growth of Tunisian piracy due to European renegades, many of whom convert to Islam

1705 Founding of the Husaynid dynasty. Stabilization of the country

1744 Beys win greater powers gaining freedom from Turkish domination

1600	1625	1650	1675	1700	1725

1628 Beginning of Muradid rule, which brings with it a period of political stability in Tunisia

1605–1691 Outbreaks of the plague occur in Maghreb every six to 12 years

Turkish-style coffee pot

1705 Increase in the country's population. An end to the run of bad luck in the production of grain

first appointed his nephew, Ali, to be his successor in 1709. However, in the same year a son, Mehmed, was born. When he reached maturity, his father made Mehmed his heir and gave him the title of Bey Mahalli. The nephew was given the title of Pasha. This situation led to five years of conflict during which Tunisian society was split into two camps, a division that lasted, in political terms, well into the 18th century. Initially Ali Pasha won the upper hand, but the descendants of Husayn bin Ali regained power with support from Algeria. During the second half of the 18th century, the country was successively ruled by three of his descendants including Husayn's two sons Ali Bey (1759–81) and Hammouda Bey (Pasha) (1781–1813). Under their rule the country prospered for a brief period but in 1819 Tunisia was forced to put an end to piracy, thus depriving it of revenue. The country ran up large debts and taxes on agriculture and trade were increased to make up for the shortfall. The economy suffered and Tunisia was forced to borrow heavily from European (mainly French) banks.

A plate with a stylized image of an antelope

Tunisia's fate was sealed at the Berlin Congress in 1878, which had been called by the Europeans to decide how best to carve up the recently defeated Ottoman Empire. The country was now bankrupt and it was only a matter of time before one power or another stepped in.

In 1881, with the spurious excuse that they were protecting French-occupied Algeria from raids by Khroumirie tribesmen, France sent 30,000 troops across the border into Tunisia from Algeria. The troops swiftly took control first of Le Kef and then of Tunis. The initial opposition was intense but short-lived and the same year the Treaty of the Bardo, signed with Mohammed el-Sadiq Bey, recognized the bey as the nominal ruler with the proviso that France was in ultimate control.

Tunisian section at the 1851 London Exhibition

View of Carthage in the early 19th century

1750	1775	1800	1825	1850	1875

1819 Tunisia outlaws piracy

1836 France becomes the advocate and the guarantor of Tunisia's independence

1814 Death of Hammouda Bey marks the end of the Husaynid's "golden age"

1824–25 Tribal revolts break out in rural regions of Tunisia: trade collapses, peasant poverty increases

1855–56 Tunisian army suffers heavy losses in the Crimean War

THE COLONIAL ERA

The French had always attached great importance to Maghreb – Tunisia, Algeria and Morocco. The history of their trade links, treaties and agreements made with these countries stretched back over three hundred years prior to taking control.

Tunisia's loss of independence was followed by reform of the central government, which, while preserving the Muslim administration with Sidi Ali Bey at its head, placed it under the control of the French civil service. On assuming the protectorate, the French made a number of key investments. By 1914, they had built oil refineries, schools and hospitals and had also embarked on the task of extending the railway network linking Tunis with Algeria, and Sousse with Sfax. In Tunis they extended La Goulette harbour and commenced the rapid development of the Ville Nouvelle (modern town) to which they moved most of the major government offices.

Souk in Tunis in the early 19th century

The walls of Tunis as seen in the mid-19th century

EARLY INDEPENDENCE MOVEMENT

These blessings of civilization served only the country's elite, however. A negative aspect was the purchase of land by rich Europeans. As a result, many Tunisian peasants were forced out to the poorer areas of the country, and the traditional way of life of stock-keeping shepherds began to disappear. At the same time, some 60,000 Tunisian troops fought in World War I – 10,000 died.

A struggle for independence was linked to growing national awareness, which in turn was brought about by better education within Arab society as a whole. One of the fathers of Arab nationalism was Jemeladdin al-Afghani whose ideology had a great influence on Tunisian activists. Two of the main architects of Tunisia's rebirth were Kheiredine Pasha (*d*.1889) and Sheikh Mohammed Kabadu (*d*.1871), who initiated a number of reforms of the religious tribunal and the Zitouna

Sidi Ali Bey and his ministers

TIMELINE

1881–1956 Establishment of the French protectorate (12 May 1881). Resistance movement fights against French rule

1892 One fifth of the area used for cultivation of olives is taken over by French settlers

1880	1890	1900	1910

Tunisian Army generals

1890–1914 Building of new schools, hospitals and railway lines (Tunis–Sfax, Tunis–Gabès)

"Arabic" pavilion in Paris in 1900, promoting the appeal of Tunisia

theological university. Kheiredine also founded the Sadiki College in 1875, an institution that was to play an important role in the cultural and intellectual life of Tunisia.

The college produced many of the later advocates of modernization of the country, as well as members of the "Unbreakable Bonds" society, founded in Tunis in 1885, which co-operated with the Egyptian reform movement. In April 1885, the first public national demonstration took place in Tunis, organized by Mohammed as-Sanusi. At that time the activists demanded not so much independence as permission for Muslims to have their say in the running of the country. The French authorities arrested the leaders. The Tunisians were forced to change their tactics and commenced

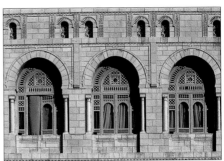

Façade of the town hall in Sfax

an intensive struggle through the media, aimed in particular at the urban population.

Social unrest continued and the year 1920 saw the foundation of the Tunisian Constitutional Party, commonly known as Destour. It demanded a constitution, and access to all state offices for Tunisians as well as public education. Ten years later, a new generation of activists came to prominence. Among them was a young lawyer, Habib Bourguiba. He founded a newspaper, *L'Action Tunisienne*, and used it to launch a struggle against the authorities.

In March 1934, Bourguiba founded the Neo-Destour Party with the main aim of fighting for the country's independence. He drew massive support and the French, sensing the danger, declared the party illegal and had Bourguiba arrested, though he was later released. By 1938, however, popular resistance to French rule had became widespread. Just before the outbreak of World War II, Bourguiba was arrested again, but by the time the authorities had acted against the nationalists the war had already begun.

French poster advertising Tunisia's attractions

1920 Founding of the Destour Party

1926 French rule puts an end to Tunisian freedom of the press, gatherings and associations

1932 Habib Bourguiba founds *L'Action Tunisienne* daily newspaper

1920	1930	1940

1914–1918 Ten thousand Tunisians are killed in World War I

1934 Founding of the Neo-Destour Party

Cavalry parade during the French Prime Minister's visit to Tunisia in 1939

WORLD WAR II

Tunisia's proximity to Italy suddenly had strategic importance for both sides. Despite aggressive German propaganda and earlier French-Tunisian tensions, the Tunisians came out in support of France and the Allies. The Germans were supporting the colonial ambitions of the Italians in Libya and the Italians, taking advantage of the situation, were also trying to gain control of Tunisia. In June 1940, after declaring war on Britain and France, Italy bombed military targets in

Allied troops liberate Tunisia in 1943

Bizerte and around Tunis. German forces landed in Tunisia in 1942 while Rommel's Africa Korps conducted a military campaign in the south. The German authorities also attempted to win Habib Bourguiba over to their side, but met with his firm refusal to co-operate.

It was not long before the Allies were marching into the country, however, and on 7 May 1943 Allied Forces commanded by General Patton and General Montgomery liberated Tunisia. The country had

suffered heavy losses: Sfax and Sousse were heavily damaged, while other towns, such as Bizerte, Gabès and Tunis suffered various degrees of bombardment. Allied casualties numbered some 15,000.

REGAINING OF INDEPENDENCE AND THE BOURGUIBA REGIME

After the war, France tried to relieve the political tensions persisting in Tunisia. It abolished censorship and installed a new Tunisian government headed by Mustapha Kaakim. But the most decisive change in Paris's attitude towards Tunisian independence occurred only in 1954, when the office of French prime minister was taken over by Pierre Mendès-France – an advocate of peaceful solutions to France's colonial conflicts. The French press published an interview with the

Habib Bourguiba after the proclamation of independence

TIMELINE

1942 Germans invade Tunisia

1943 Allied Forces liberate Tunisia

1956 Regaining of independence (20 Mar)

1959 Tunisian Republic gets its constitution (1 Jun)

1964 Bourguiba nationalizes land of remaining French settlers

1940	1950	1960	197

1957 Proclamation of the Tunisian Republic. Habib Bourguiba becomes the first president of independent Tunisia

1963 French troops leave Bizerte (15 Oct)

1967 Bourguiba refo religious teach

Bofors gun dating from World War II

imprisoned Habib Bourguiba and the convention on Tunisian autonomy was signed in June 1955. On 20 March 1956 the country regained its independence and a year later the Tunisian Republic was proclaimed. Bourguiba became the country's first president and the leader of the Neo-Destour Party, which later restyled itself and changed its name to Parti Socialiste Destourien (PSD).

Tunisia's golden beaches act as a magnet to visitors

Before this, and immediately after regaining independence, work began on drafting a new constitution, which finally came into force on 1 June 1959. Its preamble affirmed that Tunisia was a free, independent and sovereign state. Its religion was Islam and Arabic was to be given priority in schools and government offices. Its political system was to be a free republic. This same constitution granted far-reaching powers to the new president.

Trade is stimulated by tourist revenue

BEN ALI

Despite a series of reforms and increased prosperity from tourism, there was much social unrest under Bourguiba's rule. A general strike was called in 1984 demanding an end to repression and a revocation of anti-constitutional laws. On 2 October 1987, the Minister of

The incumbent President Zine el-Abidine ben Ali

the Interior, Zine el-Abidine ben Ali became the country's prime minister. On 7 November he assumed the office of PSD leader and forced President Bourguiba to give up the presidency for life. Bourguiba resigned in view of his advanced years and poor health. Ben Ali became president. He promised to abolish life presidencies, introduced a multi-party system, followed a policy of economic liberalism and set up a series of reforms which brought about democracy and social pluralism. In the 1994 and 1999 general elections, he was once again elected the country's president.

1970s Growing revenues from tourism stimulate growth of economy

1994 Zine el Abidine ben Ali is re-elected as the country's president

1999 Zine el-Abidine ben Ali is elected for a third term

1980   1990   2000

1974 Habib Bourguiba is re-elected as president

Monument to Bourguiba in Monastir

1987 Prime Minister Zine el-Abidine ben Ali becomes the country's president and commander of its armed forces

Tourism arrives

TUNISIA REGION BY REGION

TUNIS 64-89
GREATER TUNIS AND
CAP BON PENINSULA 90-121
NORTHERN TUNISIA 122-143
THE SAHEL 144-173
JERBA AND THE MEDENINE AREA 174-189
SOUTHERN TUNISIA 190-211
CENTRAL TUNISIA 212-241

Tunisia at a Glance

TUNISIA'S REGIONS DIFFER from one another not only in terms of culture, but also in terms of landscape. Travel to the north and northwest and there are forests, mountains and fertile plains. The central region is known for its historic remains dating from the Roman and early Arab eras. Jerba, the Sahel and Cap Bon peninsula, on the east coast, are famous for their magnificent beaches, while the southern section of the country is dominated by great salt flats and the vast expanse of the Sahara Desert.

NORTHERN TUNISIA
See pp122–143

CENTRAL TUNISIA
See pp212–241

Tabarka *is the main seaside resort of north-western Tunisia. It is a picturesque place, nestling beneath mountain slopes. A tourist zone is being developed around the town. This is also a favourite spot for divers who come to explore the offshore rocks and caves.*

Tamerza *is a fairly new village north of Tozeur. Nearby are the ruins of old Tamerza. Set among green palm groves, old Tamerza is a Berber village that was abandoned in 1969 after severe flooding. There are waterfalls and small lakes in which to cool off.*

Chott el-Jerid *is an extraordinary phenomenon. This vast seasonal salt-water lake is dry for much of the year and has salt piles that glitter with a multitude of colours. A trip across it is an unforgettable experience.*

Sbeïtla *lies southwest of Kairouan and is worth visiting for the nearby ruins of Sufetula, an ancient Roman town that has a number of well-preserved ruins including temples and a triumphal arch.*

0 km	75
0 miles	75

◁ **Picturesque ruins of a small town, in the south of Tunisia**

GREATER TUNIS AND CAP BON PENINSULA
See pp90–121

TUNIS
See pp64–89

THE SAHEL
See pp144–173

JERBA AND THE MEDININE AREA
See pp174–189

SOUTHERN TUNISIA
See pp190–211

Sidi Bou Saïd is a charming town just a little way to the northeast of Tunis. The whitewashed houses with their blue doors and shutters create a unique atmosphere and the café-lined cobbled square has a sense of quiet affluence and peace. Set high on a cliff, the village attracted artists and writers such as Paul Klee and André Gide and was for a time the cradle of modern Tunisian painting.

Bardo Museum in Tunis is famous for its magnificent collection of Roman artifacts. Among these are some of the finest mosaics in the world, which were found on the sites of ancient towns, including Bulla Regia in northern Tunisia.

Sfax is renowned for its medina, one of the most beautiful in the country. The 17th-century Dar Jellouli houses a museum with exhibits relating to the region's culture.

Jerba, just off Tunisia's southeast coast, attracts large numbers of visitors who come to make the most of the mild climate and glorious beaches. Despite some development, the island has kept its distinctive culture intact, and many locals can be seen in traditional dress.

The camel is one of the symbols of Tunisia. It is associated mainly with the Sahara Desert, which was once crossed by caravans. Today, a camel trip in the Sahara, lasting anything from a few hours to a few days, is a popular activity for visitors.

TUNIS

·····················

T UNIS HAS A COMPACT CITY CENTRE *making it easy to explore on foot. There is plenty to see. The lively medina has fascinating shops and markets as well as Islamic architecture dating back a thousand years. The Bardo Museum contains the world's largest collection of Roman mosaics, while along Avenue Habib Bourguiba there are continental-style cafés and restaurants. Just a little way out of Tunis lies the ancient site of Carthage.*

The history of Tunis goes back to the early days of Carthage and it features on Roman maps dating from the first Punic War. Destroyed in 146 BC it was half-heartedly rebuilt by the Romans but remained a place of little importance until the arrival of the Arabs in the 7th century. Believing it to have a good defensive position, Hassan ibn Nooman, who had just ousted the Byzantines from Carthage, decided to build here and sited the medina on a bank of high ground next to a salt lake. The most significant work undertaken was the Great Mosque in AD 732 and the city served as the imperial capital during the last years of Aghlabid rule. From then on, Tunis was a major centre of

science, culture and religion in North Africa.

During the Hafsid era (1228–1574), with trade flourishing between Europe and the East, it became an Arab metropolis and by the 13th century the Hafsids had made it their capital. The Ottoman Turks (1580–1705) saw no reason to change this and built heavy fortifications round the city as well as a large number of mosques and palaces.

By the 19th century the population was becoming too numerous to remain inside the city walls and the French drained some of the nearby marshland to extend the city. The new part features wide avenues and some distinctly European architecture.

Place de la Kasbah, paved with local stone

◁ Entrance to one of the medina's hammams (Turkish baths)

Tunis Town Centre

TWO WORLDS ARE side by side in the centre of Tunis. On the one hand, there is the historic district, almost unchanged since medieval times, on the other, a modern metropolis. The western area of the centre is occupied by the medina, full of ancient palaces, mosques, medersas and souks. The eastern part comprises the Ville Nouvelle with the National Theatre, high-rise buildings, Art Deco houses, cinemas, a railway station and busy cafés and bars.

Palm trees and fountain for washing, in the arcaded courtyard of Sidi Mehrez Mosque

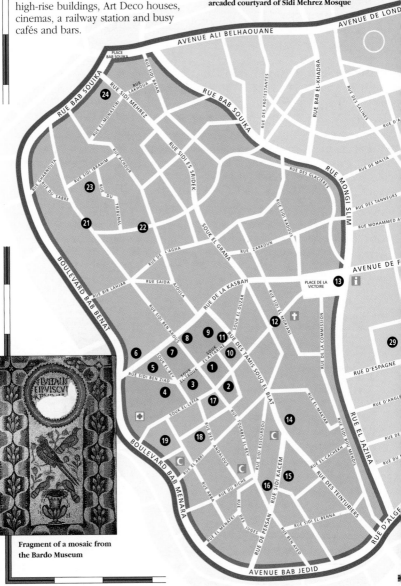

Fragment of a mosaic from the Bardo Museum

SEE ALSO

- **Where to Stay** pp248–250
- **Where to Eat** pp272–5

SIGHTS AT A GLANCE

Areas, Streets and Squares

Avenue Habib Bourguiba **28**
Bab el-Bahr **13**
Belvedere Park **30**
Place du Gouvernement **6**
Rue de la Hafsia **22**
Rue du Pasha **21**
Rue Jemaa Zitouna **12**

Markets

The Great Souk **7**
Main Market **29**
Souk el-Attarine **10**
Souk et-Trouk **3**

Museums & Historic Buildings

Bardo Museum pp88–9 **32**
Dar ben Abdallah **15**
Dar el-Bey **5**

Dar el-Haddad **19**
Dar Hussein **18**
Dar Lasram **23**
Dar Othman **14**
Hôtel Majestic **25**
National Library **11**
Théâtre Municipal **27**
Tourbet el-Bey **16**
Tourbet of Aziza Othmana **9**

Religious Buildings

Cathedral **26**
The Great Mosque (Zitouna Mosque) pp70–71 **1**
Hammouda Pasha Mosque **8**
Jellaz Cemetery **31**
Kasbah Mosque **20**
Medersa Mouradia **17**
Sidi Mehrez Mosque **24**
Sidi Youssef Mosque **4**
The Three Medersas **2**

GETTING AROUND

The most convenient way of exploring Tunis is on foot. The buses and trams can be crowded, but are useful for reaching sites further out, such as the Bardo Museum. The TGM train's main station is at the end of Avenue Habib Bourgiba and links the centre of Tunis to the suburbs. See pp326–7 for more details.

0 m   200
0 yards   200

KEY

Street-by-Street: The Medina
See pp68–9

Medina wall

Tourist information

Church

Mosque

Hospital

Post office

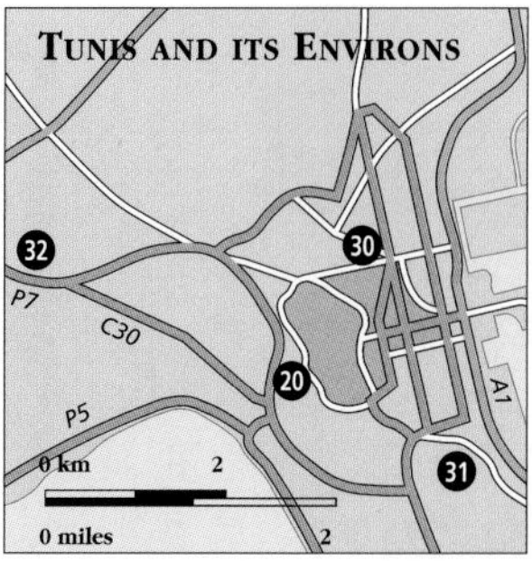

TUNIS AND ITS ENVIRONS

0 km   2
0 miles   2

Street-by-Street: The Medina

Tunis's ancient medina is classed by UNESCO as a World Heritage Site. Bustling with life for over one thousand years, it is full of narrow alleys, mosques, oriental markets and unexpected courtyards. It also has many mysterious and colourful doorways beyond which are ancient palaces and wealthy homes. The medina is centred on an axis formed by the Great Mosque and its many surrounding souks.

The Great Souk
The animated market has kept much of its traditional atmosphere and was used for scenes in the film The English Patient ❼

Place du Gouvernement *is the town's main square. It can be used as the starting point for exploring the medina* ❻

PLACE DU GOUVERNEMENT

RUE DE LA KASBAH

SOUK EL-BEY

Dar el-Bey *is the former beys' palace and is now the prime minister's office* ❺

RUE SIDI BEN ZIAD

SOUK ET-T

Sidi Youssef Mosque
This distinctive mosque has the oldest Ottoman-style minaret in the medina (1616) and is crowned with a balustrade and a wooden roof ❹

SOUK EL-BERKA

STAR SIGHTS

★ The Great Mosque

★ Souk et-Trouk

★ The Three Medersas

★ **Souk et-Trouk**
Built in 1630 by Sidi Youssef, this is one of the medina's most colourful rows of shops offering carpets, clothes and souvenirs. One shop has a terrace that provides a view of the medina ❸

Hammouda Pasha Mosque
The main feature of this mosque (1665) is the octagonal minaret, which is built in the Turkish style. It is one of the most beautiful mosques in Tunis ❽

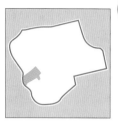

Tourbet of Aziza Othmana *is the tomb of Aziza – daughter of Othman, a bey of Tunis* ❾

National Library
The National Library contains over two million volumes. It is located at the heart of the medina, in the former military barracks built by Hammouda Pasha ⓫

SOUK BLAGHIJA

SIDI BEN AROUS

SOUK EL-ATTARINE (SUK AL-ATTARIN)

AL-TURK)

RUE JAMAA ZITOUNA

Souk el-Attarine *has traded in perfumes, incense, henna, candles and herbs since the 13th century* ❿

RUE DES LIBRAIRES

| 0 m | 50 |
| 0 yards | 50 |

★ The Three Medersas
These three Muslim schools comprise the Medersa of the Palm Tree, the Bachia and the Slimania ❷

★ The Great Mosque
This is the largest mosque in Tunis. Its construction was begun in the 8th century ❶

KEY

– – – Suggested route

The Great Mosque ❶

THE GREAT MOSQUE has been at the heart of Tunis since it was begun in the 8th century and towers over the souks that crowd around it. Aptly named, its striking east gallery opens up suddenly when proceeding up the final yards of Rue Jemaa Zitouna. Though parts of the mosque have been remodelled many times, its vast courtyard of polished marble is in its original form and is surrounded on three sides by graceful arcades.

★ Courtyard
Shaded by simple arcades, the courtyard is based on Kairouan's Great Mosque.

The Capitals
These ornate decorations can be seen crowning the many columns surrounding the inner courtyard of the complex.

★ Minaret
This stands on the site of a former defensive tower. It has been extended to a height of 44 m (144 ft).

Minaret Decorations
These were built to resemble the decorations in the Kasbah Mosque. The upper parts are lined with ceramic tiles.

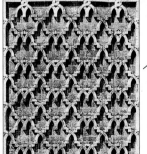

STAR SIGHTS
★ Courtyard
★ Minaret

Door to the Prayer Hall

The geometric patterns decorating the entrance to the prayer hall are based on Spanish designs.

Minbar

Standing to the right of the mihrab (indicating the direction of Mecca), this is a pulpit from which the khutba (weekly sermon) is delivered.

Prayer Hall

At the far end of the courtyard, the prayer hall must be kept ritually pure. Non-Muslims are not allowed to enter.

14th-century Gothic tower

Arcades

The three arcaded galleries in the main courtyard were built during the Husaynid dynasty (18th century).

The Dome

Since AD 864, this dome has topped the vestibule of the prayer hall.

The Three Medersas ❷

Rue des Libraires 11, 19 & Rue de la Medersa 13.

THE GREAT MOSQUE is adjoined by a group of three medersas. Built by the Husaynids as residential Islamic schools in the 18th century, each of them has a similar layout, with a courtyard flanked on three sides by students' cells. Used by students studying the Koran, the fourth side of the medersas' courtyards adjoin the mosque.

The oldest of them is the **Medersa of the Palm Tree** (1714). Its name derives from the palm tree that stands at the centre of the courtyard surrounded by arcaded galleries. The arcades, with their horseshoe arches, have columns with richly ornamented capitals. The Medersa of the Palm Tree now houses the headquarters of the organization concerned with Koranic law.

Bachia, the second in the group, was built in 1752 by Ali Pasha. Standing next to the entrance is a small fountain with miniature pools that are always full of water. The adjacent *tourbet* (mausoleum) houses the Cultural Society. **Slimania** also owes its existence to Ali Pasha, who built it in memory of his son Suleyman who had been murdered by his younger brother.

Inside a carpet shop in Souk et-Trouk

Souk et-Trouk ❸

THIS 17TH-CENTURY Turkish market is situated between Souk el-Attarine (the scent market) and Souk el-Berka (formerly the site of the old slave market). It contains the north gateway to the Great Mosque and also **Au Palais d'Orient** – one of Tunis's best-known carpet shops and viewing points. Here, visitors will also find **Café M. Rabet** with its miniature garden (a kind of verandah) and a more expensive restaurant on the first floor (overlooking a section of the Great Mosque). This is the place to come to enjoy some traditional Tunisian music, a cup of tea and, for those that want it, a puff of tobacco through a *chicha* (hookah).

Sidi Youssef Mosque ❹

Rue Sidi ben Ziad.

THIS BUILDING IS located on the first floor above the shops, which provided Muslim mosques with a revenue during the Turkish era. One of the most interesting Ottoman sacred buildings, the mosque has the the oldest Turkish minaret in the medina (1616). The octagonal minaret is set on a square base and is typical of Ottoman architecture. Most of the 48 columns (eight rows of six columns) in the prayer hall feature antique capitals and are North African in design. Adjacent to the mosque is the mausoleum of its founder – Sidi Youssef – which has a pyramid roof of green tiles. The complex is completed by the medersa, which was built in 1622.

Sidi Youssef Mosque with its 17th-century minaret

Dar el-Bey ❺

Place du Gouvernement.
🚫 to visitors.

THE FORMER SEAT of the bey rulers, and later of the French Protectorate administration, this is now the prime minister's office. Dar el-Bey, with its imposing 18th- and 19th-century façade, is the most important building in Tunis's Place du Gouvernement. Next to the west wing of the government's seat (in Rue Sidi ben Ziad) is the start of a marked walking route that leads towards the Great Mosque and further, to

Arcaded courtyard in the Medersa of the Palm Tree

Tourbet el-Bey and Dar ben Abdallah, in the south of the medina. At the start of the route there is a detailed map with the main sights and other points of interest clearly marked on it.

The palace was built as a guest house by a Husaynid monarch in 1795, on the ruins of a royal residence dating from the Muradid period. It was extensively remodelled in 1876 when it was used by the Bey of Tunis as a place to receive important visitors. It was here that he received many heads of state from Germany, England, France and the Ottoman Empire.

The bey himself lived outside Tunis in the Bardo area at this time. Prior to that, until the Husaynid period (18th century), the sultan's main residence was the nearby kasbah. The change was partly brought about by the fashion for building summer residences that prevailed at the beginning of the 19th century.

Place du Gouvernement ❻

THIS BUSY square is full of government buildings, fountains, palm trees and flowers. It is also a popular meeting place for young people and serves as a useful starting point for expeditions into the heart of the medina (it is just a short distance from the Great Mosque).

Place du Gouvernement is situated in what would once have been the western limit of the medina. It is flanked on the west by the Boulevard Bab Benat (Tunis's local government building stands on the opposite side of the avenue), and on the east and north by the Government Secretariat and the Ministry of Religious Affairs.

The Dar el-Bey *(see opposite)* stands at its southern end on the side of the Sidi Youssef Mosque. This former bey's residence has been renovated several times and now houses the offices of Tunisia's prime minister.

Busy alley in one of the medina's souks

The Great Souk ❼

THE MEDINA IN Tunis has more than 20 souks. The major ones are adjacent to the Great Mosque and together form one vast, colourful, animated marketplace. Two terms, both meaning "market", compete with each other in the Muslim world: the bazaar (from the Persian) and the souk (from the Arabic). For centuries a souk had a distinct, cohesive character based on the traditions of the eastern and Mediterranean nations, and featured clearly identified places for various types of goods. From the beginning, this was a venue for trading in goods and conducting financial transactions, as well as being the centre of social life. Arab souks, as opposed to European markets, were never places of residence for the merchants. The Great Mosque was always the seat of learning and faith, while the souks constituted the town's economic centre. Souks may seem chaotic but actually have a strict hierarchy. The immediate vicinity of the Great Mosque was reserved for the up-market bazaars selling articles such as religious books, perfumes, carpets and jewellery. In Muslim countries, the market was, and continues to be, an important element of Islamic life. The souk is a place where people come to shop, trade and meet friends. According to Muslim tradition, trading is the sweetest occupation. The medieval Arab scholar al-Ghazali, for instance, considered commerce as a form of preparation for the rewards of the next world.

Haggling is a strictly scripted performance: both parties must end up believing that they have struck a good bargain. Any customer who engages in a long bargaining process should not pull out of the deal at the end *(see p291).*

Fountain in Place du Gouvernement

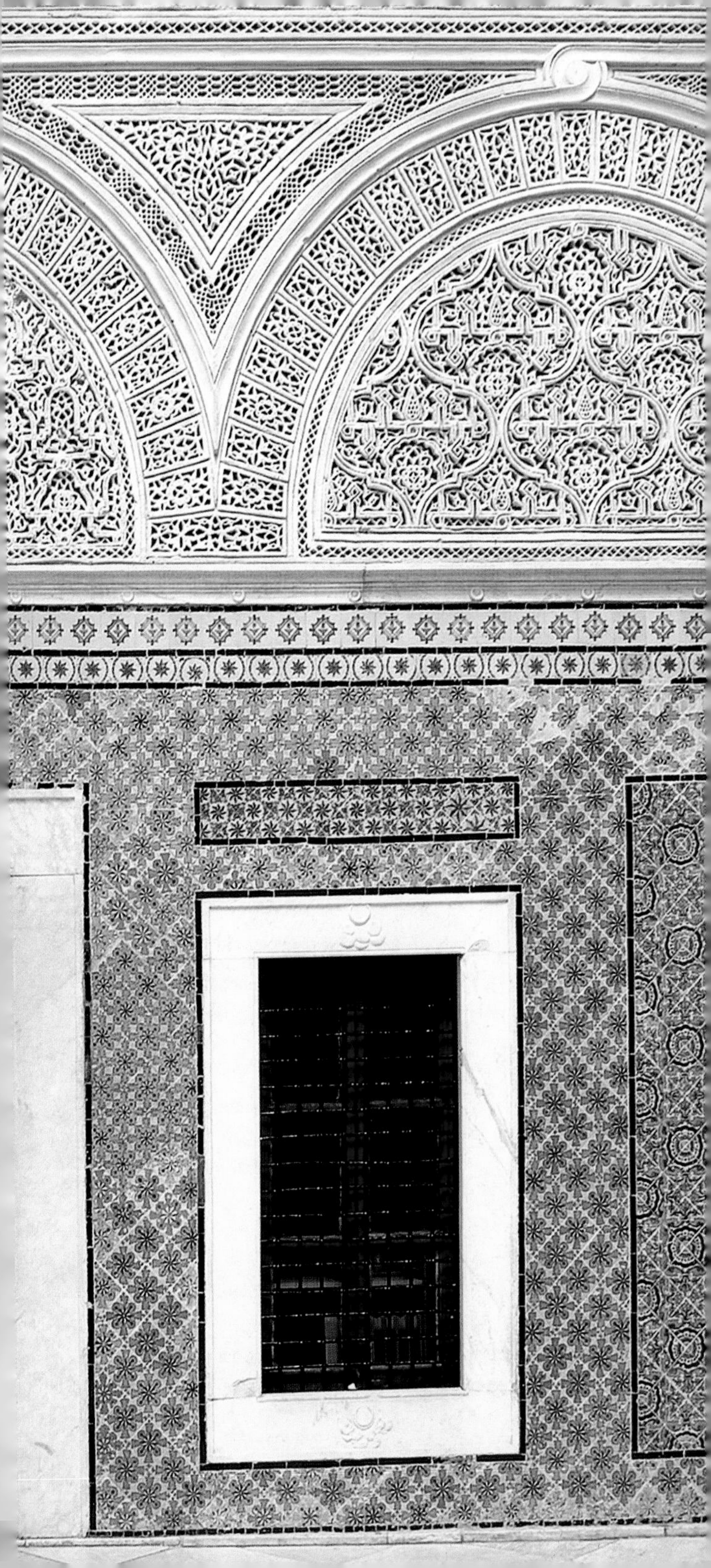

Hammouda Pasha Mosque **8**

Corner of Rue Sidi ben Arous and Rue de la Kasbah.

ONE OF THE MEDINA'S most distinctive buildings, this mosque attracts a large number of the Muslim faithful for the all-important Friday prayers. The entire complex includes the mosque and the *tourbet* (tomb) of its founder, Hammouda Pasha, one of the early Ottoman rulers and the founder of the Muradid dynasty. The mosque was completed in 1665, a year before the monarch's death, and was lavishly decorated by craftsmen from Italy.

Two gates lead to the mosque, which is easily recognisable by its sandstone walls. The main one is the northern gate from Rue de la Kasbah while the side entrance is from Rue Sidi ben Arous. Inside the mosque is a courtyard surrounded with arcades, which are towered over by one of Tunis's most distinctive minarets – an octagonal, Turkish-style structure with black and white arches. The minaret's balcony would originally have been used by the muezzin to call the faithful to prayer, though this role has now been replaced by using loudspeakers.

Tourbet of Aziza Othmana **9**

Rue Sidi ben Arous 23.

NOT FAR from the Great Mosque stands the mausoleum of Aziza, daughter of Bey Othman, who has been revered by the people of Tunis for over 300 years. It was erected following the princess's death in 1669. Aziza was renowned for her charity work. Towards the end of her life, she freed her slaves and left her estate to charitable foundations that helped the poor, supported medersas, financed hospitals, and provided dowries for impoverished girls. The entrance leads first to the *zaouia* of Sidi ben Arous, where a doorman will show visitors the way to the *tourbet* of Aziza Othmana.

Souk el-Attarine **10**

THE SCENT OF perfume and aromatic oils has long hung in the air around this perfume market. The immediate neighbourhood was reserved exclusively for rich souks that did not produce noise or offensive smells (butcher's and blacksmith's souks were always tucked far away from the Great Mosque). The 13th-century Souk el-Attarine owes its existence to the early Hafsid rulers. For centuries it was a venue for trading in perfumes, incense, aromatic essence, henna, candles, wax, as well as a mixture of herbs, flowers and resins. The market no longer specializes in perfume but visitors can still buy scent here and even have a special mixture made up to an individual

A perfume vendor in Souk el-Attarine

recipe. Well-known scents, such as Chanel No. 5, can also be approximately reproduced. For Tunisians, scents have symbolic meanings. To this day, wedding guests are sprinkled with essence of orange, newborn babies with geranium oil, and arriving guests with rose essence. The use of scents is given up only during the month of Ramadan.

Illuminated manuscript from the National Library's collection

National Library **11**

Souk el-Attarine 20. **(71) 325 338.** *to visitors.*

TUNISIA'S National Library contains over two million volumes and manuscripts. It is at the very heart of the medina and occupies the former army barracks built by Hammouda Pasha. Before

Interior of the Hammouda Pasha Mosque

◁ **Ceramic and stonemasonry decorations in Dar Lasram**

becoming a library, the colonial administration had turned the building into the Department of Antiquities and then added a library just for good measure. Following Tunisia's regained independence, in 1956, the Department of Antiquities was moved to Dar Hussein, while the library was reorganized and its collection increased with thousands of Arab manuscripts that were collected together from the medina's many mosques and medersas. Unfortunately, the library is not open to visitors and entry requires permission from the Ministry of Culture.

Bab el-Bahr connecting the medina with the Ville Nouvelle

Rue Jemaa Zitouna ⓬

THIS IS ONE of the medina's main streets (after Rue de la Kasbah). There are plenty of souvenir shops here but the same souvenirs can be bought much cheaper, and without haggling, in the side-streets or the souks in the south or north of the medina.

The street runs steeply upwards, from Place de la Victoire and the Bab el-Bahr gate to the Great Mosque where the souks are some of the oldest in Tunis. The place is crowded and noisy from morning until 6pm, except for Ramadan, when it comes alive at dusk and continues until 1 or 2am. The shops that line the street on both sides offer Nabeul ceramics, "Hand of Fatima"

talismans, birdcages, camel mascots, and hookahs or hubble-bubble pipes. The shopkeepers here are a multilingual lot and advertise their wares in most languages – German, English, French, Polish, Czech and Hungarian are all heard.

The top portion of the street has a number of shops selling Tunisian cakes. The **Café Ez-Zitouna** serves coffee and tea and provides the wherewithal for hookahs. The end of Rue Jamaa Zitouna provides a view of the east gallery of the Great Mosque, which is illuminated at night. From here, turn right, then left and climb to the viewing roof of the **Au Palais d'Orient** carpet shop from where it is possible to look down on the Great Mosque's courtyard and the medina's roofs and minarets.

Bab el-Bahr ⓭

Place de la Victoire.

THE BAB EL-BAHR gate marks the symbolic border between the old quarter of Tunis and the Ville Nouvelle that was built by the French during the colonial era. This vast arch standing in Place de la Victoire was once the east gate in the wall that encircled the medina and would have been surrounded by huts and stalls.

Bab el-Bahr is the Arabic for "the Sea Gate" and is so named because of its close proximity to the sea. In the 19th century, the waters of Lake Tunis almost lapped up against the walls of the medina, though today its shores are about 1.5 km (1 mile) away. This is thanks to the French who drained much of the ground in order to lay foundations for the new town. As the Ville Nouvelle prospered, the Bab el-Bahr became a link between two worlds and a symbol of progress and of the new era. During the French protectorate, its name changed to the French Gate and only reverted to its old name after Tunisia regained independence. The present gate was built in 1848 on the orders of Ahmed Bey, who was inspired by the Arc de Triomphe and had the old gate demolished. It stands at the end of Avenue de France, which leads to the harbour.

HAND OF FATIMA

The "Hand of Fatima" is a common talisman that is thought to ward off bad luck. Many Muslims believe that the hand has the power to protect and bestow blessings. Fatima was the daughter of the Prophet Mohammed. An idealized mother and wife, the Fatimid dynasty claimed descent from her. The five fingers symbolize not only the five pillars of Islam, but also the Muslim prayer that is repeated five times a day.

"Fatima's hand" on a house wall

Garden in the inner courtyard of Dar Othman

Dar Othman ⓮

Rue el-M'Bazza 16.

ONE OF THE MEDINA'S oldest and most stately palaces, Dar Othman's façade is fashioned from black and white marble; the interior has a rich array of mosaics, wooden ceiling decorations covered with magnificent paintings and a small garden in the inner courtyard. Located in the southern part of the medina, not far from Dar ben Abdallah, the palace was built by Othman Bey who resided here from 1594 until his death in 1610. The first owner of the palace became famous for his unswerving principle of separating state affairs from his private life and this palace was designed to provide him with a haven in which he could take a rest from his daily work, while separate sections were allocated for receiving visitors. The subsequent inhabitants of the palace included Bey Hussein and Ibd Mahmud. Now the restored palace houses the headquarters of the Medina Conservation Department.

Dar ben Abdallah ⓯

Museum of Popular Arts and Traditions, entrance from Rue ben Abdallah. ☐ *(71) 256 195.* ☐ *9:30am-4:30pm daily.* ● *Sun.* 🖼 🖾

THIS 18TH-CENTURY palace, located in the southern part of the medina, has a fine courtyard, surrounded by tall arcaded galleries with walls that are decorated with colourful ceramic tiles. One

of the finest palaces in the medina, it was built by Slimane Kahia el-Hanafi, a government official responsible for the collection of taxes during the reign of Hammouda Pasha. The entrance from the courtyard leads to the inner rooms of the palace, where the **Museum of Popular Arts and Traditions** has displays illustrating the lives of the medina's wealthy 19th-century inhabitants.

Visitors can still see some of the rooms that were used by the owner, his wife and children, plus additional guest rooms and the kitchens. The interior furnishings include Venetian mirrors, crystal chandeliers and candelabras. The palace, originally called Dar Kahia, got its new name from its later owner – Ben Abdallah, a merchant, who lived here from 1875–99.

Tourbet el-Bey ⓰

Museum–mausoleum, Rue Tourbet el-Bey 62. ☐ *9am-4:30pm daily.* ● *Sun.* 🖼 🖾

THIS ROYAL MAUSOLEUM of the Husaynids was built by Ali Pasha II (1758–82). It is not far from Dar ben Abdallah and Dar Othman (a marked trail leads to all three sights, starting from Place du Gouvernement). Although Islam – and particularly the Malekite school – calls for simple burials, with the

Mannequins in one of the museum rooms in Dar ben Abdallah

arrival of the Turkish Ottomans the Hanefite school began to gain influence. This allowed for far more fanciful, richly ornamented and opulent mausoleums.

Tourbet el-Bey is an entire architectural complex, covered with several domes of different sizes, and includes two inner courtyards (orange trees grow in the smaller of these), and is reminiscent of palace architecture.

Entrance to Tourbet el-Bey

Medersa Mouradia ⑰

Souk des Etoffes 37.

JUST A SHORT DISTANCE from the Great Mosque, this 18th-century Muslim residential school is entered through a large and ornately studded wooden door. Its inner courtyard is surrounded by an arcaded gallery. The courtyard is typically Tunisian in style and features an entrance to the prayer hall, marked by an arcade, which is horseshoe-shaped and in black and white marble. Wooden doors lead to the cells of the older students. The medersa was built in 1637 by Murad II, on the site of some Turkish army barracks that were destroyed during a rebellion.

Dar Hussein ⑱

Place du Château. ◯ (courtyard only) 8:30am–1pm and 3–6pm. ● Fri. Admission free.

THIS IS ONE OF the finest restored palaces of the medina. Built in the 18th century, it is a stately place, and was erected on the site an 11th-century palace. Today it houses the National Institute of Arts and Archaeology and the present owners are happy to let visitors look around. It is reached via the short and narrow Rue du Château. Having passed through the *skifa* (vestibule), enter the spacious palace courtyard, which has been covered with a modern, sloping glazed roof since its restoration. The courtyard is surrounded by cloisters with columns topped with Corinthian capitals. The walls are covered in colourful ceramic tiles (the work of Italian artisans) that feature floral motifs and intricate geometrical patterns. The wooden vaults have also been beautifully decorated.

Dar el-Haddad ⑲

Impasse de l'Artillerie 9.
🞜 (71) 570 937. ◯ (courtyard only) 8:30am–1pm & 3–6pm. ● Fri. Admission free.

HIDDEN AWAY IN a labyrinth of narrow alleys, this is one of the oldest palaces in the medina and was built in the late 16th century. Restored in 1966, it now houses a

Cloisters around Dar Hussein's arcaded courtyard

branch of the National Heritage Institute. The easiest way to get here is from the west (from Boulevard Bab Menara), via Souk Sekkajine (from which it is necessary to turn into Rue ben Mahmoud), or via Rue du Château (also turning into Rue ben Mahmoud). From the 18th century, the palace belonged to the wealthy Haddad family, who originally arrived from Andalusia following the fall of Granada. The courtyard is surrounded by porticoes on three sides and its columns are topped with capitals from the period of the Hafsids.

Exquisitely decorated arcades around the patio of Dar el-Haddad

The minaret of the Kasbah Mosque

Kasbah Mosque ⑳

Place de la Kasbah.

THE KASBAH MOSQUE gets its name from the fort that stood above the medina during the Hafsid reign. Badly damaged during a revolt by Turkish troops in 1811, only the mosque and parts of the wall running along Rue el-Zouaoui have survived. Protected by mighty walls, the kasbah was once the venue of the sultan's council gatherings and was where the sultan held audiences.

Adjacent to the kasbah were the army barracks and city guard quarters. These were used as the sultan's residence until Husaynid times (18th century) and continued to retain a military function. During the time of the French Protectorate, they were occupied by French troops. The barracks were eventually demolished in 1957.

The mosque is well worth visiting, if only to see its minaret (the tallest in the medina), which served as the model for the Great Mosque's Malekite minaret. Five times a day, the call to prayer is signalled by briefly flying a white flag from the minaret.

Rue du Pasha ㉑

DURING THE Ottoman period, this cobbled street bisected the town's smartest district. Today, it is a popular tourist route and divides the medina from north to south. It is worth taking a closer look at the small courtyards, window shutters, and the main doors along its route. The size and grandeur of each door is directly related to the size and grandeur of the residence behind it. Almost every door in this street is still furnished with its traditional doorknocker. Some of the houses have more than one knocker. These used to indicate the number of people who once lived inside and date from a time when different sounding "knocks" were used to signal the identity and gender of guests (men, women and children each had different doorknockers). One of the most elaborate of these doors can be found at No. 29.

Rue du Pasha is also full of intricately decorated façades and window shutters, and is an ideal place for taking some photographs.

Visitors can discover a variety of unusual places, such as the former palace at No. 71. Dilapidated but full of charm this once-grand building stands beyond a small garden planted with jasmine and banana trees. It now houses the headquarters of the Tunisian Red Crescent (volunteers are pleased to show visitors around).

Rue de la Hafsia ㉒

THIS DISTRICT occupies the northern part of the medina. It was once inhabited by Jews, who towards the end of the 19th century moved to the Ville Nouvelle. Neglected and derelict, it gained a reputation as one of the seedier parts of town. During the 1950s there were calls to demolish it but recently a plan to renovate and rebuild the Rue de la Hafsia has been given the go-ahead.

Dar Lasram ㉓

Rue du Tribunal 24.
⊙ during office hours of the Association de Sauvegarde de la Medina (selected rooms).

DAR LASRAM is one of the most stately and expertly renovated palaces in the entire medina. Visitors have access to the courtyard as well as some of the main rooms including the library, which has several displays of maps, plans and photographs.

Construction of the palace began in the latter part of the 18th century and was continued by Hammoud Lasram, a rich landowner and high-ranking officer. His descendants inhabited it until 1964. The palace is arranged over three storeys: the ground floor was occupied by the servants, the raised first floor was the main portion of the house, and the top floor was set aside for guests.

Rue du Pasha – an ancient alleyway

Magnificently decorated rooms of Dar Lasram

Visiting the palace offers a unique insight into how the wealthy lived in 19th-century Tunis. The main door opens up to the *driba* (entrance hall), which was used by the owner of the house to receive visitors. The room to the right of the entrance is the *bayt-al-sahra* (evening room). During the day, it was used by teachers but in the evening it became a venue for all-male gatherings, which were livened up by female dancers.

Women also had their own soirees. For these, the servants would sprinkle the carpets and pond with rose and jasmine petals, fill the censers with ambergris, incense and aloe and arrange cushions on the floor. After the women had taken their seats, a large tray would be brought in, laden with sweets and glasses of tea.

Much of the decoration is in keeping with this lavish lifestyle. The wall containing the door to the *dar al-kebira* (state rooms) is lined with pink sandstone while the white stuccowork above the door resembles intricate lace. Look out for the arches supported by Doric columns that feature charming stucco decorations.

It is perhaps no surprise that such a stunning palace is now the home of the Association de Sauvegarde de la Medina (The Medina Conservation Society).

Sidi Mehrez Mosque ㉔

Rue Sidi Mehrez.

THIS MOSQUE STANDS in the northern part of the medina, in the El-Hafsia district. Begun in 1675, it was named after the town's patron saint – Sidi Mehrez – a prominent 10th-century marabout (Islamic holy man) and theologian, who arrived here from Kairouan. It was to him that Tunis owed its recovery in 944. The mosque architecture and decorations are reminiscent of the traditional Muslim buildings of Istanbul. One of the best views is to be had from the north side of Bab Souika.

Richly ornamented interior of Sidi Mehrez Mosque

THE CORSAIRS

The glamorous but violent world of the corsairs played a significant role in shaping the history of Tunisia from the mid-16th century until the early 19th century. The most notorious corsair was the Turkish-born Khair ed-Din Barbarossa (Red Beard), who based himself on the island of Jerba and in 1534 captured Tunis. Under the Ottomans there was great wealth to be taken at sea and corsairs flourished during the Husaynid period as a major Tunisian enterprise. During the late 17th and early 18th centuries some maritime nations even paid bribes to Tunisia so that their ships would not be attacked.

Barbarossa, once the most notorious corsair in Tunisia

The whole building is topped by a large white dome, surrounded by four smaller ones (also white). The courtyard is surrounded on three sides by arcades; and the walls of the prayer hall are richly ornamented.

Opposite the entrance to the mosque is the mausoleum of Sidi Mehrez (also known as Mehrez ibn Chalaf). The tomb is revered by Muslims and Jews alike. Sidi Mehrez was famous for his tolerance and won a number of concessions for the Jews. Thanks to him, those who traded in the local souks were granted the right to settle within the city walls and no longer had to leave the city at nightfall.

Hôtel Majestic 25

Avenue de Paris.

THE HÔTEL MAJESTIC stands in Avenue de Paris, in the Ville Nouvelle. Built in 1914, it has a beautiful white façade with gently curved corners typical of Art Nouveau architecture. It also boasts several lovely balconies. The hotel is built over four-storeys: the first floor has a terrace where guests once took afternoon tea. The restaurant and hotel remain open to this day but the surroundings have changed: the once quiet street is now a busy avenue, full of shops, people and cars. Nevertheless, the hotel retains some of its old charm. A ten-minute walk along Avenue de Paris will bring visitors to Avenue Habib Bourguiba.

Hôtel Majestic, once among the best hotels in Tunis

Cathedral 26

Place de l'Indépendance.

THE CATHEDRAL OF St Vincent de Paul and St Olive, to give it its full name, stands at the very centre of the Ville Nouvelle, close to Bab el-Bahr. It was built in 1882, on the site of a Catholic cemetery dedicated to St Antoine. Mentioned in a number of early 17th-century texts, this cemetery was originally destined for deceased slaves who had previously been captured by corsairs operating out of Tunis. The cathedral, with its tall twin towers which

Façade of the Cathedral of St Vincent de Paul

form the entrance, is an odd mix of Byzantine, Gothic and North African architecture. This echoes the muddled history of Christianity in the region and resembles the Christian basilica in Henchir Khira, near Béja, with a Byzantine-style dome rising above the nave and the transept intersection. A mosaic above the main entrance depicts Christ.

Inside, the church has a broad mix of styles and imagery. The arcade is crowned with the figure of Abraham blessing the Jews, the Christians and the Muslims. The painting in the apse depicts the Assumption of St Vincent de Paul who is surrounded by the figures of North African saints and

martyrs, led by the famous bishop of Carthage – St Cyprian. The green-blue stained-glass window on the left (south transept) depicts the Assumption of the Virgin Mary, while the red-gold window on the right (north transept) shows the descent of the Holy Spirit at Pentecost.

The main altarpiece mosaics are composed of alabaster and marble, and are fashioned in a typical Tunisian style. Built in 1921, the cathedral's organ is generally regarded as the finest in North Africa. The cathedral is occasionally used as a venue for concerts.

Théâtre Municipal 27

Avenue Habib Bourguiba.

THIS THEATRE WAS built by the French in the early 20th century and is a classic example of Art Nouveau, with distinctive white stucco, soft flowing floral forms and fantastic carved figures. It is still used as a theatre today and is a good venue for concerts of both classical and Arabic music as well as films and talks.

Ornate stuccowork on the façade of the Théâtre Municipal

Ville Nouvelle Architecture

Dᵁᴿᴵᴺᴳ ᵀᴴᴱ ᴾᴱᴿᴵᴼᴰ of the French Protectorate (1881–1956), the population of Tunis began to move beyond the walls of the medina. New structures appeared and wealthy Tunisians gave up the narrow labyrinthine alleys of the medina for the wide avenues and apartments of the Ville Nouvelle. The building of the new town coincided with the development of Art Nouveau in France and Italy, followed later by Art Deco. Perhaps no other European style has merged so successfully with Islamic architecture as Art Nouveau. The arabesque, an ornament typical of Islamic art, blended perfectly with the curves and undulating surfaces of Art Nouveau, as did the Islamic taste for ornate stuccowork and florid decorations.

Street lamps *with fanciful decorations protecting their glass shades illuminate and decorate Avenue Habib Bourguiba – one of the finest streets in the European district of Tunis.*

The Oriental style *featuring domes, arched windows and courtyards, combines with European elements and can be seen in the buildings around Place du Gouvernement.*

Art Nouveau *houses, adorned with stunning balconies are common on Avenue de Paris, Rue ibn Khaldun and Rue Charles de Gaulle.*

Architecture *inspired by Baroque and Renaissance styles is the most prevalent in Tunis's modern town. Frequently, each storey of a building is constructed in the style of a different era. The extremely rich, heavily ornamented façades are also reminiscent of Islamic architecture.*

The colonial style *is represented mainly by apartment blocks and public buildings. These were built in clusters in styles fashionable in Europe during the late 19th century.*

Architectural details *including floral motifs and figures adorn the façades of most houses built during the colonial era.*

Imposing clock tower standing at the end of Avenue Habib Bourguiba

Avenue Habib Bourguiba ㉘

THE MAIN STREET of Tunis's Ville Nouvelle, Avenue Habib Bourguiba runs like an artery through the city linking the harbour and TGM train station with the medina. Along the way it cuts through Place du 7 Novembre 1987 (which commemorates the day when Bourguiba was replaced by Zine el-Abidine ben Ali) and Place de l'Indépendance. From here it becomes Avenue de France. About half way along, Place du 7 Novembre has a fountain and a prominent clock tower decorated with fine tracery. In the evenings the illuminated clock and the multicoloured fountain become a popular meeting places for the youth of Tunis.

The section between here and the cathedral is the busiest part of this tree-lined promenade and there are plenty of smart cafés and fashionable restaurants to tempt visitors. Café de Paris, situated near Hôtel Africa, is the birthplace of the Ecole de Tunis, founded in 1949, which was an influential group of Tunisian painters. The café is still a popular meeting place, although little has remained of its artistic atmosphere. Moving on towards the medina, you pass on the left hand side the lovely Art Nouveau façade of the Théâtre Municipal (see pp82–3). Next to it is a large modern shopping centre, the Palmarium, on the ground floor of which is the *artisanat* (state-run) showroom of SOCOPA (see p37), where there is a good selection of Islamic art and handicrafts.

Tunis Cathedral (see p82) stands in Place de l'Indépendance, not far from Bab el-Bahr. Opposite is the French Embassy. To the left, beneath the arcades, are several smart shops selling clothes and shoes, and also Magasin Général – a large self-service store where food and drink can be purchased on the ground floor.

Main Market ㉙

Rue d'Allemagne. ⬜ from the early morning until about 2:30pm.

THIS HUGE MARKET hall is situated not far from Bab el-Bahr and is where many of the residents of Tunis come to do their weekly shopping. Built during the colonial era, it has a high-vaulted roof to protect shoppers from the rain or heat. A wide variety of goods is on offer. Articles include a large selection of excellent cheeses, dozens of varieties of the Tunisian harissa (chilli and garlic sauce), cooking oil, vegetables, fruit, meat and fish. On sale right by the entrance are flowerpots containing Tunisian herbs and other plants that include varieties of jasmine, bougainvillea, basil and rosemary. A large part of the hall is occupied by fruit and vegetable vendors trying to out-perform each other in the hope of getting passers-by to purchase their products. Any transaction may involve haggling. The market is worth visiting if only to witness these scenes of everyday Tunisian life.

Fishmonger's stall in the main market

◁ A stall with lanterns, plates and hookahs in the medina

Belvedere Park ⓷⓪

Entrance on Avenue des Etats-Unis or Place Pasteur. 🚆 🚌 📞 (71) 89 0 386. @ ami.belvedere@planet.tn

BELVEDERE PARK IS located to the north of the medina, on the slope of a hill standing some 2 km (1 mile) from the end of Avenue Habib Bourguiba. Outside rush hour it is possible to get there by TGM train (the Tunisians refer to it as the metro) from République (get off at Palestine then walk).

This is Tunis's only major park and provides an opportunity to escape from the busy and somewhat cramped streets and alleys of the medina. The park was established in 1892 by Josepha de Laforcade, a landscape artist and one of Paris's top gardeners. Initially it was closed to the public (due to construction works and the natural plant growth cycle) and the official opening did not take place until 1910.

To this day it remains the biggest park in Tunis, and the favourite place for family outings, receptions and Sunday picnics. At the last count, it had over 230,000 trees and 80 species of plants including olive trees, pines and numerous varieties of cacti. The park also plays an important educational role. A visit to the Friends of Park Belvedere Park, which has a small office on the high ground near the park's entrance will provide information on the many plants growing in the garden, and also on Tunisia's flora and fauna in general. Close to this is the **Centre d'Animation Équestre**, which organizes pony-trekking. A little higher up is a fairly gentle assault course.

There is also a zoo in the southern section of the park which has a number of birds and animals native to Africa. The zoo has a small admission charge and attracts over a million visitors a year. If visiting the zoo, look out for the Midha, a 17th-century ablutions room that was

Belvedere Park – a popular recreational area for residents of Tunis

transported here from the Souk et-Trouk in the medina and was also displayed at the World Exhibition in Paris in 1900. Not far from the zoo there is an artificial lake.

Standing at the heart of the park, on a hill, is a lovely *koubba* or pavilion. Once part of Hammouda Pasha's rose garden, it was placed here to serve as a resting place and viewpoint. It is an excellent example of Tunisian architecture. Its decoration tastefully combines a variety of styles – Italian white marble columns, Doric capitals, Moorish-Spanish ceramics and stuccoes, and Tunisian earthenware.

Belvedere's grounds also include a former casino. Originally converted into an officers' club, it has since become a museum of modern art and cinema. The museum also has two summer theatres and occasionally serves as a concert venue.

Centre d'Animation Équestre
📞 (98) 652 085.
📠 (71) 336 884.

Jellaz Cemetery ⓷⓵

Next to Bab Alleoua.

LOCATED NEXT TO the bus station, this burial ground is the largest in Tunis. Visiting the graves of one's relatives is considered a duty, especially during Aïd el-Fitr, at the end of Ramadan. At this time the cemetery is visited by family groups, who clean and whitewash the tombs, which are all arranged to face towards Mecca. The first mass demonstrations against French rule took place here in 1911, costing the lives of 30 Tunisians and nine Frenchmen in the riot that ensued.

Entrance to Jellaz Cemetery – the largest burial ground in Tunis

Bardo Museum 32

Ceramic decoration

LOCATED ON THE outskirts of Tunis, the Bardo museum occupies a former palace belonging to the Husseinite beys. The museum has an unrivalled collection of Roman mosaics dating from the 2nd to 4th centuries AD that once adorned the homes of some of Roman Africa's wealthiest citizens. As well as priceless mosaics, the Bardo contains a huge number of items from other periods including Punic funeral masks, Greek bronze statuary, Islamic tiles and finds from a ship that went down off Mahdia in the 1st century BC.

2nd floor

★ Eros
(125 BC)
This bronze statuette is one of the most precious objects that was recovered from a ship that went down off Mahdia during the 1st century BC.

Mosaic with the image of Virgil

1st floor

★ Roman Sarcophagus (3rd century AD)
The relief depicts the three Graces and the four seasons of the year – a favourite Roman motif that often appears on tombs and in mosaics.

Ground floor

Minerva (2nd century AD)
The marble statue of Minerva, goddess of wisdom and war, patron of crafts, arts and literature, stands on the ground floor, in the corridor devoted to Roman sculpture.

STAR EXHIBITS

★ Eros

★ Julius Mosaic

★ Roman Sarcophagus

MUSEUM GUIDE

The museum's Roman mosaics are spread over all three floors. Islamic art occupies several rooms on the ground floor and first floor. The first floor also has a display of underwater finds from Mahdia. Punic and early Christian exhibits can be seen on the ground floor.

Entrance

Mosaics from the Acholla baths, near Sfax

VISITORS' CHECKLIST

Bardo 2000. 🚌 from Bab el-Khadra, Nos. 3A, 3D and 30. 🚋 4 from Park Thameur. 🚍 📞 (71) 513 650. FAX (71) 514 050. ⬤ Apr–mid-Sep: 9am–5pm; mid-Sep–Mar: 9:30am–4:30pm daily. ⬤ Mon. 📷 📱 📹

Mahdia Room

In 1907 sponge divers came across the wreck of a ship near Mahdia that sank during the 1st century BC. It contained marble columns, reliefs, sculptures and bronze vases.

Carthage Room

This room has a fine collection of statuary from Roman Carthage. At its centre is a monument to Augustus from the 1st century AD. The floor mosaics date from the 3rd century AD and once decorated wealthy homes in Oudna.

★ Julius Mosaic

(3rd century AD) *This Carthaginian mosaic belongs to a series depicting farming in North Africa. Other mosaics illustrate scenes from everyday life and mythology.*

Dougga and Sousse Rooms

The Dougga Room has an intricately decorated ceiling with floral and arabesque motifs. In the adjacent Sousse Room is a fine floor mosaic. Recovered from a villa in Sousse, it represents the Triumph of Neptune.

KEY

🟨	Roman art
⬜	Christian art
⬜	Punic art
🟦	Islamic art
⬜	Objects recovered from the shipwreck off Mahdia
🟫	Prehistoric art
⬜	Non-exhibition rooms

GREATER TUNIS AND CAP BON PENINSULA

T HE COASTAL SUBURBS JUST EAST OF TUNIS, *including La Goulette, Carthage and Sidi Bou Saïd, provide an alternative to the bustle of the city. Drawn by cooling sea breezes, many locals visit this area on hot summer evenings. Further east is the Cap Bon peninsula. A major agricultural region since Carthaginian times, Cap Bon has some fine beaches and has become one of Tunisia's main resort areas.*

Poking out like a finger into the Mediterranean Sea, the Cap Bon peninsula is a mere 140 km (87 miles) from Sicily. Some geologists believe that it may once have provided a link between Africa and Europe until rising sea levels cut it off some 30,000 years ago. A range of mountains divides the peninsula lengthways into its eastern and western portions. The east coast, with its fine beaches and historic ruins, is mostly given up to resorts such as Hammamet and Nabeul while the west coast is more rugged and less frequently visited. Cap Bon is also one of the country's major industrial regions. La Goulette is a major port, and handles frequent passenger traffic from Europe.

The Carthaginians made the most of the fertile soil and by the time the Romans settled here the cape resembled a spectacular garden, and was named the Beautiful Cape or Cap Bon. When the French arrived in the 19th century they planted huge citrus groves and vineyards.

Even today, many farms thrive and, thanks to a high level of rainfall and efficient irrigation systems, Cap Bon provides the country with 80 per cent of its citrus fruit crop, 60 per cent of its grapes and almost half of its vegetables. Most Tunisian wines are also produced in this area, especially around the town of Grombalia, which has an annual wine festival in September.

Harvesting oranges in Cap Bon

◁ **Striking white minaret of a mosque in Sidi Bou Saïd**

Exploring Greater Tunis and Cap Bon Peninsula

GREATER TUNIS AND THE Cap Bon peninsula have fine beaches, fertile land and unique historic sights. A visit to the ruins of Carthage, once the second city of the Roman Empire, is unmissable for anyone interested in this period. Just north of Carthage, the charming town of Sidi Bou Saïd looks out over the Gulf of Tunis, and has some fine restaurants. The gently rolling terrain and rugged coast of Cap Bon are perfect for exploring, as are the Roman ruins in Kerkouane. Nabeul, a little way from Hammamet, has a busy market and is famous for its ceramics. Spring is a good time to visit, when the scent of orange and lemon blossom is in the air.

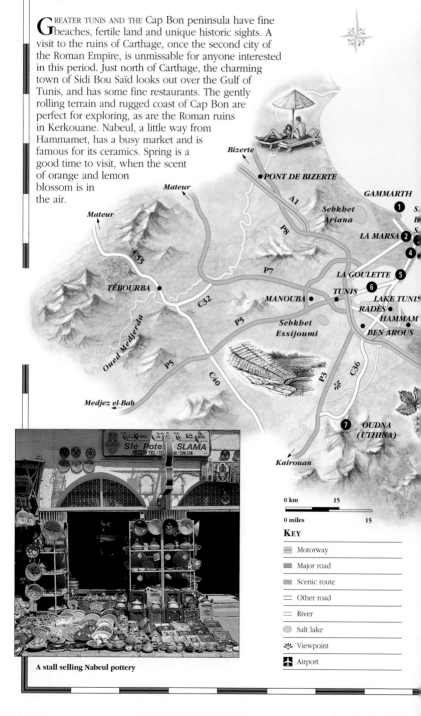

A stall selling Nabeul pottery

KEY

▬	Motorway
▬	Major road
▬	Scenic route
=	Other road
=	River
⬤	Salt lake
✹	Viewpoint
✈	Airport

0 km   15
0 miles   15

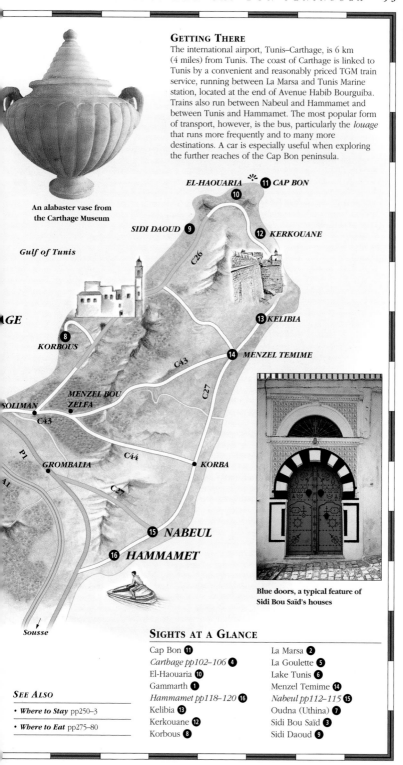

GETTING THERE

The international airport, Tunis–Carthage, is 6 km (4 miles) from Tunis. The coast of Carthage is linked to Tunis by a convenient and reasonably priced TGM train service, running between La Marsa and Tunis Marine station, located at the end of Avenue Habib Bourguiba. Trains also run between Nabeul and Hammamet and between Tunis and Hammamet. The most popular form of transport, however, is the bus, particularly the *louage* that runs more frequently and to many more destinations. A car is especially useful when exploring the further reaches of the Cap Bon peninsula.

An alabaster vase from the Carthage Museum

EL-HAOUARIA **10** **11** CAP BON

SIDI DAOUD **9** **12** KERKOUANE

Gulf of Tunis

C26

13 KELIBIA

8 KORBOUS **14** MENZEL TEMIME

CA3 C27

MENZEL BOU ZELFA

SOLIMAN C43

P1 C44 KORBA

GROMBALIA

C27

15 NABEUL

16 HAMMAMET

Sousse

Blue doors, a typical feature of Sidi Bou Saïd's houses

SIGHTS AT A GLANCE

Cap Bon **11**
Carthage pp102–106 **4**
El-Haouaria **10**
Gammarth **1**
Hammamet pp118–120 **16**
Kelibia **13**
Kerkouane **12**
Korbous **8**

La Marsa **2**
La Goulette **5**
Lake Tunis **6**
Menzel Temime **14**
Nabeul pp112–115 **15**
Oudna (Uthina) **7**
Sidi Bou Saïd **3**
Sidi Daoud **9**

SEE ALSO

• *Where to Stay* pp250–3
• *Where to Eat* pp275–80

A former bathing pavilion on La Marsa beach

Gammarth ❶

Road map C1. 24 km (15 miles) northeast of Tunis.

THE SMART SEASIDE resort of Gammarth is an upmarket place, with expensive hotels, magnificent beaches and lush greenery. In the past this was just a small fishing village nestled beneath cliffs. Holidaymakers have been visiting here since the 1950s and now tourism is the main source of the town's income. As well as the many four- and five-star hotels and some good restaurants, the town has some lovely private villas, hidden away in the hills.

Small sandy coves provide ideal conditions for swimming and most water sports. The town itself is small and its activities are firmly aimed at the holiday trade. During the high season, when it can become very busy, its narrow streets fill with boisterous visitors and those in the know often head a little way north in search of more remote and emptier beaches.

White houses perched on the high cliffs of Gammarth

La Marsa ❷

Road map C1. 22 km (14 miles) north of Tunis. 🚃 *La Marsa Nights (13 Jul & 18 Aug).*

LA MARSA WAS once a district of Punic Carthage, and known as Megara. In the 7th century it became a port – Marsa er-Rum. Today, it is known for its beaches and is the favourite weekend playground for Tunis's residents. It is easy to get to by TGM train (from the end of Avenue Bourguiba in Tunis); the journey takes half an hour. It is worth stopping for a while at Café Saf-Saf at Place Saf-Saf, to enjoy a snack, a glass of mint tea or a Turkish coffee. Look out for the well on the terrace which dates back to the Hafsid period. Sometimes a camel working the well's wheel can be seen.

In the late 19th century, the Bey of Tunis built his residence here (Abdallia Palace). In order to make it possible for the ladies of the court to bathe discreetly, the palace was fitted with a specially constructed wooden terrace that rested on pillars over the sea. Openings were built into the floor that allowed the women to get in and out of the water well away from prying eyes.

The town has some good beaches and is a popular place. Looking from the beach towards the town, there are a number of small white houses standing on hillsides, hidden amid greenery. The smart, tastefully designed hotels all have direct access to the sea. With Sidi Bou Saïd and Tunis just a short train ride away, La Marsa makes a good base for a Tunisian holiday.

PAUL KLEE IN TUNISIA

"Colour has taken possession of me. Colour and I are one. I am a painter." So wrote Paul Klee (1879–1940), the Swiss-born painter associated with Bauhaus, during his visit to Tunisia in 1912–14. Klee was taken aback by the festive colours he encountered in Tunis, Sidi Bou Saïd and Kairouan and his works from that period, such as those built up of coloured squares, were clearly influenced by the mosaics and arabesques that he so admired. His Tunisian-inspired paintings include *Sunrise over Tunis* and *Camels and Donkeys*.

Paul Klee

Beaches around Tunis

T UNIS'S SUBURBS INCLUDE over 25
kilometres (16 miles) of beaches.
They can easily be reached by car or by
TGM train from the station at the end of
Avenue Bourguiba. The coastline is
varied – flat around Carthage and La
Marsa, but rocky in the region of
Gammarth and Sidi Bou Saïd. The small
coastal towns have plenty of restaurants
and cafés and are ideal for an afternoon
or evening excursion.

Gammarth ⑤
Gammarth is famous for its exquisite fish
restaurants and its magnificent sandy
beaches. It can get busy during the summer
and many of the hotels are often fully
booked at peak times.

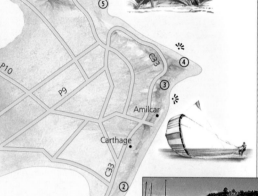

La Marsa ④
This magnificent resort is at
the end of the train line
that links the coastal towns
with Tunis. It has the
region's best beaches and
some expensive hotels.

La Goulette ①
The beaches of La Goulette, being
the closest to Tunis, can get busy at
peak times. Quieter spots can be
found a short distance further afield,
at Salambo for instance.

0 km   2

0 miles   2

Sidi Bou Saïd ③
Sidi Bou Saïd is worth
visiting at any time of the
year. The view from the main
promenade over the gulf is
truly breathtaking.

Salambo ②
This quiet little
town is full of
whitewashed villas
and colourful
flowers and makes
a welcome
alternative to the
bustle of Tunis. Its
wide, sandy beach
runs along a cove
that is protected
by a breakwater.

Raoued

Sebkhet Ariana

P10

P9

C33

Amilcar

Carthage

C33

Sidi Bou Saïd ❸

Road map C1. 20 km (12 miles)
north of Tunis. 🏛 *16,000.* 🎭 *Kharja
Festival (Jun).*

Sidi Bou Saïd's panorama, seen from the south

PERCHED ON TOP of high cliffs, Sidi Bou Saïd enjoys a commanding view over the Gulf of Tunis. It is named after Sidi Bou Saïd, a 13th-century Sufi holy man (1156–1231), who settled here on the return journey from his pilgrimage to Mecca. From then on, the village (known at the time as Jabal el-Menar) became a centre of Sufism, and attracted pilgrims from all over the country. The area around his tomb became the burial ground for other Sufis. Although there are no longer processions heading to the **tomb of Sidi Bou Saïd**, the grave and its adjacent small mosque are still visited by the Muslim faithful. It is

BLUE DOORS

A blue door with studded ornamentation

It was Baron d'Erlanger who gave Sidi Bou Saïd its blue and white colour scheme. The scores of blue doors in the village are only superficially identical. In reality, they differ from each other in terms of size and their ornamentation. The most popular motifs include moon crescents, stars and minarets. Blue and white dominate the streets and courtyards. The white walls provide a striking background for the deep blue shutters, ornate window grilles and colourful doorways.

accessed via the narrow stairs, right behind Café des Nattes (see below).

In the early 18th century, Hassan ibn Ali Bey ordered a mosque to be built here, which was entered via a magnificent gate and stairway. Today, the stairway and entrance to Café des Nattes stand on exactly the same spot. In the 19th century Mahmoud Bey built his summer residence here. Soon afterwards, the charms of this pretty town, with its cobbled streets and narrow alleyways, were discovered by the wealthy residents of Tunis who came here hoping to escape the summer heat.

The **Café des Nattes** is the village's hot spot and was the favourite haunt of the 1920s avant-garde artists who came here. It remains highly popular to this day and a traditional glass of mint tea with pine kernels can still be enjoyed. During the day the café can get busy as tour buses stop off to explore the town. Early in the morning and later at night, it is a much quieter place and is taken over by locals who sit quietly reading their newspapers. The café's decor has not changed in years and the yellowed photographs lining the walls bear witness to its famous guests including Simone de Beauvoir, André Gide

and Jean-Paul Sartre. But, as the present owner of the café says, "The foreigners were only passing through here. They came and they went. But to our family, this place has always been a symbol of continuity and tradition."

Since the days when Paul Klee visited, the village has grown in size and beauty. Its smart streets are full of flowers; the freshly whitewashed walls reflect the strong midday light. Yet it remains an artists' village, full of galleries and studios, while the former palace of Baron d'Erlanger (now the Centre of Arab and Mediterranean Music) stages concerts of *malouf* music *(see opposite).*

A summer day in Sidi Bou is broken by a long siesta, when a drowsy silence and calm descends upon its streets and

The main street leading to Café des Nattes

alleyways. The hum ceases and the women, shrouded in white veils, disappear behind the houses' blue doors. It is only along the steep, main street of the village that shopkeepers remain open, waiting for holidaymakers to whom they offer Bedouin jewellery, intricate scent boxes and aromatic oils. Heat permitting, this can be a good time to explore the cobbled streets and alleys of Sidi Bou. The pretty, whitewashed houses rise and fall in line with the cobbled streets that climb the ridge of the hill. Their white walls are covered with purple bougainvillea and their gates are garlanded with scented jasmine.

A number of Sidi Bou's mansions are open to visitors. One of these is **Dar el-Annabi** at 18 Rue Docteur Habib Thameur, just off Place 7 Novembre. Several of the 55 rooms of this 300-year-old house are open to the public and a terrace offers magnificent views of the town and the gulf beyond.

Not far from Café des Nattes, the street turns into a promenade with an amazing view over the bay. From here head for the magnificently sited **Café Sidi Chabaane**. The zaouia (tomb) built here in 1870 is associated with Sidi Sheb'an – a mystic, poet and musician. Today, his tomb stands almost on the site of the café. Standing here, and looking in the direction of the sea, it is easy to see how much has remained from bygone days. It is also worth visiting the **fishing harbour** and the **yacht marina**. From here the whole village can be seen resting on the slope of a hill, amidst lush greenery.

Another place to look out for is Dar Ennejma Ezzahra, a former palace which now houses the **Centre of Arab and Mediterranean Music**. It was built between 1912–22 for Baron Rodolphe d'Erlanger, a member of a

Yachts in Sidi Bou Saïd's marina

rich French banking family of German descent. The Baron first visited Tunisia at the age of 16, fell in love with the country and swapped his

A watercolour from a Sidi Bou Saïd gallery

banking career for a painter's easel. The site of the palace, which was built for his wife Elizabeth, was carefully chosen so as not to upset the character of the village. Built on the hillside, it overlooks the sea and village. As well as the architecture and wonderful gardens, the museum has a good selection of traditional musical instruments and some

rare recordings of Arab music.

An enthusiastic musicologist, the Baron was a major force behind the first Congress of Arab Music, which was held in Cairo in 1932 and it is possible to hear wonderful concerts of rare Arab music performed here. The Baron's tomb stands in the park that surrounds the palace.

Sidi Bou Saïd is easily reached by TGM train, which runs between Tunis and La Marsa. On leaving the small station, follow the road uphill and the street leads to Café des Nattes. Alternatively, climb up through the small, beautifully kept park on the right-hand side of the street that leads up to the village centre.

Most visitors stop here just for a few hours, but in order to soak up the atmosphere of the place it is well worth spending a night here. An overnight stay allows time to attend a concert of malouf music in the evening, and in the morning enjoy a drink of strong mint tea on the terrace of Café des Nattes.

🏛 The Centre of Arab and Mediterranean Music
⬛ Tue–Sun: 9am–noon & 2–7pm (summer); 2–5pm (winter). 🏷

BIRDCAGES

Sidi Bou Saïd is famous for its beautiful birdcages. Made of wire and often painted white, they look like miniature mausoleums. The design of the birdcages resembles the curved window grilles found in the wooden shutters of traditional Arab houses. Tunisians are fond of pet birds, particularly canaries. Empty cages can often be seen in hotel reception areas, serving as decorations or as mailboxes for residents' letters and postcards.

An ornate wire birdcage

Artists in Sidi Bou Saïd

Among Tunisian artists, Sidi Bou Saïd enjoyed a reputation as an "artist's village" long before the arrival of the European painters, but it was the latter who made it world-famous. Enchanted with the place, artists such as Paul Klee, August Macke and Louis Moillet usually stayed much longer than they originally planned. The Tunisian light transformed their painting. In the works of Paul Klee, for

Painting of flower-seller

instance, brown and black graphics gave way to vivid colours. The arrival of European artists was to have a significant effect on Tunisian painting, and prompted the emergence of a salon that included European, Muslim and Jewish artists. Out of this grew the École de Tunis which took Tunisian daily life as its subject matter and included paintings of cafés, markets and hammams.

A traditional lifestyle was a frequent theme of painters from the École de Tunis. This picture by Ammar Farhat conveys the colour and mood of the Tunisian siesta splendidly. His paintings may be far removed from the popular image of Tunisia, but are essentially true.

Brahim Dhahak (1931–2004) was one of the most outstanding artists of the École de Tunis, although he is less well known than Yahia Turki.

Portrait of an Old Woman is the work of Yahia Turki (1902–69), one of the early members of the École de Tunis. The expressive sketch, drawn with ink and crayon, depicts in great detail not only a person but also her emotions. In the context of Tunisian art, this is an extraordinary work.

Still Life with Fish by Dhahak is proof that Tunisian artists are also skilled in the use of engraving techniques. This lithograph clearly shows the influence of modernist European artists.

The Night Scene is painted in pastels. The expressive power of many École de Tunis artists lies in their ability to depict mood through colour.

Man on a Donkey is the work of Brahim Dhahak. It captures the magnificent light and wonderful colours that once so entranced Paul Klee and August Macke.

Remains of an 18th-century arsenal, constructed by Hammouda ibn Ali Bey, in La Goulette

Carthage ❹

See pp102–106.

La Goulette ❺

Road map C1. 15 km (9 miles) northeast of Tunis.

L A GOULETTE – an old fort and the harbour for Tunis – lies a short distance from the capital. The town was first developed as a port and strategic outpost by the Arabs in the 7th century after they had captured Tunis. In the 16th century it was a stronghold for pirates who were allowed to stay here by the Hafsid sultan, Mohammed V, who feared an attack by the Spanish. The attack duly came and the pirates proved to be no match for the Spanish forces. In 1535 the Spanish King Charles V built a fort here. The fort was later destroyed and in its place the Ottomans built a massive kasbah, which remains to this day.

La Goulette began to grow rapidly in the 17th century, due to the construction of the harbour. Led by Dutch engineers, the development included the canal, the basin and the arsenal. The numbers of Europeans living in the town gradually increased from year to year. During the French Protectorate, the kasbah was used as a temporary prison. The name La Goulette – "the gullet" or "throat" that separates the sea from Lake Tunis – dates from those days.

Today La Goulette (along with Mahdia, Sfax, Kelibia, Tabarka and Bizerte) is a major fishing port and the coastal section of Tunis harbour. Here, fishermen can be seen returning with their catch. Nearly half of them still use traditional rowing boats.

The country's long shoreline (over 1,300 km/800 miles) means that fishing still plays an important part in Tunisia's economy. Many of La Goulette's fishermen can be seen in the evenings, heading out to sea where they fish at night with lights, returning in the morning in time to deliver their valuable catch to the town's restaurants and markets.

Many Tunis residents come here to enjoy fish and seafood in one of the local restaurants as La Goulette is reputed to have the best fish restaurants in Tunisia. Depending on the season, fresh gilthead, bream or tuna are excellent.

La Goulette is also a major passenger port – almost all ferries going to Italy and France set off from here.

At one time La Goulette was also renowned for its tolerance. This is vividly illustrated by the 1995 Franco-Tunisian comedy *Un été à la Goulette*, which is set in 1960. The film tells the story of three teenage girls – one Christian, one Jewish and one Muslim – who decide to undergo their sexual initiation, each with a boy of a different faith. The girls' plan becomes public knowledge and causes a temporary upset in the staid life of the village.

La Goulette can be reached in less than ten minutes by TGM train from Tunis. The best time to visit the village is in the late afternoon or evening, on the way back from La Marsa's beach or a trip to Carthage. There is a beach near La Goulette, but in view of the harbour's proximity and the resulting pollution, it is better to swim elsewhere.

Lake Tunis ❻

Road map C1.

I N THE 9TH CENTURY, the Arabs dug a canal about 10 km (6 miles) long to link Tunis with the sea. This created the artificial Lake Tunis. The widening of its mouth allowed two harbours to be built – one on each side of the canal. The lake – not particularly picturesque in itself – is now a brackish lagoon attracting various species of bird, including seagulls, white and grey heron, and, during the winter months – flocks of flamingoes and cormorants. The lake can be crossed by TGM train (Tunis-La Goulette-La Marsa) or by car.

Angler on the shores of Lake Tunis

Carthage ❹

SCATTERED RUINS are all that remain of one of the most powerful cities of the ancient world. Carthage was founded in 814 BC by Phoenician colonizers. By the 4th century BC it had become the major force in this part of the Mediterranean. The Punic wars led to the destruction of the city although it rose again under Roman rule. It was subsequently conquered by the Vandals, who were replaced by the Byzantines in the 6th century. Following its capture by the Arabs in AD 695, Carthage gradually fell into ruins.

St Louis Cathedral towering over the ancient city

Exploring Carthage

Carthage Museum stands on Byrsa Hill, right next to the Cathedral of St Louis. To the north of the museum, close by, is the 2nd-century Theatre of Hadrian, which stages performances in summer during the International Cultural Festival. Sights that should not be missed include the ruins of the Roman amphitheatre, the remains of the Roman villas, and the ruins of the Basilica of St Cyprian. From here, a road leads to the best-preserved fragment of Carthage – the Antonine Baths. In summer, there is a horse-drawn carriage that tours the main sites. It can be hired near Carthage Hannibal station. The trip lasts two hours and the price should be settled in advance.

HANNIBAL (247–182 BC)

Hannibal was one of the greatest military commanders of the ancient world. In the course of the Second Punic War he embarked upon a long and arduous march across the Pyrenees, southern Gaul and the Alps. Although his army was not large, it was exceptionally well trained. Following his legendary crossing of the Alps, Hannibal took on the might of the Roman army. Despite early successes, the Carthaginians were eventually defeated and made to pay huge reparations. At home, an attempt to introduce democratic reforms brought Hannibal into opposition with the ruling classes and he was forced to flee Carthage. Unable to reconcile himself to the loss of his homeland, he committed suicide.

A marble bust of Hannibal

◁ **Sun-drenched villa in Sidi Bou Saïd**

🏠🖼 Cathedral of St Louis

Byrsa Hill. 📞 (71) 733 866. ⏰ daily: 7:30am–7pm (summer); 9am–5pm (winter). 🎫

The cathedral was built in 1890 by Cardinal Lavigerie. It was dedicated to the French King Louis IX who died of the plague while laying siege to Carthage in 1270. Cardinal Lavigerie was an enterprising person – he founded the Order of the White Fathers, which was active throughout Africa. Its nuns and monks proved to be outstanding archaeologists and were the first to begin investigations into Tunisia's past. Lavigerie was also responsible for resurrecting the Carthage bishopric.

The building has not served as a place of worship since 1964 and was rebranded in the 1990s as the **Acropolium de Byrsa**. It is now used as a venue for classical concerts and exhibitions.

🏛 Carthage Museum

See pp104–105.

Foundations of Punic houses unearthed on Byrsa Hill

⋔ Byrsa Hill

Climbing to the top of Byrsa Hill affords a magnificent view of the area and makes this a good place to begin a visit to Carthage. Under Punic rule it was the heart of the city and had a temple dedicated to the Carthaginian god Eschmoun. The Romans, after razing Carthage to the ground, levelled the top of the hill to accommodate their capitol and forum. In the process they buried some

Carthage's amphitheatre, capable of seating 3,000 spectators

VISITORS' CHECKLIST

Road map C1. 17 km (11 miles) north of Tunis. 🚉 *TGM Carthage–Hannibal.* 🚌 *41.* 🎬 *International Film Festival (Oct every 2 years).*

Several Christians were put to death on that occasion including St Perpetua who was gored by "a most savage cow" before being run through by a sword.

Punic villas that were later uncovered by French archaeologists. Byrsa Hill is now dominated by the Cathedral of St Louis and the Carthage Museum.

🏛 Antonine Baths
Avenue des Thermes d'Antonin.
🕐 *Apr–mid-Sep: 8am–7pm Tue–Sun; mid-Sep–Mar: 8:30am–5:30pm.* 💶
These 2nd-century baths were once the largest in Africa. Their soaring vaults rested on eight lofty columns made of grey sandstone, and the *frigidarium* was the size of a cathedral. Destroyed by the Vandals in AD 439, all that is left are ruins, including a handful of rooms and the remains of the vaults. Nevertheless, the complex still makes a deep impression.

🏛 Amphitheatre
Avenue du 7 Novembre.
🕐 *Apr–mid-Sep: 8am–7pm Tue–Sun; mid-Sep–Mar: 8:30am–5:30pm.* 💶
The amphitheatre was one of the largest in the Roman Empire. Games were the favourite recreation of the Carthaginians. In AD 203 a show was staged to celebrate the birth of the emperor's son.

The impressive ruins of the Antonine Baths

🏛 Roman Villas
🕐 *Apr–mid-Sep: 8am–7pm Tue–Sun; mid-Sep–Mar: 8:30am–5:30pm.* 💶
The reign of Caesar Augustus brought with it stability and economic growth. The emperor created favourable conditions for land and sea trade, which resulted in the growing prosperity of the urban upper and middle classes, including natives of Tunisia. In the 2nd century AD, Carthage reached the peak of its development. The villas date from this period. Much of the site is overgrown, though the restored 3rd-century Villa de la Volières still has its original floor mosaics.

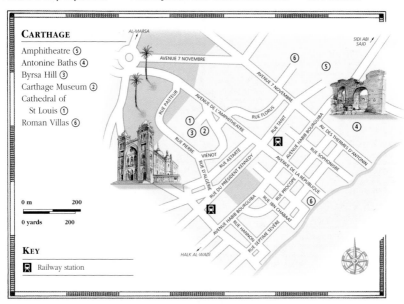

CARTHAGE

Amphitheatre ⑤
Antonine Baths ④
Byrsa Hill ③
Carthage Museum ②
Cathedral of St Louis ①
Roman Villas ⑥

0 m   200
0 yards   200

KEY

🚉 Railway station

Carthage Museum

THE MUSEUM STANDS on top of a hill, surrounded by a beautiful expanse of grass. One of its terraces adjoins the foundations of the Punic villas, which were discovered by French archaeologists. The museum is arranged chronologically with Punic, Roman, Christian and Arab displays. Among these are inscriptions, marble sarcophagi, everyday objects from Punic and Roman Carthage, and colourful Phoenician masks.

Model of Carthage
Situated on the first floor of the museum, this model provides a good basis for appreciating the sheer scale of Carthage and its ports.

★ Mosaics
The museum displays only a handful of mosaics but all are very well preserved. Most are from the Roman-African period. The mosaic pictured here depicts a woman gathering fruit which symbolizes summer.

GALLERY LAYOUT

The museum houses exhibits dating from the Phoenician-Punic, Roman-African and Arab eras. The Phoenician-Punic exhibits occupy the ground floor. Here there are, among other things, Punic ceramics and Punic sarcophagi. The first floor is mostly devoted to exhibits from the Roman and Arab periods and includes some fine Roman sculptures and mosaics.

Jug (11th century BC)
Terracotta vessels were already being produced in the early days of Carthage. The most popular items included candlesticks, lamps and jugs made in fanciful shapes and decorated in blue and crimson.

Ground floor

PHOENICIAN ART

Characteristic of Phoenician art are sarcophagi with a human figure on the lid; other typical objects include terracotta figurines, jewellery products, ivory items and masks. Vast numbers of amulets made of a glass and silica compound bear witness to the important role played by magic in everyday life, as well as to the influence of Egyptian art and religion.

Punic tombstone of a man, from the Carthage Museum (not on display)

KEY

☐	Mosaics
☐	Ceramics
☐	Archaeological finds

STAR EXHIBITS

★ Mosaics

★ Phoenician Coin

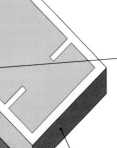

★ **Phoenician Coin**
Phoenician coin dating from the 5th century BC from Tyre. Coins also appeared in Ardos, Sydon and Byblos at this time.

VISITORS' CHECKLIST

Byrsa Hill. ((71) 730 036.
Carthage–Hannibal. 🚌 41.
Apr–mid-Sep: 8am–7pm; mid-Sep–Mar: 8:30am–5:30pm.

Jug (7th century BC)
Carthaginian ceramics include jugs with an upturned top and triple spouts. These items began to appear in the late 8th century and were produced until the end of the 6th century BC.

1st floor

Punic Vase
Phoenician vessels were made using a simple potter's wheel and fired in tall round furnaces which were built of brick. The typical colour of Punic ceramics was light red.

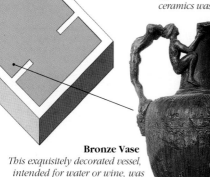

Bronze Vase
This exquisitely decorated vessel, intended for water or wine, was made in the 5th century BC. Objects of this type were very highly valued by the Phoenicians as well as by their trading partners.

Further Afield
On the other side of Avenue Bourguiba is the Magon Quarter where there are some Punic floor mosaics. Further on, along the main road to Tunis, is the Roman and Paleo-Christian Museum. A little to the east of this are the remains of the Punic Ports. Another very interesting site is the nearby Tophet (Phoenician burial place), which is also known as the Tanit and Baal Hammon sanctuary *(see p106)*.

St Cyprian Basilica
TGM Carthage–Amilcar.
St Cyprian, a prominent writer and a theologian of great standing, was a bishop of Carthage. He preached church unity based on the unity of the College of Bishops and was an advocate of the bishop's power in his own local community. He died a martyr's death during the persecution of Christians under Emperor Valerian's rule, in AD 258.

This Byzantine basilica that bears his name was probably the initial resting-place of the saint, though that is open to dispute. Situated at the north end of the town, this eight-aisle church is one of a handful of the Christian historic remains in Carthage, along with the mighty Damous el-Karita Basilica.

Presidential Palace
Avenue Habib Bourguiba. *TGM Carthage–Presidence.*
The Presidential Palace stands on a hill above the Gulf of Tunis, near the Antonine Baths. It is from here that the best view of the palace, engulfed by the greenery of its vast garden, can be found. When photographing the Roman baths remember not to point the camera at the palace. In Tunisia it is prohibited to photograph government buildings, soldiers and policemen. In this case the law is strictly enforced. The main entrance to the palace is through the gate at Avenue Bourguiba. There are always guards on duty, regardless of whether the president is currently in residence or not.

Former Punic Port at the south end of Carthage

🏛 Roman and Paleo-Christian Museum

🔲 *Apr–mid-Sep: 8am–7pm Tue–Sun; mid-Sep–Mar: 8:30am–5:30pm.* 📷

This museum has objects dating from the Roman period of Carthage's history (5th–7th century AD). Also among the exhibits are some early Christian remains and some mosaic fragments. The origins of Christianity in the Roman Province of Proconsular Africa probably go back to the late 1st century. In the museum grounds are what little remains of the Basilica of Carthagenna (6th century AD).

⋔ Punic Ports

Avenue du Mars 1934.
🔲 *Carthage–Byrsa.*

Unfortunately, not much remains of these two ports which were once the powerhouse of Carthage's prosperity and the envy of Rome. Imagination is needed, therefore, to visualize the pride of the Punic fleet in these two small ponds. In

their heyday, these ports could accommodate 220 vessels. The southern square-shaped basin was for commercial shipping, while the northern circular basin was used as the naval harbour. The two harbours would have been linked. The entrance was via a channel in the sea which led to the commercial port. A scale model at the edge of the naval harbour gives some idea of just what a wonder these ports once were.

Between the two ports is an **Oceanographic Museum** which has aquariums and some new interactive displays.

⋔ Tophet

Rue Hannibal. 🔲 *Carthage–Salambo.*
🔲 *Apr–mid-Sep: 8am–7pm Tue–Sun; mid-Sep–Mar: 8:30am–5:30pm.* 📷

These ruins are all that remains of the Tophet, or sanctuary, that was dedicated to the Carthaginian divinities Tanit and Baal Hammon (*see p110*). Sacrifice may well have

been the main act of this ancient Phoenician cult and this is the oldest surviving site of its kind in Carthage. Although no-one knows for certain, it is believed that offerings were made of animals, people (often foreigners and enemies), and most of all children. They were sacrificed to the goddess (originally the offerings were made to Baal Hammon, and only later to Tanit). According to some theories, the children were laid in the arms of a bronze statue, from where they fell into the flames. The parents were not allowed to cry, as their grief was believed to diminish the sacrifice.

When Agathocles defeated the Carthaginians in 310 BC, the town citizens reputedly sacrificed 300 children in order to appease the gods.

The oldest part of the Tophet includes the tiny Cintas shrine with a small niche carved into the rock where some 8th-century pots were found. In front of the building is a courtyard with an altar and three concentric walls forming a kind of labyrinth through which everyone wishing to enter the sanctuary had to pass.

DIDO AND AENEAS

According to Virgil's epic poem the *Aeneid*, Aeneas fled Troy after its destruction by the Greeks and set sail with a handful of refugees on a divine mission to found a new Troy in Italy. He was shipwrecked off Carthage and taken in by the Phoenician Princess Dido. Soon they fell passionately in love. Torn between his love for Dido and the will of the gods, Aeneas left to fulfil his destiny and began a series of adventures that ended with the founding of Rome. Heartbroken, Dido stabbed herself, offering her life to Carthage. Her body was burned on a funeral pyre.

***Dido Receiving Aeneas**, Francesco Solimena*

Tophet – a magnificent and tragic monument to Punic culture

Phoenician Culture

Coin dating from the Punic era

THE PHOENICIANS were great explorers and during the early years of the first millennium BC they ventured as far as Spain and into the Atlantic, establishing a number of colonies including the one at Carthage. The Phoenicians brought with them a culture based on a blend of Egyptian, Anatolian, Greek and Mesopotamian influences. One of their greatest contributions was the alphabet, which was adapted by the Greeks, and spread with the rise of the Roman Empire. The Phoenicians were also skilled in carving, metalwork, sculpture and jewellery. Many Phoenician remains were found at Carthage, and excavations carried out in Kairouan also reveal Punic houses containing well-preserved mosaics. Phoenician tombs have also been found in Cap Bon and in Utica.

Phoenician cemeteries *show that the Phoenicians and their Punic descendants believed in an afterlife. Embalmed bodies, elaborate sarcophagi and inscriptions warning against disturbing the dead indicate just how strong this belief was.*

The Punic alphabet, *with its elongated, gently curving letters, was widely used in Carthage and throughout the western Phoenician colonies.*

Altars *in the form of shrines (cippi) gave way in the 5th century BC to steles, with triangular tops. These often bear an engraved motif of a moon crescent or a stylized figure.*

Necklaces *made of glass compound were popular adornments. Jewellery played an important role in Carthage. Miniature masks, amulets, scarabs and golden plates were often added to necklaces.*

Terracotta female figures *were first produced around the 6th century BC. They may have been inspired by Egyptian art as figures unearthed at Carthage resemble those found on Egyptian sarcophagi. The use of masks in religious ceremonies was also widespread in Carthage.*

Oudna (Uthina), one of the oldest Roman colonies in Africa

Oudna (Uthina) ❼

Road map C2. *30 km (19 miles) south of Tunis.* ◻ *Apr–mid-Sep: 9am–7pm Tue–Sun; mid-Sep–Mar: 8:30am–5:30pm Tue–Sun.* 🏛

THIS FORMER Berber settlement is one of the oldest Roman colonies in Africa, and was founded during the reign of Octavian Augustus. The modern-day ruins of Roman Uthina (now called Oudna) divide into two main sections. Immediately by the entrance stands a complex of buildings, some of which have been reconstructed, including Roman villas, private and public baths, cisterns, a theatre and a 2nd-century amphitheatre. The second part, which includes the capitol, has been largely unexcavated and lies a few hundred yards away, adjoining a small village and the remains of the colonial buildings. This part of Oudna can be visited free of charge.

Founded at the beginning of the 1st century AD, Uthina was a typical Roman town and attracted wealthy veterans from the Roman army. The hub of its public life was the market square (forum), which was surrounded by the town's most important buildings including the capitol (the seat of the local authorities), a courthouse and the marketplace. One of the corners of the forum usually adjoined by a smaller market square, known as the *macellum.*

The most valuable mosaics, including one depicting Venus bathing, are now on display in the Bardo Museum.

ENVIRONS: Before reaching Oudna, it is worth stopping in **Mohammedia** to see the ruins of the Palace of Ahmed Bey (1837–56) which was intended to rival Versailles in its grandeur. About 2 km (1 mile) from the village, running parallel to the Tunis–Zaghouan road, are the remains of a Roman aqueduct that once carried water to Carthage.

Bathers in the hot springs in Korbous

Korbous ❽

Road map C2. *50 km (31 miles) northeast of Tunis.*

KORBOUS LIES ON the Cap Bon peninsula and is set in a deep ravine that opens to the sea near the village of Sidi Rais. Popular as a health resort since Roman times when it was known as Aquae Calidau Carpitanae, the waters here are believed by many Tunisians to to have health-giving properties.

In the late 19th century, Korbous was developed by the French, while Ahmed Bey founded a spa resort here in 1901. Korbous is today Tunisia's main health resort and many of the local hotels and sanatoriums offer water and steam treatments to elderly Tunisians. The natural hot springs bubble up out of the ground at about 44–60° C (112–140° F) and contain high levels of sulphur.

Korbous is an unassuming place though there are now plans to convert this hitherto quiet resort into a large spa, with a marina and luxury hotels. The main attraction of the town is the **hammam** (bath), located in the former bey's palace.

Public bathing played a prominent role in the life of the Roman towns in North Africa. The custom of using alternate hot and cold baths, borrowed from the Greeks, assumed great importance in Rome and its dominions. Bath complexes were the centre of town life and often included playing fields, libraries and relaxation rooms with mosaic floors and frescoes. Wealthy people sometimes spent whole days in the baths – resting and enjoying discussions.

The local waters are thought to be good for curing arthritis and beneficial in cases of gastric ailments.

One famous landmark to look out for in Korbous is the **Zarziha Rock**, which can be found near the presidential palace. According to legend, it is supposed to cure infertility. The edges of the stone have been polished smooth by the hands of those seeking help.

Not much remains here of the old buildings. The fortress that towers over the town dates back to the Roman period. A hot spring, **Aïn el-Atrous**, can be found a short way north of town. Here water at 50° C (122° F) shoots out of the ground via an underground pipe and falls over steps down to the sea. This is a very popular picnic spot, particularly at weekends

Sidi Daoud ❾

Road map D1.

THIS FISHING VILLAGE located on the peninsula's headland, opposite the island of Zembra, is famous for tuna fishing. To this day the locals use an old-fashioned method known as *Matanza* that dates back to Roman times. This technique employs a huge net containing a series of chambers of decreasing sizes which is laid some 4 km (2 miles) out to sea. The fish are caught and swim from chamber to chamber until they all reach the smallest one. The net is closed and dragged to the surface. The fishermen then jump into the nets and set about the tuna with clubs, knives and harpoons. The *Matanza* takes place in May and June during the spawning season. For the rest of the year the village is quiet.

El-Haouaria ❿

Road map D1. ☐ daily: 8am–7pm (summer); 8:30am–5:30pm (winter). 🦅 Falconry Festival (Jun).

EL-HAOUARIA IS perched high on the rugged headland of Cap Bon, surrounded by a

turquoise sea. The view from here over the sea and its breaking waves is truly awe-inspiring. Two kilometres (1 mile) from the centre of the modern village is the site of the old Roman quarries from which marble was cut and transported by slaves to Carthage, El-Jem and other Roman towns. All that remains of them now are two dozen vermilion caves running along the coast. Some of these are 30 metres (98 ft) high. A little further out of town, the Chauves-Souris cave is inhabited by hundreds of bats. Visitors should make sure they have a guide – and a torch! The village is famous for its June falconry show held on its outskirts, opposite the island of Zembra, during

which trained birds are used for hunting.

ENVIRONS: Almost directly opposite El-Haouaria, 15 km (9 miles) from Sidi Daoud, lies the picturesque island of **Zembra** and, separated from it by 5 km (3 miles) of water, the tiny island of **Zembretta**. Zembra was once popular with scuba divers but both islands and the waters that surround them have been declared a nature reserve and are now off-limits to visitors. In the spring and summer they provide resting points for migrating birds. They are also home to 260 species of plants, four of which are endemic. The surrounding waters support many types of fish and shellfish.

El-Haouaria, site of a lifetime of slavery in the quarries

Peppers – one of Cap Bon's main crops

Cap Bon ⓫

Road map D1, D2.

A SHORT WAY from Europe and within easy reach of Carthage, Cap Bon has long had an economic importance. Its main ports were once used as harbours for Phoenician ships, while the fertile coastal areas supported agriculture. Here, the Phoenicians cultivated cereals and grapes from which they produced wine. The Romans continued these traditions and it was only the Arab conquest that put an end to wine production. Under French rule, the Cap Bon peninsula was revived once again when it became an important area of European settlement. More vineyards were planted at this time, along with huge citrus groves.

Although tourism plays an increasingly important role, especially around the beaches of Hammamet and Nabeul, the production of vegetables and fruit still provides the main source of income. For this reason, the peninsula has preserved a quiet, rural character, particularly inland. In the small village of **Soliman** for instance, with its beds of spinach, beans and potatoes, time seems to have ground to a halt. In **Menzel Bou Zelfa**, orange and lemon groves fill the spring air with the heady scent of blossom.

On the east coast, Kelibia and Menzel Temime are famous for their colourful markets while the busy resort town of Nabeul is known for its ceramics and its magnificent beach. Just along the coast from Nabeul is Hammamet, once called the Tunisian Saint Tropez, although it is rather less exclusive than it once was. The main road along the rugged west coast runs inland where the scattered villages are isolated and little visited, apart from Korbous, which is renowned for its hot springs.

Kerkouane ⓬

Road map D1. ⬚ *9am–6pm daily.*

K ERKOUANE IS situated on the high cliffs of Cap Bon. Between the 4th and the 2nd century BC this was a Punic town with a population of 2,000 and was controlled by Carthage. The Second Punic War put an end to the town's existence when it was abandoned. The town was rediscovered in 1952 by a French archaeologist.

Kerkouane has been remarkably well preserved and, from the remaining foundations, it is easy to see the checkerboard layout of the streets. Little was known about Punic architecture before the discovery of Kerkouane, but from the size of the houses and the wide streets, it is apparent that the town's inhabitants were not only sophisticated but also had a high standard of living.

GODDESS TANIT

From the 5th century onwards, the goddess Tanit occupied the highest position in the pantheon of the Punic gods. Associated with the cult of fertility, she was believed to be the personification of both the sun and the moon. Sometimes she is depicted by a crescent moon turned upside down and joined onto the disc of the sun. At other times, her image is formed from a triangle, a horizontal line and a circle.

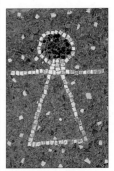

Mosaic with the stylized symbol of the goddess Tanit

Most impressive of all are the houses' baths, with their well-preserved floors, walls and sanitary equipment. Many of the houses have their own bath, suggesting that the owners liked to bathe in private.

Very little is known about this town and it was named Kerkouane by the French

Kerkouane and its ruins of a Punic town

archaeologist who found it.
From the artifacts that have
been found here, it is
probable that much of
Kerkouane's wealth was
based on the production of a
dye, highly prized at the time,
known as Tyrian purple (after
Tyre, the Phoenician capital).

Kelibia ⑬

Road map D1. 50 km (31 miles)
along the coast from Nabeul.
◻ 8am–6pm daily . 🎬 Amateur
Film Festival (Jul).

SET AT THE VERY TIP of Cap
Bon, on its eastern side,
this small town gives the
impression of being fully
surrounded by water. It dates
back to Punic times (being
for a while a trading outpost
of Syracuse); as well as to the
Roman Empire (as the Roman
settlement of Clupea).

Its history resembles that of
many other Punic hamlets in
that it began life as a Berber
settlement. Conquered by
Agathocles in 310 BC, and by
Regulus in 256 BC, it suffered
devastating damage in the
course of the Third Punic
War, when the Romans
nearly demolished it. Almost
nothing remains from Punic
and Roman times. The only
relic that has survived is the
late 6th-century Byzantine
fortress. The lighthouse,
dating from the early years of
Arab rule, now houses a
meteorological station and
provides a magnificent
panoramic view of the
surrounding country. Kelibia
is also known for its white
wines, particularly the dry
muscat.

The town's main sight is the
old **fort** that overlooks the
harbour. The present building
was erected by the Byzantines
in the 6th century AD and
was further modified by the
Spanish and the Turkish. The
gun emplacements were laid
here by German forces during
World War II.

Next to Lake Ichkeul,
Kelibia is the most important
bird-breeding ground in
Tunisia. The local lake
changes its size and shape
depending on the amount of

rain. At times of high annual
rainfall its area grows to
include the surrounding
marshes. During the high
season, the lake may attract
over a quarter of a million
birds. Unfortunately, in recent
years low water levels have
caused the number of birds
to decrease. Species still seen
include heron and flamingo.
The area around the lake is
also visited by many species
of birds that inhabit dry and
desert areas. The best view
of the lake is from its northeastern end, from the road
near the GP2 and MC 48
junction. Kelibia's beach is
small and can often have
seaweed. But **Mansourah
beach**, 2 km (1 mile) to the
north, is long, sandy and
often almost deserted.

Kelibia – situated at the tip of Cap Bon

Market stalls in Menzel Temime

Menzel Temime ⑭

Road map D1. 🚍 Tue.

DURING THE PERIOD of the
Roman Empire, the
wealth of this area was based
almost entirely on the
cultivation of cereals and
olives, vineyards and fig
orchards. Vast country estates
brought great fortunes to their
owners. It was here that the
new colonial system was first
introduced. It involved an
annual tax, paid in kind – in
the form of grain and oil –
that was levied on large
estates and used to feed the
Roman populace.

Located a short way from
Kelibia, Menzel Temime is
known for its spices, the
strings of sun-dried red
peppers, and above all
for its huge Tuesday
market where farmers
from the entire
peninsula congregate.
Pyramids of fruit and
vegetables create
fantastic multicoloured
mosaics.

ENVIRONS: A little
further away lies the
picturesque village of
Korba. Korba is
nicknamed the "red
village" because of
the quantity of
tomatoes, peppers and
strawberries that are
grown here. The local
produce worth buying
in the village includes
the homemade hot
and spicy Tunisian
sauce called harissa.

Nabeul ⑮

House in Avenue Habib Thameur

JUST UP THE COAST from Hammamet, Nabeul is the administrative centre of Cap Bon and is known for its beautiful beaches, busy market and wonderful ceramics. The original Punic town was destroyed by the Romans. Later on, Julius Caesar established a colony here, the ruins of which were accidentally discovered in 1964 during the construction of the first tourist hotel in town. With the arrival of the Arabs, the town centred around the *ksar* (fortified granary). Today, this is the town's oldest district.

Shops along Rue el-Arbi Zarouk, the site of the market

Exploring Nabeul
Most people visit Nabeul on Friday and come for the weekly market. Virtually anything can be bought here from colourful spices, bowls and spoons to music cassettes and cotton shawls. Nabeul's large medina, with its complex network of narrow streets, gates and alleyways, is well worth exploring. Walking along Avenues Habib Thameur, Farhat Hached or Hedi Chaker takes the visitor past scores of shops and ceramic workshops selling

Decorative panel on the façade of the Great Mosque

colourful crockery, tiles, lamps, candlesticks, goblets and couscous dishes.

▦ Market
Rue el-Arbi Zarouk. ◯ *6–10am Fri.*
The market is held every Friday and attracts huge numbers of visitors. Originally it was a camel market, but camels are not usually on sale unless they are stuffed toys. During the peak season, however, there is the opportunity of paying for a camel ride. The thousands of day-trippers who visit here each week can be overwhelming and stall holders have no need to lower their prices. Little is to be gained from haggling.

◖ Great Mosque
Rue de L'Orient and Rue Habib Karma. ◖ *to non-Muslims.*
Nabeul's mosque, hidden by the souk's arcades, is a typical example of sacral Islamic architecture. Its layout includes a courtyard and a large prayer hall decorated with some magnificent ceramic tiles and crystal chandeliers. Its green-white minaret is reminiscent of the mosque in Kairouan.

Avenue Habib Thameur
Avenue Habib Thameur, whose continuation is Avenue Farhat Hached, runs in the direction of the souk and the market. Together with Avenue Hedi Chaker, it forms the town's commercial centre and is crammed with workshops and small shops selling ceramics. The heart of the town is Place du 7 Novembre, at the junction of Avenue Habib Thameur and Avenue Habib Bourguiba. The vast clay jug vessel here is meant to symbolize Nabeul's pottery traditions.

Ceramic bric-a-brac, such as ashtrays, small jars and plates can be bought fairly cheaply. Even larger plates or a beautifully decorated dish cost just a few dinars.

Although Nabeul is famous mainly for its pottery, it has also developed other forms of craft, including embroidery, wickerwork (straw mats) and stone carving. Nabeul embroidery is white or light blue and uses cotton or silk yarns. At one time it was used only on women's clothes but now it can also be found decorating tablecloths and linen napkins.

Courtyard of a pottery shop in Avenue Habib Thameur

Avenue Habib Bourguiba
Avenue Bourguiba, lined with palm trees and oleanders, is the town's swankiest street. It starts at the town centre and runs towards the sea, reaching the local beaches. It is over 2 km (1 mile) long. Along it are situated the station and the archaeology museum. Its northern section is full of shops. Heading south, it is worth taking a look at the beautiful villas belonging to the wealthy citizens of Nabeul.

🏛 Archaeology Museum

Av. Habib Bourguiba 44.
⬜ *Apr–mid-Sep: 9am–1pm & 3–7pm Tue–Sun; mid-Sep–Mar: 9:30am–4:30pm.*

Several well-lit rooms in this small but interesting museum house items unearthed during archaeological excavations, including Carthaginian sculptures and Roman mosaics. The first room, immediately by the entrance, includes the plan of Roman Neapolis *(see below)* and a map of Cap Bon, showing the major archaeological sites. To the left of the entrance, in Room 1, are displays of Punic objects (7th–4th centuries BC) including oil lamps, jewellery and coins, mainly from the excavations in Kerkouane. Here vessels from Kelibia can also be found.

Along the corridor that links the rooms there are further displays of Punic and Roman objects. Look out for the clay statuettes of Baal Hammon and the Carthaginian goddess Tanit. The remaining rooms house a large collection of Roman mosaics excavated

Statue from the Archaeology Museum

from Kelibia (1st–3rd century AD) and Roman Neapolis (4th century).

⋔ Neapolis

⬜ *1–5pm Tue–Sun.*

This ancient site stands in the town suburbs, within the tourist zone, close to the Hotel Neapolis and opposite Pension Monia Club. Not much is left of the Roman town whose ruins were discovered accidentally when building the Hotel Neapolis and its large, fenced-off grounds are overgrown with grass and olive trees.

Nabeul was once a part of the senate province of Proconsular Africa. It was governed by the proconsul residing in Carthage. The reign of Caesar Augustus marked a period of stability, when colonies began to grow and new towns intended for Roman war veterans were established. Caesar ensured favourable conditions for trade, which resulted in the growing wealth of the

VISITORS' CHECKLIST

Road map D2. 🏠 *60,000.*
🚌 *ONTT: Av. Taieb Mehiri; Av. H. Bourguiba, (72) 286 800.*
🌐 *www.nabeul.net.* 🎉 *Orange Blossom Festival (Mar/Apr); Summer Festival (Jul/Aug).*

urban upper and middle classes, as well as of the native population. One of these towns was Nabeul.

Increasing wealth was accompanied by the growing influence of Roman culture. Not much has survived from ancient Nabeul, which the Romans called Neapolis, and all that can be seen is a handful of scattered stones and the remains of a wall that probably once surrounded a palace.

Excavation site in Neapolis

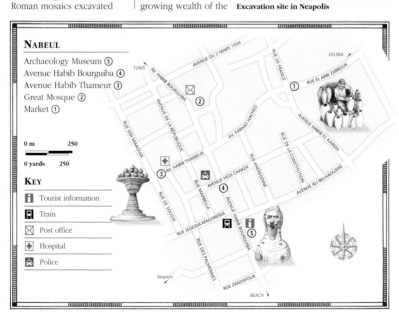

NABEUL

Archaeology Museum ⑤
Avenue Habib Bourguiba ④
Avenue Habib Thameur ③
Great Mosque ②
Market ①

0 m   250

0 yards   250

KEY

🛈 Tourist information

🚉 Train

✉ Post office

✚ Hospital

👮 Police

TUNIS

KELIBIA

AVENUE DU 2 MARS 1934

AV. HABIB BOURGUIBA

RUE DE FRANCE

RUE EL ARBI ZARROUK

AVENUE HABIB EL KARMA

RUE SIDI MAAOUIA

AVENUE DE LA RÉPUBLIQUE

AV. FARHAT HACHED

RUE DE LA CONSTITUTION

RUE DE SOUSSE

AV. HABIB THAMEUR

RUE MARBELLA

AVENUE HEDI CHAKER

RUE KHEIREDINE

AVENUE ALI BELHOUANE

RUE JEDEIDA MAGHREBIA

AVENUE HABIB BOURGUIBA

RUE DES PALMIERS

RUE ZANZAFOUR

Neapolis

BEACH ↘

Nabeul Pottery

T UNISIAN POTTERY GOES BACK to the Neolithic period when large jugs and vases were used for storage. In the early years of the Muslim era, during the Aghlabid dynasty (649–909), a new technique was introduced known as "mirror" dyeing that involved the use of metallic dyes. The periods of the Fatimids and Zirids (10th and 11th centuries) mark a revolution in the decorative arts of this region when figurative images began to appear on vases and mosaics. During those days, Tunisian ceramics were in high demand and were exported to Andalusia and Sicily.

Abstract designs– arabesque and geometric patterns – first appeared during the Hafsid dynasty (1159–1534). At that time, the popular colours were cobalt blue and brown. These designs have survived though the range of colours has increased.

Turkish influences are in evidence from the 16th century onwards. The Ottoman Turks introduced polychromatic (many coloured) designs, with flowers being a frequently used motif. These techniques produced brightly-coloured designs on bowls, jugs, tiles, vases and all kinds of other vessels.

POTTERY WORKSHOP

Workshops that produce ceramics are generally small. They employ a handful of people, often members of one family. Separate rooms are used for moulding, firing and decorating the items. Visiting tourists are generally invited to see the final stages of the process when artists decorate the bowls and jugs.

CERAMIC DECORATION

Craftsman decorating a bowl

The centre of Tunisian ceramics was once Guellala, on the island of Jerba. Its local craftsmen arrived at Nabeul in the 15th century, possibly attracted by the quality of the local clay. The Guellala potters often use Berber motifs and favour brown and beige colours. Nabeul craftsmen prefer floral designs. Each item is hand-decorated by an artist.

Nabeul pottery uses a lively mix of colours but is predominantly in strong blues and greens.

Andalusian, Turkish and Italian influences are evident in 17th-century ceramics. Today, traditional green and yellow decorated objects, with brown motifs, are becoming increasingly rare.

Artistic pottery products are decorated with arabesques or geometric patterns combined with images of fish, birds, cypress trees and stylized flowers.

Children learn the craft from an early age.

The quality of all finished vessels is carefully checked.

All pots are moulded on a potter's wheel.

Ceramic tiles are decorated with motifs that together form large multi-coloured compositions.

Ceramics shops can be found in every street of town. Their courtyards display all possible forms of ceramics, and their small workshops are tucked away at the back.

Jugs – long and pointed – were produced during the Phoenician era. Roman times saw the introduction of red ceramics decorated with mythological and floral motifs.

Hammamet ⓰

Mermaids from the kasbah

HAMMAMET LIES ON THE COAST, half-way between Tunis and Sousse, and has some of the best beaches in Tunisia. In the 2nd century, the Romans established a settlement called Pupput, close to the present town, which was later inhabited by the Normans. It was only in the 1920s, however, that the place was really put on the map when the Romanian millionaire George Sebastian built a villa here. Where he led others soon followed and today Hammamet attracts over half a million visitors a year.

Exploring Hammamet

The most pleasant time of the day in Hammamet is the late afternoon, when the streets and cafés fill with people emerging after their afternoon siesta, and the sun casts a warm glow on the walls of houses. The compact medina, built by the Hafsids, is well worth exploring and includes ancient bathhouses and shops hidden away in the narrow alleys. The Great Mosque and the kasbah are strategically located by the medina's main entrance.

At sunset, head for the café situated by the kasbah at the entrance to the medina. This delightful spot is a pleasant place to savour a cup of mint tea or coffee and watch the world go by.

The main streets of the new section of town are Avenue Bourguiba and Avenue de la République, where most shops, banks, and some good restaurants are situated. At their junction stands the **Centre Commercial**, which was opened in 1979.

Narrow streets of the medina, providing shelter from the sun

♨ Kasbah

🕐 *Apr–Oct: 8am–1pm & 3–7pm. Outside high season: 8:30am–5:30pm.*

Built in the 15th century, the kasbah (Arab fort) stands next to the main gate leading to the medina. It is approached by high stairs; its upper terrace provides a magnificent view of the glistening sea and the roofs of the old town houses on which drying peppers, peas, sesame seeds and couscous often form colourful mosaics. Visitors can also stop for a cup of aromatic tea in the charming café next to it.

⛩ Medina

Through the main gate – Bab el-Souk – is the entrance to the medina. It is surrounded by high walls, erected in AD 904, and was rebuilt in the 13th century during the period of the Hafsid dynasty.

Immediately past the gate there are souvenir vendors with colourful stalls and small shops full of rugs, lovely oriental mirrors and old (or imitation) jewellery. In the first street to the left (counting from the gate) are the Turkish baths (open to men in the morning, and to women in the afternoon).

There is little need for a detailed map when wandering around Hammamet's medina, and it is easy to get into the rhythm of its narrow streets with its unique patchwork of alleyways. Walking around, there is a pleasant variety of details to take in – a doorknocker in the shape of the hand of Fatima, for example, or a flower-pot set against the white wall of a house. Visitors can step into **Dar Hammamet** in order to see a traditional Tunisian house with a collection of costumes which have been gathered together from all over Tunisia.

🏛 Dar Hammamet

Rue Sidi Abdallah. 📞 *(72) 281 206.* 🕐 *8:30am–7:30pm daily.* 📷

🅲 Great Mosque

🕐 *to non-Muslims.*

Standing in the medina, the Great Mosque was built in 1236 by Abu Am Othmar. Since then the mosque has been remodelled and has undergone two major renovations: one in 1727 was undertaken by Hussein Bey, the second in 1978–79 was overseen by the town authorities. The nearby Sidi Abdel Kader mosque was built in 1798; it now houses the School of Koranic Studies.

View from the kasbah walls over the medina and the sea

◁ *Chryses visiting Agamemnon* – a mosaic from Neapolis, now in the Nabeul Museum

A palm-shaded promenade on Avenue Bourguiba

Avenue Habib Bourguiba

The main thoroughfare of Hammamet, Avenue Habib Bourguiba is full of shops, narrow passageways and tourist restaurants. The adjacent central square is the site of the fish and vegetable market, held every morning. This is also the centre of Hammamet's nightlife, with clubs and restaurants open until the small hours. In order to see how the Tunisians spend their free time, take a seat for a while during the late afternoon in one of the local teahouses, in the area where Avenue Bourguiba reaches the walls of the medina. The end of siesta marks a time for coffee and *chichas* (hookahs) or for contemplating life over a cup of strong mint tea. The busiest people around this time of the day are the jasmine sellers.

Fishing boats on one of Hammamet's beaches

Men place the small fragrant posies behind their ears; women hold them in their hands, turning them around.

Beaches

Hammamet has two main tourist zones. The older, in the north, is located between Hammamet and Nabeul; the newer, in the south has been named Hammamet Jasmine and lies 8–10 km (5–6 miles) from the town centre.

Thoroughly geared up for visitors, these zones have excellent beaches, clean water and mounted police patrols. The northern zone offers a wider range of hotels and restaurants. It is also more lively, with small bars and street vendors; and it is closer to town. Hammamet Jasmine maintains a higher standard, with most hotels having four or five stars. It also has the largest Tunisian marina. Tourist zones allow visitors to behave in a more relaxed way than would be appropriate in the town.

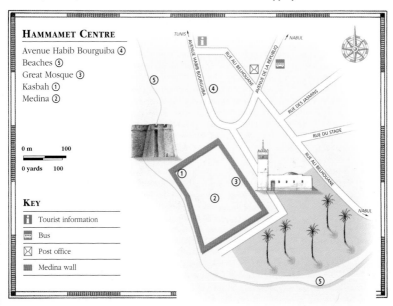

HAMMAMET CENTRE

Avenue Habib Bourguiba ④
Beaches ⑤
Great Mosque ③
Kasbah ①
Medina ②

| 0 m | 100 |
| 0 yards | 100 |

KEY

🛈 Tourist information

🚌 Bus

⊠ Post office

▦ Medina wall

The former villa of George Sebastian

Further Afield

Beaches that are further from the town centre, as well as those located in the new parts of Hammamet Jasmine, are all within easy reach by taxi. A walk to the International Cultural Centre, which hosts performances in the summer, takes about 20 minutes. Also worth exploring, particularly on market days, are the villages around Nabeul.

🏛 International Cultural Centre

Avenue des Nations Unies. 🔌 (72) 280 410. ⏱ 8:30am–7pm daily. 🎵 Jul, Aug.

The International Cultural Centre is housed in the villa that once belonged to George Sebastian, which was praised by the architect Frank Lloyd Wright as the most beautiful house he had ever seen. The ground floor is occupied by a gallery, and the house is surrounded by a beautiful park. Visitors can stop and rest in one of its delightful nooks or sit in the waterside café, although it is open only in the summer. The centre hosts an Arab Music Festival during July and August in the park's amphitheatre. The concerts, including both classical and modern popular Arab music, are great fun.

ENVIRONS: Nearby, **Pupput** is situated 6 km (4 miles) south of Hammamet, on the road to Sousse. In the 2nd century AD this was a small Roman settlement. During the Byzantine era, the site was occupied by a fortress. Although little remains of the town's former glory, it is still worth coming here to see the 4th-century mosaics from Christian tombs.

Grombalia, 30 km (19 miles) north of Hammamet, comes alive on market days, although to experience a truly festive atmosphere it is best to visit the town in September, during the wine festival that coincides with the all-important harvest.

Grombalia is one of Tunisia's wine-producing regions. Vines have been cultivated here since Punic times. In order to protect the plants from the heat, the vineyards were laid out facing north, the vines were planted in trenches and their roots were covered with stones to provide protection from rain and the summer heat. The Phoenicians were believed to have produced excellent wines. The Romans upheld these traditions, but with the arrival of Muslim civilization, wine production declined. Grapes continued to be cultivated, but on a much smaller scale. This is largely because the drinking of alcohol was not encouraged by the Prophet. This rule was strictly adhered to in the early days of Islam, but Imam ibn Hanifa and the Hanefite school of law allowed their followers to drink certain types of wine. Wine-drinking was widespread towards the end of the Ummayad dynasty. In some branches of Sufism, wine has come to symbolize the Absolute, with wine-induced intoxication regarded as a state of mystic ecstasy in which the sufi draws closer to God.

Monument to wine making, in Grombalia

Bir Bou Regba, a small town close to Nabeul, comes alive on market days. Visitors usually head for the dried-out riverbed of Faoura. The target of their trips is the small waterfall (also sometimes dry) situated a short distance up the course of the river. Water flowing from the spring runs over the stones that are believed to be the remains of a Roman aqueduct. One of the ravines in the valley used to contain a sanctuary devoted to the Punic god Baal Hammon and the goddess Tanit (see p110).

🏛 GEORGE SEBASTIAN

In the early 20th century, Hammamet became the favourite haunt of artists, aristocrats and politicians including Winston Churchill, who worked on his memoirs here. This is largely due to George Sebastian, a Romanian millionaire who liked it so much that he decided to make it his home. He built a magnificent villa (now the International Cultural Centre) set in a beautiful park. George Sebastian used it to entertain many writers and artists, including Paul Klee and André Gide. Word spread and he was soon not the only foreign resident. The town also lured the American couple John and Violet Henson and their house became a meeting place for the artistic elite from all over the world.

Bust of Sebastian

🏛 Pupput

⏱ Apr–Sep: 8am–1pm & 3–7pm daily. Oct–Mar: 8:30am–5:30pm.

Tunisian Doors

I**N TUNISIA**, doors are regarded as symbols reflecting the fortune and happiness of the households within. They are therefore solidly built of palm wood, reinforced with sheet metal and often set within richly decorated portals. They are usually painted blue, though they can be brown or yellow. Only the doors leading to public baths or marabout mausoleums are painted in green or red.

Carved portal of a house in Kairouan

Under the Hafsids (13th–16th century) Tunisian doors were almost entirely devoid of decoration. In the 16th and 17th centuries, the Moorish style introduced geometric patterns, which under Turkish rule were supplemented with stylized plants and flowers. In the 19th century, European fashion influenced the colouring and the decorative motifs of Tunisian doors.

*An **Italian influence** is clear in the semicircular wrought-iron grille in the top section of this door. The light blue colouring is inspired by the European fashion and appeared in the 20th century.*

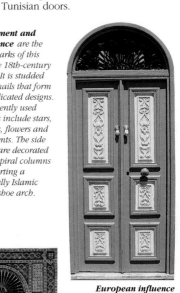

***Ornament and opulence** are the hallmarks of this sturdy 18th-century door. It is studded with nails that form complicated designs. Frequently used motifs include stars, plants, flowers and crescents. The side posts are decorated with spiral columns supporting a typically Islamic horseshoe arch.*

***European influence** led to hearts and stylized flowers on rectangular tiles replacing doorway decorations produced with studs and nails.*

***Motifs** most frequently seen on Tunisian doors include the crescent, star, minaret and stylized palm leaves.*

***Doorknockers** are present on every door. They are often in the shape of a large circle or a hand. The ones on the left are usually used by women, the ones on the right by men.*

NORTHERN TUNISIA

OR MANY YEARS *northern Tunisia was little appreciated by visitors who preferred other parts of the country such as the east coast of Cap Bon and the resorts around Tunis. This situation is gradually changing and the mild Mediterranean climate, rugged coast, magnificent beaches and Roman sites such as Bulla Regia are attracting visitors in increasing numbers.*

The indigenous population of the northern regions of Tunisia were the Berbers, but it was the Phoenicians who established the earliest settlements here – including present-day Utica, Bizerte and Tabarka. They were attracted by the fertile soil of the region and its calm bays, in which they could safely anchor their ships.

Following the downfall of Carthage, Rome took over the former Punic settlements, turning them into fast-growing military colonies. Towns such as Béja, Bulla Regia, Utica and Bizerte owe their prosperity to grain and trade. The fertile soil of the Medjerda Valley was the granary of Phoenicia and Rome, and it remains agriculturally important today. The region owes much to the Arab immigrants who arrived from Andalusia in the 17th and 18th centuries. Besides cereals and vegetables they began to grow almonds, figs, citrus fruit and grapes. The vineyards of Raf Raf and Béja produce fine Coteaux D'Utique wines.

Bizerte and Tabarka – northern Tunisia's largest towns – have long-established maritime traditions dating back to Phoenician times. Both were once major ports, pirate strongholds and naval bases. Today their economies are based on industry and on a steadily growing tourist trade, with numerous resorts and hotels springing up. Bizerte, nicknamed the "Venice of the North", has a lovely old harbour and a charming medina, while at Tabarka there is a coral reef and a first-class golf course.

Rolling hills around Testour

◁ **Working on the fishing boats in Ghar el-Melh harbour**

Exploring Northern Tunisia

T HE NORTHERN SECTION of Tunisia is not as popular as the coast of Sahel and Jerba, yet the region has a great deal to offer. Those who enjoy hiking or hunting should head for the Khroumirie Mountains where there are many trails leading through wooded hills. The beaches around Tabarka, Bizerte and Raf Raf are perfect for swimming and relaxing while Lake Ichkeul, used as winter quarters by many thousands of migrating birds, is an ornithologist's paradise. Bulla Regia, to the south, has unique underground villas and is one of the most archaeologically important Roman towns in the world.

La Galite

A ceramic statuette from Sejnane

SEE ALSO

• **Where to Stay** pp254–5

• **Where to Eat** pp280–2

CAP SERRAT 9

Les Aiguilles by the Tabarka beach

SIGHTS AT A GLANCE

Béja 6
Bizerte 12
Bulla Regia pp132–3 5
Cap Blanc 13
Cap Serrat 9
Chemtou 4
Ichkeul National Park pp136–7 10
Khroumirie Mountains 3
Menzel Bourguiba 11
Sejnane 8
Tabarka 1
Testour 7
Utica 14

Tours
Around Tabarka pp128–9 2

SEJNANE

P7

C52

TABARKA 1

El-Kala

KHROUMIRIE MOUNTAINS 3

El-Kala

AROUND TABARKA 2

BÉJA

P6

BOU SALEM

Oued Medjerda

P17

CHEMTOU 4

BULLA REGIA 5

P6

C75

DJUNDUBA

Oued Melle ue

P6

Oued Melle ue

Souk Ahras

Le Kef

GETTING THERE

The main airport for the northern coast is Tunis. Two roads link the capital with Tabarka: the northern P7 and the southern P6 from which drivers must turn north onto the P17. Bizerte can be reached by the A1 motorway or P8 highway. The scenery around Béja, Téboursouk and Testour is remarkable, although the roads are narrow. Access to the coast in places other than Tabarka and Bizerte is difficult.

An underground villa in Bulla Regia

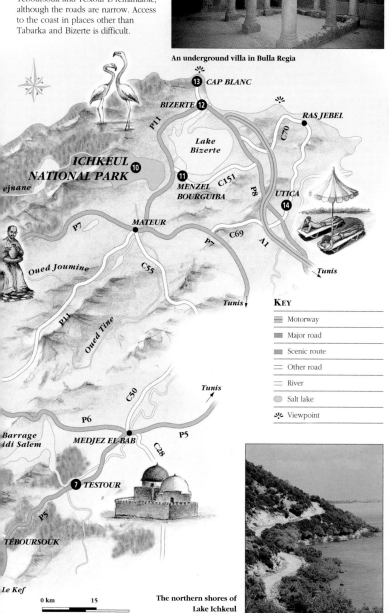

CAP BLANC ⑬

BIZERTE ⑫

P11

RAS JEBEL

C70

Lake Bizerte

ICHKEUL NATIONAL PARK ⑩

ejnane

MENZEL BOURGUIBA ⑪

C151

P8

UTICA ⑭

MATEUR

P7

C69

A1

Tunis

Oued Joumine

C55

P7

Tunis ↓

P11

Oued Tine

KEY

▬	Motorway
▬	Major road
▬	Scenic route
═	Other road
═	River
⬤	Salt lake
☀	Viewpoint

C50

Tunis ↑

P6

Barrage idi Salem

MEDJEZ EL-BAB

P5

C28

⑦ **TESTOUR**

P5

TÉBOURSOUK

Le Kef

0 km   15

0 miles   15

The northern shores of Lake Ichkeul

Fishing boats, with Tabarka's Genoese fort in the background

Tabarka ❶

Road map B1. 🏚 *13,700.*
🛈 ONTT: Commissariat regional au
tourisme, Blvd. 7 Novembre 32, *(78)*
673 555. 🎷 *International Jazz*
Festival (late Jun).

TABARKA IS JUST 22 km (14
miles) from the Algerian
border and is one of the
greenest towns in Tunisia. Its
picturesque setting includes
beaches to the north and
gentle hills overgrown with
cork oak, pine and mimosa to
the south.
   The town stands on the site
of a former Phoenician
colony, Thabraca. During
Roman times Tabarka was an
important port used for
shipping grain from Béja and
marble from Chemtou to
Rome. As well as its forests
full of game, Tabarka's
greatest asset was its coral
reef. In the 16th century the
exclusive rights to coral
fishing were granted to the
Genoese who built an
offshore fort close by. With
the advent of the French
Protectorate, in 1881, coral
rights were taken up by the
French and Tabarka and Le
Kef were two of the first
towns to be occupied.
   Tabarka is quite small. It
centres round two streets
running parallel to the coast,
where most of its restaurants
and cafés can be found. The

red-tiled roofs of the
Genoese fort can be seen
from almost any point in
town but the best view is
from the jetty. The beautifully
located hotel **Les Mimosas**
also affords a magnificent
panoramic view of the town,
the gulf and the surrounding
area. A little further west from
the harbour stands an ochre-
coloured rock formation –
Les Aiguilles (The Needles),
sharpened by the constant
erosion of wind and rain.
   A **Cork Museum** is a short
way out of town on the road
leading to Aïn Draham. It
provides information on cork
production in this area.
   Tabarka has quiet beaches
and a number of golf courses.
It also has some of Tunisia's
best diving. About 60 km (37
miles) north of Tabarka is the

CORAL

Coral, brought up by
divers and fishermen from
the seabed, has been in
high demand throughout
North Africa for many
years. Since the 15th
century, when the
Europeans discovered its
beauty, coral jewellery has
fetched a high price.
Tabarka is a centre for
jewellery made from coral
and shops sell necklaces,
pins and brooches with
coral inserts. It has long
been used as a talisman:
red coral is believed to
bestow vitality, pink coral
is conducive to pleasant
thoughts, while white coral
clears the mind. Coral is
becoming scarce, however;
some visitors choose not to
buy it for this reason.

**Coral and shell necklaces for
sale at Tabarka's market**

Galite archipelago, which can
be reached by boat from
Tabarka. Details can be
obtained from any of Tabarka's
diving clubs *(see p307).*

🏛 **Cork Museum**
◻ *8am–noon & 2–5pm daily.*

Les Aiguilles (The Needles) as seen from Tabarka's beach

Coral Reef

TABARKA'S CORAL REEF is close to the shore. Just 10 minutes away by boat is a rock surrounded by black and red corals. A little further on is a magnificent complex of tunnels, grottoes, underwater caves and caverns. Warm waters mean that the reef teems with life. Flitting between coral branches are colourful marine fish and luminescent jellyfish.

Other marine occupants include sponges, sea urchins, sea cucumbers and sea squirts. Deeper waters are inhabited by halibut, moray eel and wrasse. Diving for coral is popular along the entire northern shore of Tunisia, but the most beautiful specimens come from the waters around Tabarka. Its popularity means that coral is an endangered species.

Rainbow wrasse
is a colourful fish belonging to the perch family. Only active during the day, it buries itself in the sand at night.

Swallowtail sea perch *is a small predatory fish that lives in large shoals. Its bright colouring makes it highly conspicuous. It can be seen grazing near entrances to underwater caves in which it seeks shelter when threatened.*

Fish *graze near the bottom of the sea, searching for food in rock crevices and amongst the coral where they can hide. They often assume the colour of the reef, which makes them invisible to predators.*

The dusky grouper *is a very large, slow-swimming fish. It can sometimes be curious about divers and therefore presents an easy target for spearfishing. Reefs provide it with plenty of hiding places, although it does not have many natural enemies other than mankind.*

Wrasse
favour rocky coastal waters and reefs. Here they find the small fish, as well as snails, mussels, crabs and other invertebrates that make up their staple diet.

Red coral knolls *grow on the rocky bottom of the Mediterranean Sea. As well as being collected with nets, coral is also cut using a special device consisting of heavy, metal-reinforced beams. These are set in the shape of a cross, weighted with a stone in the centre and have loosely weighted nets at the corners. The cross is pressed into crevasses and the nets wind themselves around the coral, breaking it off the bedrock.*

Around Tabarka ❷

EL-KALA

Rising immediately behind the town are the steep slopes of the Khroumirie Mountains. These are densely forested and are a marvellous region for exploring. The deep ravines and numerous springs and streams provide welcome cool in the summer heat. Villages such as Hammam Bourguiba and Aïn Draham are long-established resorts and make good starting points for hikes. The cool climate and wonderful scenery make this area popular with Tunisians.

Hammam Bourguiba ①
The village lies in a valley surrounded by hills dense with cork oak and pine. The excellent climate combined with hot springs has made it popular with elderly Tunisians including (at one time) President Bourguiba.

Beni Metir ④
Beni Metir was built in the 1950s to house French builders. It is close to a lake and surrounded by a forest of oak and myrtle.

Bulla Regia ⑥
These Roman ruins include baths, a temple complex and theatre, as well as villas that were built underground to escape the heat.

Chemtou ⑦
These local quarries used to provide Rome with marble. On top of the hill the Numidians erected an altar to Baal. The Romans used this to worship Saturn. For the Muslims it became a centre for marabouts (Islamic holy men).

Oued Medjerda

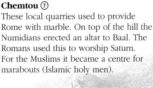

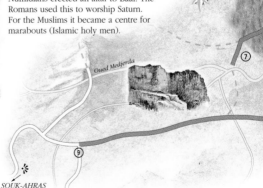

Ghardimaou ⑨
This quiet village lies almost on the border with Algeria. It is worth visiting mainly for its beautiful mountain scenery as part of a tour that also takes in Chemtou.

SOUK-AHRAS

TABARKA

Babouche ②

The road from Tabarka to Babouche runs steeply upwards. The village lies at the entrance to a gorge. From here the road leads to a deer park. This is a good starting point for hikes through the forest.

Aïn Draham ③

Perched on the western side of Jebel Bir (1,014 m/3327 ft), Aïn Draham was popular with the French. Aïn Draham's steep red-tiled roofs help cope with the winter snow and lend the town an Alpine atmosphere.

BOU SALEM

Fernana ⑤

Around Fernana the mountainous landscape gives way to a plain. Every Sunday the village holds a market selling fruit, vegetables and livestock. According to legend it was here that the Khroumirie chiefs came to ask a thousand-year-old oak tree how much tax they should pay to the Bey of Tunis. The tree would rustle its leaves in response.

C65

O. Ghezala

BOU SALEM

P17

C62

C59

BÉJA

KAIROUAN

TIPS FOR DRIVERS

Length: About 90 km (56 miles).
Stopping-off points: Jendouba, Aïn Draham and Hammam Bourguiba have accommodation. There are plenty of restaurants.
Other attractions: The road that runs between Bou Salem and Téboursouk is particularly scenic.

KEY

▬ Suggested route

═ Other road

-- Unmetalled road

☆ Viewpoint

Jendouba ⑧

The provincial capital, surrounded by fields, is half way between Tabarka and Le Kef. In the evenings the men sit down to a cup of tea and a *chicha* (hookah) in one of the small restaurants along the main road from Tabarka to Le Kef. It is a good base to visit the ruins at Bulla Regia.

0 km   3

0 miles   3

Hilltop field and olive trees, flanked by the Khroumirie Mountains

Khroumirie Mountains ❸

Road map B2.

THE KHROUMIRIE Mountains begin to rise just a few miles outside Tabarka and stretch some 50 km (31 miles) south to Fernana, reaching a height of about 1,000 m (3,281 ft). They owe their name to the Khroumirie tribes who were renowned for their bravery. When French troops invaded in 1881, it was the Khroumirie who put up the fiercest resistance. The forests were once the favourite hunting grounds of local tribes, as well as visiting Europeans. The last lion was killed in 1891; all hunters have been left with is wild boar. In summer, the forests are popular with mountain hikers.

Although holly, eucalyptus, mimosa, elm, birch and willow all grow here, the most abundant tree is the cork oak, which has been grown for its bark by the villagers of the Khroumirie for thousands of years. Used to make anything from tiles to wine corks, the red-stained trunks of freshly-stripped trees can be seen everywhere.

Chemtou ❹

Road map B2. 27 km (17 miles) north of Jendouba. 🏛 *Apr–Oct: 9am–6:30pm Tue–Sun; Nov–Mar: 9am–5pm Tue–Sun.* 📷

NOT MUCH HAS survived in Chemtou from the former Roman colony of Simithas, which was established in the 1st century BC. Chemtou owed its existence to the quarries which provided a dark-yellow marble that was highly prized by the Romans. Blocks of marble were marked with the name of the emperor and were transported on carts to Tabarka across the mountains.

The site included workers' homes, baths, a theatre and a workshop. Aerial photographs taken in the late 1960s revealed a large labour camp. It was built in AD 154 and housed the slaves who worked in the quarries. The quarries remained active until Byzantine times, but were abandoned after the arrival of the Arabs (7th century).

The site was first excavated in 1968 and many of the finds from this dig can be found in the excellent **site museum**, which was opened in 1990. Among the displays are a detailed explanation of the excavation, a working model of an ancient flour mill and over 1,600 gold coins that were discovered when the museum was being built.

One surprise of the excavation work was the discovery of a Numidian temple to Baal Hammon at the top of the hill. Dating from the 2nd century BC, the find suggests that the Numidians had a more sophisticated culture than historians had once believed.

The quarries are located opposite the museum. The huge holes dug into the rock attest to the amount of sheer effort and human endurance that went into working them.

Further on up the hill are the ruins of a temple. Originally a Numidian site, it was converted into a temple dedicated to Saturn by the Romans. Particularly interesting among Chemtou's other relics are the rock carvings found on the western and northern sides of the hill.

The ancient quarries at Chemtou

Red trunk of a freshly stripped cork oak, an important resource of the Khroumirie Mountains

Bulla Regia ❺

See pp132–133.

Béja ❻

Road map B2. 70,000.

THE ROAD FROM Tabarka to Béja (which in ancient times was called Vaga) runs amid gently rolling hills covered with eucalyptus, stone-pine and oleander. The town – the capital of the province – is 250 m (820 ft) above sea level, and lies in the valley of the Medjerda River. Béja is an important grain town and a weekly market has been held here since Roman times. The town was attacked and destroyed by the Vandals in the 5th century, only to be rebuilt by Emperor Justinian who named it Theodoriana, in honour of his wife. The ruins of the Byzantine kasbah that dominate the old town date from that period.

The most charming part of modern-day Béja is its small medina. It is a busy and atmospheric place and the many mosques, *zaouias* (tombs), Islamic schools and public baths are punctuated by colourful market stalls. Head for Rue Farhat Hached for a fine view from the medina over the town and the surrounding countryside.

ENVIRONS: Some 13 km (8 miles) south of Béja stands **Trajan's Bridge**. Built in AD 29, it linked Carthage with Bulla Regia *(see pp132–3).* Heading north, towards Beni Metir, 8 km (5 miles) beyond Béja, is **Henchir el-Fouar**. Excavations begun in 1960 unearthed the ruins of Roman villas, a small forum and two basilicas, which formed the Roman town of Belalia Major. It is worth stopping for a while in **Tebourba** – a little town on the banks of the Medjerda River, set in gardens and olive groves. Tebourba has a pleasant medina, laid out on a regular grid pattern. As well as a number of market stalls, the town has a 17th-century Great Mosque and a handful of smaller mosques and *zaouias*. The oldest of the *zaouias* is dedicated to Sidi Thabet and dates from the 7th century.

A medersa's green-tiled dome, Testour

Testour ❼

Road map C2. 8,000.
Malouf Music Festival (Jun).

TESTOUR IS ONE of Tunisia's Andalusian Muslim towns. In the 17th century, 80,000 Arabs who were expelled from Andalusia after the Christian reconquest arrived in Tunisia. The wealthier refugees were allowed to settle in Tunis but the poorer farmers had to make do with the uninhabited regions of the country's interior. After petitioning the authorities they were granted the right to settle on the Roman site of Tichilla, which became present-day Testour.

The farming techniques brought from Andalusia helped the newcomers turn the barren land into fertile oases and their attachment to Andalusian traditions injected a European flavour into the Arab settlements. Testour's central square became the focal point of the town layout. Windows now faced the streets and mosques acquired their distinctive arches. Testour's main square is one of the earliest products of the 17th-century Spanish influence. It contains several cafés, the Great Mosque and the hammam and is planted with numerous orange trees and jasmine shrubs. Leading to the square is the town's main street – Avenue Habib Bourguiba.

Testour used to have 14 mosques. Five of them remain open to this day. The main one – the **Great Mosque** (17th century) is open only to Muslims and is a good example of Tunisian Moorish architecture. The square base of the tiled minaret is crowned with two octagonal towers, one built into the other, and is reminiscent of a Castilian bell tower. The most striking evidence of Andalusian influence is the clock on the minaret's south face. Besides the fact that a clock is not seen on a minaret anywhere else in the world, the other surprising feature is the hours, which go backwards, revealing, perhaps, the refugees' desire to turn back time and return to their homeland.

Nearby, in El-Andalouse Square, are the ruins of the first Great Mosque (1610). Rue du Mars, running parallel to Avenue Bourguiba, contains the Abdellatif Mosque, also known as the Hanefite mosque.

For most of the year, Testour is a quiet town but it can get busy in June during the Festival of Malouf music.

Green fields dotted with olive trees near Béja

Bulla Regia ❺

THE IMPORTANT ARCHAEOLOGICAL SITE of Bulla Regia is famous for its underground villas, which were built by the Romans in the 2nd and 3rd centuries AD to escape the fierce heat of the Tunisian sun. The site also includes a temple, baths, fort and a market square, but it is the houses which are the main attraction. Each of the villas has been named after the mosaics that were found within them. Some of these beautiful mosaics are still *in situ*, while others have been moved to museums such as the Bardo in Tunis *(see pp88–9).*

★ **House of Amphitrite**
The house, found at the north end of the cluster of underground villas, is famous for its exquisite mosaics, which are in the basement.

The Byzantine fort is a very modest structure, devoid of any defensive features. It was erected in the 6th century.

★ **House of the Hunt**
Of all the surviving underground houses this one is the most striking. Its colonnaded basement courtyard is especially impressive.

Byzantine Church
The church was built in the 6th century. Visible among the fallen columns are fragments of the floor mosaics featuring Christian motifs.

Roman cisterns were later used to store food.

Southern baths

STAR SIGHTS
★ **House of Amphitrite**
★ **House of the Hunt**

0 m   50

0 yards   50

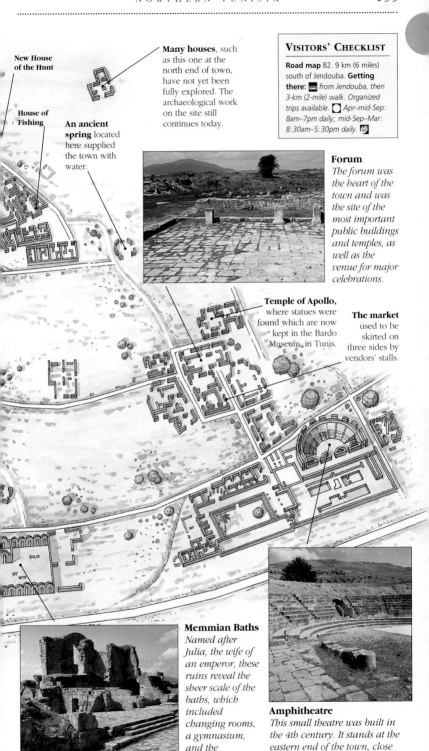

New House of the Hunt

House of Fishing

An ancient spring located here supplied the town with water.

Many houses, such as this one at the north end of town, have not yet been fully explored. The archaeological work on the site still continues today.

VISITORS' CHECKLIST

Road map B2. 9 km (6 miles) south of Jendouba. **Getting there:** from Jendouba, then 3-km (2-mile) walk. Organized trips available. ◯ Apr–mid-Sep: 8am–7pm daily; mid-Sep–Mar: 8:30am–5:30pm daily.

Forum
The forum was the heart of the town and was the site of the most important public buildings and temples, as well as the venue for major celebrations.

Temple of Apollo, where statues were found which are now kept in the Bardo Museum, in Tunis.

The market used to be skirted on three sides by vendors' stalls.

Memmian Baths
Named after Julia, the wife of an emperor, these ruins reveal the sheer scale of the baths, which included changing rooms, a gymnasium, and the frigidarium.

Amphitheatre
This small theatre was built in the 4th century. It stands at the eastern end of the town, close to the forum.

Sejnane ⑧

Road map B1. 🏚 *2,000.*

SEJNANE – a small village hidden among the hills overgrown with laurel, oleander and eucalyptus – lies along the road that links Bizerte with Tabarka. Quite close to Béja and Cap Serrat, the village is inhabited by Berber tribes who lead a semi-nomadic life. The air here is suffused with the smell of pine resin and the bread baking in outdoor ovens.

Sejnane is famous for two things: its lovely beige pottery and its numerous storks' nests. The storks, of which there were twenty-four pairs at the last count, build their nests each spring. The birds seem fairly indiscriminate as to where they site their nests and can be seen on the roofs of the local houses, the train station, and (behind the station) on some abandoned mining apparatus.

The techniques used to create the pottery made here date back thousands of years. The clay is shaped by hand, then decorated. Some of the decorations are drawn directly onto the wet clay and the grooves are filled with a black resin from the mastic tree. The items are baked on open fires in the yards of the houses. Pots of various shapes and sizes and animal figurines, which are painted by hand by the Berber women using traditional motifs, are most common. The typical colours of the Sejnane products are beige, rust-red and black.

Originally, such pottery was intended for domestic use or as talismans created to bring success and happiness. Sejnane pottery includes heavy plates, water jugs, deep platters, animal statuettes and censers. These are filled with herbs and aromatic resins,

Berber ceramics from Sejnane region

and the sweet-smelling smoke is believed to purify the house of all evil influences. The women also purify their skirts and dresses with the smoke.

The decorative patterns on the vessels all have symbolic meanings. The stylized triangles symbolize fertility; the crosses, large and small, are intended for protection and healing. A wavy line placed on a dish will ensure the abundance of water.

Much of the pottery produced here is from the outlying villages and is sold on roadside stalls. Many of these can be found on the road to Bizerte.

North from Sejnane, across the wooded hills, are the beautiful Sidi Mechrig beach and Cap Serrat.

Cap Serrat ⑨

Road map B1.

CAP SERRAT IS situated away from the busy tourist centres. Its steep cliffs drop down to the sea and the views from the top are truly breathtaking. The remote beach on the eastern side of this little peninsula is long, sandy and, for much of the time, virtually deserted. It is visited mainly by local Tunisians who come here in

family groups. A small café next to the beach caters for campers during the summer.

The road between Cap Serrat and Cap Negro is an exceptionally scenic one. It is fringed with laurel, mimosa and pine trees. Cap Negro (its name is associated with the Genoese settlers) is an old trading post, built in the 16th century by the French who traded in grain. It is now occupied by the National Guard. The area is beautiful, but has virtually no roads and is best explored on foot.

The region between Cap Serrat and Tabarka is full of pine, eucalyptus, mimosa, oleander, cork oak and fruit orchards. Sometimes described in brochures as "Green Tunisia", it is a long way from the typical Tunisian image of desert and beaches.

ENVIRONS: About 40 km (25 miles) off the coast from Cap Serrat is the volcanic archipelago of **La Galite**. Consisting of seven volcanic islands, this was already known to the Phoenicians. During Roman times it was called Galathea. The waters around the islands are rich in marine life and are a superb place to go diving. There is no regular transport between the islands and the mainland, but it is possible to get here by boat from Tabarka. Details can be obtained from one of Tabarka's diving clubs (see p307). Although remote, the islands are inhabited by a handful of families who make their living from fishing and cultivating grapes.

Leading a horse to water in Cap Serrat

Tunisian Birds

Tunisia is visited by many migrating birds that fly here from the north for the winter. The Gulf of Gabès is the winter home of some 350,000 birds – almost half of the bird population that winter in the Mediterranean region. Here flamingoes and many

Thekla lark in full song

varieties of shorebirds, such as curlew, plover and dunlin, can be seen. Lake Ichkeul is a perfect habitat for waterfowl and a paradise for ornithologists. About 200,000 ducks, geese and coots also settle here during the winter. Birdwatchers tend to visit Tunisia in March.

Flamingoes live in colonies, feeding on small water animals and plants. In Tunisia they can be seen in and around the Gulf of Gabès and also in Ichkeul National Park.

Lesser black-backed gulls are the most commonly seen bird on the Tunisian coast. The biggest flocks of these birds can be seen around the Gulf of Gabès.

Lanner falcons live in the border areas, between the mountains and the desert. This bird of prey builds its nest in rock crevices and hunts in open spaces. It catches birds and small rodents. Unlike many other species of falcon it can also catch its prey on the ground.

Boobys are among the largest birds that can be seen on the Tunisian coast. They inhabit the steep craggy shores in the north of the country.

Common cranes can be seen in many parts of northern Tunisia, including the salt lake at Sebkha Kelbia. They feed on plants and small animals.

Houbara bustards inhabit the edges of the desert, in areas of low-growing vegetation where they can hide. Although a protected species, hunting for bustards with falcons is a popular local sport.

Ichkeul National Park ⓾

THIS GOVERNMENT-PROTECTED nature reserve was
established in 1980. Covering 60 sq km (23 sq
miles), it is one of the main wintering grounds for
migrating waterfowl in the entire Mediterranean
basin. The shallow, freshwater lake and its
surrounding marshes are a sanctuary to thousands of
waterfowl which nest here during the mild winter
(see p135). Other animals inhabiting the reserve
include toads, terrapins,
porcupines, jackals,
wild boar and foxes.
There is even a herd
of water buffalo,
which is descended
from Asian buffaloes
brought here in the
19th century.

Otter
*This predator inhabits low-
lying areas surrounding the
lake; it feeds mainly on fish.*

Lake Ichkeul

Greylag Goose
*Some 10,000 of these birds arrive here
each year. Wintering on the waters of
the lake, the geese can easily find food.*

Genet
*Genets hate water.
Their hunting
grounds are the
shrubs that cover
the hillsides. They
hunt for small
birds and rodents
and also feed on
birds' eggs.*

JEBEL ICH

TABARKA   P7

TUNIS

0 km   2

0 miles   2

KEY

— Minor road

— Other road

— Park boundary

⌇ River

⚹ Viewpoint

Jebel Ichkeul
*Several sandy footpaths lead through the hills, which are
overgrown with wild olive trees, pistachio and euphorbia
shrubs. The best view of the lake is from here.*

Water Buffalo
A pair of buffalo was introduced here in the 19th century. Hunters brought the animal to the verge of extinction in the 1960s. Now it can be seen on the northern shore of the lake.

Grey Heron
This species can be seen from the lakeshore throughout the year, although they are more plentiful during the winter.

Tinja

Kestrel
This small falcon is one of the few birds of prey that can be seen in the park.

oldjane

Eco–museum
Displays illustrate the natural assets of the region, which in 1996 was placed on the UNESCO List of World Cultural and Natural Heritage Sites.

Coastal Marshes
The marshes dry out in the summer as waters fall below the level of the sea that feeds the lake.

Fishing boats in Bizerte's Old Port

Menzel Bourguiba ⓫

Road map C1. 🏚 *30,000.*

MENZEL BOURGUIBA is a small industrial town situated 24 km (15 miles) south of Bizerte. To get here take a car or *louage* (shared taxi) which can be hired in front of Bizerte's railway station. The town was established by the French in 1897. Originally called Ferryville, it was built on the ruins of a Spanish fortress, and was intended for European immigrants. The French built an arsenal and five dry docks here that were once the biggest in Africa. In the early 20th century the small town that sprung up around the arsenal was nicknamed "Little Paris".

Not much remains of the original provincial town. Since 1963 Menzel Bourguiba has been developing as an important centre of the textile and metal industries. It has a large harbour that links directly with the Mediterranean through the Bizerte Canal. Menzel Bourguiba's main street has an impressive modern mosque.

Bizerte ⓬

Road map C1. 65 km (40 miles) northwest of Tunis. 🏚 *90,000.* 🛈 *Quai Khemais Ternan (Vieux Port), (72) 432 897.* 📷 *Bizerte International Festival (17 Jul–17 Aug).*

BIZERTE IS THE principal town on the northeast coast of Tunisia and is situated on the canal that links Lake Bizerte

with the sea. A modern-day commercial port, Bizerte has long had a strategic importance. It was the Phoenicians who first settled here and dug a channel linking the lake to the sea, thus producing one of the safest harbours in the Mediterranean. They named their town Hippo Zarytus. The Romans destroyed it in 146 BC only to rebuild it again as Hippo Diarrhytus. It was subsequently renamed Benzert by the Arabs. Under the French Protectorate the town became a major naval base. During World War II it was occupied by German troops and suffered considerable damage in the course of Allied bombardments. In the past decade Bizerte has developed its tourist infrastructure. The magnificent, almost empty beaches and scenic dunes stretching along the Corniche

Top of the Great Mosque's minaret

(the road that runs parallel to the coast) have prompted the building of many modern hotels. The picturesque old town and the fishing harbour run along the canal. The newer, European, part of the town begins at the point where the canal joins up with Lake Bizerte.

The most attractive part of Bizerte is its **Old Port**, built on the canal that links the lake with the sea. Here, the quay is lined with quaint cafés where it is pleasant to sit out and watch the boats heading out to sea. The Old Port is entered through a huge gate, 35 m (115 ft) wide. The promenade that starts by the kasbah runs in a gentle arc along the canal. The kasbah and the small 11th-century citadel, standing on the opposite side, once formed parts of the fortifications that guarded the medina and the harbour. Built by the Arabs on the site of a

Seaside promenade beside the beach in Bizerte

◁ **Green hills between Testour and Téboursouk**

Byzantine fortress, the traditional Byzantine brick arrangement can be seen to this day.

The **kasbah** dates from the 17th century. Behind its huge walls, which are up to 10 m (33 ft) high in places, is a self-contained town within a town which includes atmospheric streets and alleys, a mosque, baths and a number of homes. The Fort Sidi el-Hanni tower now houses the **Oceanography Museum**, which has a small collection of sea creatures.

Originally, there was only one gate leading to the medina, which is now hidden behind the façades of the houses that line the banks of the canal. Until the 19th century it was surrounded by a 6-m (20-ft) high wall that was 3.5 m (11 ft) thick. All that remains of it now is the segment between the Andalusian district and the so-called Spanish Fort.

The **Spanish Fort** is actually Turkish in origin and was built in the 16th century. Little of its original structure remains, though a Muslim cemetery lies within its defensive walls. The fort's terrace offers a magnificent view over the surrounding area, including the Old Port and the modern harbour. In summer it serves as a venue for concerts.

The **Great Mosque** at the centre of the medina was built in the 17th century. Its octagonal minaret is crowned with a balcony that can be seen from every point along the promenade. The mosque is surrounded by a number of small *zaouias* (tombs), but the most important of them, the Zaouia of Sidi Mostari, is situated some distance away.

This tomb was built on the orders of Murad Bey, in 1673. It features an ablutions room, a dome-covered sanctuary containing El-Mostari's tomb, and a beautiful galleried courtyard.

It is worth visiting the Andalusian quarter where the Arab refugees from Spain settled in the 17th century. Once situated beyond the town walls, it had its own

The kasbah defending the harbour entrance, Bizerte

mosque, with a square minaret topped by a roof of green tiles. The houses here also have a distinctly Spanish character with light blue doors decorated with studs and nails. However, with the passage of time, the town wall vanished and the Andalusian quarter lost much of its identity.

Returning to the medina, to the quayside promenade, it is worth stopping in **Café Le Pasha**. In the evening its terrace provides a lovely view of the canal and the colourful lights of the nearby cafés. Immediately behind the café, situated between the souks, the Old Port and the

Picturesque houses of the medina, Bizerte

harbour, is **Place Lahedine Bouchoucha**. Here, a 17th-century mosque featuring an octagonal minaret is decorated with an external gallery. One section of the square is occupied by a market selling fish, fruit and vegetables.

A short distance further on is the **Tourist Information Bureau**. Immediately behind it the canal walk ends, but continue walking along its opposite side and there is a good view of the kasbah walls. The main street that runs along the quay leads to the beach, and further on to the tourist zone.

Head west from the town centre along Avenue Habib Bourguiba to reach the Military Academy and, further on, the European cemetery with the nearby Martyrs' Monument commemorating victims of the 1961 pitched battle between the French garrison and Tunisian forces that included many barely-trained volunteers. The road leading to the new part of town and the Ras Jebel peninsula goes over a vast drawbridge. Cap Blanc, situated 10 km (6 miles) away is often taken as the northernmost point of the African continent.

**Craggy coastline around
Cap Blanc**

Cap Blanc ⑬

Road map C1. 10 km (6 miles) north
of Bizerte.

Cap Blanc is often given the
title of the northernmost
point of Africa, though a map
reveals that this claim to fame
should actually go to Ras ben
Sekka situated just a short
distance to the west.

The road from Bizerte runs
along Habib Bougatfa,
following the coast. Passing
the tourist zone and the
pebbly beaches, the road
climbs gently upwards. The
greater the height, the lovelier
the views become. Seen from
the beach or the road, Cap
Blanc appears to be a big
green mountain whose
summit has been replaced by
a sugar-loaf. The mountain
drops sharply towards the
sea. The surrounding waters
are much favoured by divers.
The area is quiet and can be
windy. It is possible to stop
for a while in Nador (the last
village before Cap Blanc) to
rest and have a bite to eat in
the Rif Rif restaurant.

Utica ⑭

Road map C1.

Utica is an older sister of
Carthage. It lies 10 km (6
miles) from the sea, southeast
of Bizerte. The Phoenicians
established Utica as their
trading post perhaps as early
as the 10th century BC. The
site's main feature is the
House of Cascades, named
after the fountains that once

decorated this palace. Other
objects found here include
amulets, rings, scarabs,
painted vessels, lamps and
numerous amphorae.

Not much is known about
the early days of Utica's
history. Scarce information
began to appear in ancient
Greek texts but only after
the founding of Carthage.
Utica is regarded as the
second most important
ancient town after
Carthage in this
region. At its height, it
had its own harbour
and merchant fleet
and fought alongside
Carthage against
Greece and Rome.
However, in the
course of the Third
Punic War (149–146
BC) it switched
allegiance, declaring
itself on the side of
Rome. Following
the destruction of
Carthage it was
granted autonomy in AD 146
and became the capital of the
Province of Africa. It remained
as such until the rebuilding of
Carthage. The town's economic
growth reached its zenith in
the 2nd and 3rd centuries
when it derived most of its
revenue from trade. Today
Utica no longer borders the
sea as the deposits carried by
the Medjerda River have
clogged up the bay.

**Statue of Hercules in
the Utica museum**

Reminders of the town's
Punic heritage include a
pottery workshop and the
necropolis. The **baths** and
two **theatres** date from
Roman times as do the
Treasury Building, the
House of the Hunt and the
House of the Cascades.
The latter has a
colonnaded inner
courtyard and was once
a villa belonging to a
wealthy Roman
citizen. Its other
features of note
include a fountain and
marble slabs with
mosaics portraying
maritime themes. One of
the loveliest mosaics,
depicting a dolphin
playing with a cherub,
was taken from here to
the Louvre.

The **House of the
Historic Capitals** is
a spacious villa built
on the site of a
Punic structure. The
inner court is surrounded by
colonnades.

Utica's **museum** is also
worth visiting. It displays some
interesting mosaics, jewellery,
funeral accessories and Punic
sarcophagi of children that
were probably sacrificed.

🏛 Museum

By the entrance to the town.
🕐 Apr–mid-Sep: 8am–7pm daily; mid-
Sep–Mar: 8:30am–5:30pm daily. 📷

Ancient ruins in Utica

Northern Tunisia's Beaches

EAST OF BIZERTE is a range of hills covered with olive groves, vineyards and orchards of almond and fig trees. In spring the entire area blossoms and resembles one big colourful garden. The local beaches are, for the most part, undeveloped, empty and incredibly picturesque. The shore falls steeply into the crystal clear water. The most beautiful beaches of the region are to be found in Raf Raf and Sidi el-Mekki.

Ras Jebel ①

The small farming town of Ras Jebel has its own beach. The water here is clear, but the currents are very strong. The beach has not been developed. It is popular as an unnofficial campsite.

Raf Raf ②

The coast here is craggy, and the beach is relatively narrow, but it is a beautiful setting. The place is ideal for diving. The village is known for its grapes which make an excellent Muscat wine.

Sidi el-Mekki ③

Sidi el-Mekki is famous for its lovely quiet beach and the tomb of Sidi Ali el-Mekki. A network of caves leads to the tomb hidden deep in the mountain.

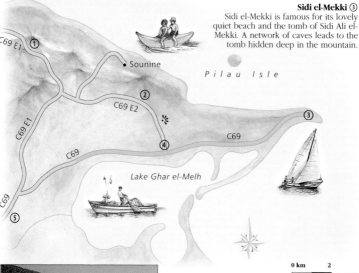

Sounine

Pilau Isle

C69 E1 ①

C69 E1

C69 E2 ②

C69 ③

C69

④

Lake Ghar el-Melh

C69

⑤

0 km 2

0 miles 2

Ghar el-Melh ④

This small town, sometimes referred to as Porto Farina, has been here since Punic times. Sites worth visiting include the fortress of Osta Murad Dey and the old port. The town lies on the shores of a lake and is linked to the sea by a canal.

Aousia ⑤

The best time to visit this picturesque village, situated some 2 km (1 mile) southwest of Ghar el-Melh, is in August, during its festival. There is a local restaurant that serves tasty fish caught by the village fishermen.

THE SAHEL

Long sandy beaches, *sparkling emerald waters, jasmine-scented nights: these are the images usually associated with the Sahel. The eastern coast of Tunisia (Sahel is Arabic for coast) stretches from Nabeul, through Sfax and the Gulf of Gabès, to Libya. It is here that Tunisia's most famous resorts and yacht harbours are found, as well as the historic towns of Mahdia, Sfax and Sousse.*

To the Phoenicians and Romans the Sahel was one of the most important regions with thriving Roman towns and colonies including Hadrumetum (Sousse) and El-Jem, which was one of the richest towns in Roman Africa. Such municipia were able to fund ambitious construction projects including the amphitheatre at El-Jem, which is one of the most impressive monuments of Roman civilization in Africa. The citizens of El-Jem had their own administration and possessed civic rights on a par with the citizens of Rome.

The wealth of the region was based on the trade in olives. The oil was valued by the Romans for its flavour but was also used in lamps. With some 15 million olive trees, the Sahel accounts for over two-thirds of Tunisia's olive oil production.

Great towns such as Mahdia, the former capital of Tunisia, and the Sahel's ribats (fortified Islamic monasteries) are a reminder of the region's past when it was under constant threat from piracy and Christian invaders. Monastir's historic ribat is particularly interesting as it is not only the oldest and the best-preserved in present-day Tunisia, but is also one of the few along the entire African coast that admitted women as teachers and students. Islamic holy men are still held in great esteem in this part of the country and the *zaouias* (tombs) are more than mere relics of the past.

French influence can be seen in the new towns (*villes nouvelles*) of Sousse and Sfax although the ancient medinas of these two ports still have much of their maritime atmosphere.

Fishing boats in Mahdia's harbour

◁ Hotel bungalows in one of the Sahel's tourist zones

Exploring the Sahel

SITUATED ALONG TUNISIA'S EAST COAST, the Sahel has the country's best beaches, an abundance of wildlife, and numerous historic sites. Located between Hammamet and Mahdia are Tunisia's most popular resorts, while Port el-Kantaoui and Hammamet Jasmine have the country's biggest marinas. The once-isolated Kerkennah Islands, near Sfax, have been steadily developing their tourist infrastructure. Sousse and Sfax are the region's major towns and have ancient walled medinas and interesting museums. Magnificent examples of Islamic architecture can be seen in Monastir, Sousse and Mahdia.

Woman from Hergla selling wicker baskets

The distinctive dome of Khalaout el-Koubba in Sousse

GETTING THERE

The Sahel region has two airports – one in Monastir and one in Sfax. Monastir's airport handles the majority of charter flights. The Métro du Sahel (which has a stop-off at Monastir's airport) provides a comfortable transport link between Monastir, Mahdia and Sousse. The entire coast up to Sfax has railway links with Tunis; many trains run from Hammamet to Sousse (change at Bir Bou Regba). The *louage* (shared taxi) also provides a convenient means of transport; private taxis are popular on the route between Sousse and Monastir. A hired car is best for a trip inland.

KEY

▬	Motorway
▬	Major road
▬	Scenic route
=	Other road
=	River
⬤	Salt lake
☀	Viewpoint
✈	Airport

SEE ALSO

- *Where to Stay* pp255–9
- *Where to Eat* pp282–5

Kairo

Kairo

Sbeïtla

Gafsa

Gafsa

P15

Tozeur

P16

EL-HAM

MATM

C105

Gulf of Hammamet

unis

DA

GLA

1

2 PORT EL-KANTAOUI

3 *SOUSSE*

KHA
IBIA

4 *MONASTIR*

✈

KSAR HELLAL

DŽAMMAL

MOKNINE

kba de
el-Hani

MAHDIA **5**

C87

KSOUR ESSAF

EL-JEM
6

C87

C82

JEBENIANA

P13

P1

7 *SFAX*
✈

8

KERKENNAH
ISLANDS

MAHRÈS

P1

9 *GULF OF GABÈS*

BÉS

P1

Medenine

A 19th-century house in Sfax

SIGHTS AT A GLANCE

El-Jem **6**
Gulf of Gabès **9**
Hergla **1**
Kerkennah Islands **8**
Mahdia pp160–162 **5**
Matmata **10**
Monastir pp154–7 **4**
Port el-Kantaoui **2**
Sfax pp164–9 **7**
Sousse pp150–153 **3**

0 km	30
0 miles	30

Beach in Chafaar, on the Gulf of Gabès

Hergla **❶**

Road map D2. 32 km (20 miles) north of Sousse. **👤** *6,000.* **🚢** *Thu.*

PERCHED ON A CLIFF, Hergla spreads out on both sides of a fishing harbour. The original village, known as Horraea Coelia, was founded in the 2nd century AD by the Romans. Its remains are a short way from the village centre. The village was totally destroyed in the course of the Arab invasion, but with time it rose from the ashes. In the 18th century it acquired an attractive mosque.

Today this pleasant seaside village is quiet and largely undiscovered, with pretty, whitewashed houses and a sandy beach. In the town's 18th-century mosque is the tomb of Sidi Bou Mendil, a 10th-century holy man who is said to have flown back from Mecca on his handkerchief.

A cemetery on the outskirts of Hergla

Fountain at the centre of Port el-Kantaoui

Port el-Kantaoui **❷**

Road map D2. 10 km (6 miles) north of Sousse. **👤** *6,000.* **ℹ** *tourist train.* **ℹ** *ONTT: Marina Kantaoui, (73) 348 799, Port el-Kantaoui (73) 241 799.*

THIS GARDEN harbour (el-Kantaoui means "garden") of the Mediterranean fully deserves its name. It is immersed in flowers, while its marina is the second largest in Tunisia. Port el-Kantaoui was built in the late 1970s as a tourist zone and represents the up-market end of Tunisia's thriving holiday machine, with a complex of smart hotels that is situated directly on the beach.

Not surprisingly, there is plenty for holidaymakers to enjoy. The beach, of course, is first class, although much of it is taken up exclusively by the five-star hotels. The hotels, built in an Arab style, are surrounded by lush greenery such as jasmine and bougainvillea. In the evenings most of them put on their own entertainment including concerts, folk shows and belly dancing. The town's championship quality golf club has a course that winds through the olive groves next to the marina. Cruises are popular, with many agencies organizing sea trips. Club Sdanek can provide information about diving and also offers lessons.

For children, there is **Hannibal Park**, which has a merry-go-round and other rides. Next to this, **Acqua Palace** has water chutes, slides and pools.

At the heart of Port el-Kantaoui lies its colourful marina. The yacht basin is full of boats swaying gently on their moorings. A replica of a pirate ship takes visitors on sailing trips. The marina is fringed by restaurants, cafés and shops selling souvenirs. Street vendors sell fruit juice and posies of fresh jasmine.

Yachts moored in Port el-Kantaoui's busy marina

JASMINE

The white jasmine plant was probably brought to Tunisia from Arabia, Persia or India. The strong fragrance of its delicate flowers is believed to lift the spirits and act as an aphrodisiac. Tunisians can often be seen carrying small posies of jasmine when out strolling or when sitting down to dinner. Posies are some-times given as welcoming or parting gifts. Men place them behind their ears or carry them in their hands. Women frequently wear garlands of threaded flowers made into fragrant white necklaces. Small bottles of jasmine oil are readily available.

Street vendor selling posies of white jasmine

Beaches of the Sahel

The SAHEL'S BEACHES ARE among the most visited in Tunisia; many of the region's hotels can be found close by. Yasmine Hammamet, a new tourist area, opened in Hammamet in 2001, and includes Tunisia's largest marina. The resort town of Port el-Kantaoui has a long stretch of pristine sand. The once-deserted beaches on the Kerkennah Islands are gradually becoming popular with visitors.

Hergla ①
Visitors to Hergla's beach are mainly Tunisian. The village is perched on a cliff and is quiet and picturesque.

Port el-Kantaoui ②
Here, the stretches of beach are mostly owned by the hotels, though parts are open to the public. The facilities include hire of diving equipment and water bikes.

Hammam Sousse ③
The beaches of this popular tourist zone, northwest of Sousse, offer fine sand and good facilities for windsurfing and paragliding.

Sebkhet Halk el-Menzel

Sousse ④
Sousse's main beach is wide and long and runs next to the town's main promenade. The white sandy beach close to the main high-rise hotels can get very busy, though there are some quieter parts further out of town.

0 km 3
0 miles 3

Skanès ⑤
The beaches of this tourist zone have fine sand and are within easy reach of the hotels.

Monastir ⑥
Curving round a bay, Monastir's main beach provides a good view of the ribat and the Great Mosque. The hotel beaches are west of town.

Sousse ❸

THE CAPITAL OF THE SAHEL and the third largest town in Tunisia, Sousse was founded by the Phoenicians in the 9th century BC and was, for a time, Hannibal's naval base. Throughout the Punic wars it was one of the Phoenicians' most important towns, along with Carthage and Utica. Modern-day Sousse is a popular resort town with a sandy beach, an historic walled medina and, occupying part of the kasbah, an excellent museum with mosaics from the 2nd and 3rd centuries AD.

Exploring Sousse

The medina is entered from Place Farhat Hached or from Place des Martyrs. The medina includes the 9th-century Great Mosque and the ribat (fortified monastery). Nearby is the Turkish-built Zaouia Zakkak. One of the more picturesque fragments of the medina starts uphill, near Bab el-Gharbi. Down towards El-Caid souk are antique stores, workshops and cafés. Not far from here is the Sofra cistern complex. Narrow streets lead down towards the main market. Near Bab el-Gharbi is the kasbah and museum.

Interior of the Great Mosque, viewed from the courtyard arcades

🏛 Place Farhat Hached

This colourful square is the centre of Sousse and the entrance to the medina. This is where the town's main streets originate (even the railway cuts through it). It is a popular meeting place for the young people of Sousse and is also busy with street vendors. To the north of the square, beyond the railway line, is Avenue Bourguiba, a modern thoroughfare with shops, banks and department stores. This runs down to the coast and to the seashore boulevard – Avenue Hedi Cheker. Entering the square from Avenue Bourguiba there is a several-storey-high **Artisanat** on the right. It is a good idea to step in here for a while before entering the medina, to get some idea of the prices. To the southeast of the square is Sousse's harbour.

🏛 Place des Martyrs

Adjoining Place Farhat Hached is Place des Martyrs. The 16th-century Sea Gate – Bab el-Bahr – provided entry to the inner harbour. The 18th-century fort that once stood on this site was destroyed during a World War II bombing raid.

Monument to the 1943 bombardment, on Place des Martyrs

◪ Great Mosque

Rue el-Aghlaba. ◯ 8am–1pm Sat–Thu (to courtyard). 🖼

The Great Mosque stands at the edge of the medina and not – as is more common – at its centre. Together with the ribat and the medina walls it formed part of the town's defensive system. This is reflected in its architectural design that resembles a fortress rather than a mosque. Built in 851, at the peak of the Aghlabids' golden age, it was modelled on Kairouan's mosque. Its vast courtyard (the only part open to visitors) is surrounded by columns; carved above them are words from the Koran, the date of completion and the names of the mosque's builders. From one corner of the building high stairs lead to an octagonal sundial. The minaret that rises above the mosque was built two centuries later. Before that time, the faithful were called to prayer from the tower of the neighbouring ribat. The prayer hall's arched vault rests on massive supports. Its walls are built of stones laid out in an intricate pattern providing an austere decoration for the interior.

♟ Ribat

Rue de Smyrne. ◯ Apr–mid-Sep: 8am–7pm daily; mid-Sep–Mar: 8:30am–5:30pm daily. 🖼

Sousse's ribat, dating from the Aghlabid period, is one of the most famous and best-preserved monastic fortresses in Tunisia. Work on its construction began probably in AD 787 and was completed in AD 821. It was then that the Nador – the 27-m (89-ft) high watchtower – was added at the southwest corner. The ribat was built at a time when Christians invading from Italy were a constant threat and the tower would have been used as a lookout point as well as a beacon for passing on messages. Today it offers a view over the entire town.

The garrison consisted of mercenaries paid by the state. A ribat offered shelter to travellers and merchants and,

The unassuming main entrance to the ribat

at times of extreme danger, to the local population as well. The square-shaped structure is surrounded by walls over 13 m (43 ft) high. Vast bastions were placed at the corners and halfway along each wall. The inner yard is skirted by rows of portico-shaded cells. On the ground floor these surround the yard on all four sides; on the first floor – on three sides only; the fourth side is taken up by a large oratory that confirms the religious character of the building. During times of peace, the ribat was used as a place of study. Following the

building of the kasbah in the southwest part of the medina, the ribat lost some of its military importance and began to fall into ruin. It was restored in 1722 and turned into a Koranic school. Some additional restoration work was carried out in the 1950s.

C Zaouia Zakkak
Rue Tazerka. ●

A little way west of the ribat stands an octagonal minaret whose style is reminiscent of Renaissance architecture. It belongs to the Zaouia Zakkak complex, which was built during the Ottoman era. The complex includes a mosque, a medersa (school) and a mausoleum and owes its name to the holy man who lived and worked here in the 10th century. On his death he was buried in his own house, which was later turned into a medersa. The porticoed entrance leads to the courtyard that is flanked on three sides by students' cells. The south end of the *zaouia*

Octagonal minaret of Zaouia Zakkak

VISITORS' CHECKLIST

Road map D3. 🚶 492,000.
🚌 🚉 ✈ Skanès/Monastir.
ℹ ONTT: Avenue Habib
Bourguiba 1, (73) 225 157.
🎭 Sidi el-Kantaoui Festival (Jul);
International Sousse Festival
(Jul–Aug); Folklore Festival (Aug).

(tomb) was destroyed in 1943 during a bombing raid. The dome-covered mausoleum, built in the 18th century, stands in the northeast corner of the complex.

🕌 Rue el-Aghlaba

Rue el-Aghlaba – one of the medina's most picturesque streets – starts immediately beyond the ribat and runs westwards, past the Great Mosque, going deep into the medina. One of its offshoots is Rue d'Angleterre that runs southwards to the covered markets. The many stalls and shops found here form the commercial heart of Sousse and are a riot of colour and activity.

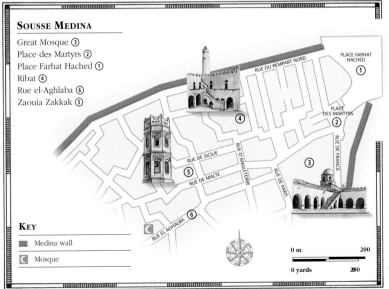

SOUSSE MEDINA

Great Mosque ③
Place des Martyrs ②
Place Farhat Hached ①
Ribat ④
Rue el-Aghlaba ⑥
Zaouia Zakkak ⑤

RUE DU REMPART NORD

PLACE FARHAT HACHED ①

PLACE DES MARTYRS ②

RUE DE SICILIE
RUE D'ANGLETERRE
RUE DE MALTE
RUE DE PARIS
RUE DE FRANCE
RUE EL AGHLABA

KEY

▪ Medina wall

C Mosque

0 m 200
0 yards 200

100 m

Walls of the medina, dating from the 9th century

♣ Medina Walls

The medina's western and southern extremes are well preserved and exceptionally picturesque. It is worth taking a stroll around here to get a taste of the everyday life of the medina's inhabitants.

In the 7th century Oqba ibn Nafi's army destroyed the Roman town of Hadrumetum. In its place, the Arabs built Soussa and, some 200 years later, during the Aghlabid period Soussa (which was renamed Sousse) became a major port for the Aghlabid capital – Kairouan.

The 9th-century walls that surround the medina date from this time. They were built to replace the earlier Byzantine walls. To this day they encircle the town with a ring of stone that is broken only near Place des Martyrs, which was bombed during World War II. At one time there were eight gates. Only four now remain standing – Bab el-Gharbi, Bab el-Finga, Bab el-Jerid and Bab el-Khabli. The only section of wall open to the public is within the kasbah's museum (*see below*).

♣ Kasbah

Boulevard Maréchal Tito.
[C] *(73) 219 011.* ◯ *Apr–mid-Sep: 8am–noon & 3–7pm Tue–Sun; mid-Sep–Mar: 9am–noon & 2–6pm Tue–Sun.* 🗟
A visit to the kasbah, which is located just outside the medina's walls to the south, should also include a tour of the **Archaeology Museum**.

Built originally in 1100 it was rebuilt and reinforced around 1600. It houses an excellent museum that

displays mosaics dating from the Roman and Byzantine periods, and has a variety of objects found in the vicinity of the Great Mosque and the harbour. Set under the arcades of its small courtyard are some fine mosaics displaying geometric patterns, animal and mythological motifs and Christian symbols that were found in the city's Christian catacombs (*see opposite*).

Roman mosaic from the kasbah's museum

Room No. 3 houses the most precious mosaics including a 3rd-century AD depiction of Bacchus in Triumph being drawn along in a chariot by lions and tigers. At the north end of the courtyard there are some Christian epitaphs taken from the catacombs and also the sarcophagus of a woman named Theodora.

The large, garden-like courtyard of the kasbah, where there is some pleasant

shade during summer, contains an exhibition of sculptures, sarcophagi, columns and capitals. The roof terrace provides a good view of the medina.

🏛 Khalaout el-Koubba

Rue Zarrouk. ◯ *9am–1pm & 3–5:30pm Mon–Thu, 10am–2pm Sat–Sun.* 🗟
Not far from the covered souks and stalls on Rue d'Angleterre is the Khalaout el-Koubba. This building, crowned with a distinctive *koubba* (dome), dates from the 11th or 12th century. Its original purpose remains a mystery. It was probably some kind of tomb for a major spiritual leader or a meeting place. The most distinctive feature of the Koubba is its dome, which is decorated with a zigzag frieze. This type of decoration can also be found on some of the domes in Fès and Marrakech (Morocco), dating from the Almoravid period. The central court was added at some later date, probably in the 17th or the 18th century.

The building was used as a *fondouk* (inn) in the 14th century and later became a café. It was restored in 1980 and today houses the **Museum of Popular Arts and Traditions**, which is devoted to the history of the medina with life-size tableaux illustrating marriage customs and everyday activities.

Zig-zag patterned dome of Khalaout el-Koubba

🏛 Dar Essid

Rue du Rempart-Nord 65.
📞 *(73) 220 529.* ⏰ *10am–7pm daily (summer); 10am–6pm daily (winter).* 📷

This fascinating museum is situated in a beautiful home that adjoins the walls of Sousse's medina. A small, private museum, its collections include costumes, jewellery and everyday items. The decor has been recreated in the style of a well-to-do Arab household from the 19th century and includes family rooms surrounding a tiled courtyard. It is a charming place and succeeds admirably in conjuring up the atmosphere of an affluent Arab home. The house itself dates from AD 928 and is one of the medina's oldest homes.

The walled-off area between Bab el-Finga and Dar Essid is Sousse's red-light district.

Catacombs – the final resting place for 15,000 Christians

Catacombs

About 2 km/1 mile from the town centre, close to Rue Hamed el-Ghazali. The easiest way to get to the catacombs is from the bus station or the louage stand in Avenue des Catacombes. ⏰ *Apr–mid-Sep: 9am–7pm Tue–Sun; mid-Sep–Mar: 9am–5pm Tue–Sun.*

In 1888 a vast complex of Christian catacombs was discovered on the outskirts of Sousse in the west part of the town. This labyrinth of chambers and corridors was carved out of the soft rock between the 3rd and 4th century AD. Its wall niches contain the remains of 15,000 Christians. The galleries stretch over 5 km (3 miles), though only a small fraction is open to the public. The **Catacombs of the Good Shepherd** date from the late 3rd century. They are 1.6 km (1 mile) long and include 6,000 graves; the **Hermes Catacombs** date from the 3rd century and contain 2,200 graves.

The section of catacombs open to the public consists of a 100-m (328-ft) long segment of the Catacombs of the Good Shepherd. Most of the graves are bricked up, but a few have glass windows displaying the human remains.

ENVIRONS: The areas around Sousse are planted with olive groves that have been cultivated here since Punic times. Although the Romans used oil mainly for industrial purposes, it was – along with wheat – Tunisia's main agricultural product. Now over 50 varieties of olive trees are grown here.

Some 43 km (27 miles) northwest of Sousse is **Enfida**, which is worth visiting, particularly during its Sunday market. The town also has a Christian church that has been turned into a museum, where you can see early Christian mosaics from

Ken village – a handicraft centre

the nearby site of Upenna. In July, Hammam Sousse hosts the Sidi el-Kantaoui Festival.

The village of **Ken**, 20 km (12 miles) north of Sousse, has an exhibition centre that produces and sells a variety of handicraft items including blown glass, textiles and furniture. The village itself is an example of an eclectic architecture that embraces a variety of traditional Tunisian building styles and methods.

Park Friguia, situated in Bou Ficha, 58 km (36 miles) from Sousse, is a large recreation area that combines a zoo with an amusement park. Run in collaboration with the Tunisian forestry commission, the zoo is home to some 25 species of African animals including giraffes and elephants. The zoo also has a restaurant and puts on folk shows at peak times.

TUNISIAN DOLLS

This warrior-doll is a typical Tunisian souvenir. The dolls are made by hand and come in a variety of colours and sizes but always include the same basic elements. The head is carved from wood and sports bushy whiskers, while its trunk is fashioned from wood and wire. The warrior is dressed in wide trousers with a colourful tunic over the top. In his hand he holds a metal sword. The origin of the doll is not clear, though its clothes would suggest that it comes from Turkey. Wooden puppets such as these are hung on metal wires and can be seen in almost all Tunisian markets.

Tunisian doll dressed in a colourful costume

Ribat

THE HOLY WAR AGAINST CHRISTIANS, the constant skirmishes with the Berbers and the plans to carry out military forays to Europe prompted the building of ribats from the 8th century onwards. Monastir's defensive fortress was originally known as the Ribat de Harthama and combined religious and military functions by assembling soldiers and mystics under the same roof. It is one of the oldest and best preserved in Tunisia and was used for scenes in Zeffirelli's *Life of Christ* and *Monty Python's Life of Brian.*

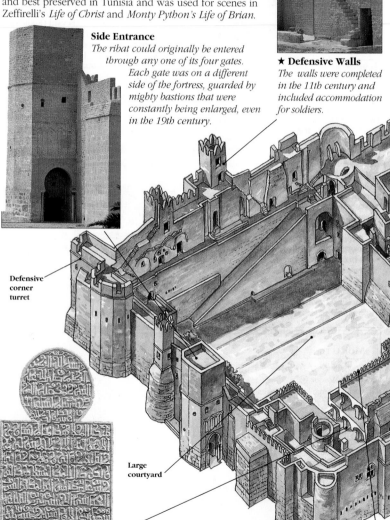

Side Entrance
The ribat could originally be entered through any one of its four gates. Each gate was on a different side of the fortress, guarded by mighty bastions that were constantly being enlarged, even in the 19th century.

★ Defensive Walls
The walls were completed in the 11th century and included accommodation for soldiers.

Defensive corner turret

Large courtyard

Islamic Art Centre
A museum devoted to Islamic art is in the ribat's prayer room and includes Arab coins, fabrics and pottery.

Battlements
Some sections of the walls are crenellated. The battlements were usually simple, but provided protection for archers shooting from the walls.

Parasols on a Monastir beach

Decorative Details
As in many ribats,
there is little in the way
of decoration. Most
heavily decorated are
the window surrounds
and column capitals;
much of this has worn
away over the years.

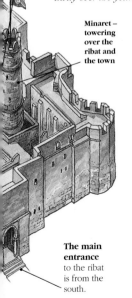

Minaret –
towering
over the
ribat and
the town

The main
entrance
to the ribat
is from the
south.

STAR SIGHT

★ **Defensive Walls**

Further Afield
The area around Monastir
abounds in olive trees, which
have been cultivated here
since Roman times. Of more
interest to the visitor,
Monastir has several long,
sandy beaches and small
coves. The most popular of
them are around Skanès.

⚓ Port
Route de la Falaise.
A little way to the southeast
of Monastir, the old fishing
harbour is no longer very
important to the economy of
the town, which derives its
main revenue from tourism,
olive oil production and sea
salt excavation. There is,
however, an attractive marina
not far from the ribat. Fringed
by restaurants and cafés, it
provides a pleasant place to
escape from the summer heat.

🏖 Beaches
The town's main tourist
complex is around Skanès.
This tourist zone provides

9,000 hotel beds. The beach
is wide and well kept. As
well as bathing, equipment
can be hired on the beach
for water sports such as
paragliding. A frequent train
service and taxis provide easy
access to town. There are
numerous beach bars. Beach
vendors offer light snacks and
ensure that no-one goes
hungry. The beaches around
Khniss are quieter.

ENVIRONS: It is worth
stopping for a while in
Lamta, some 15 km (9 miles)
southeast of Monastir – which
was once the Roman colony
of Leptis Minor, the smaller
sibling of Leptis Magna,
which can be found in Libya.
Following the downfall of
Carthage, this was one of the
six free towns. Even then, the
region was famous for its
olive groves. Another local
speciality was the fish sauce
called *garum*, which was
much valued throughout the
Roman world.

MARABOUTS

Marabouts were mostly members of Sufi brotherhoods, or
soldiers. Revered as mystics and Islamic holy men or
saints, many were believed to have divine powers. To this
day many Tunisians believe that a
marabout has received a special gift
from God, allowing him to plead
successfully for Allah's mercy
(*baraka*) on their behalf.
Many muslims make
pilgrimages to a marabout's
tomb (also known as a
marabout). One of the most
revered of Tunisia's
marabouts is Sidi Mehrez
– the patron of Tunis.

A plain marabout in Blidet

Mahdia ●

T HE FIRST FATIMID CALIPH, Obeid Allah, known as El-Mahdi (the Saviour of the World), waited until the astrologers identified the most propitious moment before founding this coastal town. Work started in AD 916 and the town was given the name of Mahdia, in honour of the charismatic caliph. Today Mahdia is a major port. It is one of Tunisia's most attractive towns and is famous for its house decorations. The busy quayside is lined with palms and has an engaging maritime atmosphere.

Rue Obeid Allah el-Mahdi – the main shopping street in Mahdia

Exploring Mahdia

Mahdia has retained much of its medieval charm. Its medina is entered by a vast gate, Skifa el-Kahla. Standing close to Place du Caire is the Mustapha Hamza Mosque and the Great Mosque. Further along the narrow boulevard are the Municipal Museum, the ruins of the former docks, the armoury, the emir's palace and the Great Tower – Borj el-Kebir, which provides a splendid view of the town and the bay beyond *(see p162)*.

⚐ Rue Obeid Allah el-Mahdi

This is one of Mahdia's main streets and leads through the heart of the medina. The bright house walls stand in contrast with the colourful shops selling ceramics, carpets and leather goods. Along its side streets are workshops where weavers work on upright looms making silk fabrics destined for wedding dresses. Silk weaving is a big business in Mahdia and was brought here by Jewish immigrants from Libya in the 19th century. The loom workers are highly skilled and are usually happy to talk to visitors about their work.

🏛 Municipal Museum

Rue Obeid Allah el-Mahdi.
◯ *Apr–mid-Sep: 9am–1pm & 3–7pm Tue–Sun; mid-Sep–Mar: 9am–4pm Tue–Sun.*
This modern archaeological museum houses some fine Punic, Roman and Christian statues and ceramics, mosaics from El-Jem *(see p163)* as well as a number of oil lamps and a delightful collection of perfumes in intricate bottles made of coloured glass, which are arranged on brightly painted, wooden shelves. A section is devoted to Islamic art and includes mosaics, calligraphy *(see p167)* and some examples of local costumes including exhibits relating to their manufacture. Mahdia is famous for its house decorations and the museum also has some good examples of the local passion for interior decoration.

◖ Mustapha Hamza Mosque

Rue Obeid Allah el-Mahdi. ◗
This mosque, with its lovely façade, was built in the 18th century during the town's Ottoman period. Its octagonal minaret towers over the entire district and is typical of Turkish design.

Minaret of the Mustapha Hamza Mosque

⚐ Skifa el-Kahla

Rue Obeid Allah el-Mahdi.
The huge gate that leads to the town was built in the 10th century by Obeid Allah. Its "dark passage" (which gave the gate its name) was once the only entrance to the city and led through a wall that was 10 m (33 ft) thick in places. At the time, Mahdia was the private property of its ruler. All who did not belong to the court were forced to live outside the walls and huge iron grilles were lowered to deny anyone else access to the city. The original gate was destroyed by the Spanish in 1554 but rebuilt the same year. The former city entrance today contains a covered market selling perfume and items of jewellery.

⚐ Place du Caire

This small square at the centre of the medina functions almost as a salon. The locals, especially the old

Relaxing in the shade of the trees in Place du Caire

◁ **Habib Bourguiba Mausoleum in Monastir**

men, gather here to discuss the latest events, to meet with friends, read a newspaper or simply ponder over a glass of tea. It is pleasant to stop here for a while and survey the proceedings from one of the cafés overlooking the Mustapha Hamza mosque.

Detail, façade of the Slimen Hamza Mosque

More attention is paid to the light and the mosque contains stained-glass windows and exquisite lamps. A lamp in the mosque is the symbol of God's presence and appears on the prayer mats.

◖ Slimen Hamza Mosque
Place Kadhi en-Noamine. ◖

This building, which stands facing the Great Mosque, is in an Ottoman-style design. Mosques of this kind generally have a rectangular structure that is crowned with a dome and include a slim minaret, which is usually octagonal in shape. Tunisian minarets dating from the Ottoman period have a much greater diameter than their Turkish counterparts, however. The prayer hall is large and much brighter than those found in Kairouan-type mosques. There is very little ornamentation and the only furnishings and decorations consist of carpets and calligraphic inscriptions.

◖ Great Mosque
Rue de Borj. ◖ to non-Muslims.

The Great Mosque was founded by Obeid Allah in AD 921. Destroyed when Charles V and his troops entered the town, little of the original building remains and what is seen today is a reconstruction from the 1960s and 1970s that was designed as a replica of the original Fatimid mosque. The most obvious Fatimid element is the monumental entrance gate, which was used exclusively by the caliph's family. In the prayer hall this segregation is also apparent, with a central aisle that was reserved for the ruler

VISITORS' CHECKLIST
Road map D3. 27,000. ONTT: Rue el-Moez, (73) 680 663. Fête de la Mer (Jul), International Festival of Symphonic Music, also at El-Jem (Jul–Aug). Fri.

and his privileged entourage. The only parts of the original structure that can be seen now are the remains of the mihrab (niche indicating the direction of Mecca) and the monumental portal leading to the courtyard.

Arcaded walkway of the Great Mosque

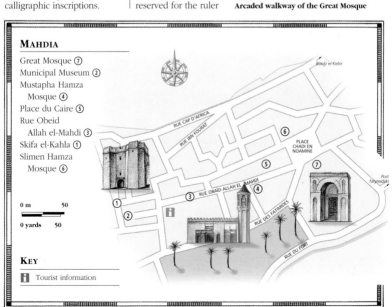

MAHDIA

Great Mosque ⑦
Municipal Museum ②
Mustapha Hamza Mosque ④
Place du Caire ⑤
Rue Obeid Allah el-Mahdi ③
Skifa el-Kahla ①
Slimen Hamza Mosque ⑥

0 m   50
0 yards 50

KEY
ℹ Tourist information

Further Afield
Standing beyond the walls of
the medina is an old Fatimid
port, a Muslim cemetery
established in the 16th
century, scenically located on
top of a hill, and the Punic
necropolis – the second
largest after Carthage. Among
the objects discovered here is
a clay statuette of a naked
goddess, wearing a crown. A
short way southwest, in
Ksour Essaf, is the *zaouia*
(tomb) of Sidi Ali Mahjub.

Muslim necropolis near a lighthouse

♣ **Borj el-Kebir**
Rue de Borj. ☐ *Apr–mid-Sep:
9am–noon & 2–6pm Tue–Sun;
mid-Sep–Mar: 9:30am–4:30pm
Tue–Sun.* 📷
This 16th-century Turkish fort
stands on the site of Obeid
Allah's palace. A narrow
corridor leads to the courtyard
flanked by rows of small cells
and a mosque. The fortress
was rebuilt several times. Until
the 16th century it had a
rectangular ground plan; the
mighty bastions were added
in the 18th century. The
southwestern bastion includes
the entrance, from which a
gently curving corridor leads
to a gate adorned with a stone
rosette. The gate opens to
a barrel-vault passage
resembling Skifa el-Kahla,
which leads to the reception
hall that was restored during
the colonial days. Stairs from
the small courtyard lead to the
first floor, where the fort's
commander had his quarters.

The castle's terrace provides
a wonderful view of the
surrounding area. In the 16th
century Mahdia was a pirate
stronghold and became
closely linked with the
intrigues of the superpowers
of the day such as Spain and
Turkey. The most famous
corsair residing in Mahdia
was Dragut.

♫ **Fatimid Port**
The port's construction is
generally attributed to caliph
Obeid Allah. It was most
probably built on the site of
the old Punic port. The
Fatimids had a very strong
fleet, which they inherited
from the Aghlabids. Obeid
Allah wanted Mahdia to be
both a fortress and a strong
naval base. The 15-m (49-ft)
long canal that leads to the
port was guarded by two
towers. Fragments of their
foundations can be seen

today. The basin was a
rectangle and could
accommodate 30 ships.
During the times of Obeid
Allah the port had its own
defensive walls. Now only
a small section of them
remains, on the south side.

**Remains of 10th-century
Fatimid fortifications**

ENVIRONS: The small town of
Ksour Essaf, 11 km (7 miles)
south of Mahdia, is famous
for its textiles and contains
the 18th-century *zaouia*
(tomb) of Sidi Ali Mahjub.
The dome of the sanctuary is
decorated with grooved
terracotta ornaments. Inside
the mosque is an unusual
mihrab, placed on wheels.
   In **Salakta**, 14 km (9 miles)
from Mahdia and a short taxi
ride from Ksour Essaf, are the
ruins of the Roman port and
fishing village of Sullectum.
The port was probably used
for shipping lions that were
destined for the gladiatorial
arena at El-Jem. The nearby
beach is a pleasant place to
stroll and has some further
Roman remains including a
bath and some villa walls.

Bastion of Mahdia's main fort – Borj el-Kebir

El-Jem ⑥

THIS FORMER PUNIC TOWN – Thysdrus – declared itself on the side of Rome during the Third Punic War in AD 146. It proved to be a wise move and after the fall of Carthage El-Jem was awarded the status of a free town. In the mid-3rd century it became a Roman colony. It was among the richest towns in Roman Africa. The most magnificent historic relic of El-Jem is its 3rd-century amphitheatre.

VISITORS' CHECKLIST

Road map D3. 🚶 12,000. ☐ ☐
⋔ Amphitheatre. ☐ Apr–mid-Sep: 7am–7pm Tue–Sun; mid-Sep–Mar: 8am–5:30pm Tue–Sun.
🏛 Museum ☐ As above. 🎫 Symphonic (Jul–Aug). 🎫

★ Amphitheatre
Built in 230–238 this is the world's third largest Roman amphitheatre and the best-preserved Roman relic to be found in Africa.

Corridors
The corridors lead to all levels of the auditorium, which measures 427 m (1,401 ft) in diameter.

Elliptical arena, measuring 65 x 39 m (213 x 128 ft)

★Museum
The museum is housed in one of Tunisia's best-preserved Roman villas, on the outskirts of El-Jem.

The highest seats provide a breathtaking view. The games could be watched by over 30,000 spectators.

Mosaics
As well as some gladiatorial scenes, the mosaics displayed in the museum have some more abstract and stylized designs.

STAR SIGHTS

★ Amphitheatre

★ Museum

Sfax ❼

A mosque decoration

Tʜᴇ ᴘᴏʀᴛ ᴏꜰ sғᴀx is Tunisia's second largest city and its major commercial centre. Once a Roman settlement, its prosperity was founded on its shipping fleet and the trade in olive oil. Sfax is known for its unhurried atmosphere and has a compact medina with wonderful covered souks and two excellent museums. A regular ferry route runs from the port to the Kerkennah Islands *(see p172)*.

Bab Diwan standing at the end of Avenue Hedi Chaker

Exploring Sfax

The city stretches between the medina walls and the harbour. Rebuilt in the late 1940s, modern Sfax resembles any large European city, with wide avenues, squares and public parks. Hedi Chaker Avenue runs from Hedi Chaker Square to Bab Diwan – one of two gates leading to the old town. Beyond it lies the medina. It is well worth taking a stroll along Rue Mongi Slim, stopping for a while at the colourful spice market in Rue des Aghlabites.

Rue de la Grande Mosquée – full of shops and always busy

♣ Bab Diwan

Bab Diwan is the medina's main entrance and is located on the south side. It was built in the early 14th century, but was extensively remodelled in the 17th and 18th centuries. It was finally restored in the 20th century.

Along with Bab Jebli in the north, Bab Diwan was once one of only two entrances to the city. Its ironclad doors would have been closed tightly at night to protect Sfax from intruders.

Bab Diwan was designed to complement the 9th-century walls built by the Aghlabids. These walls originally marked the boundaries of the city, although modern Sfax has long since outgrown these limits. Beyond the walls were olive groves, which flourished thanks to earlier Roman irrigation systems. One of the gate's towers now houses a charming Moorish-style café.

▦ Rue de la Grande Mosquée

One of the main streets of the medina, it starts at the Grand Mosque and runs south in a straight line towards the medina walls, which are parallel to Rue Mongi Slim.

🇨 Great Mosque

🚫 *to non-Muslims.*

Begun in AD 849 by the Aghlabids, the Great Mosque was modelled on its famous contemporary in Kairouan. It stands at the heart of the medina, at the junction of its two main roads. The mosque has been modified several times and was rebuilt extensively in 988 and 1035. In the 12th century the courtyard was reduced by half, allowing for the enlargement of the prayer hall, which still maintains an L-shaped layout. By the 18th century the mosque was in its present form.

The minaret, rising at the north end of the courtyard, is a replica of the minaret adorning Kairouan's Great Mosque. It is three storeys high and is richly decorated with Kufic script and floral motifs. The mosque is closed to non-Muslims, its eastern wall being the only section that is visible. The best view of the minaret can be had from Rue des Aghlabites, which runs along the north side of the mosque.

Men relaxing inside the Great Mosque

⛫ Dar Jellouli Museum

See pp168–9.

▦ Rue Borj Ennar

This narrow street follows the southern section of the walls, from Rue de la Grande Mosquée to the fortress of Borj Ennar. This is a typical medina street, lined with workshops, small shops and rows of unassuming doors

Borj Ennar, built into a section of the city wall

district of Sfax. Borj Ennar now houses the Association de Sauvegarde de la Médina, a group responsible for preserving the medina, where a detailed street map of the old town and also more about the medina's history can be obtained.

VISITORS' CHECKLIST

Road map D4. 🏠 *340,000*.
🚌 🚉 ℹ️ *ONTT: Avenue Mohammed Hedi Khefacha, (74) 497 041.* 🎫 *(Jul–Aug).* 🛍️ *Fri.*

leading to private homes. It also contains a number of small mosques such as Amar Kamoun mosque, between Nos. 50 and 52, which was built in the 14th century and substantially modified four centuries later.

♨ Borj Ennar

Rue Borj Ennar. ⏰ *8:30am–1pm & 3–6pm daily.* ● *Fri.*

Borj Ennar – the "Tower of Fire" – owes its name to the beacons that used to be lit on its tower as signals. Located at the southeast corner of the medina walls, this was one of the main defensive towers of old Sfax, and was built at the same time as the medina walls. From the top, there is a splendid view over the entire medina and the French

Further Afield

Other places worth visiting include Sidi Abu el-Hasan's mausoleum, located a short distance to the west of the

A small mosque in a row of houses in Rue Borj Ennar

mosque; and the blacksmiths' souk, situated to the north. In the 10th century this was a *fondouk* (inn) and featured in Anthony Minghella's 1996 film *The English Patient*. Beyond the walls, stretching out to the north, is the new town, which suffered heavy damage during World War II. Hedi Chaker and Avenue Habib Bourguiba are streets with beautiful 19th-century houses. A little further on, to the southwest, is Sfax's port and a thriving daily fish market.

🏛 Place de la République

Place de la République is at the junction of Avenue Habib Bourguiba and Avenue Hedi Chaker and dates back to the French Protectorate, when the administration centre was built outside the medina walls. Much of this area was destroyed during wartime bombing raids, although several colonial buildings have survived. The square contains a monument to Habib Bourguiba.

SFAX MEDINA

Bab Diwan and
  the medina walls ①
Borj Ennar ⑥
Dar Jellouli Museum ④
Rue Borj Ennar ⑤
Rue de la Grande
  Mosquée ②
Great Mosque ③

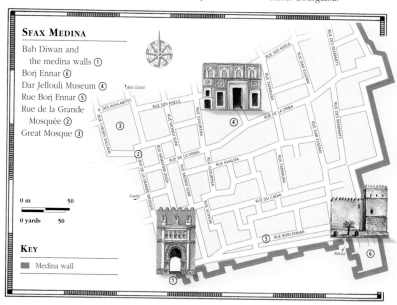

0 m   50

0 yards   50

KEY

▨ Medina wall

Kasbah

○ *9:30am–4:30pm Tue–Sun.* 📷

Sfax's kasbah can be found in the medina's southern quarter. Part of the building is 12th century but it was gradually extended until, by the 17th century, it had reached the size of a large fortress. Initially it served as a watchtower and later as the residence of the Hafsid governor. After that, it became the headquarters of Sfax's military commander.

Today, the kasbah houses the **Museum of Traditional Architecture** and contains exhibits on religious, private and public Tunisian building. A number of the exhibits are outdoors. These include a model illustrating the design of the medina walls and the construction methods used by their builders. Best of all, a trip to the kasbah provides an opportunity to walk along the battlements.

Shady entrance to Sfax's historic kasbah

The Souks

Strolling through the shady streets and alleyways it is not hard to see that Sfax's medina is one of the loveliest and best preserved in the whole of Tunisia. Indeed, much of Sfax's market district was used as a stand-in for Cairo in the film *The English Patient*.

The narrow alleys can be crowded but become quieter during siesta hours. The old town is divided into markets (souks) – specializing in perfumes, spices, textiles, bags, gold, carpets and food.

Souk ar-Rabi, situated in the northern part of the medina, specializes in the production of *chechia* hats, while the former Rue el-Bey is now the blacksmiths' souk and rings to the sound of hammering.

When shopping for a carpet, head for Souk des Etoffes, which was also used as a setting in *The English Patient*. The narrow streets surrounding Rue des Aghlabites are full of stalls and shops selling a variety of spices, herbs, gum arabic and blue talismans that protect the wearer against the "evil eye". Squeezing through a narrow medina entrance at the end of Rue Mongi Slim, visitors emerge into a modern, but very pleasant, covered market where fruit, vegetables and spices are on sale. At the back is a butcher's hall.

In Rue de la Driba, not far from Dar Jellouli Museum, there is Hammam Sultan, which is Sfax's oldest bathhouse. It was restored in the 18th century and is still open to the public.

Avenue Hedi Chaker

Hedi Chaker is one of Sfax's smartest streets. It runs from the square in front of the town hall to Bab Diwan – the main gate leading to the medina. Along it there are travel agents, pharmacies, restaurants, music shops, banks and a theatre.

Vegetable souk at the edge of the medina

Two-colour façade of the modern town hall

Town Hall

Place de la République. 📞 *(74) 229 744.* **Archaeological Museum** ○ *Sep–Jun: 8:30am–1pm & 3–6pm; Jul–Aug: 8am–3pm.* ● *Sun.*

The town hall was erected during the French Protectorate in the early 20th century. Built in a Moorish style it features a tall, minaret-like clock tower at the corner. A dome covers the main hall.

The ground floor of the building now houses a small **Archaeological Museum**, with exhibits ranging from prehistoric to Roman and Arab times. These include flint items, pottery, glass, tomb steles (grave stones) and a variety of objects dating from the Punic, Byzantine and Roman periods.

The most interesting sections include the collections of coins, frescoes, terracotta, Roman drinking vessels, Muslim books, jewellery and mosaics.

Avenue Habib Bourguiba

Situated in the new part of town, this runs from the railway station in the east to the harbour in the west and crosses Avenue Hedi Chaker. It is one of the town's main thoroughfares and is lined with restaurants and hotels as well as nightclubs, banks, travel agents' offices and a post office. Here, modern offices stand next to stylish apartment blocks reminiscent of 19th-century Parisian architecture.

Arabic Calligraphy

For ISLAMIC COUNTRIES calligraphy, or the art of handwriting, has a special importance and copying the Koran is a highly esteemed skill. The Islamic edict prohibiting representation of the human form further promoted calligraphy as a kind of decoration. Arabic calligraphy is based on the Kufic script. This almost geometric style was ideal for carving in stone. Some fine examples of Kufic script can be seen on the eastern wall of Sfax's Great Mosque. By the end of the 12th century, Kufic had been largely replaced in North Africa by a style of calligraphy known as Maghribi, which arrived in Tunisia via Granada (Spain) and Fès (Morocco).

Kufic script *was used as a highly decorative element in Islamic architecture. Its earliest forms were characterized by rigid, angular lines.*

Tomb steles *were often decorated with Kufic script. Its appearance evolved with time, tending towards richer forms. This resulted in a variety of types, including floral kufi, interwoven kufi, and kufi enclosed within floral or geometric borders. From the 12th century onwards the Kufic script was used only for decoration.*

Decorative calligraphic compositions *painted on glass became popular in the 19th century. Their roots can be found in Ottoman art. Highly colourful, they were often used to display Koranic verses.*

Paper *was first used by the Arabs in the 8th century. Blue paper is very rare and surviving examples of early Arab script on blue paper are highly valued by collectors.*

El-bijazi, *though not ornamental, is a popular form of the Arabic script. This private letter was written on parchment using sepia ink.*

The most valuable copies of the Koran *are embellished with gold letters. From the 13th century onwards, literary and scientific works were also decorated.*

Dar Jellouli Museum

OCCUPYING A 17th-century courtyard house in Sfax that once belonged to the wealthy Jellouli family is the Dar Jellouli Regional Museum of Popular Arts and Traditions. The building has a classic layout with an arched entrance and a porticoed courtyard surrounded by rooms. The first floor features a lovely wooden balustrade. From the magnificently decorated ceilings to the walls lined with faience tiles and the doors painted in bright colours, the interiors conjure up a period of opulence and affluent ease.

Colonnades
surround the courtyard at the first floor level.

★ Costumes
Tunisians attached great importance to their clothes, which also marked the social rank of the wearer. A typical woman's outfit consisted of a tunic, a scarf and a veil, complemented with items of jewellery.

The kitchen has been reconstructed with the same degree of precision as the other rooms.

Ceilings
Houses belonging to the wealthy were heavily decorated. Window and door frames were intricately carved; ceilings were decorated in geometric or other patterns.

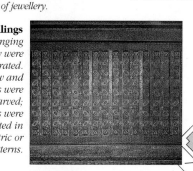

1st floor

Rooms
Rooms within grand houses had a T-shaped floor layout. Wall shelves were used as cabinets and displayed bric-a-brac and lamps. Low sofas were usually arranged facing each other, or placed around the walls of a niche.

GALLERY LAYOUT
Many of the museum's exhibits have been designed to create the impression that the Jellouli family still live here. The ground floor contains furniture, kitchen appliances and vessels. Here visitors can learn how to make harissa, the traditional spicy Tunisian sauce, or study the art of creating aromatic oils used for producing perfumes. The first floor is given over to a collection of traditional costumes (including wedding garments) and jewellery.

STAR EXHIBITS

- ★ **Alcove**
- ★ **Costumes**
- ★ **Jewellery**

★ Jewellery
Women always wore plenty of jewellery. Jewelled headgear was a standard piece of attire for a wedding or other formal occasion.

VISITORS' CHECKLIST

Rue de la Driba. 📞 (74) 221 186.
🕐 9:30am–4:30pm Tue–Sun
(earlier during Ramadan). 📷 📷
The museum is situated in the eastern part of the medina; the way to it from Rue de la Grande Mosquée is marked with arrows.

Glass Paintings
Dar Jellouli houses an interesting collection of glass decoration. This includes quotes from the Koran and decorative calligraphic characters of symbolic significance.

★ Alcove
Dar Jellouli would have had a strictly divided space. The upper floors were used mainly by women. The ground floor rooms (apart from the kitchen) were the male section. Women were not admitted to most gatherings held in the house.

Chest
Richly ornamented chests were used by the family to store valuable fabrics, clothes and thick quilts, which were used as beds.

Windows
Windows were fitted with intricate wooden grilles, which were designed to protect women from the gaze of strangers.

Ground floor

Entrance

KEY

☐ Jewellery
☐ Costumes
☐ Calligraphy
☐ Historic interiors
☐ Non-exhibition rooms

A Traditional Arab Town

IN THE 9TH AND THE 10TH centuries a new type of Arab town emerged, laid out on a grid pattern. The towns built in this style include Kairouan and Mahdia. In order to protect their population from invasion, towns began to develop districts known as medinas in the 11th and 12th centuries that were guarded by gates and surrounded by a high wall. At the medina's centre stood the Great Mosque, with markets and public baths nearby. The urban landscape was enriched by further religious buildings, including Islamic schools and *zaouias* (tombs).

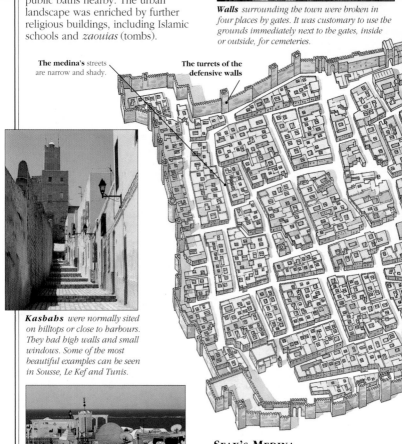

Walls *surrounding the town were broken in four places by gates. It was customary to use the grounds immediately next to the gates, inside or outside, for cemeteries.*

The medina's streets are narrow and shady.

The turrets of the defensive walls

Kasbahs *were normally sited on hilltops or close to harbours. They had high walls and small windows. Some of the most beautiful examples can be seen in Sousse, Le Kef and Tunis.*

The roof *was and still is an integral part of a Tunisian house and a scene of everyday life for its inhabitants with tables and a carpet on the floor. This is where family and friends might meet over coffee.*

SFAX'S MEDINA

This is one of Tunisia's best-preserved old quarters and conforms to Islamic principles of architecture. At its centre is the Great Mosque, which is surrounded by the town's souks. The souks, according to custom, are located in a hierarchy. Incense and candle dealers are closest to the mosque while noisy blacksmiths and vendors serving the caravan trade were located at the medina's edge.

The towers at the four corners of the medina walls were supported by buttresses and crenellated; they were built into the walls that formed part of the fortifications.

Souks, besides being markets, were also scenes of political discussions and plotting. They also included a wide variety of places where people could go for a glass of mint tea and listen to professional storytellers.

Dars were homes of the medina's elite. Externally they did not differ much from the surrounding buildings but the beauty and the riches of their interiors were stunning.

The gates guarding the entrance to towns usually numbered between two and six. During the day markets would be held close by. At night the gates were closed.

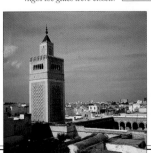

The Great Mosque was and still is the most important and usually the most beautiful of an Arab town's mosques. Communal Friday prayers are the busiest time. In the early days of Islam this was the only mosque that had a minbar (pulpit).

Smaller mosques (some the size of a living room) were often situated on the ground floors of other buildings. They were used for Friday prayers from the 12th century onwards.

Interior of the 12th-century Sidi Driss Mosque

Kerkennah Islands ⑧

Road map E4. 🏛 *15,000.*
🚌 *Av. Mohammed Hedi Khefacha.*
🎭 *Festival of Octopus (Mar); Festival of Mermaid (Jun).*

LOCATED JUST 20 km (12 miles) off the coast of Sfax, the Kerkennah Islands were once a place of exile. Hannibal was sent here, as were Roman outlaws and, much later, Habib Bourguiba. Even today the 180 sq km (70 sq miles) of archipelago, comprising seven islands, has a desolate feel and only two of the islands (Gharbi and Chergui) are inhabited.

Depending on the time of year, up to five car ferries provide daily transport links with the mainland. The journey takes about 75 minutes. The ferries sail to Sidi Youssef on Gharbi. On the northeastern coast lies the islands' capital – El-Attaia. The main attractions include fine white sand, quiet surroundings and excellent conditions for snorkelling. The islands are flat (the highest point is only 13 m/43 ft above sea level) and are therefore ideally suited for cycling. The main resort is Sidi Frej on Chergui, which lies west of Ouled Kacem. From here it is possible to walk along the beach to the Roman ruins at Borj el-Hissar.

Gulf of Gabès ⑨

Road map D4, D5.

STRETCHING SOUTH from Sfax all the way to the Libyan border, the Gulf of Gabès's sandy marshes provide a winter home for half of the entire bird population that migrates to the Mediterranean basin from the north. The winter migrants number around 400,000 and include several varieties of gull and heron as well as tern, plover, oystercatcher and flamingo.

The main town on the shores of the gulf is Gabès. Its foremost historic relic is the 12th-century **Sidi Driss Mosque**. Other attractions include a **Museum of Popular Arts and Traditions**, which is housed in a former medersa, and a trip to the local oasis. For visitors and Tunisians alike, however, Gabès is famous mainly as the centre of henna production, which can be purchased here cheaply.

Underground houses in Matmata, providing shelter from the heat

Matmata ⑩

Road map D5. 🏛 *8,500.* 🏢

THE BERBER village of Matmata lies 650 m (2,133 ft) above sea level and is 40 km (25 miles) south of Gabès. This is the biggest and best known of the troglodyte villages, where the houses have been dug out of the rock to escape the intense daytime heat. This building tradition, which allows the rooms to maintain an even temperature of about 17° C (63° F) throughout the year, goes back hundreds of years. In the 1960s the three biggest cave compounds were turned into hotels. Many houses are still occupied and they inspired George Lucas, the creator of the *Star Wars* films, to spend many days shooting here.

The current centre of the region is New Matmata, which is situated about 15 km (9 miles) from old Matmata.

SPONGES

Tunisia is a good place to purchase real sponges, which have been collected for hundreds of years from the Gulf of Gabès. Sponges are marine creatures and spend their lives

Cutting sponges in a workshop

motionless, attached to rocks or the sea bed; they do not have any nerve cells or muscles, and do not display any reaction to external stimuli. They filter organisms and organic matter by letting a constant stream of water flow through their bodies. Sponges have amazing powers of regeneration. Even a tiny fragment, consisting of just a few cells of the same kind, is able to reproduce a new sponge.

The Hammam

IT WOULD BE HARD to imagine a Tunisian town without a bathhouse. The custom of building them was passed down from antiquity and the need for them was kept up by the Islamic requirement for ritual cleanliness, particularly the ablutions carried out prior to prayers. At one time there

Women at the Baths by **Dominique Ingres**

was at least one bathhouse in every street, and in large towns they could number several hundreds. Visitors would undress in a special room, put on a thin towel and enter the water. Washing was originally carried out using dried leaves of jojoba or soapwort in place of soap.

Hammams were a vital part of life in Roman times and served a social function as well as an hygienic one. Everything needed for a bath could be bought from a vendor who stood by the front door. The attendants cleaned the rooms and scrubbed the slabs, which were heated with hot air.

Hammam rooms serve a variety of purposes. Some are used for bathing; others – filled with steam – for opening the pores and cleansing the skin.

Temperatures *in a Tunisian hammam are not as high as in a sauna. Nevertheless, the steam and the hot-water pool will warm the body in no time at all.*

Massages and haircuts *are among the treatments offered in hammams. Hammams once employed barbers who were also skilled in bloodletting. Payment for a visit is made on leaving.*

Women *used to visit hammams around midday. This provided them with an opportunity to go out (shopping was done by men). Older women would scrutinize the younger ones, searching for wives for their sons.*

JERBA AND THE MEDENINE AREA

THE ISLAND OF JERBA *lies at the southern end of the Gulf of Gabès, 5 km (3 miles) from the mainland. It is known for its wonderful sandy beaches, its warm climate and its picturesque capital of Houmt Souk. Other attractions include fortified smallholdings* (menzels) *and Ibadite mosques. Back on the mainland, the area around Medenine has scenic hills and ancient villages.*

Were it not for the dogged determination of its people, Jerba would remain no more than a scrap of desert. The inhabitants of the island have managed to turn the barren island into one big garden, however, with olive and orange groves and orchards. There are about 4,000 wells on the island, and the tourist zone is supplied with water by an aqueduct. Beautiful whitewashed mosques and traditional *menzels* hidden behind high hedges add to Jerba's charm.

According to myth, Odysseus landed here and nearly lost his crew to the amnesia-inducing food of the resident lotus-eaters. From the 4th century BC, Jerba was ruled from Carthage; later on it passed into the hands of the Romans. The island's prosperity is derived from trading in fish, olive oil and ceramics. The advent of Islam in the 7th century was accompanied by the arrival of the Ibadites, an austere Islamic school of religious thought and practice that was hostile to authority. Their descendants still inhabit western parts of the island. In the 16th century the Malekite School began to gain popularity and now the majority of Jerba's population is Sunni Muslim. There is also a small but significant Jewish contingent, whose ancestors arrived here some 2,000 years ago. Hara Sghira's synagogue is still a place of reverence for Jews.

Medenine was once an important stopping point for caravans and is a good base for forays into the villages scattered among the nearby hills.

Wickerwork products for sale in Houmt Souk

◁ **Houses in Toujane, northwest of Medenine**

Exploring Jerba and the Medenine Area

JERBA OCCUPIES AN AREA OF 538 sq km (208 sq miles) and is virtually flat. It is one of Tunisia's most popular tourist destinations. As the temperature on the island never falls below 15° C (59° F) even in winter, it is a popular resort all year round. Zarzis, on the mainland, is slowly beginning to rival Jerba as a tourist area, but it is more difficult to reach. The Zarzis peninsula is the region's main area for growing citrus fruits and olives. Medenine, 40 km (25 miles) southwest of Jerba, provides a good starting point for a tour of the *ksour* (fortified villages).

Gulf of Gabès

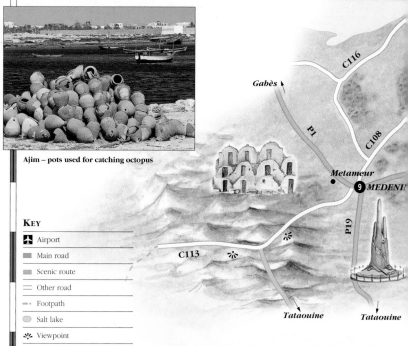

Ajim – pots used for catching octopus

KEY

✈	Airport
▬	Main road
▬	Scenic route
=	Other road
---	Footpath
○	Salt lake
☀	Viewpoint

SIGHTS AT A GLANCE

Aghir ⑥
El-Ghriba ②
El-May ③
Guellala ⑦
Houmt Souk pp178–9 ①
Medenine ⑨
Midoun ⑤
Ras Remel ④
Zarzis ⑧

Tours

Around the Gulf of Bou Grara
pp188–9 ⑩

Crocodiles in an amusement park in Jerba

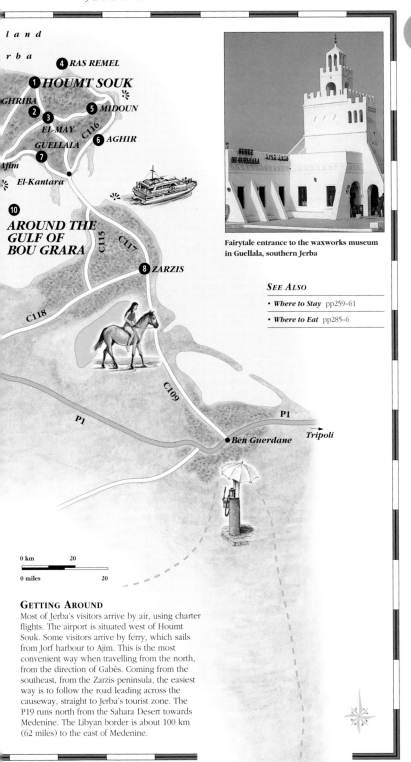

Fairytale entrance to the waxworks museum
in Guellala, southern Jerba

SEE ALSO

• *Where to Stay* pp259–61

• *Where to Eat* pp285–6

GETTING AROUND
Most of Jerba's visitors arrive by air, using charter
flights. The airport is situated west of Houmt
Souk. Some visitors arrive by ferry, which sails
from Jorf harbour to Ajim. This is the most
convenient way when travelling from the north,
from the direction of Gabès. Coming from the
southeast, from the Zarzis peninsula, the easiest
way is to follow the road leading across the
causeway, straight to Jerba's tourist zone. The
P19 runs north from the Sahara Desert towards
Medenine. The Libyan border is about 100 km
(62 miles) to the east of Medenine.

Houmt Souk ❶

JERBA'S CHARMING CAPITAL LIES ON THE island's northern shore. Houmt Souk literally means "market quarter", revealing the long-standing importance of trade to the town, and its narrow streets and ancient souks are full of shops selling jewellery, clothes and souvenirs. Also of interest are the *fondouks* that were built as inns for travelling merchants during the Ottoman period, and the 13th-century fortress, Borj el-Kebir, which provides stunning views along the coast.

Avenue Bourguiba, a thoroughfare and a place of relaxation

Exploring Houmt Souk

To the north of the town lies the harbour, and close to it the Borj el-Kebir. The old town centre is fairly compact. Rue Mohammed Ferjani leads to the shady Place Hedi Chaker. Nearby is the Mosque of the Turks, which serves as a market venue. Rue Moncef Bey, running parallel to Rue Mohammed Ferjani, has an interesting *fondouk* with a large courtyard. On the left hand side of Place Sidi Brahim is the tomb of Sidi Brahim. On the opposite side of the road is the Mosque of the Strangers. A walk along Avenue Abdel Hamid el-Kadhi leads to the Museum of Arts and Popular Traditions, housed in the mausoleum of an Islamic holy man.

🕌 Avenue Habib Bourguiba

This is the main street, cutting across the town from north to south. Its northern section is fringed with houses built in various European styles at the end of the 19th century. The street's southern section is shady.

🕌 Souks

Place Bechir Saoud, Avenue Abdel Hamid el-Kadhi.

The town's old quarter is a maze of narrow alleys and small shops selling leather goods, jewellery and handmade fabrics. The only covered souk is Souk ar-Rab. The old *fondouks* are among the most interesting and picturesque features of Houmt Souk. These former lodging houses combined the functions of stores and inns and were used by travelling merchants. Some of the *fondouks* have now been converted into hotels or youth hostels.

Fish auction at the souk

◖ Mosque of the Strangers

Avenue Abdel Hamid el-Kadhi.
◖ (75) 606 4715. ● to non-Muslims.

In Houmt Souk there are three mosques standing next to one another. Each belongs to a different Islamic school. The multi-domed Mosque of the Strangers is used by the Malekites and is topped with an ornate minaret. The El-Sheikh Mosque is the main mosque of the Ibadites, while the Mosque of the Turks is used by the Hanefites.

🕌 Zaouia of Sidi Brahim

Place Sidi Brahim. ● to non-Muslims.
The entire complex consists of a school, the tomb of Sidi Brahim, a hammam (bath) and a bakery. The school was founded in the 17th century by the Muradids, with the aim of promoting the Malekite school of Islam. The medersa's large courtyard is flanked on three sides by arcades and on the fourth by the prayer hall. Small steps lead from the courtyard to the first-floor gallery.

🕌 Place Hedi Chaker

Rue Mohammed Ferjani leads to this square, which is in the town centre. A lively place, it makes an excellent spot to sit down for a while, order a cup of coffee or tea and take in what is going on.

◖ Mosque of the Turks

Avenue Mohammed Ferjani.
● to non-Muslims.
The Mosque of the Turks, covered with seven white domes, is the town's largest mosque and dates from the 17th century. It is used by the followers of the Hanefite school of Islam, which proclaims rationalism and tolerance towards other religions. This branch of Islam reached its peak of popularity during the Ottoman period but is still popular in Tunisia.

Further Afield

The town's life centres around Avenue Bourguiba and the souks. The Museum of Arts and Popular Traditions can be found a short way to the east of the centre. To the north, a little way along the beach, is

Stone bridge leading to Borj el-Kebir

the Borj el-Kebir. Lying beyond this is the harbour.

⚖ Museum of Arts and Popular Traditions

📞 *(75) 650 450.* ⊘ *Apr–mid-Sep: 8am–noon & 3–7pm; mid-Sep–Mar: 9am–4pm.* ● *Mon.*
Occupying the Zaouia of Sidi Zitouni, this modest museum has a collection of traditional costumes and other items illustrating various aspects of the traditions and customs of Jerba's population.

⊞ Borj el-Kebir

⊘ *Apr–mid-Sep: 8am–noon & 3–7pm; mid-Sep–Mar: 9am-6pm* ● *Mon.* ⊟ *Mon & Thu.*
This fort stands on the seafront. Its foundations date back to

Roman times, but the first fortress on the island was built by the king of Sicily, Roger de Lluria, in 1289. It was reinforced in the 14th century. In its design, the fortress combined defensive elements with religious features and was the most important part of the island's defence system. In the 16th century the famous pirate Dragut reinforced its walls and extended the entire structure.

⊞ The Monument of Skulls

Situated between the harbour and Borj el-Kebir is a small obelisk. The site was formerly occupied by a gruesome 11-m (36-ft) high pyramid of human skulls placed here by Dragut following a massacre of Spanish Christians in 1560.

VISITORS' CHECKLIST

Road map D5. 🏠 *63,000.* ✈
ℹ *(75) 650 016.* ⊟ *Mon., Thu.*

The pyramid stood here until 1848, when the human remains were buried at the local cemetery.

Harbour
Houmt Souk's small harbour looks its best at sunset, when the fishermen return with their day's catch. The local fish include tuna, gilthead and shrimp. In winter, fishermen use clay pots to catch squid and octopus. The harbour is located at the end of Rue du Port, which is an extension of Avenue Bourguiba.

Fishing boats moored at Houmt Souk

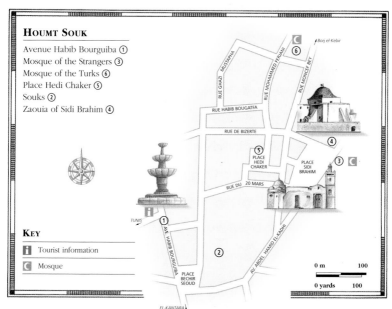

HOUMT SOUK

Avenue Habib Bourguiba ①
Mosque of the Strangers ③
Mosque of the Turks ⑥
Place Hedi Chaker ⑤
Souks ②
Zaouia of Sidi Brahim ④

KEY

ℹ Tourist information

C Mosque

0 m   100

0 yards   100

El-Ghriba ❷

Road map D5. ☐ *Sun–Fri*
9:30am–5pm.

THE COUNTRY'S most famous
synagogue is El-Ghriba,
which is a short way south of
Hara Sghira. This is the oldest
site of a synagogue in the
world and dates back to 586
BC; the present structure was
built in the 20th century. It is
an important place of
pilgrimage for Jews from all
over North Africa, especially
during the Passover Festival.
Although relations between
Muslims and Jews are
generally good on the island,
El-Ghriba was subject to a
terrorist attack in 2002 which
killed 21 people and
damaged part of the interior.

The interior of the El-Ghriba synagogue

The prayer hall's 12 windows
allude to the Zohar – the
principal book of the Kabbala
– and symbolize the 12 tribes
of Israel. The interior is
decorated with rich fabrics,
wood-carvings and ceramic
tiles. It houses many items
donated by pilgrims from all
over the world. In order to
maintain the high status of the
synagogue, the Rabbi of Jerba
decreed it to be the only place
on the island where religious
scrolls are to be kept.
Particularly striking elements
of the interior furnishings
include a beautiful Torah
cabinet and Hanukkah lamps
made of wood and silver.

El-Ghriba ("the miracle") is
said to have been founded on
the spot where a holy stone
fell from heaven. A mysterious
woman arrived at the same
time to oversee construction.

Jerba's Jewish community is
concentrated mainly in two
villages – Hara Sghira (Er
Riadh) and Hara Kebira (Es
Souani). At first glance these
two villages (which are
about 5 km/3 miles apart)
are identical to any other
Tunisian village with palm
trees and white houses with
distinctive blue doors and
windows. It is only when
the streets fill with boys
returning from school
wearing skull-
caps,

or when Sabbath
candles are lit
inside the houses,
that visitors may get
the impression of
being in a district of
Jerusalem rather
than in a Tunisian
village.

The two villages
have a number of
synagogues. Some
of the synagogues'
walls bear stern
notices: "If you talk
in the synagogue,
where do you pray?"

The island's Jewish
community is mainly middle-
class and continues to
celebrate the Sabbath and
other Jewish festivals and
observe the main rituals. For
a son's circumcision, for
instance, a red blanket is hung
on the door as a sign of
invitation to everyone to come
and witness the ceremony.

El-May ❸

Road map D5.

THIS VILLAGE LIES at the
centre of Jerba and is
9 km (6 miles) south of
Houmt Souk. Once it used to
separate the eastern part of
the island, inhabited by the
Ibadites, from its western
part, populated by the
Wahbis. The Ibadites
(a moderate faction of
Kharijism) recognized man's
free will. The Wahbis, who
renounced all other factions
of Islam, proclaimed the
necessity for *jihad* –
holy war. The 16th-
century Mosque of
Umm et-Turkia
(closed to non-
Muslims) was
formerly also
a fort.

FORTIFIED MOSQUES

**The nave of an underground
mosque**

Besides being important
spiritual centres, Jerba's
mosques were also
military defence
establishments. Their thick
walls provided shelter
from attacks, while their
minarets were used as
watchtowers. As well as
fortress-style minarets, the
local population also built
underground mosques. It
is likely that these were
used by the Ibadites for
secret prayer meetings.
One such mosque –
Jama'a el-Baldawi – can
be found near the village
of Ajim. Its façade was
built in modern times.
Underground mosques are
distinguished by their
austerity and functionality.
Ibadite doctrine does not
permit any ornamentation
within the mosque, as this
could distract the faithful
from prayer.

The mosque in El-May, at the centre of the island.

Ras Remel – a site of wintering birds and a weekend recreation spot

Ras Remel ❹

Road map D5.

THE RAS REMEL peninsula in the north of Jerba is just under 10 km (6 miles) from Houmt Souk, and is an ideal spot for daytrips and picnics. Its main attractions are the wintering flocks of pink flamingoes that migrate here from southern France and Spain, joining the fledglings who spend the entire year here. The waters surrounding Ras Remel are shallow and the muddy bottom provides the birds with plenty of food. A short distance from the headland lies Flamingo Island. Most hotels situated in Houmt Souk's tourist zone organize trips to the island, which are often combined with lunch and swimming.

ENVIRONS: At the furthest northwestern tip of the island is **Borj Jillij**, a mere 3 km (2 miles) from Mellita Airport. A lighthouse was first built here in the 16th century. This was replaced in the 18th century by a fort, which is once again being used as a lighthouse. From here it is possible to walk to Ajim along a narrow and quiet country road.

Ajim – ancient Tipasa – is situated 22 km (14 miles) southwest of Houmt Souk. Occupying the point closest to the mainland it has regular ferry links with Jorf (the ferry can be busy, especially at weekends). The village is also a centre for sponge diving *(see p172)*. The MC116 road runs among palm and olive groves. Fans of the first *Star Wars* film may want to search out the mosque that is 3 km (2 miles) up the coast towards Borj Jillij – this was used as the exterior of Obiwan Kenobi's house.

The small village of **Mahboubine** lies in the eastern part of the island, 3 km (2 miles) southwest of Midoun, and is surrounded by green fields and gardens. Its El-Katib Mosque is a copy of the Hagia Sophia in Istanbul. It was built in the 19th century by Ali el-Katib.

The village of **Arku** lies at the centre of the island, not far from the coastal town of Aghir, which marks the end of the tourist zone. The village's population consist mainly of the descendants of former slaves, who were brought to Jerba from Central Africa. Following the abolition of slavery in 1846, the majority of the island's black inhabitants chose to stay. Some adopted the surnames of families for whom they worked. Today their main occupation is agriculture, as well as basket- and mat-weaving. They are also renowned as outstanding musicians and dancers.

Unlike the centre of Jerba, which resembles one big garden, with palm, fig and olive groves, as well as orange and apple orchards, Jerba's **west coast** is largely uninhabited. A dirt road runs from Ajim to Borj Jillij with traditional Jerban houses and small fields scattered here and there. The coastline is rocky and not good for swimming, which means that there are few tourists. The dirt roads and lack of facilities, however, make it popular with campers and cyclists who don't mind putting up with a little hardship in order to get away from the bustle of the resort areas.

Ras Remel flamingo

MENZELS

Menzels are self-sufficient agricultural smallholdings. Although many have been abandoned, some remain in use. The internal area consists of a yard surrounded by white walls and buildings. The buildings provide accommodation for people and domestic animals; the yard also contains a granary and a water cistern. The entire area is surrounded by a garden and a palm grove. *Menzels* used to be interconnected with a maze of roads to other *menzels* and the mosque. In this way, news of approaching danger could be passed around instantly.

A fortress-like *menzel* on Jerba

Midoun ❺

Road map D5. 👥 48,000. 🚌 Fri.

SURROUNDED BY GARDENS, and orange and palm groves, this is Jerba's second town, after Houmt Souk. Midoun's population includes many descendants of African slaves, who were brought here from sub-Saharan Africa. The weekly Friday market attracts crowds of people from all over the island, as well as from the nearby mainland villages. The market is held at the centre of the town's small medina. It sells a variety of souvenirs, including local ceramics, wood carvings, leather goods and olive oil.

The other local event – "Fantasia" – is staged every Tuesday during the summer and includes a mock wedding ceremony accompanied by music and folk dancing, as well as displays of horse and camel riding. At the centre of Midoun, close to the junction that leads to Houmt Souk and the tourist zone, is an underground *massera* (oil press), covered with a white dome at ground level.

Mosque and fountain in front of the town hall, Midoun

Aghir ❻

Road map E5.

THE HOTEL ZONE that starts about 8 km (5 miles) east of Houmt Souk stretches up to the village of Aghir, on the eastern side of the island, which has been transformed into a hotel resort. Even so, as well as the souvenirs sold

Reconstructed dye-works in Guellala's waxworks museum

by local shops everyday groceries can also be bought. There is a regular bus service to Houmt Souk and Midoun.

From Aghir it is not far to Ras Taguerness, which is distinguished by a 54-m (177-ft) tall lighthouse. Aghir is also convenient for a visit to the small village of Arku *(see p181)* or for a walk along the beach to other complexes in Séguia or Ras Lalla Hadria. Aghir's sandy beach has been divided into a public area and a number of private sections belonging to local hotels.

Guellala ❼

Road map D5.

GUELLALA, the ancient town of Haribus (meaning a "pot"), owes its name to the skill of the local potters, who mastered the potter's wheel several thousand years ago. The village lies on the south coast of Jerba and is the only place on the island where the Berber language is spoken.

Since ancient times this was the island's main pottery centre. Jerba was for centuries the sole manufacturer of ceramics in Tunisia, and its products were famous throughout the Saharan region. Even as late as the 19th century the island paid the beys tax, which was paid in kind, in the form of jars and pots that were used for storing food.

The range of Jerba's traditional ceramics includes amphora-like jars, which are still used today. Most of the production now centres on enamelled goods that are intended for visitors, however. There are about 450 small pottery shops working in this area.

Traditional Jerba ceramics are made of clay that is excavated from mines up to 80 m (262 ft) deep. It is dried for two to three days and then mixed with water. The products are left out to dry for a further 60 days, and only after that are they fired for four days in kilns, which are half-buried in soil.

Guellala's **museum** is a little way north of the village on the road to Cedouikech. The colourful displays, using waxwork tableaux, attempt to conjure up scenes of traditional Tunisian life such as a shepherd with his flock or a weaver at work.

🏛 **Guellala Museum of Popular Traditions**
📞 (75) 761 114. ⏰ 9am–6pm. 📷

Ceramic workshop and retailer, Guellala

Jerba's Jewish Community

THERE ARE LESS THAN 1,000 Jews living in Jerba. According to legend, a group of Jewish clerics arrived on the island following the fall of Jerusalem in 586 BC. They brought with them a door from the destroyed Jewish temple and included it in the new El-Ghriba synagogue. From Jerba, Jewish colonies sprang up across Tunisia and by the 2nd century AD Tunisia was the home of the

A Jewish resident

majority of North African Jews. Many Jews worked as jewellers and established Jerba's reputation as a commercial centre. During the 19th century Jews here were forced to wear distinctive black clothes to mark them out and anti-Jewish discrimination only lessened with the arrival of the French in 1881. Many Jews left Jerba for a new life in Israel and France in the 1950s and 60s.

El-Ghriba is the most important synagogue on the island and is open to visitors. It is closed only on the Sabbath, when it is used by the Jewish islanders for services.

Lag Ba'omer is a major festival and an occasion when several thousand Jews from all over the world congregate in Jerba. The holiday celebrates the 33rd day of Omer, a period of abstention and mourning, that is counted from Passover.

Pilgrimage – *El-Ghriba (the miracle) is an important site of pilgrimage for Jews from all over North Africa.*

Library – *this is the place for studying the Torah (Jewish holy book). El-Ghriba has one of the oldest Torahs in the world and is a centre of Jewish study.*

Sabbath services *take place once a week, on Saturday, when Jerban synagogues fill with the faithful. The service is short, since the main celebrations traditionally take place at home.*

Zarzis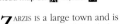

Road map E5. 🚶 *11,000.* 🚌

Zarzis is a large town and is located 20 km (12 miles) southeast of Jerba. In geographical terms this area belongs to the Jaffara Plains that stretch between Gabès and the Libyan border. Since the 7th century this region has been inhabited by Arab nomads and a population that led a semi-nomadic lifestyle.

Zarzis is surrounded by vast olive and palm groves, with about 700,000 olive trees and 110,000 date palms. The town itself was built in the 19th century by the French, who established their garrison here. The tourist zone has fine sandy beaches and starts 4 km (2 miles) outside town. The zone stretches for about 8 km (5 miles) along the coast. It is becoming increasingly important as one of Tunisia's tourist regions.

Medenine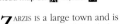

Road map E6. 🚶 *18,000.* 🚌

This is an excellent base from which to explore the outlying villages. The town, which is split into two by a river bed (the Arab word "medenijin" means "two towns"), was once an important stopping point for caravans. During the French Protectorate it housed a military garrison. As the main market town, to which goods were brought from the entire southern region, it became

Beach in Zarzis's tourist zone

the administrative centre of southern Tunisia.

Initially Medenine consisted of a large *ksar*, which in total had over 6,000 *ghorfas* (rooms). The nomads used them for storing valuables, mainly corn, seed and vegetables, but they also left in them articles that were not needed on the journey.

Each family had its own *ghorfa*. During the 1960s most of the *ghorfas* were demolished. Today the handful of remaining *ghorfas* have been turned into tourist souvenir shops.

Such *ksour* (plural of *ksar*) are symbols of an old way of life, although they are increasingly being abandoned and falling into ruin, as the villagers store their grain in

modern silos on the outskirts of the towns. Nevertheless, there are still many well-preserved *ksour* in the neighbouring area. The best way to get to them is by car *(see pp196–7)*.

Environs: A large *ghorfa* complex can be seen in **Metameur**, 6 km (4 miles) west of Medenine. The village inhabitants are semi-nomadic. Some of them are descended from Sidi Ahmed ben Adjel, a holy man who founded the village in the 13th century. The best time to visit Metameur is on Friday, when the nomads leave their pastures and gather here for their Friday prayers. The most important building in town is the 600-year-old *ksar*, which has three storeys of *ghorfas* built around three courtyards.

From Metameur a road (MC104) leads to **Toujane**, a small half-deserted village below the ruins of a kasbah. Its flat roofs, made of olive wood, resemble terraces.

Some 80 km (50 miles) southeast of Medenine is the small town of **Ben Guerdane**, which has 3,000 inhabitants. Every Friday there is a market here. As with Zarzis and Medenine, it was founded by the French in the late 19th century. From here it is only 32 km (20 miles) to the Libyan border.

Souvenir shop in a *ghorfa* in the centre of Medenine

◁ **Traditional Jerba pottery**

Jerba's Beaches

JERBA'S BEAUTIFUL BEACHES stretch along the northeast coast of the island, all the way from Ras Remel to Ras Taguerness. However, access to them is often restricted by a virtually unbroken line of hotels. There are some attractive beaches on the east coast, in the region of Aghir. The less-frequented beaches on the island can be found around Ras Remel.

Ras Remel ①
This beach lying at the tip of the headland is often deserted and can only be reached by car over unmetalled roads. It is best to travel with a guide to avoid getting lost.

Bravo Club ②
Most hotels have their own stretch of beach, with umbrellas, loungers and other facilities including paragliding and water bicycles for the sole use of guests.

Beach Traders ③
Vendors can often be seen roaming the tourist zone beaches. They offer drinks, ice cream and fruit and also sell beach toys and souvenirs.

Ras Remel

①
②
③
④
⑤ ⑥

Ras Taguerness

C209

• Midoun

Sport ④
Banana rides, sailing and a variety of other attractions are available on the tourist zone beaches.

• Mahboubine

0 km   1
0 miles   1

Beach Rides ⑤
The most popular local activities include camel rides along the beach. On some parts of the beach horse riding is also available.

Dar Jerba ⑥
The gardens and terraces of this large hotel complex, which has bars, restaurants and nightly entertainment, lead directly to the sandy beach.

Around the Gulf of Bou Grara ⑩

A JOURNEY AROUND THE Gulf of Bou Grara reveals just how diverse and attractive this section of the coastline is. As well as ancient ruins, picturesque floodplains and golden beaches, there are high rugged cliffs, a modern tourist zone and hundreds of acres planted with olive and orange trees. It is also worth venturing a little further to visit the exotic bazaar in Ben Guerdane, which sells a variety of Libyan-made goods.

El-Kantara ①
This is the starting point for the causeway leading to Jerba. It provides a lovely panoramic view of the island.

Jorf ⑧
Visitors have to pass Jorf when travelling to Jerba from the direction of Gabès. Every quarter of an hour or so the only ferry to the island leaves from here.

Bou Grara ⑦
This tiny fishing village would not have much to recommend it were it not for the magnificent scenery, which includes a high shore line and sandy beaches.

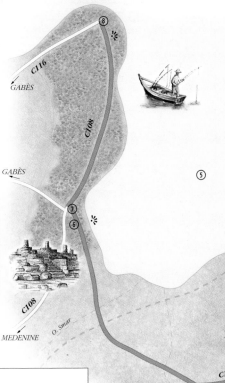

BEN GUERDANE

A small town, 33 km (20 miles) from the border with Libya, Ben Guerdane has a good market where almost anything can be bought, though not always at a low price. The market is used mainly by Tunisians. Along the road to Ben Guerdane are small petrol stations, which also sell inexpensive Libyan jewellery.

Rug stall at Ben Guerdane

Gightis ⑥
This ancient village, on the shore of the bay, was founded by the Phoenicians. The existing ruins represent a later period dating from the 2nd century AD.

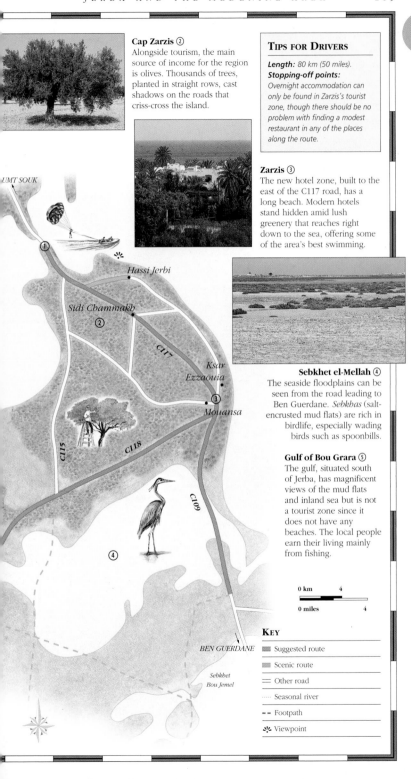

Cap Zarzis ②

Alongside tourism, the main source of income for the region is olives. Thousands of trees, planted in straight rows, cast shadows on the roads that criss-cross the island.

TIPS FOR DRIVERS

Length: 80 km (50 miles).
Stopping-off points:
Overnight accommodation can only be found in Zarzis's tourist zone, though there should be no problem with a modest restaurant in any of the places along the route.

Zarzis ③

The new hotel zone, built to the east of the C117 road, has a long beach. Modern hotels stand hidden amid lush greenery that reaches right down to the sea, offering some of the area's best swimming.

Sebkhet el-Mellah ④

The seaside floodplains can be seen from the road leading to Ben Guerdane. *Sebkhas* (salt-encrusted mud flats) are rich in birdlife, especially wading birds such as spoonbills.

Gulf of Bou Grara ⑤

The gulf, situated south of Jerba, has magnificent views of the mud flats and inland sea but is not a tourist zone since it does not have any beaches. The local people earn their living mainly from fishing.

UMT SOUK

Hassi Jerbi

Sidi Chammakh

C117

Ksar Ezzaouia

Mouansa

C115

C118

C109

BEN GUERDANE

Sebkhet Bou Jemel

0 km   4

0 miles   4

KEY

	Suggested route
	Scenic route
=	Other road
····	Seasonal river
– –	Footpath
☀	Viewpoint

SOUTHERN TUNISIA

SOME OF THE COUNTRY'S MOST INTERESTING SIGHTS *are to be found in this part of Tunisia. Oases and ancient* ksour*; a sea of golden sand and green palm groves; troglodyte houses; Bedouin bread baked on the scorching sand; modern musicals performed in the desert and the largest salt lake in Africa – all these make a visit to southern Tunisia a truly unique experience.*

Southern Tunisia lures visitors with the sheer diversity of its landscape. It holds special appeal to holidaymakers who simply wish to relax on the beaches of the Sahel but is also increasingly popular with adventure-seekers. Only a small section of the Sahara – the world's largest desert, shared by 11 African countries – belongs to Tunisia. Nevertheless, in view of its relative safety, transport facilities and tourist infrastructure, it is this section of the Sahara that is most easily accessible.

Here, visitors can journey along the routes of former trade-caravans or choose to follow in the footsteps of *Star Wars* director George Lucas. Nights can be spent in Bedouin tents, remote mountain oases or luxury hotels that resemble oriental palaces. Pomegranates and dates can be picked ripe from the tree. Some visitors choose to spend several days touring the desert on camelback. Others prefer to relax in ancient Berber villages or lose themselves in meditation amid the ancient mosques of Sufi Nefta.

The Tunisian section of the Sahara comprises three main types of desert: the rocky *hamada*; the pebbly *serir* and the sandy *erg*. The latter is the most picturesque and occupies the eastern end of the Great Eastern Erg. Its most impressive dunes can be seen around Ksar Ghilane.

During the summer, this region can become unbearably hot. For this reason, spring and autumn are the best times to visit.

The main courtyard of Ksar Ouled Soltane

◁ **Palm trees of a Saharan oasis**

Exploring Southern Tunisia

WITH SO MUCH CHOICE, it could be difficult to decide what to see in southern Tunisia. Visitors keen on ancient ruins will find little of interest here, but those who seek spectacular, breathtaking scenery cannot fail to be enchanted with the region, which includes ancient mountain oases; the shifting colours of Chott el-Jerid, and the green oases of Nefta – the cradle of Tunisian Sufism. Ksar Ouled Soltane, perched on top of a mountain, has some extremely well-preserved *ghorfas*. Most impressive of all, perhaps, is the Sahara Desert which can be admired while perched on a camel's back or from a hot-air balloon floating above the sands.

Chott el-Jerid – a seasonal salt lake

KEY

▬	Major road
▬	Scenic route
═	Other road
--	Unmetalled road
◯	Salt lake
✲	Viewpoint

SIGHTS AT A GLANCE

Chebika **12**
Chott el-Jerid **9**
Douz **6**
Ksar Ghilane **5**
Ksar Haddada **1**
Ksar Ouled Soltane **3**
Midès **14**
Nefta **11**
Remada **4**
The Sahara pp200–1 **7**
Tamerza **13**
Tataouine **2**
Tozeur **10**

Trips

Douz to Tozeur pp206–7 **8**

Ksar Ouled Soltane – the best-known *ksar*

SEE ALSO

• *Where to Stay* pp261–4

• *Where to Eat* pp287–8

Camel-train waiting for tourists in front of a Douz hotel, on the edge of the Sahara Desert

GETTING THERE

The Tunisian Sahara is skirted by roads on its northern and eastern sides. Douz – the northern gate of the Sahara – can be reached from Gabès via the P16, or from the direction of the mountain oases via the causeway that runs across Chott el-Jerid. From here on, visitors can explore the Sahara only with a guide. To reach Ksar Ghilane turn west from the P19. Finding this, the most popular oasis, is no easy task, since during high winds the roads become covered in sand. The P19 road running from Medenine ends in the south at Remada.

0 km 30

0 miles 30

A maze of alleys in Ksar Haddada

Ksar Haddada ❶

Road map D6. 29 km (18 miles) northwest of Tataouine.

THE MAIN POINT of interest of this small village is its superbly restored *ksar*, which is one of the most striking complexes of former fortress-granaries to be found in southern Tunisia. It stands at the very centre of the village, in close proximity to the mosque, which is across the road.

A large notice in front of the main gate informs visitors that in 1997 George Lucas used this place as a location for the *Star Wars* prequel, *The Phantom Menace.*

It is worth diving deeper into the maze of stairways, terraces and small courtyards and peeping into some of the granary niches known as *ghorfas*. These were once used to store food by the local Haddada and Hamdoun tribes, and by two other tribes which probably arrived here from Libyan and Moroccan territories.

Today, a section of the *ksar* has been converted into a small hotel, which combines the unique atmosphere of an ancient *ksar* with a tinge of Hollywood. The hotel's kitchen offers a simple menu; the rooms, although equipped with bathrooms, are fairly austere. Right by the entrance to the *ksar* is a pleasant little café where a glass of mint tea can be enjoyed with a puff on a hookah if desired.

Tataouine ❷

Road map D6. 125 km (78 miles) south of Gabès. 🏠 7,000. 🛈 ONTT: Avenue Habib Bourguiba, (75) 850 686. 🎦 International Saharan Ksour Festival (Mar–Apr); Festival of the Olives (Dec). 🛒 Mon, Thu.

VARIOUSLY KNOWN as the "gateway to the Sahara" and the "mouth of the springs" (from the Berber "foum tataouine"), this is Tunisia's southernmost tourist base. It is situated 50 km (31 miles) from the Mediterranean coast, along the popular tourist trail that links Jerba with Matmata and Douz with the Saharan oasis of Ksar Ghilane. Some fans of *Star Wars* may also realize that Tataouine provided the name for Luke Skywalker's mythical and wind-blown home planet of Tatooine.

Traditional flutes on sale at Tataouine's market

Some 150 million years ago this area was inhabited by dinosaurs before being flooded by the sea. Mankind has been forced to adapt to the barren land and arid climate. To this day the Berbers show great respect for the natural environment. Berber women occupy themselves with handicrafts, weaving rugs and carpets and sewing warm camel-wool cloaks. The men produce shoes called *balgha* which have flattened toe-ends.

Tataouine was founded in 1892 by the French and is today a major administration centre of this region. It is known for its hotels which are distinguished by their interesting architectural style and locations, and for its colourful markets selling fruit, olives and Berber fabrics. There is also a weekly livestock market during the early part of summer which is popular with tribespeople from the outlying villages.

Apart fromt the hotels and markets Tataouine has little tourist appeal though it does provide a very convenient base for exploring the local *ksour*, such as Ksar Haddada (29 km/18 miles), Ksar Ouled Soltane (20 km/12 miles), and Remada (78 km/48 miles). The nearest one is Ksar Megabla – only 2 km (1 mile) from the centre of Tataouine (in the direction of Remada). Though this former fortified village has been largely destroyed, it does offer a lovely view of the surrounding area.

The local delicacy is the sweet honey-and-almond bread *(kab el-ghazal)* baked in the shape of a gazelle horn. The annual Saharan Ksour Festival (a five-day event at the end of March/beginning of April) provides an opportunity to witness camel races and Berber wedding ceremonies and to sample some of the delicious local cuisine.

Tataouine is also only 18 km (11 miles) from **Chenini**, a Berber village occupying a scenic position on a high hill, which is famous for its ancient cave dwellings.

Ksar Ouled Soltane ❸

Road map D6.

K SAR OULED SOLTANE is the most interesting and best-preserved fortified village in Tunisia, and is situated 20 km (12 miles) south of Tataouine. It is still used to store grain and olives and is inhabited by the Ouled Chehida tribesmen (in between their regular migration to pasturelands to tend their sheep, goats and camels). Surrounded by an additional set of defensive walls, the complex consists of over 300 granaries – *ghorfas*. Rising up to four storeys they are set round two courtyards that are linked by a narrow corridor made of palm wood. The older courtyard dates from the 15th century; the newer one was built in 1881. The place is worth visiting particularly on Friday, after the main Muslim prayer session, to witness the lively discussions between the Ouled Chehida tribesmen.

The larger of the two *ksar* courtyards is also sometimes used as a venue for folk shows, especially during the Ksour Festival. The traditional Berber music and dancing of the ancient community are in perfect harmony with the architecture of this beautifully restored fortified village.

Steep stairs leading to upper floors in Ksar Ouled Soltane

Remada ❹

Road map D6.

T HIS SMALL OASIS lies 50 km (31 miles) from the Libyan border. A smallish Roman fort once stood here. Under the French Protectorate, the town once again became a military base. Due to its close proximity to Libya, Remada has remained a garrison town. The only eye-catching feature in the central Place de l'Indépendance is a former abattoir building, covered with 15 small domes. This is a border zone, and any trip to the desert requires special permission from the military authorities.

Borj Bourguiba, 41 km (25 miles) southwest of Remada, is where the first president of Tunisia, Habib Bourguiba, was kept prisoner during the early 1950s.

STAR WARS

George Lucas – the creator of *Star Wars* films – was fascinated by the landscape of southern Tunisia and used many of its most exotic sights and interiors as locations for his epic space adventures. Luke Skywalker's home at the beginning of the first *Star Wars* movie was actually the interior of the Sidi Driss Hotel in Matmata for instance, while the natural features of Ksar Haddada were used to conjure up slave quarters in *The Phantom Menace*. The worldwide success of *Star Wars* helped to

Remaining fragments of *Star Wars* film set

promote many of Tunisia's tourist attractions and a percentage of the revenue obtained from the sale of tickets when the first film was released in 1977 went to the National Solidarity Fund that helps the poorest regions of the country in their fight against the desert. Newly-established tourist agencies have since begun to offer trips that follow in the footsteps of George Lucas – there are even some local road signs that point to *Star Wars* sites.

***Star Wars* robot**

The Ksar

THIS CENTURIES-OLD FEATURE of the Tunisian landscape is a strongly fortified Berber village that is difficult to access. Originally the word *ksar* (or *ksour* in the plural) meant a fortified granary with *ghorfas* (rooms), which were placed cylindrically around an inner courtyard with a well-concealed entrance. Later on, *ghorfas* came to be used as dwelling places for local tribes. Ksar Ouled Soltane is considered to be Tunisia's best-preserved fortified village, and is still used by the Ouled Chehida tribe as a home and granary.

Berber fortified villages and granaries *have for centuries been part of the everyday life of people in southern Tunisia.*

Courtyards *were a feature of every* ksar. *Some larger* ksour *had more than one courtyard, linked with a special passage. Surrounded by ghorfas, courtyards were the main scene of Berber social life.*

Stairs *provided internal connections within a* ksar. *This was particularly important since ghorfas were usually two to four storeys high.*

The well in a *ksar*'s courtyard was surrounded by green plants.

External walls *ensured the safety of the inhabitants and protected their granaries. The ghorfas facing the courtyard also provided a natural defence with no access via their back walls. For added security, an additional wall was sometimes added.*

KSAR OULED SOLTANE

This is one of the most southerly *ksour* and has been restored to its original state. The *ksar* is still inhabited by a Berber tribe. The entrance to it is from the plateau, through a small courtyard. The *ksar* is at its best at sunset.

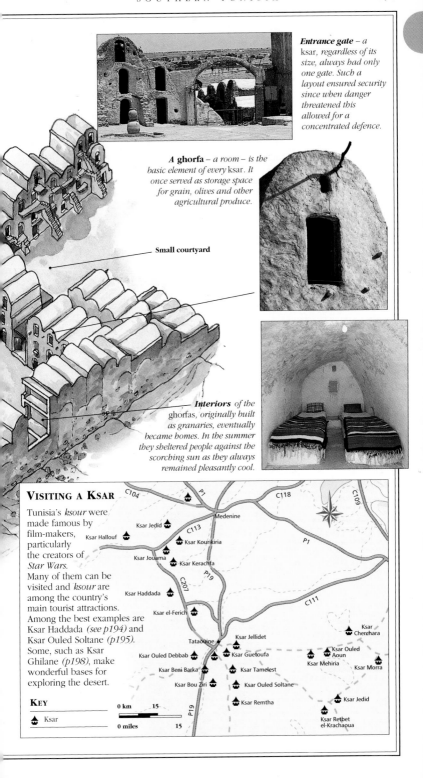

Entrance gate – *a* ksar, *regardless of its size, always had only one gate. Such a layout ensured security since when danger threatened this allowed for a concentrated defence.*

A ghorfa – *a room – is the basic element of every* ksar. *It once served as storage space for grain, olives and other agricultural produce.*

Small courtyard

Interiors *of the ghorfas, originally built as granaries, eventually became homes. In the summer they sheltered people against the scorching sun as they always remained pleasantly cool.*

VISITING A KSAR

Tunisia's *ksour* were made famous by film-makers, particularly the creators of *Star Wars*. Many of them can be visited and *ksour* are among the country's main tourist attractions. Among the best examples are Ksar Haddada *(see p194)* and Ksar Ouled Soltane *(p195)*. Some, such as Ksar Ghilane *(p198)*, make wonderful bases for exploring the desert.

C104
P1
C118
C109
Medenine
Ksar Jedid
C113
Ksar Hallouf
Ksar Kourikiria
P1
Ksar Jouama
Ksar Kerachfa
C207
P19
Ksar Haddada
C111
Ksar el-Ferich
Ksar Cherchara
Ksar Jellidet
Ksar Ouled Aoun
Tataouine
Ksar Guetoufa
Ksar Ouled Debbab
Ksar Mehiria
Ksar Morra
Ksar Beni Barka
Ksar Tamelest
Ksar Bou Ziri
Ksar Ouled Soltane
Ksar Remtha
Ksar Jedid
Ksar Retbet el-Krachaoua

KEY

🔺 Ksar

0 km   15
0 miles   15
P19

Camels resting at a desert watering place

Ksar Ghilane ❺

Road map C6.

Surrounded by the dunes of the Great Eastern Erg, this small Saharan oasis is 147 km (91 miles) southeast of Douz and 100 km (62 miles) west of Chenini. The Romans built a frontier fort on this desolate spot and the ruins of a citadel can still be seen close by. The only way to get to Ksar Ghilane is by four-wheel-drive car or by camel. It is well worth stopping here for a few days to see the shifting reds, golds and yellows of the desert sand.

Accommodation is not a problem. Tourist camps with Bedouin tents are furnished with camp-beds and blankets. Some campsites have canteens offering a limited menu; some even have showers (though these are not always working). For more fastidious visitors there is a luxury campsite with air-conditioned Bedouin-style tents, complete with refrigerators and satellite TV. Some meals are served with genuine Bedouin bread – a large flat cake that is tossed into fire embers. After ten minutes it is turned over and left for a while longer. Bread baked this way is delicious.

One special attraction of Ksar Ghilane is bathing in the palm-fringed pool that is fed by the waters of a natural hot sulphur spring. In the winter, when the night temperature drops to just a few degrees above freezing (from over 20° C/68° F during the day),

bathing in the desert, amid swaying palm trees under starry skies, is a unique experience. The pool is surrounded by small cafés and restaurants where souvenirs can be purchased such as a desert rose or a warm woollen cloak with a hood – the traditional clothing of the desert people.

Market stall selling locally-made footwear in Douz

Douz ❻

Road map C6. *123 km (76 miles) southwest of Tozeur.* 🏛 *7,000.* ℹ *ONTT: Avenue des Martyrs, (75) 470 351.* 🎭 *International Festival of the Sahara (Nov–Dec).* 🛒 *Thu.*

Nicknamed "the gateway to the Sahara", this small town lies on the edge of the Great Eastern Erg that stretches westwards, all the way to Morocco. The oasis, which is literally on the verge of the vast desert dunes, is a major springboard for exploring the Sahara. This is where the asphalt road ends and any further journey southwards can be made only by a four-wheel-drive vehicle (approximately seven hours to Ksar Ghilane) or on camelback (five days to Ksar Ghilane).

A good time to visit is during the International Festival of the Sahara, normally in November or December. The festival, which has been taking place for over 30 years, is an opportunity to witness the ceremonies that have marked the pace of life of the local nomadic tribes. These include wedding ceremonies, sheep-shearing, duels, hunting and camel races. From Douz, groups can go for a balloon flight over the Sahara, or ride scooters over the dunes. Sweet dates can be bought here, as well as Berber jewellery and leather goods. The tourist zone starts a short way from the centre, on the edge of the dunes.

TUNISIAN CONDIMENTS

Harissa – a traditional Berber paste made with hot red pepper, garlic, tomato puree and olive oil – appears on every Tunisian table and is eaten with almost everything. It it thought to strengthen the appetite and invigorate and disinfect the body – including the respiratory tract. Harissa

is sometimes served with small pieces of tuna and olives. Other herbs and spices used in Tunisian cuisine include fresh and dried mint leaves, coriander, aniseed, saffron, cinnamon and caraway.

Multicoloured herbs and spices

Caravans

In ancient times groups of merchants travelled along the Silk Road that linked China with the West. During the Middle Ages such caravans provided the only safe way of travelling across North Africa and were the sole means of transporting goods and merchants, troops and pilgrims. Tunisia lay at the crossroads of major caravan routes to the far corners of the African continent.

Warning sign: Attention! Camels!

Caravans also used mules and donkeys, but in the harsh desert environment the camel proved to be the most effective. As well as goods, caravans helped the spread of Islam, the scriptures and the written language. Many of the roads that were once travelled by caravans have now become highways. It is possible, however, to join an adventure caravan and travel over the desert dunes.

Camels *have been domesticated for thousands of years. They can drink 130 litres (28.6 gallons) of water at a time and go for up to two weeks without drinking again. Much of the camel's fat is in its hump, enabling it to lose heat more easily. The Arabic language has over one hundred terms to describe camels.*

Special contraptions *facilitated travel on camelback, while at the same time protecting the rider against sun and sand. The most difficult operations are mounting and dismounting. Riders must hold on tight to the horn of the saddle that is placed in front of the hump.*

Oases *and deep wells hidden among the desert sands ensured a caravan's survival. Any camel-driver is able to lead the caravan to an oasis or a well, without needing to refer to a map.*

Present-day caravans *still travel over the sands of the desert. Their nomadic owners are able to recognize their camels just from the camel's footprints.*

Visitors *may go for short trips or embark on camel treks lasting several days between oases and* ksours, *stopping at night in* ghorfas *or pitched Bedouin tents.*

Typical desert terrain near Gabès

The Sahara ❼

Road map B6, C6, D6.

THE SAHARA IS THE world's largest desert and occupies one third of the African continent (9,000,000 sq km/ 3,474,000 sq miles). It stretches from the west coast of Africa to the Red Sea. Its area lies within 11 African states, one of them being Tunisia, which controls only a small section of the desert. However, in terms of safety, transport facilities and tourist infrastructure this section of the Sahara is the most accessible. It is also the patch of desert that most often features in the movies.

The image of a desert as an ocean of sand, stretching off to the horizon, was created by fiction writers and film-makers such as Bernardo Bertolucci in *The Sheltering Sky*. In reality the desert is more often than not a stony plain – grey and dull, or an arid land criss-crossed with mountain ranges that are punctuated by mountain oases such as Chebika, Tamerza and Midès.

The Tunisian section of the Sahara features all three main types of desert: the rocky *hamada*; the pebbly *serir* and the sandy *erg*. The latter, most frequently associated with the image of the Sahara portrayed in films and literature, lies at the eastern end of the Great Eastern Erg,

A palm-shaded oasis in the middle of the desert

which runs all the way from Morocco. It starts south of Douz and its most striking sand dunes can be seen in the vicinity of Ksar Ghilane. In the north they are preceded by vast steppes occasionally interspersed with sand dunes which are bordered by vast, dry salt lakes. The causeway that crosses the largest of these – Chott el-Jerid – is the spot where mirages are most likely to occur.

Wildlife is scarce in the desert. Wild camels are rarely encountered in Tunisia's arid areas. The ones that are seen are usually part of someone's herd. The North African fox, its ears pointing up like radar aerials, can now be seen only in zoos. At times a gazelle can be spotted. There is no shortage of desert lizards, poisonous adders and scorpions. Here and there, desert areas feature clumps of esparto grass, which is used to make paper and mats.

The driest areas of the Sahara have no more than 25 mm (0.985 inches) of annual rainfall. The oases are surrounded by a sea of sand. Every scrap of greenery, every well or pasture, once belonged to a clan or a tribe and was cherished, cared for and fought over. Strangers were perceived as a threat and as competition. Even the *sa'alik* – the knight errant of the desert, the intractable outcast of various tribes – would join in groups in order to survive. An expulsion from a community meant death amid the sands. Tribal awareness, although not as

SAFETY IN THE SAHARA

The rule is never travel alone in the desert, even when using a four-wheel-drive jeep. There must be at least two cars, preferably driven by Tunisian drivers. Any excursion made by car or on camelback must always be reported to the National Guard and may only be made with their permission (travel agents can usually arrange these formalities). Excursions made on foot also have to be reported and are best made with a guide. It is essential to take sunscreen products. Also useful are wraparound sunglasses, a down-filled sleeping bag, a groundsheet, a pair of loose trousers, a large cotton headscarf that can cover the entire head and neck from sun and wind, and as much water as you can carry. High-sided shoes will provide protection against scorpions.

vital as in the old days, is still strong. The ties of blood protected people and gave them a feeling of security. Several families descending from a common ancestor formed a clan. A group of related clans formed a *kabila* – a tribe. A tribe used to surround the home of their chieftain with a circle of tents – the *dawwar* – creating something like a small, sovereign autonomous state.

Family, tribes and the association of tribes formed the bedrock of Bedouin society. Warrior-sons and guards led the caravans, procured domestic animals and, in the course of plundering raids, defended the honour of their clans and took women captives. Their bravery and courage ensured the clan's safety and prosperity. Women were regarded as the property of their families. They were expected to be obedient and bear the maximum possible number of sons. Their situation changed for the better with the arrival of Islam, for although Mohammed preserved the form of marriage that left a woman in the power of her husband, he nevertheless set

Camel train travelling across the desert

Horses – a frequent sight on the edges of the Sahara

out a number of rules aimed at protecting women. He made the woman the owner of her own dowry and regulated the legal position of orphans, of women abandoned by their husbands and of widows, granting to all of them rights to at least some portion of the estate.

Time seems to flow slowly in the desert. Sand shifts from one dune to another. Colours also shift: white, occasionally yellow and golden-red mounds move along, changing their shape and position.

Though beautiful, the desert can be treacherous. Sand immobilizes vehicle wheels and hinders travellers' legs, while its minute grains find their way into camera lenses, even without a sandstorm. At the same time the sand is so velvety that it can be rubbed against the cheek without causing a scratch.

Tozeur, Nefta and Jerba all represent convenient starting points for forays into the Sahara, but to truly savour the desert adventure, the best places to start are Douz, Zaafrane and Ksar Ghilane. The sense of wonder will not be limited to sleeping in Bedouin

tents, the proximity of the desert or the taste of Bedouin bread baked in the hot sand – it will also include the sight of quirky cafés built of old metal cans or palms, appearing unexpectedly over dune tops.

TRIPS TO THE SAHARA FROM DOUZ

Ghilane Travel Services,
Avenue Taieb Mehiri 38, Douz.
☎ (75) 470 692.
FAX (75) 470 682.
@ gts@planet.tn

Horizons Deserts Voyages,
Rue el-Hanni 9, Douz.
☎ (75) 471 688.
FAX (75) 470 088.
@ h.deserts@planet.tn
w www.horizons-deserts.com

Libre Espace Voyages,
Avenue Mohamed,
Marzougi, Douz.
☎ (75) 470 620.
FAX (75) 470 622.
@ contact@libre-espace-voyages.com
w www.libre-espace-voyages.com

Mrazig Voyages,
Avenue 7 Novembre, BP 126, Douz.
☎ (75) 470 255.
FAX (75) 470 515.
@ mrazig_voyages@hexabyte.tn

Zaied Travel Agency,
Avenue Taieb Mehiri, Douz.
☎ (75) 491 918.
FAX (75) 470 584.
@ info@zaiedtravel.com
w www.zaiedtravel.com

Sand dunes in the Sahara

Desert Oases

THE OASIS WAS ONCE a haven for caravans and lost travellers and was used by tribes who lived in the desert. Even today, oases are a vital lifeline for people who must survive in extreme conditions. Desert oases have grown up around natural springs, ground water and wells. The typical desert oasis consists of cultivated plots of land shaded by palms and screened with palm-frond fences. Some oases, such as Gabès and Douz, have grown into large towns.

Berber tents, *put up specially for visitors, are a popular way to experience life in the desert oases. Some luxury tents are even air-conditioned.*

A sophisticated irrigation system *is indispensable to the life of an oasis. It must ensure an even distribution of water. In large oases, such as Nefta and Tozeur, water must be collected from hundreds of sources.*

The date harvest *in Tunisia is one of the biggest in the world. Dates are both sweet and nutritious and are an essential part of the staple diet of the oasis's inhabitants. Three dates and a spoonful of water mark the end of the Ramadan fast.*

Arable fields under palm trees *are possible as a result of irrigation. Crops that can be cultivated include carrots and semolina, which is used to make couscous.*

THE OASIS
The modern oasis exists purely thanks to human intervention. Irrigation systems make the most of natural water sources, making it possible not only to water the camels, but also to grow plants.

Shaft craters collect valuable rainwater.

Camels that live in Tunisia have only one hump. The oases provide them with places of rest and shade, where they can also top up their stores of water.

Underground springs also supply the oasis with water.

The pathways that criss-cross the oasis are not only used for transport, but also mark out the watered plots. The locals travel around on foot, on camelback or on donkeys.

Life in an oasis revolves around the tending of crops and animals (camels, horses, sheep and goats). The irrigation systems are vital and require constant attention.

Figs, oranges and pomegranates ripen in the shade of the palm trees.

Deep wells exploit water held in rock or soil layers far below the surface. The wells provide water for oases and caravans – and also now for visitors. Although there are no maps marking such wells, every good camel driver knows their locations by heart.

Natural pools, fed by deep underground springs and artificial reservoirs, provide oases with a constant supply of water for bathing.

Douz to Tozeur ●

THIS IS ONE OF THE most interesting routes in Tunisia and crosses the Chott el-Jerid – a vast, glittering salt lake that stretches as far as the eye can see. The route forms an important section of a longer tourist trail that leads from Tozeur (via Matmata) to Jerba. Until the mid-19th century it was used to transport slaves to the vast slave market in Kebili. The road is remarkably scenic, and it is worth allocating extra time for the journey.

Chott el-Jerid ⑦
The contours of salt lakes as drawn on most maps correspond with the winter rains season. The actual sight seen by visitors is usually only the dry bottom of the lake.

TAMERZA

GAFSA

P16   P3

Chott el-Gharsa

El-Mahassen

El-Hamma du Jerid   ⑩   P16

P3   ⑪

NEFTA

Causeway ⑨
This is where desert mirages are most often seen in Tunisia. Some people imagine they see passing caravans of camels, or even a railway train.

Chott el-Fejej ⑧
This is a natural offshoot of the Chott el-Jerid, and forms a narrow corridor running to the desert oasis of El-Hamma, near the shore of the Gulf of Gabès.

Degache ⑩
Oases such as Degache are inhabited by descendants of ancient nomadic tribes who still travel with their herds of camels, sheep and goats in search of fresh pastures. Life in this arid land is only possible thanks to the existence of oases.

DESERT ROSE

This is the most famous and least expensive souvenir of a visit to southern Tunisia. Sometimes artificially coloured (in shades of light green, blue and red) its beauty nevertheless resides in its natural colour – grey bordering on brown. It is usually found under several metres of sand. In chemical terms this is made of gypsum (crystals of calcium sulphate) that crystallizes from underground water and takes on the form of an open rose flower.

Desert rose – a symbol of the Sahara

Tozeur ⑪
Tunisia's "Hollywood" is the town of poets and of unusual yellow brick architecture. It is also a good base for trips to the mountain oases, to Nefta and to the dunes of the Great Eastern Erg.

◁ **Camel train making its way across the desert**

Bechri ⑥
This 64-km (40-mile) long causeway crosses the Chott el-Jerid. It links Bechri (near Kebili) with Kriz (near Tozeur).

Kebili ⑤
Kebili is the main market town of the Nefzaoua oases (market day is Tuesday). It is an important oasis along a former caravan route.

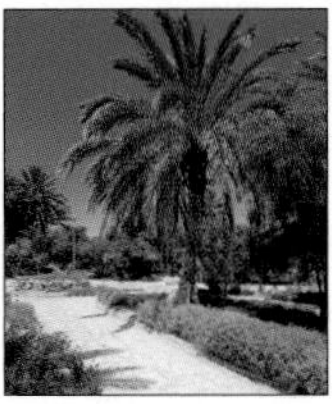

Tips for Drivers

Length: *161 km (100 miles).*
Stopping-off points: *Hotels can be found in Douz, Tozeur, Nefta and Bechri. A cup of coffee and a light meal are available anywhere, even on the causeway.*

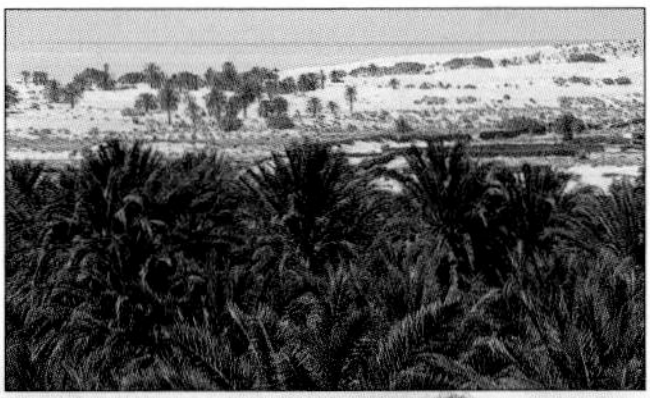

Blidet ④
This hill surrounded by palm groves, on which the village stands, is one of the better places from which visitors can admire the panoramic view of the Chott el-Jerid.

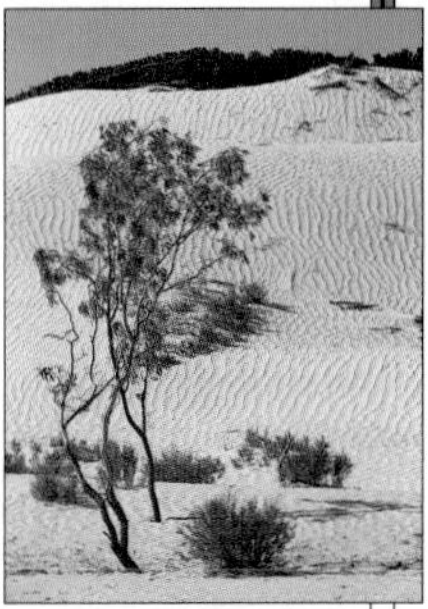

El-Faouar ③
El-Faouar – an oasis on the southern shore of the Chott el-Jerid – gives a foretaste of the great adventure.

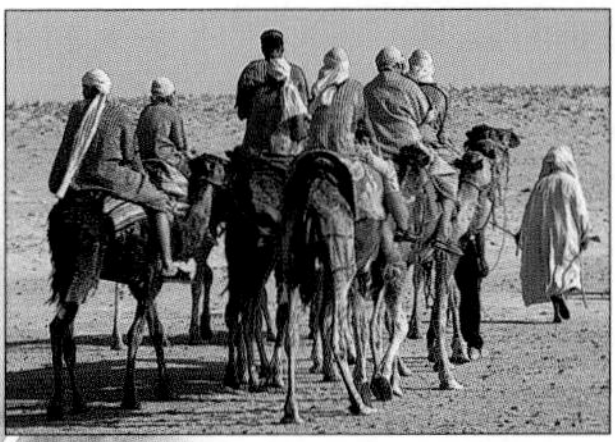

Zaafrane ②
Along with nearby Douz and Ksar Ghilane, Zaafrane is a major tourist centre from where classic camelback expeditions to the desert can be embarked upon.

Douz ①
Douz is the main springboard for desert trips. Any further journey south requires the use of a four-wheel-drive vehicle. Douz is also the venue for the International Festival of the Sahara.

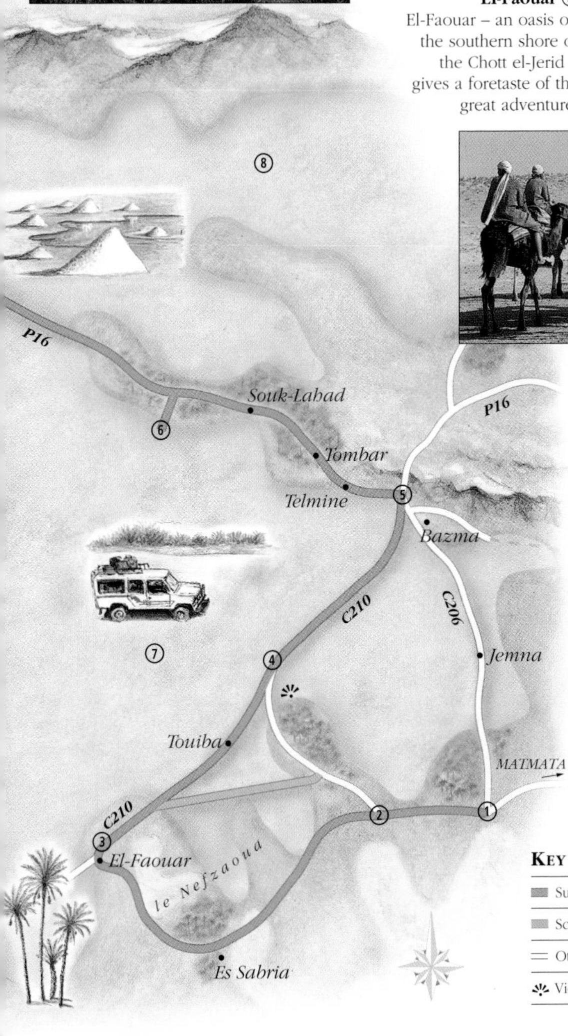
⑧
P16
Souk-Lahad
⑥
Tombar
Telmine
⑤
P16
Bazma
C206
C210
⑦
④
Jemna
Touiba
MATMATA
C210
③
El-Faouar
le Nefzaoua
②
①
Es Sabria

0 km 10
0 miles 10

Key

- Suggested route
- Scenic route
- Other road
- Viewpoint

Chott el-Jerid �ⓐ

Road map B5.

ONE OF TUNISIA'S several salt lakes, Chott el-Jerid was created by tectonic movements of the earth's crust some 1.5 million years ago. It is the largest of the North African salt lakes (51,280 sq km/19,794 sq miles) and lies between the Gulf of Gabès and the Algerian border. For most of the year it is dry, with only a thin layer of water remaining here and there, becoming an intriguing desert "carpet" that consists of minute salt crystals shimmering with blue, white and pale-green hues. The view of the lake at sunset is unforgettable. Mirages are a common occurrence.

The lake can be crossed on a 64-km (40-mile) long causeway that is open all year round. The route links Kriz (near Tozeur), with Bechri (near Kebili). It is best not to stray away from the road, as the lake bed in this area may be dangerous.

Halfway along the causeway there is a handful of small cafés, built of reed, where souvenirs such as amethyst and desert rose stones (*see p206*) can be bought. These can also provide toilet facilities. A trip on the causeway is one of the main tourist attractions along the Douz-Tozeur route.

Museum courtyard in Tozeur

The lake is also a venue for sand regattas where the yachts can reach speeds in excess of 70 km/h (43 mph).

Tozeur 🟉ⓑ

Road map B5. 🏠 21,000.
🛈 Avenue Bourguiba, (76) 454 503 and (76) 454 088. 🚩 Tue, Sun.
🎪 Festival of the Oases (Nov–Dec).

TOZEUR IS A MAJOR town and tourist centre. It is also one of the country's most beautiful oases and contains some 3,000 palm trees as well as fig and pomegranate trees and banana groves. The town is also known for growing the best dates in Tunisia. They are translucent, sweet and juicy; nearby Nefta is also famous for them.

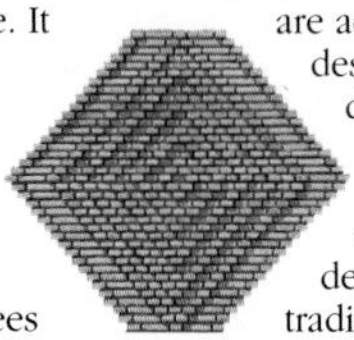

The oldest part of town is Ouled el-Hadef, which dates from the 14th century and has a distinctive high wall made of handmade bricks. The yellow stones of Ouled el-Hadef's houses are arranged so that they form Koranic verses and floral motifs.

On the outskirts of Tozeur is a private museum, **Dar Cheraït**, which is devoted to southern Tunisia's history and everyday life.

Tozeur house decoration

A separate section of the museum transports visitors to the realm of the *Thousand and One Nights*. This collection of anonymous tales written over several centuries includes traces of Indian, Persian, Egyptian, Greek, Mesopotamian and Arab influences. In the Arabian Nights grotto visitors can meet, among others, Ali Baba, Sinbad the Sailor and Scheherazade. The folk tales are accompanied by descriptions of every-day Tunisian life.

A separate **museum** on Rue de Kairouan is devoted to local traditions and includes costumes used in circumcision ceremonies and a collection of door knockers that produce a variety of sounds (making it possible to identify the caller).

Tozeur also has a **botanical garden** and a **zoo**. The latter provides a rare chance to see some desert wildlife.

Planet Oasis, a vast cultural centre, opened near Tozeur in 2001. Its huge stage, set on the Saharan sand, has state-of-the-art laser effects to accompany musical shows and other entertainment. The centre also claims "the largest Berber tent in the world".

🏛 **Dar Cheraït**
Rue Touristique. 🕐 8am–midnight.
📞 (76) 452 100.
🏛 **Museum of Popular Arts and Traditions**
Rue de Kairouan. 🕐 8am–noon & 2–6pm.

Salt on the edge of Chott el-Jerid

Nefta

Road map A5. 23 km (14 miles)
southwest of Tozeur. 🏛 *18,000.*
🛈 *ONTT: Avenue Bourguiba, (76)
457 184.* 🎪 *Festival of the Dates
(Nov–Dec).* 🛒 *Thu.*

T HE OASIS TOWN OF Nefta is
Tunisia's second holiest
site after Kairouan. It is
situated on the shores of the
Chott el-Jerid, near Tozeur.
During the Roman occupation
it was known as Aggasel
Nepte; in the 16th century it
became a centre of Sufism *(see
below)*. At that time Nefta had
100 mosques, dozens of
Islamic schools and a *zaouia*.
Today, it is frequently visited
by film-makers who come for
the unique scenery. It is worth
stopping here, even if only for
one night, to make a trip in a
horse and cart around the
entire oasis or to stroll along
the narrow alleys of Ouled
ech-Cherif.

Ouled ech-Cherif is the
oldest part of Nefta and lies in
the western portion of the
town. There are some
interesting streets and alleys to
be explored here and many of
the houses repay a second
glance. The doors and
window shutters have been
built in a wide range of shapes
and colours and have intricate
fixtures and door handles. The
door handles are often in the
shape of the Hand of Fatima.

The town wakes up after
siesta, two hours before
sunset. At the foot of the
ancient mosques young boys

Palm trees in La Corbeille gulley in Nefta

play football, vendors open
their shops and old men sit on
street benches. With a bit of
luck it may be possible to
strike up an acquaintance with
a local, get invited to a typical
Arab house and in its
courtyard be treated to fresh
dates and camel milk. The row
of restored mosques towering
over La Corbeille – a deep,
palm-filled gulley – is well
worth a photograph. The best
views are to be had from the
Café de la Corbeille.

In the heart of Nefta's oasis
is the **mausoleum of Sidi Bou
Ali**, a Moroccan-born 13th-
century mystic who founded
one of the earliest Sufi
brotherhoods. It was his fame
that turned Nefta into a major
spiritual centre of the Islamic
world. The reverence which
many Muslims pay to Sidi Bou
Ali is still strong today and his
mystical powers of healing,
passed on to his successors,
continue to attract people to
Nefta. The mausoleum is not
open to non-Muslims.

The date plantations in the
oasis belong to many private
owners. Some will invite
visitors (for a small fee) to
taste the drinks made of palm
juice, or try a cigar wrapped in
palm leaves. Here, visitors can
also find one of the many
oasis springs or go for a stroll
along the shady country lane
that crosses the entire valley.

SUFISM

Sufism is a branch of Islam
that originated in the
Middle East in the late 8th
to early 9th century and
spread to Central Asia and
India. Followers of Sufism
attempt to arrive at the
Ultimate Truth through the
"shedding of the veil" –
discarding the shackles of
everyday reason and
senses that constrain us.
Some of these devotional
practices, such as walking
on hot coals, have led to
Sufis being distrusted by
other Muslims.

**Whirling dervishes: the best-
known followers of Sufism**

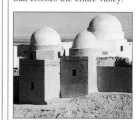

**Mosques towering over the oasis
in Nefta**

Chebika – a mountain oasis shaded by palm trees

Chebika ⑫

Road map A5. 60 km (37 miles) northwest of Tozeur; 5 km (3 miles) south of Tamerza. 👥 35,900.

THIS IS ONE of the three best-known Tunisian mountain oases (along with Tamerza and Midès). All three villages are situated near Tozeur, close to the border with Algeria. As recently as the 19th century they were major stopping-off points along one of the two main caravan routes that linked the east and west coasts of the African continent. During the years of the Roman Empire they were used as military forts where the legionnaires, making use of high-rise sentry posts, communicated with each other using mirrors.

For centuries the villages produced only what they needed to feed their population. This balance was upset when phosphate deposits were discovered nearby and many people left their homes to work in the mines. This also brought about changes in the local customs and traditions as agricultural production gradually diminished. Even greater changes were caused by the onset of mass tourism. Today, visitors travel in large numbers to this area, arriving by jeep for a day trip from Tozeur. This is also the destination for those wishing to take the Lézard Rouge train route *(see p216)*.

Chebika is a small village, built of stone and clay and clinging to the side of a mountain. It was probably built on the site of an earlier Roman outpost, Ad Speculum. Following severe flooding in 1969, the old village was abandoned. Now the village layout is almost the same as that of nearby Tamerza. Small side streets branch off the main road that leads to the market. The main point of interest in Chebika is its picturesque spring featuring a small palm grove and a waterfall, which can be found a little way beyond the village. The spring is fed by a series of small underground mountain streams (and the network of underground canals that feed the wells). This supply of water means that the otherwise barren land can produce apricots, peaches, pomegranates, citrus fruit, bananas and olives. Tobacco is grown in the shade of the palm trees.

According to a Tunisian proverb, the ultimate ruler here is the rain, and in day-to-day life water is more precious than petrol. The reason the oasis flourishes is its sophisticated irrigation system. To ensure local harmony, the system must maintain an even distribution of water to all plots. To meet this need, Chebika once had a curious "hourglass room" (it can still be seen behind the village's only public toilet). It contains a simple timer, consisting of two large jugs with handles, painted yellow with a green stripe (typical of Berber style). The jugs were hung from a rope and the water poured from one jug into the other. Based on the time it took for the lower jug to fill, an attendant would open and close appropriate gates within the irrigation system, sending water to each arable plot in turn.

Tamerza ⑬

Road map A5. 65 km (40 miles) northwest of Tozeur. 👥 1,500.
🎭 *Festival of the Mountain Oases (Mar).*

Tamerza's waterfall

KNOWN AS the "hanging balcony overlooking the Sahara Desert", Tamerza (sometimes spelt "Tameghza") is the largest of the mountain oases and is the only one that has a public transport link with the outside world (buses leave daily for Redeyef, Touzeur and Tunis). It is renowned not only for its scenic views but also for the most beautifully situated hotels in Tunisia. The four-star Tamerza Palace towers majestically over a large gorge (a dry river bed), facing the white houses and domes of the old town standing on the opposite side. Guest hotels and terraces look out onto magnificent scenery made famous by the film *The English Patient*. Tamerza, like Chebika, was abandoned following floods in 1969. The old village is now falling into ruin but maintains the general layout of an oasis, including the main road running from east to west and a labyrinth of narrow alleys that branch off it, climbing upwards.

Several marabouts (Islamic mausoleums) are still maintained in the abandoned village. The most interesting of these is the **mausoleum of Sidi Tuati**, which stands out clearly amid the devastated houses. It contains the holy man's tomb and rooms for pilgrims.

The present sanctuary is supposed to have been formerly occupied by a church. This claim was made by, among others, the medieval Arab traveller and author Tidjani. His belief may be supported by the presence of Christian churches which were active in the Jerid region in the 14th century. Some of these inspired the style of several mosques built in this area, which clearly display the influence of an 18th-century Italian style. Nevertheless the building materials are mainly local, including palm tree wood, typical of the Jerid region.

Another interesting sight in Tamerza is the pointed dome of the prayer hall belonging to the **mausoleum of Sidi Dar ben Dhahara**. The

Steep walls of the gorge surrounding Midès

mihrab (niche indicating the direction of prayer) of this sanctuary has been incorrectly placed and does not point accurately towards Mecca, a rare thing in Islamic art.

The abandoned houses and ruins of old Tamerza are increasingly visited by hikers and photographers. They are most impressive when the town becomes illuminated by the light of the setting sun.

New Tamerza has been built just above a waterfall. Close to its top stands the Hotel des Cascades, which is popular with globetrotters. Another waterfall can be seen a short way out of town on the road to Chebika.

Midès

Road map A4.

MIDÈS IS THE smallest mountain oasis in this area and is situated just a short walk from the Algerian border. The village is perched on the edge of a deep gorge (it flanks it on three sides). The gorge's red-soil floor is overgrown with lush green palm trees. The wavy vertical walls of the gorge present a particularly impressive sight. As with Tamerza and Chebika, the production of pomegranates, citrus fruit and dates plays an important role in the village economy.

Close to the new settlement is an abandoned **Berber village**. The deserted houses can be seen on the other side of the gorge. Next to the village is a café and stalls selling souvenirs, such as desert roses and semi-precious stones, as well as cold drinks and mint tea, indicating that tourism is becoming increasingly important to the economy here.

The area around Midès was used as a location for the aircraft crash scenes involving the main character in the film *The English Patient*.

The ruins of old Tamerza

CENTRAL TUNISIA

THE CENTRAL REGION OF THE COUNTRY *is dominated by vast mountainous areas of the Tell and Saharan Atlas ranges. Its extraordinary scenery includes the flat-topped Jugurtha's Table and the green hills of Jebel Zaghouan. Kairouan, one of Islam's four holiest cities, is well worth exploring, as are the Roman remains at Dougga, Sbeïtla and Thuburbo Majus.*

The hills of Jebel Zaghouan and Jebel Chambi are covered in dense forest dominated by Aleppo pine. The oases of Gafsa grow date palms, and the fertile areas around Kasserine are the country's second major bread-basket, after the Medjerda Valley. Little grows in the harsher parts of the interior apart from thick clumps of esparto grass, which is used for making paper and household items such as baskets.

Central Tunisia has four major national parks including Chambi, where hyena, gazelle and a variety of birds can be seen as well as many species of plant.

Central Tunisia's watercourses often dry out, but during the rainy season they rapidly fill with water. Numerous dams are built to prevent flooding and to stop the waters from rising too rapidly. These also preserve much-needed fresh water. Temperatures in this part of the country are higher than in the Sahel.

Kairouan is the largest town of the central region. It has the country's most famous mosque and is also a centre for carpet making. Kairouan is followed by Le Kef, 45 km (28 miles) east of the Algerian border, which has always been an important political centre. During World War II it was the seat of government in areas liberated from German occupation.

Central Tunisia has some of the country's most important historic sites where ancient temples, theatres and baths from the period of the Roman Empire can be explored.

Berber women walking near Sbeïtla

◁ Interior of the Great Mosque in Kairouan

Exploring Central Tunisia

KAIROUAN IS CENTRAL TUNISIA's largest town and, along with Mecca, Medina and Jerusalem, one of Islam's four holy cities. Kairouan's original Great Mosque was the first of its kind to be built in North Africa. The fortress town of Le Kef, to the south, includes a mighty kasbah and the sanctuary of Sidi Bou Makhlouf. Situated towards the Algerian border are some magnificent rock formations, including an extraordinary mountain known as Jugurtha's Table. The Roman sites in this region are some of the most impressive in Tunisia. Dougga, for instance, is North Africa's best-preserved Roman town, while the ruins at Sbeïtla include ancient temples, baths and a theatre built in the 3rd century AD.

Interior of the mosque of Sidi Sahab in Kairouan

SEE ALSO

- **Where to Stay** pp264–5
- **Where to Eat** pp288–9

SIGHTS AT A GLANCE

Dougga pp228–9 **11**
Gafsa **1**
Haïdra **7**
Jebel Zaghouan **14**
Jugurtha's Table **8**
Kairouan pp232–41 **15**
Kasserine **6**
Le Kef **10**
Makthar **9**
Metlaoui **2**
Sbeïtla pp218–19 **5**
Sened **3**
Sidi Bouzid **4**
Thuburbo Majus **12**
Zaghouan **13**

Jendouba

Oued Tassa

Oued Mellegue

P17

LE KEF **10**

P5

P12

P12

Souk Ahras

DAHMANI ●

EL-KSOUR ●

P17

C79

8 JUGURTHA'S TABLE

C85

P4

● TALA

7 HAÏDRA

Tebessa

P17

Tebessa

JEBEL CHAMBI ▲

KASSERINE **6**

P17

P15

FURRIJANA ●

P15

C122

1 GAF

C79

Tamerza

0 km   25

0 miles   25

2 METLAOUI

P3

Tozeur

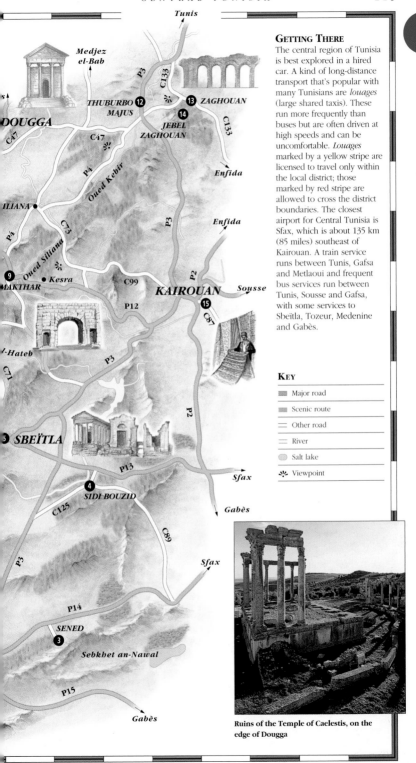

Tunis

Medjez
el-Bab

P5

C133

THUBURBO **12**
MAJUS

13 ZAGHOUAN

14

C133

JEBEL
ZAGHOUAN

DOUGGA

C47

C47

P4

Oued Kebir

Enfida

ILIANA

C75

P4

Enfida

P3

9
MAKTHAR

Kesra

Oued Siliana

C99

KAIROUAN

P2

Sousse

P12

15

C87

l-Hateb

C71

P3

SBEÏTLA **3**

P2

P13

Sfax

4
SIDI BOUZID

Gabès

C125

C89

P3

Sfax

P14

SENED

3

Sebkhet an-Nawal

P15

Gabès

GETTING THERE

The central region of Tunisia is best explored in a hired car. A kind of long-distance transport that's popular with many Tunisians are *louages* (large shared taxis). These run more frequently than buses but are often driven at high speeds and can be uncomfortable. *Louages* marked by a yellow stripe are licensed to travel only within the local district; those marked by red stripe are allowed to cross the district boundaries. The closest airport for Central Tunisia is Sfax, which is about 135 km (85 miles) southeast of Kairouan. A train service runs between Tunis, Gafsa and Metlaoui and frequent bus services run between Tunis, Sousse and Gafsa, with some services to Sbeïtla, Tozeur, Medenine and Gabès.

KEY

▦	Major road
▦	Scenic route
=	Other road
=	River
⬤	Salt lake
✳	Viewpoint

Ruins of the Temple of Caelestis, on the edge of Dougga

Gafsa

Road map B4. 93 km (58 miles) from Tozeur. 🏃 61,000. 🚌 🚆 🛈 ONTT: Place des Piscines Romaines, (76) 221 664. 🛒 Tue.

BUILT ROUND a large oasis on the border between the mountain and the desert, Gafsa is the main transport hub for the region. It isn't the most inspiring of Tunisia's towns but the surrounding area has vineyards, olive plantations and some striking scenery. Gafsa itself has a handful of attractions including restored palaces and some baths left behind by the Romans.

Gafsa has a long history. In the 2nd century BC this was a settlement belonging to the Kingdom of Numidia. Destroyed in 106 BC by the Roman commander Marius, it was subsequently rebuilt and turned into a garrison. Under the Emperor Trajan it acquired the status of a colony and became an important Roman town. It was destroyed in 680 in the course of an Arab raid but rebuilt by the Hafsids in the 15th century.

Situated at the southwest end of Avenue Habib Bourguiba are the **Roman Pools** (Piscines Romaines). These are two 4-m (13-ft) deep reservoirs, linked by a

The Roman Pools in Gafsa

tunnel and filled with water from a warm spring. Though it is not encouraged, the youth of Gafsa can often be seen diving in. Nearby is a small museum, which has some mosaics from Sousse.

The minaret attached to the Great Mosque dominates Gafsa's skyline. The mosque probably dates from the Aghlabid dynasty (9th–10th centuries), although a large section of the complex was

added in the 14th century. The prayer hall is decorated with blue ceramic tiles.

At the heart of Gafsa is Habib Bourguiba square, situated in the eastern part of the town. It contains a variety of shops, government offices and a pleasant small park.

When exploring the medina, it is worth stepping into **Dar Loungo**, a traditional 17th-century house, and **Dar el-Shariff**, which was built by a wealthy 18th-century landlord Haj Osman el-Shariff.

🏛 **Dar Loungo**
Adjacent to the National Museum of Gafsa.
◯ 8:30am–noon & 3–6pm Tue–Sun. ◉ Mon.

🏛 **Dar el-Shariff**
Rue Mohammad Khodouma.
◯ Oct–May: 8am–noon & 3–5pm; Jun–Sep: 8am–1pm.

Metlaoui ❷

Road map B5. 42 km (26 miles) southwest of Gafsa. 🏃 43,500. 🚌 🚆

METLAOUI IS Tunisia's main centre of phosphate mining. It was built by the French at the end of the 19th century and lies at the foot of the Tell Atlas.

The phosphate deposits were discovered in 1886 by Philippe Thomas, a veterinary surgeon in the French army and amateur palaeontologist. In 1896 a mining licence was granted to the Compagnie des Phosphates de Gafsa.

The main reason to come to Metlaoui is to climb aboard the **Lézard Rouge**, a narrow-gauge railway line, which was opened in 1899 by the Bey of Tunis. The train runs through the 15-km (9-mile) long Seldja Gorge and takes one and a half hours for the round trip. The carriages are early 20th century and are fitted with red leather seats. Tickets can be obtained from Metlaoui's main train station.

Lézard Rouge in the Seldja Gorge, near Metlaoui

Sened village, scenically located in a valley

Sened ❸

Road map C4.

THE EASIEST WAY of getting to Sened is from the modern Sened Gare hamlet, which once had a railway station. The village of Sened is tucked away among the hills of Jebel Biada (1,163 m/3,816 ft above sea level). Sened's houses are unusual in that they are built from stone with gypsum mortar – Berber houses are usually built with clay. After they have been harvested, red peppers are sometimes laid out to dry on flat roofs. This area has been inhabited for thousands of years and nearby caves were once the dwellings of prehistoric humans.

ENVIRONS: Some 30 km (19 miles) to the southwest of Sened and 18 km (11 miles) southeast of Gafsa is El-Guettar, a busy oasis town on the road from Gafsa to Gabès. A further 7 km (4 miles) to the southeast from Sened is the beautiful oasis of Lalla. During the 1880s the nomads of this region put up fierce resistance to the French army before escaping to the Turkish territory of Libya. It was several years before the nomads returned. As well as refreshments, the café just beyond the river provides a good view of the oasis.

Sidi Bouzid ❹

Road map C4. 🏠 112,000

IN SIDI BOUZID – a small district capital town – life passes slowly. Having a glass of mint tea, a *chicha* (hookah), or a game of cards are all long-drawn out activities. Much time is spent just talking. This is not surprising, since in the summer the scorching sun can raise the temperature to 45° C (113° F).

The centre of town has several modern buildings, which include offices, shops, a post office and a hotel. Most of the town buildings are single-storey, modest houses with solid doors.

Sidi Bouzid and the surrounding area played an important role during World War II. In late December 1942 and in the early part of 1943 Sidi Bouzid was the scene of fierce fighting between the British 8th Army led by General Montgomery, and the Afrika Korps, commanded by Field Marshal Rommel.

South of Sidi Bouzid, on the way to Gafsa, there are some old Berber settlements spread along the mountain range that runs from Gafsa to Sfax. Situated away from well-trodden paths, this region has some excellent hiking areas. Many of the villages are semi-deserted and can be reached only on foot or in a four-wheel-drive car.

THE DAKAR RALLY

In 1977 a French motorcyclist, Thierry Sabine, was taking part in the Abidjan-Nice motorcycle rally and lost his way. After wandering about for several days amid the sands of the Libyan Desert, he was miraculously found at the last moment. Thierry Sabine returned to France and decided to organize a rally that would provide its participants with a chance to challenge the forces of nature and their own limitations. He achieved his aim on 26 December the same year when drivers competing in the first staging of the event set off from Paris heading for Dakar. The rally was open to anyone who had a vehicle able to travel over the sands. The race still takes place and anybody who has suitable equipment may take part.

Racing in the Dakar Rally

Sbeïtla ❺

Arch of Diocletian, to the south of town

SBEÏTLA IS A MODERN TOWN 30 km (19 miles) east of Kasserine and is fringed with olive groves and arable fields. Close by is the site of the Roman town of Sufetula. Initially Sufetula had the status of a municipium (independent city) and later became a Roman colony. In the 3rd century Christians settled here; most of the local churches date from that period. The ruins are particularly well-preserved and include baths, a stunning forum and a capitol containing temples to Juno, Jupiter and Minerva.

The small baths are among several of their types in Sbeïtla.

★ St Vitalis Basilica
The church was built in the late 5th century on the site of a large villa. This five-aisle edifice is 50 m (164 ft) wide. One of its best-preserved sections is the baptistry with an oval basin decorated with mosaics.

STAR SIGHTS

★ **Capitol**

★ **Entrance to Forum**

★ **St Vitalis Basilica**

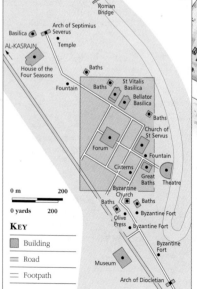

Roman Bridge
Basilica
Arch of Septimius Severus
AL-KASRAIN
Temple
House of the Four Seasons
Baths
Fountain
Baths
St Vitalis Basilica
Bellator Basilica
Baths
Church of St Servus
Forum
Fountain
Cisterns
Great Baths
Theatre
Byzantine Church
Baths
Baths
Olive Press
Byzantine Fort
Byzantine Fort
Byzantine Fort
Museum
Arch of Diocletian

0 m 200
0 yards 200

KEY

Building

Road

Footpath

0 m 50
0 yards 50

★ Capitol
The northwestern corner of the forum is occupied by the capitol consisting of three temples dedicated to Juno, Jupiter and Minerva. The forecourt of Jupiter's temple once had a speaker's podium (rostrum).

Bellator Basilica
The church was built in the early 4th century AD on the foundations of a Roman temple. Its name comes from an inscription found on the site

VISITORS' CHECKLIST

Road map B3, B4.
Sbeïtla–Kasserine road.
Rue du 2 Mars. **Ruins and museum:** ◯ 7am–7pm daily (summer); 8:30am–5:30pm (winter). 🖼 ⊙

★ Entrance to Forum
The forum is among the best-preserved in North Africa. The entrance to it was through the Arch of Antoninus Pius (AD 139) and led onto a paved area. During the Byzantine era it was surrounded by a 4-m (13-ft) high wall.

Church of St Servus
Recognizable by its four surviving pillars, this church was erected on the site of a pagan temple. It is likely that this was the cathedral of the Donatists who were active in the early 4th century (see p50). To the south are the Great Baths and an amphitheatre.

The cistern
was a tank intended for storing water, which would have fed the baths.

Vendors' Stalls
The remains of market stalls can be seen around the forum. Here, a variety of goods was sold, but mainly oil (the remains of an olive oil press are near to the fort). Equally well-preserved are pavement slabs that lead to the stalls.

The main square at the centre of Kasserine

Kasserine ❻

Road map B3. 120 km (75 miles) south of Le Kef. 🚂 🏍 *40,000.* 🚌 *Tue.*

KASSERINE LIES ON the central Tunisian upland, on the banks of the Oued el-Habeb. This is a major industrial town and transport hub. Since 1963 the town has produced cellulose and paper made from the local esparto grass. Kasserine was established by the Romans in

BATTLE OF KASSERINE

During World War II, on 18 January 1943, the German 21st Panzer division, supported by an air task force, broke through American positions at Kasserine, and advanced towards the Algerian border. US troops bore the brunt of the onslaught and it took a week of hard fighting and the arrival of British reinforcements to halt what proved to be one of the last German offensives in North Africa.

British tank in Kasserine

the 2nd century AD, and named Cillium. Following the fall of the Roman Empire it lost its status and remained an insignificant centre for local villages until it regained some of its lustre during the period of the French Protectorate. The French built a railway line and expanded the town. In its eastern section they erected a new colonial town, cut across by the long main street (Avenue Habib Bourguiba). Even today this area has most of the town's administrative buildings. It also contains the railway station (goods trains only), bus station and numerous shops. Ancient monuments, including a large mausoleum, are found on the other side of town (towards Gafsa).

A short way out of Kasserine, next to the Oued Derb, is the well-preserved **Mausoleum of the Flavii**. The walls of this triple-tiered monument are covered with a poetic inscription consisting of 110 lines; the middle section has Corinthian pilasters; above this is a niche that once housed a statue of Flavius. The whole structure was once covered with a triangular roof. In the western part of Kasserine, on the edge of the dry river bed, there is another mausoleum, which is now in ruins.

South of the town, to the left of the road leading to Gafsa, are the ruins of **Roman Cillium**, standing on top of a hill. Only a small section of the site has been unearthed. Its best-preserved

relic is a 3rd-century Triumphal Arch. Nearby are the foundations of a Christian basilica, tombs (which are carved in rock) and a small Byzantine fortress. The 1st-century theatre situated on the slope of the hill affords a magnificent view over the surrounding area.

ENVIRONS: About 15 km (9 miles) east of town is Tunisia's highest mountain, **Jebel Chambi** (1,554 m/ 5,098 ft). In 1981 this area was declared a national park. Halfway up the slope is a tourist information bureau and a small museum. From Kasserine the GP17 road leads to the village of Chambi.

A capital from the theatre ruins in Haïdra

Haïdra ❼

Road map B3. **Archaeological station** ☐ *daily.*

SITUATED CLOSE TO the Algerian border, Haïdra – formerly the Berber settlement of Ammaedara – was on the trade route that linked Hadrumetum (Sousse) with Carthage and Theveste (Tebessa) in Algeria. The Romans took control of it around AD 75 and established a camp here, which was used to station the famous Third Augustan Legion. Soldiers' graves can be seen beside the road.

An ancient road runs parallel to the modern one that leads to the site of the ruins. It is worth visiting the three-aisle **Basilica of the Martyrs** (5th–7th century).

Jugurtha's Table – a conspicuous flat rock jutting above the plain

The mosaics that once decorated the floor are now kept in Tunis's Bardo Museum. Standing to the northeast of the basilica is the **Arch of Septimius Severus** (AD 195) that was later included in the Byzantine citadel. This is the best-preserved Roman relic in Haïdra. On the other side of the road are the ruins of a late 3rd-century theatre, and further north are the remains of a basilica dating from Vandal times.

The best-known historic relic of Haïdra is the **Byzantine Fort** built during the reign of Justinian (527–565). This is the largest fortress to be found in any of the Maghreb countries. The north side of the fort was rebuilt in 1840; the south side was destroyed a few years ago by floods. At the centre of the fort are the remains of the Byzantine Chapel of the Citadel. To the north of the chapel are the ruins of the 4th-century Mellus Basilica, in which four tombs were discovered including that of Bishop Mellus; it is possible that the tomb of St Cyprian is also situated here.

Jugurtha's Table ❽

Road map B3

CLOSE TO THE SMALL town of Kalaat es-Senam, this flat-topped mountain rises abruptly out of the slightly undulating landscape that surrounds it. It owes its name to the Numidian king Jugurtha who held out against the Romans here between 112 and 105 BC. Numidia's kingdom was situated in what is now present-day Algeria and western Tunisia and competed with Carthage. In about 300 BC Numidia fell under the control of Carthage. The Numidian leader, Massinissa, supported Rome during the Second Punic War, which ensured a high degree of political freedom after the fall of Carthage. Massinissa's successor, Micipsa, continued with this policy. Following the death of Micipsa, however, Rome imposed Jugurtha (illegitimate grandson of Massinissa) as ruler.

The Arab name of the mountain (and also the nearby town) is Kalaat es-Senam or "Senam's Citadel", which originates from the chief of the bandits who used this mountain as his stronghold.

From Kasserine the GP17 road runs towards Tajerouine. Immediately past the mosque in Kalaat es-Senam, the road climbs up towards Aïn Senan. From there a narrow footpath leads to the top of Jugurtha's Table. The climb takes about an hour and a half. The trail leading up the side of the mountain is spectacular. Its last section (a 15-minute climb) is steep and requires the use of hands. Standing immediately before the summit is a gate built by the bandit chief. At the top, at 1,271 m (4,169 ft), are the ruins of a Byzantine fortress, some troglodyte caves and a tiny shrine containing the tomb of an Islamic holy man – Sidi Abd el-Juada. This is a popular local pilgrimage destination. The shrine is open to non-Muslims.

When setting out, be sure to take along plenty of drinking water (it is not possible to buy anything along the route). On reaching the summit, stop for a picnic and enjoy the view.

BERBER TATTOOS

Berber tattoos are often associated with magic. The first tattoo – *ayasha* (the one that protects life) – is introduced immediately after birth. It is cross-shaped and usually placed on the cheeks or forehead. Tattoos are used for protection, to ensure good luck and prosperity, and also as an adornment. They are also placed on wrists and the chest. Women like to sport *fula* (triangles) on their chins.

Tattooed Berber woman

Roman Baths with well-preserved floor mosaics

Makthar ❾

Road map B3. 114 km (71 miles) west of Kairouan. 🏛 19,600. 🚌 Mon.

MAKTHAR IS SITUATED between the steppes and the upland in Tunisia's second largest agricultural region (after the Medjerda Valley). It has splendid Roman remains, which are the most important in Tunisia along with Dougga and Bulla Regia.

In the 2nd century BC the small town of Makthar belonged to the Numidians, who built a fort here giving them control over local trade routes. Following the fall of Carthage in 146 BC many Punic refugees arrived here, as the town lay beyond the borders of Roman Africa. However, in 46 BC it was included in the province of a new Roman territory – Africa Nova. The Punic and Roman population coexisted peacefully. Romanization was a slow process that took some 200 years to accomplish. The numerous tomb steles (grave stones) and the tophets (sacrificial sites), preserved to this day, provide evidence of a considerable Punic influence.

In the 2nd century AD, during the reign of Emperor Trajan, the town was granted independent status, and under Marcus Aurelius it became a colony. The inhabitants were granted Roman citizenship and rights on a par with those enjoyed by the Romans. Makthar rapidly became the district's richest town, and maintained considerable

influence over the surrounding villages. During the Byzantine era the town was fortified, but following the Hilalian invasions in the 11th century it was destroyed.

A small **museum** houses a collection of tomb steles (1st–3rd century BC). Some of these bear Punic inscriptions and symbols (crescents, doves, grapes, peacocks and fish). The Roman era is represented by sculptures and architectural fragments; the Byzantine by bronzes, olive lamps and some 4th-century floor mosaics.

Christian stele tomb stone

Past the museum are the remains of a temple that has been converted into a basilica. A paved Roman road leads to the amphitheatre and to the triumphal arch. Erected in AD

116 to celebrate the town being granted the status of a municipium, Trajan's Arch overlooks the forum. Beyond it are the ruins of a basilica with a baptistry flanked by four columns. Here, too, is the tomb of Hildeguns – a 5th-century king of the Vandals. South of the Basilica of Hildeguns are the ruins of the Great Baths (2nd century).

A paved road running westwards from the Great Baths leads to the old forum. Slightly to the north is the temple of Bacchus (though only its crypt remains). To the right are the North Baths, which have some attractive floor mosaics. The road running past the Punic forum leads to the Schola Juvenus (AD 88). This was a kind of youth club where well-to-do children were taught how to be good Roman citizens.

Further on is the temple of Hathor Miskar (an Egyptian goddess of love) and the temple of Venus; immediately past this is the Roman forum, paved with white marble. Other interesting sights include the 1st-century AD Punic mausoleum, which was turned into a church in the 4th century and, next to the Great Baths, some Numidian tombs. At the very end of Makthar, beyond the **excavation site**, stands Bab el-Aïn – one of the town's oldest gates. Here, close to the stream, there once stood a tophet dedicated to Baal Hammon.

This ancient site was rediscovered in 1887 by Captain Bordier, a French officer, who founded a new town that now faces old Makthar across a ravine. Set at nearly 1,000 m (3,281 ft) above sea level, it is a spectacular spot.

🏛 **Excavation Site**
🏛 Mid-Sep–Mar: 8:30am –5:30pm daily; Apr–mid-Sep: 8am–7pm daily.

Ruins of Trajan's Arch dating from AD 116

◁ **Sun setting on the Roman ruins at Sufetula**

Roman Mosaics

Mosaics were a popular decorative element during Roman times. The mosaics would have been laid by travelling teams of artisans and were used to line the floors and walls of public baths and to adorn the façades of public buildings. Mosaics were composed of *tesserae* – tiny pieces of stone, marble or brick. From the 3rd century onwards, wealthy

Colourful mosaic featuring a bird

people began to use them to decorate their houses. Subjects were taken from everyday life, religion, agriculture and so on. Later on they began to feature images from mythology as well as floral and aquatic motifs. Favourite subjects included hunting and feasting and the seasons of the year. Games, held in amphitheatres, were also a popular subject.

Virgil and the Muses – *besides realistic scenes of everyday life, mosaics often featured images of well-known artists or rulers. Virgil was the favourite author of educated North Africans.*

Animals and plants *were frequent motifs of Roman mosaics. Craftsmen often used their own colour schemes.*

Geometric patterns *represented another style of mosaic art, which was developing along with a realistic trend. This ornamentation is typical of the later mosaics, found in Christian churches.*

Neptune's Triumph – *figurative mosaics from the Roman period used mainly mythological subjects and usually portrayed gods.*

Ulysses and the Sirens – *this mosaic (AD 260) comes from Dougga. It depicts the temptation of Ulysses, a scene from Greek mythology.*

Le Kef

Road map B2. 170 km (106 miles) southwest of Tunis; 42 km (26 miles) from the Algerian border. 🚶 *30,000.*
🚌 🚉 🚐 *Thu.*

L E KEF ("the rock" in Arabic) enjoys an exceptionally scenic location on the slopes of Jebel Dyr, close to the border with Algeria. The site was occupied early and both Neolithic tools and Numidian tombs have been found here. Following the First Punic War it fell to Carthage and was known as Sicca. Later, the Romans took over the town, naming it Sicca Veneria as a mark of respect to the goddess Venus. Most of the population fled as a result of a Vandal raid but the town was slowly rebuilt and captured by the Arabs in AD 688.

With the arrival of the Ottomans in the 16th century, the town became known as Le Kef. As a border area it was a subject of contention between Algeria and Tunisia and Le Kef was the first town occupied by the French in 1881. During World War II it was the seat of the Protectorate authorities, and in 1942 it was used as the provisional headquarters of liberated Tunisia.

A tour may be started from Place de l'Indépendance, where there is an old Roman spring, Ras el-Aïn, which once supplied some huge Roman cisterns to the north of town. An open-air café here is a favourite meeting point of the locals. Close by stands a small altar

Nomadic tent in the Regional Museum in Le Kef

dedicated to Lalla Ma – goddess of water. Rue de la Source leads to an early Roman bath complex. A walk uphill, along Rue Farhat Hached, leads to the Church of St Peter, also known as Dar el-Kousse. The church dates from the 4th century and contains a well-preserved apse. Early Christian symbols can be seen on the wall by the entrance.

The town's most interesting spot is Place Bou Makhlouf, where there is a kasbah and, at the top end, the Great Mosque, known now as the Basilica. This building no longer functions as a mosque and is used as a venue for cultural events.

Nearby is the Mosque of Sidi Bou Makhlouf, which is named after the patron saint of Le Kef. Next to this is a *zaouia* (tomb) where the saint is buried along with members of his family. Inside this mausoleum is a garden, the remains of mosaics and some steles. This 17th-century *zaouia* is an interesting sight, and features two domes and an octagonal minaret. Sidi Bou Makhlouf, founder of the sanctuary, was a Sufi master, and a disciple of El-Hadi Beness el-Mekhnessi

Cannon in the kasbah's courtyard

– a Moroccan Sufi and the originator of Aissaouia, a form of religious music. Members of the Aissaouia brotherhood used music as a means of entering into a trance. Religious meetings accompanied by Aissaouia music are held near the tomb of the master every Friday.

Close to the tomb is the complex of Sidi Ali ben Aissa (1784) and the headquarters of the Rahmania Brotherhood. Today, it houses the **Regional Museum of Popular Arts and Traditions**, which has a collection of traditional costumes including wedding gowns, as well as jewellery, Bedouin tents, everyday objects, textiles and ceramics.

Below the square stands the mausoleum of Ali Turki, which also contains the tomb of his second son, Husayn bin Ali, founder of the Husaynid dynasty (1704–1881).

Le Kef's kasbah contains two forts. The smaller of the two is 12th-century and was built on the site of a Byzantine fortress. The larger one was built in 1679 by Mohammed Bey. The tower provides a spectacular view over the surrounding area. The building now houses a museum and is used as a venue for cultural events.

🏛 **Regional Museum of Popular Arts and Traditions**
⏰ *Jul–mid-Sep: 9:30am–1pm; mid-Sep–Jun: 9:30am–4:30pm.* 📷

Zaouia of Sidi Bou Makhlouf

National Parks

THE PROCESS OF founding national parks in Tunisia began in the 1980s. These parks represent a wide range of landscapes. For bird-lovers a visit to Lake Ichkeul is a must. Those interested in botany should head for Boukornine, near Tunis, especially when the cyclamens are in bloom. The islands of Zembra and Zembretta are not only oases of peace and quiet, but also veritable laboratories of natural science. A long walk through Chambi National Park and a climb up Jebel Chambi, Tunisia's highest peak, provides an opportunity to see wild gazelle and hyena, as well as a variety of birdlife.

Antelope in Bou Hedma

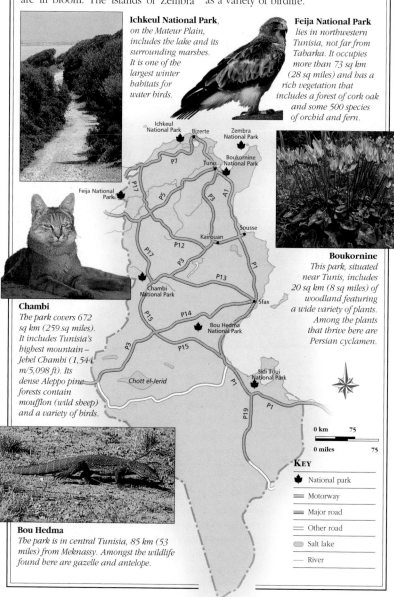

Ichkeul National Park, on the Mateur Plain, includes the lake and its surrounding marshes. It is one of the largest winter habitats for water birds.

Feija National Park lies in northwestern Tunisia, not far from Tabarka. It occupies more than 73 sq km (28 sq miles) and has a rich vegetation that includes a forest of cork oak and some 500 species of orchid and fern.

Ichkeul National Park
Bizerte
Zembra National Park
P7
Tunis
Boukornine National Park
Feija National Park
P17
P5
P3
A1
Kairouan
Sousse
P12
P17
P3
P1
P13
Chambi National Park
Sfax
P15
P14
P3
Bou Hedma National Park
P15
Chott el-Jerid
Sidi Toui National Park
P1
P19
P1

Boukornine
This park, situated near Tunis, includes 20 sq km (8 sq miles) of woodland featuring a wide variety of plants. Among the plants that thrive here are Persian cyclamen.

Chambi
The park covers 672 sq km (259 sq miles). It includes Tunisia's highest mountain – Jebel Chambi (1,544 m/5,098 ft). Its dense Aleppo pine forests contain moufflon (wild sheep) and a variety of birds.

0 km   75
0 miles   75

KEY

🍁 National park
▬ Motorway
▬ Major road
— Other road
⬭ Salt lake
— River

Bou Hedma
The park is in central Tunisia, 85 km (53 miles) from Meknassy. Amongst the wildlife found here are gazelle and antelope.

Dougga ⑪

Tympanum on Dougga's Capitol

STANDING HIGH ON THE SIDE of a valley Dougga is the best-preserved Roman city in North Africa. It was originally the seat of the Numidian king Massinissa, but was under Roman administration from the second century AD. It was accorded World Heritage Site status by UNESCO in 1997. Families continued to live among the ruins until they were relocated in the 1950s.

The forum was built in stages, between AD 14 and 34. It was flanked with columns made of red marble and crowned with Corinthian white-marble capitals.

★ Capitol
Built in AD 166, this is one of Tunisia's most impressive Roman monuments. The four front columns support the remaining fragments of the temple pediment, which features a statue of Antoninus Pius.

Dar el-Achab
Located below the forum, southwest of the Temple of Tellus, this dates from AD 164. It was probably originally a temple but is named after a family that once occupied the site.

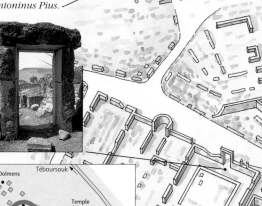

DOUGGA SITE MAP

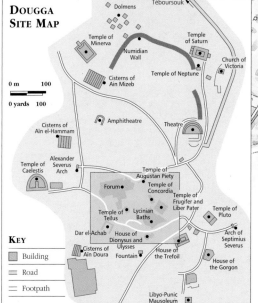

Téboursouk

Dolmens

Temple of Minerva

Numidian Wall

Temple of Saturn

Church of Victoria

Cisterns of Aïn Mizeb

Temple of Neptune

0 m 100
0 yards 100

Cisterns of Aïn el-Hammam

Amphitheatre

Theatre

Temple of Caelestis

Alexander Severus Arch

Temple of Augustan Piety

Temple of Concordia

Forum

Temple of Frugifer and Liber Pater

Temple of Pluto

Temple of Tellus

Lycinian Baths

Dar el-Achab

House of Dionysus and Ulysses

Cisterns of Aïn Doura

Fountain

House of the Trefoil

Arch of Septimius Severus

House of the Gorgon

Libyo-Punic Mausoleum

KEY
- Building
- Road
- Footpath

0 m 25
0 yards 25

STAR SIGHTS

★ Capitol

★ Lycinian Baths

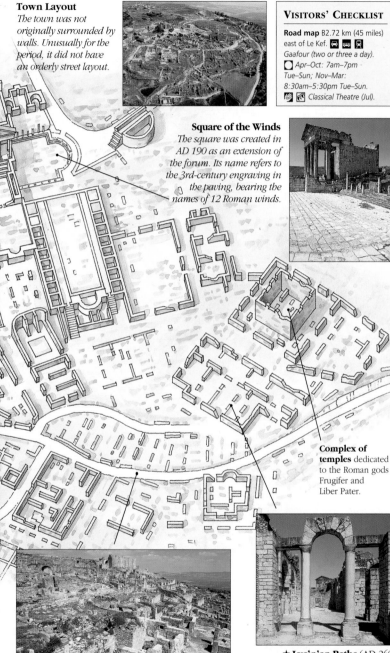

Town Layout
The town was not originally surrounded by walls. Unusually for the period, it did not have an orderly street layout.

Square of the Winds
The square was created in AD 190 as an extension of the forum. Its name refers to the 3rd-century engraving in the paving, bearing the names of 12 Roman winds.

Complex of temples dedicated to the Roman gods Frugifer and Liber Pater.

Roman Villas (3rd century AD)
The houses stand along a paved road. The most intact villas include the House of Dionysus and Ulysses, the House of the Trefoil and the House of the Seasons.

★ **Lycinian Baths** (AD 260)
Also known as the Winter Baths, this complex of cold and warm rooms and gymnasiums was richly decorated; the floors were covered in mosaics and the walls lined with marble.

Thuburbo Majus – one of the most scenic ancient ruins in Tunisia

Thuburbo Majus ⑫

Road map C2. 67 km (42 miles) west of Hammamet. ☐ *Apr–mid-Sep: 7am–7pm Tue–Sun; mid-Sep–Mar: 8:30am–5:30pm Tue–Sun.*

THUBURBO MAJUS lies in a beautiful valley surrounded by hills, and is – along with Dougga, Bulla Regia, Makthar and Sbeïtla – one of the most important Roman remains in Tunisia, with many impressive monuments. A café and toilet are at the entrance.

The Roman settlement was established in 27 BC, close to the Punic town. In AD 128, after a visit by the Emperor Hadrian, Thuburbo Majus was granted the independent status of a municipium, and later, in AD 188, it became a colony.

Located on the trading route between Sousse and Carthage, surrounded by fertile land, Thuburbo Majus grew rapidly. Most of the public buildings and homes decorated with mosaics date from the 2nd and 3rd centuries. In the 4th century some of the buildings were extended and the town's name was changed to Res Publica Felix Thuburbo Majus. However, the continuing conflicts

The colonnaded exercise yard

between Donatists and Catholics, Vandal raids and finally the Arab invasion led to the town's downfall.

On this site, immediately past the gate is the forum (each of its sides is 49 m/161 ft long), which is flanked on three sides by vast Corinthian columns. Its most important feature is the Capitol temple (one of the largest in Africa), which is dedicated to Jupiter, Juno and Minerva. Fragments of the 70-m (230-ft) statue of Jupiter are kept in the Bardo Museum, in Tunis *(see pp88–9)*. On the forum's southwestern side stands the Temple of Mercury (3rd century), which has eight column bases arranged in a circle. The southeastern side of the forum features a small temple and was once the site of the town's administrative buildings.

Beyond the forum, just to the right, are the Summer Baths. These occupy an area of 2.8 sq km (1.1 sq miles). They were once decorated with statues of Aesculapius, Hercules, Mercury and Venus and with exquisite mosaics that can now be seen in the Bardo Museum. The entrance led to the changing room; further on was the *frigidarium* with three pools, the *tepidarium* (the warm room), the *caldarium* (the steam baths) and the *sudatorium* (the sweat room). Adjacent to it was the Palaestra of the Petronii (AD 225), an exercise yard enclosed within Corinthian columns that is named after the rich family who funded it. The letters engraved on the pavement at the south end form the board of the "36 letters" game that was widely used to learn the alphabet. Higher up the hill are the Winter Baths, a well-preserved complex with a black-and-white mosaic floor.

The southern section of Thuburbo Majus contains a temple dedicated to Baal – the layout indicates Roman and Punic influence in equal measures. To the east of it stood the sanctuary of Caelestis, which was later converted into a three-aisle church. The Roman cellar became the baptistry and the forecourt of the temple was turned into a cemetery. Occasionally, a procession is held here in honour of St Perpetua, a saint who died a martyr's death at Carthage.

Zaghouan 🄱

Road map C2. 🏘 *10,000.*

ZAGHOUAN IS A charming little town that lies at the foot of Jebel Zaghouan (1,295 m/4,249 ft). During the time of Tunisia's Roman occupation the place was called Ziqua. Little remains from this period apart from the large triumphal arch standing in the main street. This street has a number of local restaurants and climbs upwards to a small square that is dominated by two minarets – one octagonal, one square. The square minaret was added to the church building that has been converted into mosque. A further climb along a narrow street to the left of the square leads to the tomb of the town's patron saint Sidi Ali Azouz (who is also venerated in Tunis). Zaghouan clearly displays Andalusian influences, following an influx of refugees in the 17th century – house windows are hung with light blue curtains and drinking fountains are decorated with mosaics.

Zaghouan is famous for the superb quality of its water and its mountain springs. It is worth taking a walk further out of town (about 1.5 km/1 mile), along the road leading through orchards and shaded

Ruins of the fountain in Zaghouan

by old trees towards the **Temple des Eaux**, a Roman fountain with 12 niches – one for each month of the year. The fountain was built in the 2nd century AD on the orders of Emperor Hadrian.

The small square hall of the fountain, framed by a portico, was built next to a spring (now, alas, dry). On the opposite side are water tanks in a figure of eight shape. This was the starting point of the 124-km (77-mile) long aqueduct that used to supply Carthage with fresh water. Its most famous sections are around the Oued Meliane, which runs along the P3 road.

Aqueduct for ancient Carthage

ENVIRONS: Some 35 km (22 miles) from Zaghouan is the spa resort of **Jebel Oust**, where the natural brine springs come out at 55° C

(131° F). The town has a small balneotherapy centre, which continues the traditions of the Roman hot baths. At the summit above Jebel Oust there is a temple devoted to Aesculapius and Hygeia, which in Christian times was turned into a church.

Jebel Zaghouan 🄲

Road map C2.

THIS CRAGGY MOUNTAIN is clearly visible behind the Temple des Eaux and its surrounding woodland. It appears to have been cut into halves. A little way up, above the fountain, is a resting point. Close to the summit, at 975 m (3,198 ft), is an excellent viewpoint and a TV transmitter. In ancient times this area was covered with cypress trees. The northern slopes of the hill are overgrown with Aleppo pine, breadfruit trees and wild olives. The scent of the pine trees blends with the fragrance of the sun-warmed meadows and rosemary. From 600 m (1,969 ft) up, green oak and turpentine trees can be seen. Maple and cherry trees become more numerous nearer the top. A hike around this area is an opportunity to admire some lovely scenery, savour exquisite scents and get away from the bustle of the tourist centres.

The mountain is rich in birdlife, especially birds of prey. Birdwatchers may be able to spot the king eagle and the Bonelli eagle, as well as vultures and falcons.

The green slopes of Jebel Zaghouan

Bir Barout

drawn by
the whee
Some bel
was foun
and that i
Mecca. T
have spe
anyone v
certain to
one day.

☐ Souk
Kairouar
the best-
The cen
once ad
Mosque
the Hafs
that is n
souks (
streets i
worksho

KA
Ave
Bir
Mec
Mo
T
Sou
Zac
S

0 m

0 y

K

Kairo...

KAIROU...
who...
goblet i...
Mecca...
from the...
Mosque...
pilgrima...
interest...
UNESC...

Ceram...

Expl...
Visito...
welco...
vast ...
entra...
surro...
walls...
throu...
The ...
Tuni...
The...
Nov...
Ali ...
of E...
tom...
littl...

The Great Mosque

A column-crowning capital

KAIROUAN'S GREAT MOSQUE, in the centre of the medina, is also known as the Mosque of Sidi Oqba after the city's founder. The original mosque was built in AD 670 but was completely destroyed. Most of what exists today dates from the 9th century, though it has been remodelled many times since then. This is one of the oldest (and largest) places of prayer in the Islamic world and the fourth most important pilgrimage destination after Mecca, Medina and Jerusalem. According to Muslims, seven visits here are equivalent to one visit to Mecca.

Capitals
Most of the column stems and their capitals were taken from other buildings, both pagan and Christian. Some, however, were produced by local craftsmen.

★ **Minaret**
The base of this minaret was built between 724 and 728 and is one of the oldest surviving structures of its kind. It set the pattern for all minarets in this part of the Islamic world. The remainder of the 35-m (115-ft) high minaret is 9th-century and towers over the mosque's vast courtyard. Stairs with 129 steps lead to the top floor.

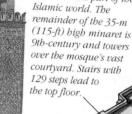

Well-heads are used to draw water from the cisterns, which is used for ritual ablutions.

The sundial in the courtyard marks the hours of prayer.

Cistern
The courtyard slopes towards the centre to deliver rainwater into a cistern below. The intricate decorations covering the hole are designed to filter out impurities before the water reaches the well.

Entrance to the Courtyard
The wall surrounding the courtyard has six gates. The main entrance is through a gate crowned with a dome.

M...
<...

Arcades
The cloisters skirt the courtyard on three sides, forming long aisles that cast a shadow and provide shelter from the sun.

Mihrab Dome
This dome marks the position of the mihrab, which points in the direction of Mecca. It has richer decorations than the mosque's other domes.

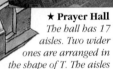

★ Prayer Hall
The hall has 17 aisles. Two wider ones are arranged in the shape of T. The aisles are separated from each other by rows of columns.

Pulpit – made of teak, this was produced around AD 863, on the orders of the Aghlabid Emir, Abu Ibrahim.

Entrance to the Mosque
There are two entrances to the mosque from the street, both leading through dome-crowned gates. One is on the southeastern side, the other on the southwestern.

Decorations
The mosque's floral motifs are inspired by ancient Hellenic traditions. The geometric patterns come mainly from early Christian and Berber designs.

STAR SIGHTS

★ **Minaret**

★ **Prayer Hall**

Pool in the courtyard of Kairouan's former kasbah

♣ Kasbah

Avenue ibn el-Jazzar.

Built into the northwestern walls of the medina, the kasbah formed part of Kairouan's defensive system. Its high walls and small windows are characteristic of this type of structure. Today, the kasbah houses a hotel. A heated pool is in the central courtyard, while a café is in the former prison.

⌗ Zaouia of Sidi Abdel Qadir el-Djilani

Rue de la Kasbah.

This architectural complex is devoted to Abdel Qadir el-Djilani – the founder of the Sufi Qadiriyya group, one of Islam's most popular spiritual groups or *tariqas* (literally spiritual "ways"). The main site of the cult is the Sidi Abdel Qadir mausoleum in Baghdad. *Zaouias* devoted to el-Qadiriyya are also found elsewhere in the Muslim world. Sufis emphasise meditation and recital of the holy text.

ENVIRONS: Some 9 km (6 miles) south of Kairouan is **Reqqada**, which contains the ruins of a former Aghlabid palace. Along with Mahdia and Abbasiya, this was one of the four Tunisian capitals. In AD 876 the Aghlabid prince, Ibrahim II, built a magnificent residence – Qasr el-Fath (the Victory Palace) – on the outskirts of Kairouan which was soon turned into a luxury summer residence. Soon

afterwards, other similar palaces were built elsewhere in the country. The building materials used, including brick and timber, were typical of the region. The ornamental motifs were mainly floral and geometric. As well as palaces, Reqqada also contains the remains of Aghlabid baths and *fondouks* (inns).

The **National Museum of Islamic Art** occupies a former presidential palace at Reqqada. It displays objects found in the palace, as well as items from other parts of the country. A special exhibition is devoted to exhibits from Sabra – a palace just outside Kairouan that was built by Caliph el-Mansour in the mid-10th century. The entrance hall to the museum has a model of Kairouan's Great Mosque and a reproduction of its mihrab (niche indicating the direction of prayer). Other rooms house a collection of Fatimid and Zirid coins, some 10th-century inscriptions from

Ancient coin from Reqqada's museum

the Koran and examples of 9th-century ceramics.

The nearby village of **Sidi Ali ben Nasrallach** is inhabited by semi-nomadic tribes and stages "Fantasia", a spectacular horse-riding show, in September.

About 60 km (37 miles) northwest of Kairouan is **Ksar Lemsa**, a 6th-century Byzantine fortress, which once guarded routes into the fertile Tell region. A few kilometres further on is the Berber village of **La Kesra** and a huge forest of Aleppo pine. Some 36 km (22 miles) west of Kairouan is the village of **Haffouz**, which has a war cemetery for Muslim soldiers who served in the French army. A short way further on, close to Oued Cherichera, are the remains of the **aqueduct** that once supplied Kairouan with water.

⌂ National Museum of Islamic Art

ℂ *(77) 323 337.* ⬤ *9:30am–4:30pm Tue–Sun.*

Entrance to the Zaouia of Sidi Abdel Qadir, close to the Great Mosque

Kairouan's Carpets

CARPET WEAVING in Kairouan goes back hundreds of years. It is said that the carpets produced here were so precious that the Aghlabid princes paid their taxes in them to the Abbasid Caliphs. Two main types of carpet are made in Kairouan – knotted and

A carpet of Berber design

woven. Woven carpets tend to be cheaper. In the 19th century a loop stitch was introduced. Camilla, daughter of the town's Turkish governor, is said to have taught this to the locals. This type of carpet features mainly red, blue and green colours and geometric patterns.

More than 4,000 women in Kairouan are employed to weave carpets (men stick to selling) and work mainly from home. At one time, brightly coloured carpets were the main part of a bridal dowry.

Buying a carpet *is a ritual, and many people visit the ONAT Museum (see p237) for advice. Visitors can also buy carpets with certificates of authenticity here.*

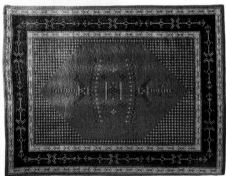

Mergoum, *or woven carpets* *are of Berber origin. This type of carpet has brighter colours and a purely geometric pattern; it is also much lighter in weight and is further decorated with embroidery.*

Carpets *sold by street vendors are predominantly of beige, white and black colouring. They are decorated with geometric patterns and floral motifs.*

The basic knot *used in Kairouan carpets is of Turkish origin. The value of a carpet depends on the number of knots per square metre, the quality of material and the weaving technique. Silk carpets can have as many as 500,000 knots per square metre.*

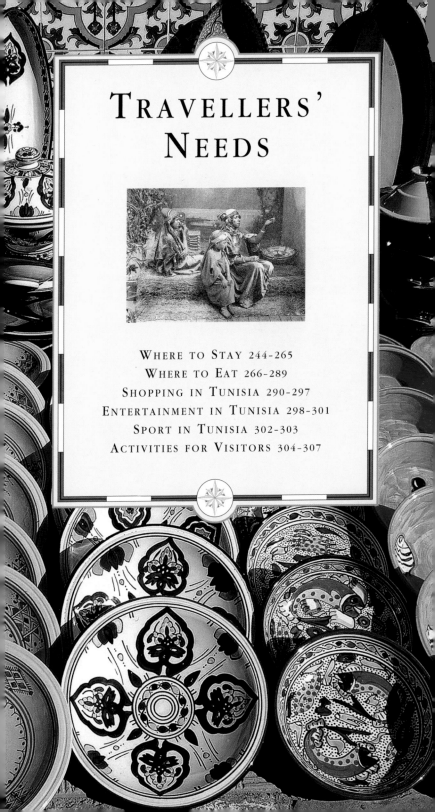

TRAVELLERS' NEEDS

WHERE TO STAY 244-265
WHERE TO EAT 266-289
SHOPPING IN TUNISIA 290-297
ENTERTAINMENT IN TUNISIA 298-301
SPORT IN TUNISIA 302-303
ACTIVITIES FOR VISITORS 304-307

WHERE TO STAY

TUNISIAN HOTELS ARE mostly of a good standard and even the more basic ones are generally perfectly clean and comfortable. Independent travellers may like to consider staying in well-kept, small family hotels that are located in old mansions or in one of the former *fondouks* (inns for travelling merchants). When visiting Berber villages it is possible to stay in a troglodyte home, as

A hotel porter in Monastir

many have been converted into small hotels. Most hotels in tourist resorts are set in scenic surroundings. Many offer extensive recreational facilities and have modern decor. Some can dazzle visitors with their exotic splendour. Hotels situated away from the main resorts are more modest. Many are aimed at Tunisian holidaymakers and do not provide the same facilities, such as nightly entertainment.

Hotel lobby in Kairouan

TYPES OF HOTEL

THE CHOICE OF hotel in Tunisia is dictated not only by its price but depends also on whether the hotel caters mainly for independent travellers or the package holiday market. As with almost everywhere in the world, a package holiday is usually a less expensive option but will not always provide the most interesting accommodation.

All hotels in tourist resorts, from three-star upwards, will have a swimming pool but in towns even a five-star hotel may not have a pool.

The choice of where to stay includes ancient *fondouks* (inns) and former palaces, troglodyte homes and Bedouin tents pitched at an oasis.

Another category is the so-called "hôtels de charme". These independently-run upmarket establishments generally have a small number of rooms and offer chic accommodation. Many distinguish themselves with stylistic flourishes such as minimalistic "designer" decor or original artwork by Tunisian artists on display in the rooms.

When checking into a less expensive hotel, particularly in the summer, check if the room is air-conditioned. At

the very least, it should have a fan and the use of a bathroom. If there is a hotel restaurant, ask for a room well away from the kitchen or dining area to avoid the potential bouquet of smells.

HOTEL CATEGORIES

HOTELS IN TUNISIA can be divided into three categories: the non-classified (NC), the classified (from one to five stars) and those classified within holiday resorts. The latter are far superior to their urban equivalents in terms of standards, comfort and recreational facilities. In addition, they usually offer a beautiful location.

One- and two-star hotels are sometimes situated in older buildings which reflect earlier colonial times. Sometimes, they are tucked away in the alleyways of ancient medinas. Most rooms have en suite bathrooms or hot showers. Three-star hotels are mostly aimed at package holidaymakers. Four- and

Hotels surrounding the harbour in Port el-Kantaoui

◁ **Colourful ceramics from Nabeul**

Swimming pool in one of Tunisia's tourist zones

five-star establishments uphold international standards and cater also for business travellers. In tourist resorts these upmarket hotels will usually have much larger rooms than the ones offered by their town equivalents, while their decor is more likely to be inspired by local designs and traditional architecture.

HOTEL CHAINS

THE MAIN hotel chain in Tunisia is Abou Nawas. It runs some good four- and five-star hotels located in many of the towns and tourist resorts. El-Mouradi is another major chain which has very good four- and five-star hotels. Several other international hotel chains operate in Tunisia, specializing in seaside holidays. These include Riu, Club Méditerranée and the Golden Tulip chain.

PRICES

PRICES CHARGED BY four- and five-star hotels are determined by the Ministry of Tourism. They depend on the time of year, the location and the overall standard. An extra surcharge may be made for a room with a sea view. In the higher category hotels the price often includes breakfast. This however is not a hard and fast rule, so check in advance. Prices charged by lower category hotels generally remain the same all year round.

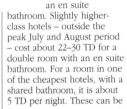

HOTEL CLASSE DE TOURISME

Plaque of a "tourist-class" hotel

Five-star hotels in towns charge about 160–230 TD per night for a double room. Ask about any special offers as there is often a substantial discount for a longer stay or an out-of-season visit.

Three-star hotels and those catering mainly for tourists offer a wide range of prices. The price of a single or double room varies between 50–75 and 100–120 TD per night, respectively. One- or two-star hotels are cheaper and cost between 40–70 TD per night. Small and non-classified hotels cost around 10–15 TD per night for a double room with an en suite bathroom. Slightly higher-class hotels – outside the peak July and August period – cost about 22–30 TD for a double room with an en suite bathroom. For a room in one of the cheapest hotels, with a shared bathroom, it is about 5 TD per night. These can be found in many parts of Tunisia, including Tunis's medina. During the peak holiday time, however, it can be difficult to find accommodation in Tunis for under 30 TD. For example, a double room in a two-star seaside hotel, with half-board, will cost about 45–50 TD during the peak season. Accommodation in a four-star hotel during peak times will be about 145 TD.

BOOKING

TUNISIA HAS A large number of hotels, particularly in the resorts, so generally speaking there is no problem securing accommodation. The best way to book a hotel room on arrival is by going to the ONTT airport desk.

In expensive hotels, even in Tunis, booking is usually not required as they always have plenty of rooms available even in high season. The situation is somewhat different with the many medium-category hotels and "hôtels de charme", where there is often a shortage of rooms.

Other than through a travel agent, the best way to book a hotel room before arriving in the country is on the Internet. However, this will involve making a credit card payment for at least one night. Booking by fax may not guarantee a room.

Booking a room in a less expensive hotel is best done by telephone. Things can go awry, however, and this method does not absolutely guarantee a room.

Rooftops among the palm trees in the tourist zone, Aghir

TOURIST ZONES

A TOURIST ZONE *(zone touristique)* is a purpose-built holiday town. The main advantages of such zones include their close proximity to entertainment, lush green surroundings and direct access to the sea and beach. Tourist zone hotels are generally of a higher standard than city hotels. Standards of behaviour are also more relaxed and visitors may act much more freely than in towns or the countryside. Nobody will raise an eyebrow at scantily dressed visitors walking in the streets, or at women going topless on the beach.

Tourist zones tend to be quieter than towns. Their location may, however, disappoint those who put sightseeing above time spent under a beach umbrella because they are rarely close to the major sights. A definite disadvantage of tourist zones is their lack of local cafés and restaurants serving traditional Tunisian cuisine. Prices in tourist zones are generally much higher than in town.

YOUTH HOSTELS

T UNISIA OFFERS A choice of two types of youth hostels: the **auberges de jeunesse** and the **maisons des jeunes**. Try to find the former because they are usually located in historic buildings such as *fondouks* (inns) or

Fairytale shapes of a tourist-zone hotel near Hammamet

palaces. The rooms, often arranged around flower-filled courtyards, differ in terms of size and furnishings. They are usually quite simple with just a bed, a wardrobe and a small table, but they are very clean. The staff contribute to a very pleasant atmosphere though the regulations and rules can be fairly strict (many hostels close at 10pm and allow a maximum stay of three nights). This type of hostel includes the charming *auberge de jeunesse* on Jerba, where small cushions embroidered with roses are placed on each bed. The hostels are also very popular with Tunisians.

The *maisons des jeunes*, on the other hand, are part of a charmless, government-run organization which in high season usually occupy schools or colleges. A major disadvantage of these hostels is their poor location, well away from town centres. A big plus is the fact that they can be found in almost every town. Many of them have small kitchens, which can be used for a small additional fee. Both types of hostel give preference to members of the International Youth Hostel Association. A night in a two- or three-bed room costs about 3–4 TD. Breakfast will cost 1 TD; the remaining meals about 3 TD.

The country's southern regions feature *marhalas*, which are slightly more expensive than the typical youth hostels found elsewhere. These are excellent places for a low-budget overnight stay and are hospitable, well-equipped and serve traditional food.

CAMP SITES

T HERE ARE FEW camp sites in Tunisia and their standard is very low. With the permission of the landowner or the local authorities a tent may be pitched on private or public land, or on a site belonging to a youth hostel. There are camp sites in Remel Plage, near Bizerte, in Hammamet (Ideal Camping), Nabeul (Les Jasmines), Sousse (Green Pub), Tozeur (Le Belvedere), Douz (Paradis), Zarzis (Sonia Camping 'n' Caravanning) and on Jerba, by the Sidi Slim Hotel. When travelling in the south of the country, it is possible to sleep in a Bedouin tent for a small fee.

DISABLED PERSONS

M OST TUNISIAN HOTELS are not accessible to wheelchairs. Modern hotels such as El-Hana Beach and Marhaba Beach in Sousse are rare exceptions. Information on facilities for the disabled can be obtained from the **Association Générale des Insuffisants Moteurs**, the main organization for people with impaired mobility in Tunisia.

Swimming pool of a hotel in Hammamet

CHILDREN

Tunisians love children and are eager to cater for their needs and wants. When planning a holiday with children ask the travel agent about hotels that offer specific entertainment for families. All tourist zone hotels will have highchairs for infants and serve special menus. They should also be able to provide a cot, though few hotels provide dedicated baby-changing rooms. Baby food, disposable nappies and food supplements can be obtained in local shops.

Most hotels offer discounts of between 30 to 40 per cent for children aged under 10.

The major resort hotels usually have well-maintained playgrounds and shallow paddling pools. The safest beaches for small children are on Jerba and in Hammamet.

Sunset over the swimming pool of a hotel in Tamerza

HOTEL ENTERTAINMENT

Most tourist zone hotels put on entertainment for their guests including social evenings, competitions and themed parties, which enable visitors to get to know the other hotel guests – this can be especially useful for those travelling with children.

However, for visitors who simply wish to relax quietly an evening's entertainment may be unwelcome. Loud music from the hotel dance floor or the amplified voice of an enthusiastic compere can penetrate even into a tightly shut room. Most entertainment programmes are run in hotels aimed at families with children; in five-star hotels the entertainment is lower key or at least avoidable.

Some hotels host evenings of cultural entertainment. This may consist of a folk show, for instance, or belly dancing or traditional *malouf* music, with the chance to try a *chicha* (hookah) in one of the hotel cafés. The larger hotels also organize excursions to some of Tunisia's most interesting sights. An additional fee is usually required for these trips.

The main pavilion of the Hammam Bourguiba resort

Choosing a Hotel

HOTELS OF VARIOUS PRICE CATEGORIES have been chosen on the grounds of their location, standard and good value. The chart below first lists hotels in Tunis, and this is followed by a list of places to stay in the rest of Tunisia. Within each region, hotels are listed in alphabetical order according to their price. Colour-coded thumb tabs correspond to the regions in this guide.

	NUMBER OF BEDS	RESTAURANT	GARDEN OR TERRACE	SWIMMING POOL	AIR CONDITIONING
TUNIS					
TUNIS: *Agriculture* ⑩ Rue Charles de Gaulle 25. 【 (71) 326 394. A comfortable hotel in the town centre, close to the medina. 📺 💇 24	57	●			■
TUNIS: *Auberge de Jeunesse* ⑩ Rue Saida Ajoula 25. 【 (71) 567 850. This medina hotel is easy to find – clear signs point the way to it from Rue de la Kasbah. The dormitory rooms are clean but are available only to Hostelling International members. Guests can stay no longer than three days.	70	●			
TUNIS: *Salammbô* ⑩ Rue de Gréce 6. 【 (71) 334 25. 📠 (71) 337 498. The service at this charming little hotel is friendly. Its location is convenient, being relatively close to the medina and the railway station. 💇 24	105	●			
TUNIS: *El-Baby* ⑩⑩ Avenue H. Bourguiba 14. 【 (71) 330 277. 📠 (71) 330 425. Located in the town centre, about 20 minutes walk away from the medina, this hotel is in an historic building and has attractive rooms. 24	124	●			■
TUNIS: *La Maison Dorée* ⑩⑩ Rue de Hollande 6 bis. 【 (71) 240 632. 📠 (71) 332 401. Close to Place Barcelone, this very pleasant hotel is run by a French family. 24	93	●			■
TUNIS: *Le Belvedere* ⑩⑩ Avenue des Etats Unis 10. 【 (71) 783 133. 📠 (71) 782 214. The hotel is situated a little way from the town centre. 🖃 P 📺 💇 🛁 💇 24	136	●			■
TUNIS: *Majestic* ⑩⑩ Avenue de Paris 36. 【 (71) 332 666. 📠 (71) 336 908. @ res@majestichotel.com.tn Ⓦ www.majestichotel.com.tn Built in 1911, this is one of the oldest hotels in Tunis. Its beautiful white façade is typical of the Art Nouveau style. The terrace and restaurant are situated on the first floor. The interior is gradually being refurbished. 📺 💇 24	44	●	■		
TUNIS: *Omrane* ⑩⑩ Avenue Farhat Hached 65. 【 (71) 345 277. 📠 (71) 354 892. @ hotelomrane@planet.tn Not far from Rue de Yougoslavie, Hôtel Omrane offers good-size rooms and is convenient for the TGM train to Carthage and Sidi Bou Saïd. 📺 24	178				■
TUNIS: *Transatlantique* ⑩⑩ Rue de Yougoslavie 106. 【 (71) 240 680. 📠 (71) 334 319. This comfortable hotel is located in an Art Nouveau building close to the medina. It has a pleasant atmosphere and friendly service. 📺 24	83	●			
TUNIS: *Carlton* ⑩⑩⑩ Avenue H. Bourguiba 31. 【 (71) 330 644. 📠 (71) 338 168. @ carlton@planet.tn Ten minutes from the medina, this hotel is in a lovely Art Nouveau building. Advance booking is necessary during the peak season. 💇	122	●			■
TUNIS: *Golf Royal* ⑩⑩⑩ Rue de Yougoslavie 51/53. 【 (71) 344 311. 📠 (71) 348 155. Set in an attractive Art Nouveau building, the rooms of this hotel are modest in terms of size and some are rather dark. Several shops are nearby. 📺	108	●			■
TUNIS: *Le Diplomat* ⑩⑩⑩ Avenue Hedi Chaker 44. 【 (71) 785 233. 📠 (71) 781 694. @ diplomat.hotel@planet.tn This popular hotel is convenient for the town centre. 24	346	●			■

		Price categories

Price categories for a standard double room, with bath or shower, including service and tax. Prices are in Tunisian dinars.
TD below 30 TD
TD TD 30–65 TD
TD TD TD 65–100 TD
TD TD TD TD 100–150 TD
TD TD TD TD TD over 150 TD

RESTAURANT
This is also open to non-residents.

GARDEN OR TERRACE
Hotel has its own garden, a terrace or a courtyard with plants.

SWIMMING POOL
Hotel has a pool for the use of its guests.

AIR CONDITIONING
All rooms are air-conditioned.

Hotel	Price	Number of Beds	Restaurant	Garden or Terrace	Swimming Pool	Air Conditioning
TUNIS: Oscar's Hotel Rue de Marseille 12/14. (71) 344 755. FAX (71) 354 311. This centrally-located hotel is convenient for the railway station. [TV] [24]	TD TD TD	95				■
TUNIS: Yadis ibn Khaldoun Rue du Kuwait 30. (71) 832 211. FAX (71) 831 689. @ yadis.hotels@planet.tn Situated in the Belvedere Park district, this hotel has numerous shops and the attractions of Ville Nouvelle close by. [TV] [24]	TD TD TD	271	●			■
TUNIS: Acropole Les Berges du Lac. (71) 750 630. FAX (71) 960 490. A modern hotel, the Acropole is located a fair distance from the centre of Tunis, making it quiet. All rooms have en suite bathrooms.	TD TD TD TD	188	●			■
TUNIS: El-Hana International Avenue H. Bourguiba 49. (71) 331 144. FAX (71) 341 199. @ inter.elhana@planet.tn This large hotel is in the modern part of the city, well away from the bustle of the medina. It has a certain charm, though some of its rooms are in need of refurbishment. [TV] [Y] [↻] [24]	TD TD TD	456	●			■
TUNIS: Grand Hôtel du Lac Rue Sindbad 2. (71) 336 100. FAX (71) 342 759. @ hotel.lac@planet.tn A little way from Avenue Habib Bourguiba, this hotel's architecture resembles an upturned pyramid. The comfortable rooms are of a reasonable size though some are perhaps in need of refurbishment. [TV] [↻] [24]	TD TD TD TD	388	●			■
TUNIS: La Maison Blanche Avenue Mohamed V 45. (71) 849 849. FAX (71) 793 842. This elegant hotel is part of the Best Western chain and enjoys a magnificent location some distance away from the town centre and the medina. The hotel has a pleasant bar that is also open to non-residents. This is one of the few luxury hotels in Tunis, so it is necessary to book well in advance. [symbols]	TD TD TD TD	96	●	■		■
TUNIS: Les Ambassadeurs Avenue Taieb Mehiri 75. (71) 846 000. FAX (71) 780 042. @ lesambassadeurs@gnet.tn This modest hotel, situated not far from Belvedere Park, represents good value for money. [P] [↻] [symbol] [24]	TD TD TD	276	●			■
TUNIS: Abou Nawas el-Mechtel Avenue Ouled Haffouz. (71) 783 200. FAX (71) 784 758. @ elmechTel@abounawas.com.tn [W] www.abounawas.com.tn This huge hotel boasts one of Tunis's better nightclubs and is popular with business travellers. The rooms are comfortable, if a little ordinary, but the facilities are excellent and include restaurants, bars and an open-air swimming pool. [symbols]	TD TD TD TD TD	998	●	■	●	■
TUNIS: Abou Nawas Tunis Avenue Mohamed V. (71) 350 355. FAX (71) 354 986. @ tunis@abounawas.com.tn. [W] www.abounawas.com.tn This large, elegant but somewhat characterless hotel is popular with business people. The rooms overlook the town and the Gulf of Tunis. [symbols]	TD TD TD TD TD	538	●	■	●	■
TUNIS: Africa el-Mouradi Avenue Bourguiba 50. (71) 347 477. FAX (71) 347 432. @ info.africa@elmouradi.com This recently refurbished hotel has good-sized rooms with en suite bathrooms and is one of the most pleasant hotels in Tunis. There are several restaurants and the service is friendly and efficient. One entire floor is reserved for non-smokers. [symbols]	TD TD TD TD TD	328	●		●	■

<table>
<tr><td>

Price categories for a standard double room, with bath or shower, including service and tax. Prices are in Tunisian dinars.
ⓉⒹ below 30 TD
ⓉⒹ ⓉⒹ 30–65 TD
ⓉⒹ ⓉⒹ ⓉⒹ 65–100 TD
ⓉⒹ ⓉⒹ ⓉⒹ ⓉⒹ 100–150 TD
ⓉⒹ ⓉⒹ ⓉⒹ ⓉⒹ ⓉⒹ over 150 TD

</td><td>

RESTAURANT
This is also open to non-residents.

GARDEN OR TERRACE
Hotel has its own garden, a terrace or a courtyard with plants.

SWIMMING POOL
Hotel has a pool for the use of its guests.

AIR CONDITIONING
All rooms are air-conditioned.

</td></tr>
</table>

	NUMBER OF BEDS	RESTAURANT	GARDEN OR TERRACE	SWIMMING POOL	AIR CONDITIONING
TUNIS: *Sheraton Tunis Hotel and Towers* ⓉⒹⓉⒹⓉⒹⓉⒹ Avenue Ligue Arabe Notre Dame. 🄲 *(71) 782 100.* FAX *(71) 782 208* W www.starwood.com/sheraton Located in the business and diplomatic district, this hotel overlooks the entire city of Tunis. All rooms have balconies with either garden or city views. Its pool is open to non-residents. TV 🍸 🎿 🛇 📺	273	●	■	●	■

GREATER TUNIS AND CAP BON PENINSULA

	NUMBER OF BEDS	RESTAURANT	GARDEN OR TERRACE	SWIMMING POOL	AIR CONDITIONING
CARTHAGE: *Amilcar* ⓉⒹⓉⒹⓉⒹ Tourist zone, Amilcar/Carthage. **Road map** C1. 🄲 *(71) 740 788.* FAX *(71) 743 139.* A large hotel with spacious, attractive rooms, the Amilcar has a freshwater swimming pool set in a well-tended garden. Other facilities include a paddling pool, a sunbathing terrace, a barbecue and a poolside bar. TV 🎿 🍸 📺 24 🏃	506	●	■	●	■
EL-HAOUARIA: *Dar Toubib* ⓉⒹ Route des Grottes. **Road map** D1. 🄲 *(72) 297 163.* This hotel's small rooms are compensated for by the price. TV 24	64	●			
EL-HAOUARIA: *Les Grottes* ⓉⒹ Route des Grottes. **Road map** D1. 🄲 *(72) 297 296.* FAX *(72) 269 070.* Situated along the road that leads to the caves, this hotel resembles a Disney-style castle. From some of the rooms there are fine views of the sunset over Zembretta island. TV 24	62	●			
EL-HAOUARIA: *Epervier* ⓉⒹⓉⒹ **Road map** D1. 🄲 *(72) 297 017.* FAX *(72) 297 258.* This modest, modern two-star hotel is situated on the main street of this small town and is handy for all the nearby amenities. The hotel's restaurant has a good reputation.	28	●			■
GAMMARTH: *Cap Carthage* ⓉⒹⓉⒹⓉⒹ Chott el-Ghaba – Gammarth. **Road map** C1. 🄲 *(71) 911 980.* FAX *(71) 911 064.* @ cap.carthage@planet.tn This modern hotel complex, not far from Tunis, has large rooms and the full range of facilities (including tennis courts). 🎿 TV 🎿 🍸 🔼 🛇 📺 24 🏃	760	●	■	●	■
GAMMARTH: *Coralia Club Acqua Viva* ⓉⒹⓉⒹⓉⒹⓉⒹ L- Raoued-Gammarth 220. **Road map** C1. 🄲 *(71) 741 374.* FAX *(71) 911 503.* @ H2976@accor-hotels.com This modern and attractive hotel has well-equipped rooms. The hotel also has its own hairdresser, masseur, and beauty salon. 🎿 TV 🍸	86	●	■	●	■
GAMMARTH: *Karim* ⓉⒹⓉⒹⓉⒹⓉⒹ **Road map** C1. 🄲 *(71) 912 188.* FAX *(71) 911 126.* @ hotel.karim@planet.tn Situated 30 minutes by road from Tunis, the Moorish-style Karim has large rooms and a pleasant lobby. 🎿 TV 🎿 🍸 🔼 🛇 📺 24 🏃	440	●	■	●	■
GAMMARTH: *Renaissance* ⓉⒹⓉⒹⓉⒹⓉⒹ Les Cotes de Carthage, 2078. **Road map** C1. 🄲 *(71) 910 900.* FAX *(71) 912 020.* @ reservations@renaissance.com.tn W www.renaissancehotels.com This business-class hotel has the full range of facilities. The rooms are comfortable and elegant and many of the sights, including Carthage and the centre of Tunis, are within easy reach. 🎿 🍸 🔼 🛇 📺 24 🏃 ♨	460	●	■	●	■
GAMMARTH: *Abou Nawas Gammarth* ⓉⒹⓉⒹⓉⒹⓉⒹⓉⒹ **Road map** C1. 🄲 *(71) 741 444.* FAX *(71) 740 400.* @ gammarth@abounawas.com.tn Situated in its own grounds and surrounded by lush greenery and flowers, this luxury hotel has a direct view of the sea. Guests are accommodated in small chalets, some of which have sea views. All of the chalets have double rooms and their own pleasant reception areas. All have en suite bathrooms. 🎿 🔼 🛇 📺 24 🏃	446	●	■	●	■

GAMMARTH: *Corinthia Khamsa*   ⓣⓓⓣⓓⓣⓓⓣⓓⓣⓓ | 618
Tourist zone. **Road map** C1. ((71) 911 100. FAX (71) 910 041.
@ reservation.corinthia@planet.tn W www.corinthia.com
The attractive rooms of this hotel each have their own sofa, en suite bathroom
and minibar. In addition, every room either has a balcony or terrace. The
hotel is convenient for the airport. ⌂ ⟱ ⌸ ⟱ 24 ⌅

GAMMARTH: *Golden Tulip*   ⓣⓓⓣⓓⓣⓓⓣⓓ | 510
Tourist zone. **Road map** C1. ((71) 913 000. FAX (71) 913 913.
@ info@gtcarthage.goldentulip.com W www.goldentulip.com
This luxurious hotel has an attractive location and offers splendid views of
Tunis and the Mediterranean. Each of the tastefully decorated rooms has an
en suite bathroom; all have a balcony or terrace. ⌂ ⟱ ⟱ 24

GAMMARTH: *Le Palace*   ⓣⓓⓣⓓⓣⓓⓣⓓ | 600
Complexe Cap Gammarth. **Road map** C1. ((71) 912 000.
FAX (71) 911 442. @ lepalace@lepalace.com.tn
This luxurious hotel has spacious rooms and all the usual facilities including
a pool and no fewer than eight restaurants. ▤ TV ⌂ ⟱ ⟱ 24

GAMMARTH: *Megara*   ⓣⓓⓣⓓⓣⓓⓣⓓ | 154
Road map C1. ((71) 740 366. FAX (71) 740 916.
@ hotelmegara@planet.tn
This attractive, small, retro-style hotel was built in the 1970s around a former
villa, close to the sea. The rooms have lovely balconies. ▤ TV ⌂ ⟱ 24

GAMMARTH: *Miramar Carthage Palace*   ⓣⓓⓣⓓⓣⓓⓣⓓ | 510
Road map C1. ((71) 910 111. FAX (71) 913 140. W www.carthagepalace.com
This five-star hotel has spacious and luxuriously furnished rooms and
beachside apartments. It has plenty of sports facilities inluding tennis courts
and a fitness centre. ⌂ ⟱ ⟱ 24 ⟱

GAMMARTH: *The Residence*   ⓣⓓⓣⓓⓣⓓⓣⓓ | 340
Tourist zone. **Road map** C1. ((71) 910 101. FAX (71) 910 144. @ residence.tun@gnet.tn
An elegant and luxurious hotel, the Residence is situated a little way from the
centre of Gammarth and can provide thalassotherapy (sea water treatments). It
is considered to be one of the area's best hotels. ▤ TV ⌂ ⟱ ⟱ ◐

HAMMAMET: *Alya*   ⓣⓓⓣⓓ | 70
Rue Ali Belhouane. **Road map** D2. ((72) 280 218. FAX (72) 282 365.
A pleasant hotel in the middle of town, it has large and airy rooms with
balconies. Some rooms look onto the medina. TV 24

HAMMAMET: *Abou Nawas*   ⓣⓓⓣⓓⓣⓓⓣⓓ | 452
Tourist zone, El-Merazka. **Road map** D2.
((72) 281 344. FAX (72) 281 089, 260 170.
W www.abounawas.com.tn
A luxurious, spacious resort hotel, the Abou Nawas has a beautiful seaside
location. Rooms with balconies and terraces overlook the sea. It is 6 km
(4 miles) from the centre of the town. ▤ TV ⌂ ⟱ ⟱ ⌅

HAMMAMET: *Africana*   ⓣⓓⓣⓓⓣⓓⓣⓓ | 502
Tourist zone, Yasmine Hammamet. **Road map** D2. ((72) 271 222.
FAX (72) 227 507. @ africana@gnet.tn
A luxurious seaside hotel, the Africana has well-appointed rooms, each of
which has an en suite bathroom, TV, telephone and small refrigerator. Most
rooms also have their own balcony. TV ⌂ ⟱ ⟱ 24 ⌅

HAMMAMET: *Anais*   ⓣⓓⓣⓓⓣⓓⓣⓓ | 140
Tourist zone, Nord. **Road map** D2.
((72) 278 488. FAX (72) 278 503.
The Anais is surrounded by greenery. The rooms are fully equipped and the
hotel has direct access to the beach. TV ⌂ ⟱ ⟱ 24 ⌅

HAMMAMET: *Aziza*   ⓣⓓⓣⓓⓣⓓⓣⓓ | 436
Tourist zone. **Road map** D2. ((72) 283 666. FAX (72) 283 099.
@ hotel.aziza@planet.tn
The Aziza is situated on a long sandy beach that gently slopes to the shore. It
is about 3 km (2 miles) away from the old town. Golfers are offered transport
to nearby Golf Citrus and Golf Yasmine. ⌂ ⟱ ⟱ ⟱ ⌸ ⟱ 24 ⌅ ⟱

HAMMAMET: *Iberotel Oceana*   ⓣⓓⓣⓓⓣⓓ |
Barakat Essahel, Yasmine Hammamet. **Road map** D2.
((72) 227 227. FAX (72) 227 003. @ riu.oceanaham@planet.tn
This hotel has luxurious rooms, all with a sea view. ⌂ ⟱ ⟱ ⟱ 24 ⌅

Price categories for a standard double room, with bath or shower, including service and tax. Prices are in Tunisian dinars.
ⓉⒹ below 30 TD
ⓉⒹⓉⒹ 30–65 TD
ⓉⒹⓉⒹⓉⒹ 65–100 TD
ⓉⒹⓉⒹⓉⒹⓉⒹ 100–150 TD
ⓉⒹⓉⒹⓉⒹⓉⒹⓉⒹ over 150 TD

RESTAURANT
This is also open to non-residents.

GARDEN OR TERRACE
Hotel has its own garden, a terrace or a courtyard with plants.

SWIMMING POOL
Hotel has a pool for the use of its guests.

AIR CONDITIONING
All rooms are air-conditioned.

	NUMBER OF BEDS	RESTAURANT	GARDEN OR TERRACE	SWIMMING POOL	AIR CONDITIONING
HAMMAMET: *Royal Azur* ⓉⒹⓉⒹⓉⒹⓉⒹ Yasmine Hammamet. **Road map** D2. ☎ (72) 278 500. FAX (72) 278 999. @ reservation.royalazur@orangers.com.tn An elegant hotel, the Royal Azur is located a short way from the old centre, and has a good range of sports facilities including swimming pools and a jogging track. The gardens lead onto the beach. 📺 🏋 🍸 🏊 🍽 🏃 🐾	446	●		●	■
HAMMAMET: *Savana* ⓉⒹⓉⒹⓉⒹⓉⒹ Yasmine Hammamet. **Road map** D2. ☎ (72) 227 733. FAX (72) 227 315. @ globalia.savana@topnet.tn Most double rooms in this elegant hotel have a balcony or a terrace. The double rooms with no balcony or terrace have similar furnishings and are a little larger. 🎫 🍸 🏊 🍽 24 🏃	290	●	■	●	■
HAMMAMET: *Shalimar* ⓉⒹⓉⒹⓉⒹ Yasmine Hammamet. **Road map** D2. ☎ (72) 226 960. FAX (72) 227 251. Located in the new tourist zone, the Shalimar is an attractive and modern hotel. The rooms are spacious and the hotel manages to combine an Arabic style with its mainly European architecture. 🏋 🍸 🏊 🍽 24 🏃	416	●	■	●	■
HAMMAMET: *Sheraton* ⓉⒹⓉⒹⓉⒹⓉⒹ Tourist zone, Nord. **Road map** D2. ☎ (72) 226 273. FAX (72) 227 301. This comfortable and elegant hotel enjoys a beautiful location in the old tourist zone. The rooms are fully equipped and the hotel, which has several good restaurants and a pretty garden, has direct access to the beach. 📺 🏋 🍸 ⚡ 🏊 🍴 🍽 24 🏃	410	●	■	●	■
HAMMAMET: *Yasmine* ⓉⒹⓉⒹⓉⒹⓉⒹ Boulevard de la Promenade, Yasmine Hammamet. **Road map** D2. ☎ (72) 249 500. FAX (72) 249 170. This beautiful hotel has its own private beach. Its design is based on traditional Islamic architecture. 📺 🏋 🍸 ⚡ 🏊 🍴 🍽 24 🏃	564	●	■	●	■
HAMMAMET: *Dar Hayet* ⓉⒹⓉⒹⓉⒹⓉⒹ Rue Akaba 78. **Road map** D2. ☎ (72) 283 399. FAX (72) 280 404. @ darhayet@planet.tn This "hôtel de charme" stands on a large site, surrounded by greenery and has a small pool and a beachside setting. 🏋 🍸 🏊 🍽 24 🏃	115	●	■	●	■
HAMMAMET: *Hammamet Serail* ⓉⒹⓉⒹⓉⒹⓉⒹ Hammamet Sud. **Road map** D2. ☎ (72) 227 333. FAX (72) 226 730. @ serail@planet.tn This hotel complex is located in the new tourist zone. It is an interesting combination of Arabian style and modern architecture. 📺 🏋 🍸 🏊 🍽 🏃	424	●		●	
HAMMAMET: *Hasdrubal Thalassa* ⓉⒹⓉⒹⓉⒹⓉⒹ Yasmine Hammamet. **Road map** D2. ☎ (72) 248 800. FAX (72) 248 893. @ asdrubal.thal@gnet.tn This hotel has its own superbly well-maintained stretch of private beach. All accommodation consists of suites. Hasdrubal Thalassa is famous for its health treatments using sea water. 🎫 P 📺 🏋 🍸 ⚡ 🏊 🍴 🍽 24 🏃 🐾	472		■	●	■
HAMMAMET: *Manar (Magic Life)* ⓉⒹⓉⒹⓉⒹⓉⒹ El-Merezka, Tourist zone, Nord. **Road map** D2. ☎ (72) 281 333. FAX (72) 280 772. @ sales.marketing@magiclife.tourism.com The hotel, situated on a long beach, offers a special programme for golfers. Golf Yasmine is about 15 km (9 miles) from the hotel. 🏋 🏊 🍴 🍽 🏃 ⛳	647	●	■	●	■
HAMMAMET: *Marina Palace* ⓉⒹⓉⒹⓉⒹⓉⒹ Hammamet Sud. **Road map** D2. ☎ (72) 248 748. FAX (72) 248 699. W www.marinapalace.tn Situated in a newly built district about 12 km (7 miles) from Hammamet, this elegant and luxurious hotel has large, comfortable rooms. 🎫 P 📺 🍸 🏊 🍴	350	●	■	●	■

HAMMAMET: *Riu Mehari* ⓉⓄⓉⓄⓉⓄⓉⓄ 434
Yasmine Hammamet. **Road map** D2. (*(72) 249 155.* FAX *(72) 249 290.*
@ riu.mehari.ham@planet.tn
A coastal road separates this hotel from the long sandy beach. The hotel has a
beautiful garden for the sole use of its guests. P 🏧 📶 🍽 24 🏃

HAMMAMET: *Sindbad* ⓉⓄⓉⓄⓉⓄⓉⓄ 335
Avenue des Nations-Unies. **Road map** D2. (*(72) 280 122.*
FAX *(72) 280 004.* @ sindbad@planet.tn
A luxurious hotel set in a lovely garden, the Sindbad has direct access to the
beach. All rooms have a sea view. P TV 🏧 Y ⚡ 📶 🛏 🍽 24 🏃

KELIBIA: *Belle Etoile* ⓉⓄⓉⓄⓉⓄ 46
Route de la Plage 93. **Road map** D1. (*(72) 274 374.* FAX *(72) 275 302.*
Centrally heated in the winter, this is a cosy, smallish hotel with pleasant
rooms. It makes a good base for an overnight stay when touring Cap Bon. TV

KELIBIA: *Kelibia Beach* ⓉⓄⓉⓄⓉⓄⓉⓄ 500
Road map D1. (*(72) 276 955.* FAX *(72) 274 779.*
The pastel-coloured rooms at this attractive new holiday centre have a good
range of facilities and splendid views of the beach. 🌐 🏧 📶 🛏 🍽 24 🏃

LA GOULETTE: *La Jetée* ⓉⓄⓉⓄⓉⓄⓉⓄ 136
Tourist zone. **Road map** C1. (*(71) 736 000.* FAX *(71) 738 396.*
A modern hotel where some of the rooms have showers and others have
baths. It is just a short way from Tunis by road. A beach is opposite the hotel.

NABEUL: *Auberge de Jeunesse* ⓉⓄ 52
Road map D2. (*(72) 285 547.*
This Berber-style hostel offers spotlessly clean and neat rooms and separate
showers and bathrooms for men and women. It is permissible to pitch a tent
in the grounds.

NABEUL: *Oliviers* ⓉⓄⓉⓄ 30
Road map D2. (*(72) 285 865.* @ pensionlesoliviers@yahoo.fr
Situated in a citrus grove, opposite Les Jasmins *(see below),* this family-run
guesthouse/hotel has pleasant and spotlessly clean rooms. TV 🏧 24

NABEUL: *Les Jasmins* ⓉⓄⓉⓄⓉⓄ 45
Avenue Habib Tameur. **Road map** D2. (*(72) 285 343.* FAX *(72) 285 073.*
@ hotel.jasmins@gnet.tn
The rooms of this hotel, which is beautifully located in an olive grove, are
pleasant but on the smallish side. P TV 24

NABEUL: *Les Pyramides* ⓉⓄⓉⓄⓉⓄ 262
Avenue Habib Bourguiba. **Road map** D2. (*(72) 285 444.*
FAX *(72) 287 461.*
This hotel complex stands by the beach. The comfortable rooms have en suite
bathrooms. The hotel has plenty of facilities for its guests including a
swimming pool, tennis courts and a disco. 🌐 🏧 Y 📶 🛏 🍽 24 🏃 🏴

NABEUL: *Club Med Aquarius* ⓉⓄⓉⓄⓉⓄⓉⓄ 682
Road map D2. (*(72) 285 777.* FAX *(72) 285 682.*
Beautifully located in an orange grove and close to the beach, Club Med
Aquarius has spacious, well-kept rooms. The resort complex is family friendly,
with water sports facilities and well-organized play areas for children. 🍽 🏃

NABEUL: *Kheops* ⓉⓄⓉⓄⓉⓄⓉⓄ 638
Av Mohamed V. **Road map** D2. (*(72) 286 555.* FAX *(72) 286 024.*
@ hotel.kheops@planet.tn W www.group-sassi.com
Situated between Nabeul and Hammamet, this hotel has spacious rooms.
Rooms with balconies face the sea. TV 🏧 Y 📶 🛏 🍽 24 🏃

SIDI BOU SAÏD: *Sidi Bou Fares* ⓉⓄⓉⓄ 44
Rue Sidi Bou Fares 15. **Road map** C1. (*(71) 740 091.*
@ hotel.boufares@gnet.tn
The small and simple rooms of this hotel are arranged around an attractive
garden courtyard. It is very popular in high season and it is necessary to book
early. P TV 24

SIDI BOU SAÏD: *Sidi Bou Saïd* ⓉⓄⓉⓄⓉⓄ 44
Rue Sidi Dhrif. **Road map** C1. (*(71) 740 411.* FAX *(71) 745 129.*
Situated a short walk from the village, in the direction of La Marsa, this hotel
has a splendid view from the terrace and the poolside. There is a good
restaurant and friendly service. P TV Y 24

For key to symbols see back flap

Price categories for a standard double room, with bath or shower, including service and tax. Prices are in Tunisian dinars.
- TD below 30 TD
- TD TD 30–65 TD
- TD TD TD 65–100 TD
- TD TD TD TD 100–150 TD
- TD TD TD TD TD over 150 TD

RESTAURANT
This is also open to non-residents.

GARDEN OR TERRACE
Hotel has its own garden, a terrace or a courtyard with plants.

SWIMMING POOL
Hotel has a pool for the use of its guests.

AIR CONDITIONING
All rooms are air-conditioned.

NORTHERN TUNISIA

	NUMBER OF BEDS	RESTAURANT	GARDEN OR TERRACE	SWIMMING POOL	AIR CONDITIONING
AÏN DRAHAM: *Beauséjour* TD TD Road map B2. (78) 655 363. This small hotel, situated right in the centre of town, is very popular with hunters. Trophies and hunting memorabilia decorate the walls. All the rooms have en suite bathrooms. P TV Y 24		●			
AÏN DRAHAM: *Les Chênes* TD TD Road map B2. (78) 655 211. FAX (78) 655 396. Occupying an old hunting lodge, this hotel is close to town. P TV 24	68	●			
AÏN DRAHAM: *Nour el-Aïn* TD TD Road map B2. (78) 655 000. FAX (78) 655 185. The hotel stands on a hill above the town and has its own traditional hammam (steam bath). P TV Y 24	122	●	■		■
BIZERTE: *Africana* TD Rue Sassi Bahri 59. Road map C1. (72) 434 412. A small hotel, the Africana is close to Bizerte's market. TV 24	50				
BIZERTE: *Hôtel Corniche* TD TD Tourist zone, Route de la Corniche. Road map C1. (72) 431 831. FAX (72) 422 515. The hotel boasts the most beautiful stretch of Bizerte's beach. There is a pleasant garden and a good restaurant. P TV ⬛ Y 24	438	●	■	●	■
BIZERTE: *Hôtel de la Plage* TD TD Avenue Mohamed Rejiba 34. Road map C1. (72) 436 510. FAX (72) 420 161. Standing in the town centre, this hotel has a good range of room sizes. Despite its name it is not situated on the beach but in an alley, a short walk from the sea. The rooms are simple but clean. TV 24	50				■
BIZERTE: *Residence ain Meriem* TD TD Tourist zone, Route de la Corniche. Road map C1. (72) 422 615. FAX (72) 432 459. The hotel stands next to a sandy beach, 4 km (2 miles) from Bizerte. The comfortable rooms have their own kitchenettes. Up to a maximum of four people are allowed to occupy one room. TV ⬛ Y ⬛ 24	295	●	■	●	■
BIZERTE: *Sidi Salem* TD TD Tourist zone, Route de la Corniche. Road map C1. (72) 420 365. FAX (72) 420 380. @ hsalem.bizerte@planet.tn Almost opposite the Old Port and the kasbah, this hotel has an enviable location. The large rooms face the beach and the sea. It is a very popular place, so book ahead. P TV Y ⬛ 24 ⬛	80	●	■	●	■
BIZERTE: *Petit Mousse* TD TD TD Tourist zone, Route de la Corniche. Road map C1. (72) 432 185. FAX (72) 438 871. This family-run seaside hotel is situated about 4 km (2 miles) from Bizerte.	24	●	■		■
BIZERTE: *Bizerte Resort* TD TD TD TD Tourist zone, Route de la Corniche. Road map C1. (72) 436 966. FAX (72) 422 955. @ hbizerta@gnet.tn This large and modern hotel is within easy reach of the sea and is close to the kasbah and the Old Port. All rooms benefit from a sea view. ⬛ ⬛ ⬛	208	●	■	●	■
HAMMAM BOURGUIBA: *Spa Hammam Bourguiba* TD TD TD TD Road map B2. (78) 602 517. FAX (78) 602 497. This hot-spring resort is not far from the Algerian border and just 15 km (9 miles) from Aïn Draham. It is popular with Tunisians and was thoroughly refurbished in 2003. P TV Y ⬛ 24	116	●	■	●	■
JENDOUBA: *Atlas* TD Rue Juin 1955 1. Road map B2. (78) 602 217. This small hotel has simply-furnished rooms. TV 24	32				

JENDOUBA: *Simithu* ⓣⓣ 54 ●
Blvd. 9 April 1938. **Road map** B2. 【 *(78) 604 043.* **FAX** *(78) 602 595.*
All of the Simithu's modern rooms have en suite bathrooms. The price is not prohibitive and includes breakfast. **TV** **24**

RAF RAF: *Dalia* ⓣⓣ 24 ● ■
Raf Raf Plage. **Road map** C1. 【 *(72) 441 630.*
This pleasant hotel is the only one in the village. Some rooms have a view of the sea. In addition, beach huts are available for hire. **TV** **24**

TABARKA: *Mamia* ⓣⓣ 36 ● ■
Rue de Tunis 3. **Road map** B1. 【 *(78) 671 058.* **FAX** *(78) 670 638.*
The Mamia provides simple but spotlessly clean accommodation and friendly service. The rooms are arranged around a quiet courtyard. **TV** **⊞** **24**

TABARKA: *Mimosas* ⓣⓣ 154 ● ■ ● ■
Avenue H. Bourguiba. **Road map** B1. 【 *(78) 673 018/028.* **FAX** *(78) 673 276.*
This charming hotel is in a traditional residence and has a well-kept garden that affords a fantastic view of both the sea and the town. The garden has a small swimming pool. The rooms all have en suite bathrooms. **TV** **Y** **24**

TABARKA: *Les Aiguilles* ⓣⓣⓣ 38 ● ■ ■
Avenue H. Bourguiba 18. **Road map** B1. 【 *(78) 673 789.*
FAX *(78) 673 604.*
The hotel is situated in an old colonial building and stands close to the beach. Rooms are large and clean and have en suite bathrooms. **P** **TV** **⊞** **24**

TABARKA: *Abou Nawas Montazah* ⓣⓣⓣⓣ 612 ● ■ ● ■
Tourist route. **Road map** B1. 【 *(78) 673 514.* **FAX** *(78) 673 530.*
A very popular place, with its own scuba diving club.
P **TV** **⊞** **Y** **⤢** **⬛** **⬛** **24** **⌖** **●** *winter.*

TABARKA: *Dar Ismail* ⓣⓣⓣⓣ 360 ● ■ ● ■
Tourist zone. **Road map** B1. 【 *(78) 670 188.* **FAX** *(78) 670 343.*
Situated close to Tabarka, this smart hotel is close to the beach. Its spacious rooms benefit from a sea view. **⬛** **P** **TV** **⊞** **Y** **⤢** **⬛** **⬛** **24**

TABARKA: *Royal Golf Marhaba* ⓣⓣⓣⓣ 320 ● ■ ● ■
Tourist zone. **Road map** B1. 【 *(78) 673 899.* **FAX** *(78) 673 838.*
@ royal.golf@gnet.tn
The hotel enjoys a lovely location, about 5 km (3 miles) from the centre of Tabarka and close to a golf course. All the rooms have a view of the sea and the hotel offers direct access to the beach. **⬛** **TV** **⊞** **Y** **⤢** **⬛** **⬛** **24** **⬛**

TABARKA: *Riu Hôtel Mehari* ⓣⓣⓣⓣⓣ 400 ● ■ ● ■
Tourist zone, Côte de la Corniche. **Road map** B1. 【 *(78) 670 185.* **FAX** *(78) 673 943.*
@ riu.meharitabarka@planet.tn.
This large hotel represents a typical holiday venue. Standing on the shore, it is popular with families with children. **⬛** **⊞** **Y** **⤢** **⬛** **⬛** **24** **⌖**

THE SAHEL

EL-JEM: *Ksar El-Jem* ⓣⓣ 16 ●
Road map D3. 【 *(73) 632 800.* **FAX** *(73) 630 390/602.*
This is the best hotel in El-Jem. All the tastefully furnished rooms have en suite bathrooms. In summer it is necessary to book well in advance. **TV** **24**

EL-JEM: *Julius* ⓣⓣⓣ 30 ●
Place de La Grace. **Road map** D3. 【 *(73) 630 044/419.* **FAX** *(73) 630 523.*
The hotel stands near the amphitheatre. The rooms, although of a modest size, are pleasant and clean. In summer it can be difficult to get a room. **TV** **24**

GABÈS: *Atlantic* ⓣ 56 ● ■
Avenue H. Bourguiba. **Road map** D5. 【 *(75) 272 417.*
This large colonial building has an attractive façade. The rooms are pleasant with attractive furnishings.

GABÈS: *Néjib* ⓣⓣ 128 ●
Avenue Farhat Hached. **Road map** D5. 【 *(75) 271 547.* **FAX** *(75) 274 488.*
A large and modern hotel, the Néjib is situated in the centre of town.

GABÈS: *Oasis* ⓣⓣⓣ 212 ● ■ ● ■
Route de la Plage. **Road map** D5. 【 *(75) 270 782.* **FAX** *(75) 271 749.*
Situated right by the beach, this elegant and modern hotel has comfortable rooms. Hot springs are nearby. **P** **TV** **⊞** **Y** **⬛** **24** **⌖**

Price categories for a standard double room, with bath or shower, including service and tax. Prices are in Tunisian dinars.
(TD) below 30 TD
(TD)(TD) 30–65 TD
(TD)(TD)(TD) 65–100 TD
(TD)(TD)(TD)(TD) 100–150 TD
(TD)(TD)(TD)(TD)(TD) over 150 TD

RESTAURANT
This is also open to non-residents.

GARDEN OR TERRACE
Hotel has its own garden, a terrace or a courtyard with plants.

SWIMMING POOL
Hotel has a pool for the use of its guests.

AIR CONDITIONING
All rooms are air-conditioned.

	NUMBER OF BEDS	RESTAURANT	GARDEN OR TERRACE	SWIMMING POOL	AIR CONDITIONING
GABÈS: *Chems* (TD)(TD)(TD) Tourist zone, Gabès Plage. **Road map** D5. *(75) 270 547.* FAX *(75) 274 485.* This large hotel complex consists of chalets set along the beach. There is a good pool and many of the rooms face the sea.	517	●	■	●	■
KERKENNAH ISLANDS: *Residence Cercina* (TD)(TD) Tourist zone. **Road map** E4. *(74) 489 953.* FAX *(74) 489 878.* Overnight accommodation is available in simply furnished chalets. Sea-facing chalets usually require advance booking.	32	●	■		■
KERKENNAH ISLANDS: *Grand Hotel* (TD)(TD)(TD) **Road map** E4. *(74) 489 864.* FAX *(74) 489 866.* The hotel, situated in the Sidi Frej tourist zone, offers comfortable rooms. In the summer it mainly serves package holidaymakers.	225	●	■	●	■
KSAR GHILANE: *Erg* (TD) **Road map** C6. *(75) 434 108.* FAX *(75) 434 017.* This oasis site provides the opportunity to spend the night in a Bedouin tent. There is a picnic area and a small restaurant in the middle of the palm grove.	120	●			
KSAR GHILANE: *Ksar Ghilane* (TD) Ksar Ghilane. **Road map** C6. *(75) 460 462.* This campsite, which has Bedouin tents equipped with bathrooms, is close to the hot springs. Traditional shows are regularly staged in the evenings.	120	●	■		
KSAR GHILANE: *Le Paradis* (TD) **Road map** C6. *(75) 470 225.* A campsite with Bedouin tents, this is situated a little way from the spring. It has a simple restaurant and clean bathrooms with hot showers.	120	●	■		
KSAR GHILANE: *Pansea* (TD)(TD)(TD) Ksar Ghilane. **Road map** D5. *(75) 900 506.* @ tunisia@pansea.com The Pansea offers luxurious overnight accommodation in air-conditioned tents, which have their own bathrooms. An open-air swimming pool provides a chance to cool off. Camel rides into the desert can also be arranged.	120	●	■	●	■
MAHDIA: *La Medina* (TD) Rue el-Bey. **Road map** D3. *(73) 694 664.* FAX *(73) 696 384.* The light, very clean rooms of this small and pleasant hotel are set around a courtyard. The hotel is convenient for the medina.	14	●			
MAHDIA: *Abou Nawas Cap Mahdia* (TD)(TD)(TD) B.P.38 – Route de la Corniche. **Road map** D3. *(73) 680 300.* FAX *(73) 680 405.* @ capmahdia@abounawas.com.tn Situated in the tourist zone, this attractively designed hotel has good amenities for families with young children including a "mini-club" and a games room.	526	●	■	●	■
MAHDIA: *Mahdia Palace* (TD)(TD)(TD)(TD) **Road map** D3. *(73) 696 777.* FAX *(73) 696 810.* This top-range hotel has magnificent Moorish architecture, outdoor and indoor swimming pools, a vast garden and large rooms with Arabian furnishings. The interior decor is warm and very attractive.	660	●	■	●	■
MAHDIA: *Riu el-Mansour* (TD)(TD)(TD)(TD) Tourist zone. **Road map** D3. *(73) 696 696.* FAX *(73) 696 669.* This luxurious hotel is aimed at families with children. The large rooms all have balconies overlooking the beach.	498	●	■	●	■
MAHDIA: *Dar Sidi* (TD)(TD)(TD)(TD)(TD) Rue de la Corniche – Rejicha. **Road map** D3. *(73) 687 002.* FAX *(73) 687 003.* This small and quiet "hôtel de charme" is situated not far from the beach. It consists of ten well-decorated bungalows, a pool and restaurant.	20	●		●	■

MAHDIA: *Iberostar el-Fatimi* ⓣⓣⓣⓣ 580
Tourist zone. **Road map** D3. ((73) 696 733. FAX (73) 696 731.
This smart hotel is aimed squarely at holidaymakers. Its large rooms have
balconies overlooking the beach. 🖥 P TV 🏊 Y 🌊 🍴 💺 24 🚶

MAHDIA: *Melia el-Mouradi Mahdia* ⓣⓣⓣⓣⓣ 594
Tourist zone. **Road map** D3. ((73) 692 111. FAX (73) 692 120.
@ elmouradi.mahdia@planet.tn
This hotel's large rooms have Arabian-style sofas. Surrounded by a garden, the
hotel has access to a lovely beach. P Y 🌊 🍴 💺 24 🚶

MATMATA: *Kousseila* ⓣ 67
Road map D5. ((75) 230 355. FAX (75) 230 265.
This pleasant and well-appointed hotel stands opposite the bus station. TV 24

MATMATA: *Ksar Amazigh* ⓣ 100
Route de Tamazrat. **Road map** D5. ((75) 230 088. FAX (75) 230 273.
The hotel is situated outside the town, in a traditional underground house.
The rooms are arranged around a courtyard with whitewashed walls.

MONASTIR: *Kahla* ⓣⓣⓣ
Avenue 7 Novembre. **Road map** D3. ((73) 467 881.
This attractive hotel is popular with visitors. Suites are also available. TV 24

MONASTIR: *Emir Palace* ⓣⓣⓣⓣ 648
Tourist zone. **Road map** D3. ((73) 520 900. FAX (73) 521 823.
@ dm.amir/orient@zenit.tn
Situated about 4 km (2 miles) from the centre, this is one of the best hotels in
Monastir. Spacious and elegant, it resembles a palace surrounded by
magnificent gardens. 🖥 P TV 🏊 Y 🌊 🍴 💺 24 🚶

MONASTIR: *Esplanade* ⓣⓣⓣⓣ 260
Route de la Corniche. **Road map** D3. ((73) 460 148. FAX (73) 460 050.
Situated in town, close to the Great Mosque, the Esplanade has comfortable,
modern rooms. TV 24

MONASTIR: *Abou Nawas Monastir* ⓣⓣⓣⓣⓣ 628
La Dkhila – 5000. **Road map** D3. ((73) 521 940. FAX (73) 521 948.
@ monastir@abounawas.com.tn
This smart hotel belongs to the Abou Nawas chain and has masses of flowers
and greenery. The decor is modern with just a dash of Arabian elements. The
comfortable rooms all have a sea view. 🖥 P TV 🏊 Y 🌊 🍴 💺 24 🚶

PORT EL-KANTAOUI: *Abou Nawas Diar Andalous* ⓣⓣⓣⓣ 609
Tourist zone. **Road map** D2. ((73) 246 200. FAX (73) 246 348.
@ abounawasdiarandalous@abounawas.com.tn
This luxurious, smart hotel has several bars and restaurants, and features all
the usual facilities including tennis courts and a delightful Moorish café, which
plays folk music in the evenings. It is a short way from Sousse, close to the
Port el-Kantaoui yachting marina. The nearby beach is lovely. All the rooms
have balconies or terraces. P Y 🌊 🍴 24 🌿 🚶

PORT EL-KANTAOUI: *Golf Residence* ⓣⓣⓣⓣ 491
Tourist zone. **Road map** D2. ((73) 348 833. FAX (73) 348 847.
The attractive one-, two- or three-room apartments of this resort hotel have
their own kitchens or kitchenettes. The surroundings are lush and the
complex has its own swimming pool. 🖥 P TV 🏊 Y 🌊 24

PORT EL-KANTAOUI: *Marhaba Palace* ⓣⓣⓣⓣⓣ 600
Tourist zone. **Road map** D2. ((73) 347 076. FAX (73) 347 077.
@ marhabapalace@planet.tn
This impressive, high-class hotel is located in a park. The rooms and grounds
are spacious and the hotel has six restaurants. 🖥 P 🏊 Y 🌊 🍴 💺 24 🚶

PORT EL-KANTAOUI: *Melia el-Mouradi Palace* ⓣⓣⓣⓣⓣ 577
Tourist zone. **Road map** D2. ((73) 246 500. FAX (73) 246 520.
@ elmouradi.palace@planet.tn
A former palace, this hotel has spacious rooms, all of which have a balcony or
a terrace. The hotel has a beautiful garden. P 🏊 🌊 🍴 💺 24 🚶

PORT EL-KANTAOUI: *Riu Bellevue Park* ⓣⓣⓣⓣⓣ 600
B.P. 344, 4089. **Road map** D2. ((73) 246 300. FAX (73) 246 392.
@ riu.bellevuepark@planet.tn
This hotel complex is squarely aimed at families with children and includes a
children's pool and expansive gardens. 🖥 P TV 🏊 Y 🌊 🍴 💺 24 🚶

For key to symbols see back flap

Price categories for a standard double room, with bath or shower, including service and tax. Prices are in Tunisian dinars.
- (TD) below 30 TD
- (TD)(TD) 30–65 TD
- (TD)(TD)(TD) 65–100 TD
- (TD)(TD)(TD)(TD) 100–150 TD
- (TD)(TD)(TD)(TD)(TD) over 150 TD

RESTAURANT
This is also open to non-residents.

GARDEN OR TERRACE
Hotel has its own garden, a terrace or a courtyard with plants.

SWIMMING POOL
Hotel has a pool for the use of its guests.

AIR CONDITIONING
All rooms are air-conditioned.

	Number of Beds	Restaurant	Garden or Terrace	Swimming Pool	Air Conditioning
SFAX: *Ennaser* (TD) Rue des Notaires 100. Road map D4. (74) 299 019. This small, clean hotel stands in the town centre, close to Bab Jebli. TV 24	18		■		
SFAX: *El-Andalous* (TD)(TD) Blvd. des Martyres. Road map D4. (74) 405 406. FAX (74) 406 425. Catering for both tourists and business travellers, this modern hotel is at the centre of town and offers good value for money.	184	●			■
SFAX: *Novotel Syphax* (TD)(TD)(TD) Road map D3. (74) 243 333. FAX (74) 245 226. This hotel is situated away from the town centre, along the road to the airport. The rooms are pleasant and attractive.	254	●	■	●	
SFAX: *Abou Nawas Sfax* (TD)(TD)(TD)(TD) Avenue H. Bourguiba. Road map D4. (74) 225 700. FAX (74) 225 521. @ abounawas.sfax@abounawas.com.tn W www.abounawas.com.tn This modern hotel is suitable for people wishing to make the most of Sfax's shopping. The hotel has a rooftop pool.	260	●	■	●	■
SKANÈS: *Skanès el-Hana* (TD)(TD)(TD) Road map D3. (73) 521 666. FAX (73) 520 709. @ skanes.elhana@planet.tn Standing directly on a sandy beach, this well-appointed hotel has good play areas for children.	474	●	■	●	
SKANÈS: *El-Mouradi Skanès Beach* (TD)(TD)(TD)(TD) Tourist zone. Road map D3. (73) 521 999. FAX (73) 521 208. @ info@skanesbeach@elmouradi.com A very attractive hotel situated within Monastir's tourist zone. Facilities include a fitness club and tennis courts.	428	●	■	●	■
SOUSSE: *Amira* (TD) Road map D3. & FAX (73) 226 325. The rooms are small but clean in this tiny hotel in the centre of Sousse. TV 24	30				
SOUSSE: *Ennacim* (TD)(TD) Route de la Corniche. Road map D3. (73) 227 100. FAX (73) 224 488. A modestly furnished hotel that caters exclusively for long-stay visitors. All rooms have en suite bathrooms.	80	●	■	●	■
SOUSSE: *Medina* (TD)(TD) Rue de Paris. Road map D3. (73) 221 722. FAX (73) 221 794. Situated close to the Great Mosque, the Medina is popular with visitors – advance booking is necessary in summer. TV 24	100	●			
SOUSSE: *Justinia Nour* (TD)(TD)(TD) Blvd. 7 Novembre. Road map D3. (73) 226 381. FAX (73) 225 993. The hotel is situated near the entrance to the tourist zone, close to Avenue Bourguiba. The hotel has its own facilities for water sports.	316	●	■	●	■
SOUSSE: *Abou Nawas Boujaafar* (TD)(TD)(TD)(TD) Avenue H. Bourguiba. Road map D3. (73) 226 030. FAX (73) 226 595. @ abnboujaafar.ssc@planet.tn This well-appointed hotel stands directly on a sandy beach but is also convenient for the town centre. The hotel has two swimming pools, a fitness centre and a thalassotherapy centre.	474	●	■	●	■
SOUSSE: *El-Hana* (TD)(TD)(TD)(TD) Route de la Corniche. Road map D3. (73) 225 818. FAX (73) 226 076. @ beach.elhana@planet.tn The comfortable rooms of this large hotel have a pastel decor and balconies that overlook the beach.	258	●	■	●	■

SOUSSE: *Orient Palace* (TD)(TD)(TD)(TD) | 806
Tourist zone, 2 km (1 mile) from the centre of Sousse. **Road map** D3.
(*(73) 242 888.* FAX *(73) 243 345.*
This spacious and luxurious hotel offers all possible amenities including a disco, fitness club and a tennis court. It stands directly on a sandy beach.
P Y ⚑ ⚑ ⚑ ⚑

SOUSSE: *Carthago el-Ksar* (TD)(TD)(TD)(TD) | 688
Blvd. 7 Novembre, Khezama. **Road map** D3. **(** *(73) 240 460.*
FAX *(73) 244 600.* @ dg.elksar@carthago.com.tn. W www.corinthiahotels.com
An impressive high-class hotel set in a magnificent park, this hotel has easy access to a sandy beach. All the rooms are furnished to a high standard and have en suite bathrooms. P ⚑ Y ⚑ ⚑ ⚑ ⚑

SOUSSE: *Coralia Club Palm Beach (Jawhara)* (TD)(TD)(TD)(TD) | 688
Blvd. 7 Novembre. **Road map** D3. **(** *(73) 225 611.* FAX *(73) 225 442.*
@ h2860gm@accord.hotel.com
This large hotel has a good garden, clean rooms and puts on plenty of entertainment. ⚑ P ⚑ Y ⚑ 24 ⚑

SOUSSE: *Hill Diar* (TD)(TD)(TD)(TD) | 416
Blvd. 7 Novembre. **Road map** D3. **(** *(73) 241 811.* FAX *(73) 242 836.*
Just 3 km (2 miles) from the town centre, this attractive hotel is by the beach. All the rooms have a sea view and the large garden includes a small zoo.
⚑ TV ⚑ Y ⚑ ⚑ ⚑ 24 ⚑

SOUSSE: *Marhaba Beach* (TD)(TD)(TD)(TD) | 506
Blvd. 7 Novembre. **Road map** D3. **(** *(73) 240 112.* FAX *(73) 240 688.*
This smart hotel has the full range of amenities and is handy for the beach. It is situated within the tourist zone, between Sousse and Port el-Kantaoui.
⚑ ⚑ ⚑ Y ⚑ ⚑ ⚑ 24 ⚑

SOUSSE: *Royal Salem* (TD)(TD)(TD)(TD)(TD) | 300
Blvd. 7 Novembre. **Road map** D3. **(** *(73) 271 589.* FAX *(73) 271 595.*
@ hroyal.salem@planet.tn. W www.marhabahotels.com
This luxurious hotel has large, air-conditioned rooms, all of which have their own balconies. Adult and children's swimming pools, a discotheque and a fitness room are just some of the amenities on offer. P Y ⚑ ⚑ ⚑ 24 ⚑

JERBA AND THE MEDENINE AREA

HOUMT SOUK: *Arischa* (TD) | 44
Rue Ghazi Mustapha. **Road map** D5. **(** *(75) 650 384.*
This *fondouk* (inn) has a flower-filled courtyard and its own roof terrace. The hotel has a good reputation. The rooms have only basic amenities. TV 24

HOUMT SOUK: *Auberge de Jeunesse* (TD) | 62
Rue Moncef Bey. **Road map** D5. **(** & FAX *(75) 650 619.*
The hostel boasts an excellent location in an old inn, set in a quiet alley. The spotlessly clean rooms are arranged around an inner courtyard. TV 24

HOUMT SOUK: *Erriadh* (TD) | 58
Rue M. Ferjani. **Road map** D5. **(** *(75) 650 756.* FAX *(75) 650 487.*
The double rooms in this charming old *fondouk* (inn) are arranged around the shady inner courtyard. TV 24

HOUMT SOUK: *Dar Faiza* (TD)(TD) | 48
Road map D5. **(** *(75) 650 083.* FAX *(75) 651 763.*
This attractive place overlooks the beach. Garden bungalows and a good restaurant mean it gets booked up. P TV ⚑ Y ⚑

JERBA: *Bougainvilliers* (TD)(TD)(TD) | 192
Tourist zone. **Road map** E5. **(** *(75) 745 692.* FAX *(75) 745 685.* @ htl.boug@planet.tn
All the rooms in this hotel have their own balconies. P ⚑ Y ⚑ 24 ⚑

JERBA: *Iberostar Djerba Beach* (TD)(TD)(TD) | 366
Tourist zone. **Road map** E5. **(** *(75) 731 200.* FAX *(75) 730 357.*
This hotel has a swimming pool, bar and a children's playground. Shrubs and flowers give the place a colourful setting. TV P ⚑ ⚑ ⚑ 24 ⚑ ⚑

JERBA: *Abou Nawas* (TD)(TD)(TD)(TD) | 498
Tourist zone. **Road map** E5. **(** *(75) 757 022.* FAX *(75) 757 700.*
This beautifully designed hotel has spacious rooms and all the amenities including a traditional hammam (steam bath) and a fitness centre. The garden is magnificent with several swimming pools. ⚑ P TV ⚑ Y ⚑ ⚑ 24 ⚑

For key to symbols see back flap

Price categories for a standard double room, with bath or shower, including service and tax. Prices are in Tunisian dinars.
ⓉⒹ below 30 TD
ⓉⒹⓉⒹ 30–65 TD
ⓉⒹⓉⒹⓉⒹ 65–100 TD
ⓉⒹⓉⒹⓉⒹⓉⒹ 100–150 TD
ⓉⒹⓉⒹⓉⒹⓉⒹⓉⒹ over 150 TD

RESTAURANT
This is also open to non-residents.

GARDEN OR TERRACE
Hotel has its own garden, a terrace or a courtyard with plants.

SWIMMING POOL
Hotel has a pool for the use of its guests.

AIR CONDITIONING
All rooms are air-conditioned.

	NUMBER OF BEDS	RESTAURANT	GARDEN OR TERRACE	SWIMMING POOL	AIR CONDITIONING
JERBA: Abou Nawas Golf ⓉⒹⓉⒹⓉⒹ Tourist zone. **Road map** E5. ((75) 746 910. FAX (75) 746 918. @ golfdjerba@abounawas.com.tn This hotel combines a Tunisian style of decor with European architecture. An 18-hole golf course is close by.	500	●	■	●	■
JERBA: Ksar Jerba ⓉⒹⓉⒹⓉⒹⓉⒹ Tourist zone. **Road map** E5. ((75) 732 541. FAX (75) 731 546. The hotel is based on traditional Tunisian architecture. The pleasant rooms all have a sea view.	268	●	■	●	■
JERBA: Al Jazira Beach ⓉⒹⓉⒹⓉⒹⓉⒹ Tourist zone. **Road map** E5. ((75) 758 860. FAX (75) 758 810. This hotel complex is ideal for families with children and has swimming pools and playgrounds. All the rooms have balconies.	550	●	■	●	■
JERBA: Athenee Palace Club Robinson ⓉⒹⓉⒹⓉⒹⓉⒹⓉⒹ Tourist zone. **Road map** E5. ((75) 757 600. FAX (75) 757 601. This smart hotel stands in a vast garden, right by the beach. The beautifully designed rooms have their own terraces with sea views. A thalassotherapy is in the hotel grounds.	566		■	●	
JERBA: Coralia Club Palm Beach ⓉⒹⓉⒹⓉⒹⓉⒹⓉⒹ Tourist zone. **Road map** E5. ((75) 757 404. FAX (75) 757 410. @ palmbeach.palace@gnet.tn This modern and spacious hotel complex has been beautifully designed and has all possible amenities including tennis and live entertainment.	562	●	■	●	■
JERBA: Hasdrubal Thalassa ⓉⒹⓉⒹⓉⒹⓉⒹⓉⒹ Tourist zone. **Road map** E5. ((75) 730 650. FAX (75) 730 730. @ asdrubal.djerba@gnet.tn W www.hasdrubal.com Surrounded by a garden, this elegant seaside hotel has a sense of luxury about it. It has facilities for water sports, a beauty salon and its own thalassotherapy (sea water therapy) centre.	430	●	■	●	■
JERBA: Melia Djerba Menzel ⓉⒹⓉⒹⓉⒹⓉⒹⓉⒹ Tourist zone. **Road map** E5. ((75) 750 300. FAX (75) 750 490. @ elmouradimenzel@planet.tn The comfortable rooms complement the unusual architecture of this traditional Jerban dwelling place.	1262	●	■	●	■
JERBA: Movenpick Ulysse Palace & Thalasso ⓉⒹⓉⒹⓉⒹⓉⒹⓉⒹ Tourist zone, Plage de Sidi Mehrez. **Road map** E5. ((75) 758 777. FAX (75) 757 850. @ resort.djerba@movenpick.com Swimming pools, bars, a small Moorish café and a thalassotherapy (sea water therapy) centre make this elegant luxury hotel complex a very pleasant place to stay.	528	●	■	●	■
JERBA: Riu Mehari Beach ⓉⒹⓉⒹⓉⒹⓉⒹⓉⒹ Tourist zone. **Road map** E5. ((75) 745 239. FAX (75) 746 238. @ riu.meharidjerba@planet.tn This spacious hotel has good-sized rooms. There is a well-kept garden with a swimming pool and a separate paddling pool for children as well as terraces and a lawn for sunbathing.	600	●	■	●	■
JERBA: Rym Beach ⓉⒹⓉⒹⓉⒹⓉⒹⓉⒹ Tourist zone. **Road map** E5. ((75) 745 614. FAX (75) 745 070. This hotel complex has good rooms with a sea view.	724	●	■	●	■
MEDENINE: Ibis ⓉⒹⓉⒹⓉⒹ Place 7 Novembre. **Road map** D5. ((75) 640 546. FAX (75) 640 550. This is the smartest hotel in town. It is modern, with attractive rooms and friendly service.	92	●			

ZARZIS: *Giktis Zarzis* ⓣⓣⓣ 409
Tourist zone. **Road map** E5. ☎ *(75) 705 800.* **FAX** *(75) 705 002.*
Located on a beach, all of this hotel's well-appointed rooms have sea views.
Evening entertainment is provided and there are playgrounds for the children.
P Y 🛁 🍴 24 🏊 🏃

ZARZIS: *Iberostar Zephyr* ⓣⓣⓣ 652
Tourist zone. **Road map** E5. ☎ *(75) 784 026.* **FAX** *(75) 780 071.*
This complex is situated close to a pleasant beach. The well-appointed rooms
all benefit from a sea view. P Y 🏊 🛁 🍴 24 🏃

ZARZIS: *Sangho* ⓣⓣⓣ 722
Tourist zone. **Road map** E5. ☎ *(75) 705 124.* **FAX** *(75) 705 715.*
@ sangho.zarziz@planet.tn
One of the dozen or so hotels situated in the tourist zone, this is attractively
designed and has a good range of facilities. P TV Y 🏊 🛁 🍴 24 🏃

SOUTHERN TUNISIA

DOUZ: *Hôtel 20 Mars* ⓣ
Rue 20 Mars. **Road map** C6. ☎ *(75) 470 269.*
This charming place is in the centre of Douz and handy for the surrounding
area. It is very good value and the management are extremely friendly. The
rooms are arranged around a shady inner courtyard. TV 24

DOUZ: *Rose de Sables* ⓣ 200
Tourist zone. **Road map** C6. ☎ *(75) 470 597.* **FAX** *(75) 471 366.*
A pleasant, modest hotel, Rose de Sables is situated in the tourist zone, just off
Avenue des Martyrs. Its clean, well-kept rooms are arranged around a pleasant
inner courtyard. TV Y 24

DOUZ: *Mehari* ⓣⓣⓣ 252
Tourist zone. **Road map** C6. ☎ *(75) 470 481.* **FAX** *(75) 471 589.*
The architecture of this hotel is traditional Tunisian with some interesting
communal areas. The hotel has two swimming pools. 🌐 P TV Y 🏊 🍴 24

DOUZ: *Saharien Paradise* ⓣⓣⓣ 300
Tourist zone. **Road map** C6. ☎ *(75) 471 337.* **FAX** *(75) 470 339.*
@ hotoasis@gnet.tn
The chalets, set in a delightful palm grove, and no fewer than four swimming
pools (one indoors) make this a popular place with tour operators. TV Y 24

DOUZ: *Touareg* ⓣⓣⓣ 315
Tourist zone. **Road map** C6. ☎ *(75) 470 245.* **FAX** *(75) 470 313.*
@ hotel.touareg@gnet.tn
This modern complex in the tourist zone resembles an old kasbah. The rooms
are attractive and stylish. The swimming pool contains a small central island
with a palm tree. TV Y 24 🏃

DOUZ: *El-Mouradi Oasis* ⓣⓣⓣⓣ 342
Tourist zone. **Road map** C6. ☎ *(75) 470 303.* **FAX** *(75) 470 906.*
@ elmouradi.douz@planet.tn
El-Mouradi is elegant and luxurious and stands at the gateway to the desert.
The oriental-style rooms contain some lovely furniture and the hotel also has a
small but extremely pleasant hammam. 🌐 P TV Y 🏊 🛁 🍴 24

DOUZ: *Sahara* ⓣⓣⓣⓣ 300
Tourist zone. **Road map** C6. ☎ *(75) 470 865.* **FAX** *(75) 470 566.*
This friendly hotel lies in the heart of the tourist zone. The rooms have all
been tastefully furnished. 🌐 P TV Y 🏊 🍴 24

KEBILI: *Kitam* ⓣ 64
Road map D1. ☎ *(75) 491 338.* **FAX** *(75) 491 076.*
This pleasant and modern hotel is on the road into town. The rooms are large
and bright. TV 24

KEBILI: *Fort des Autruches* ⓣⓣ
Road map D1. ☎ *(75) 490 233.* **FAX** *(75) 728 258.*
This hotel enjoys a magnificent location in a former fort.

KEBILI: *Les Dunes* ⓣⓣ 176
Bechri, Souk Lahad. **Road map** D1. ☎ *(75) 480 711.*
FAX *(75) 480 653.*
The hotel is situated 22 km (14 miles) from Kebili, near the village of Bechri.
It has a magnificent location on the edge of the Chott el-Jerid salt lake.

For key to symbols see back flap

<table>
<tr><td colspan="2">

Price categories for a standard double room, with bath or shower, including service and tax. Prices are in Tunisian dinars.
ⓉⒹ below 30 TD
ⓉⒹⓉⒹ 30–65 TD
ⓉⒹⓉⒹⓉⒹ 65–100 TD
ⓉⒹⓉⒹⓉⒹⓉⒹ 100–150 TD
ⓉⒹⓉⒹⓉⒹⓉⒹⓉⒹ over 150 TD

</td><td colspan="2">

RESTAURANT
This is also open to non-residents.

GARDEN OR TERRACE
Hotel has its own garden, a terrace or a courtyard with plants.

SWIMMING POOL
Hotel has a pool for the use of its guests.

AIR CONDITIONING
All rooms are air-conditioned.

</td></tr>
</table>

	NUMBER OF BEDS	RESTAURANT	GARDEN OR TERRACE	SWIMMING POOL	AIR CONDITIONING
KEBILI: *Oasis Dar Kebili* ⓉⒹⓉⒹⓉⒹⓉⒹ **Road map** D1. 📞 (75) 491 436. **FAX** (75) 491 295. This new, luxury hotel boasts an attractive location, pleasant rooms and a good range of facilities including a swimming pool and minibars in all the rooms. 🗎 📺 🕓	248	●	■	●	■
NEFTA: *El-Habib* ⓉⒹ **Place de la Libération. Road map** A5. 📞 (76) 430 497. This unassuming hotel has simple rooms and friendly service.	30				
NEFTA: *Neptus* ⓉⒹⓉⒹ **Tourist zone. Road map** A5. 📞 (76) 430 698. **FAX** (76) 430 647. Beautifully situated, on the edge of a palm grove, Neptus is similar to La Rosa *(see below)* in terms of character and price. The rooms are clean, well-appointed and comfortable.	154	●	■	●	■
NEFTA: *Bel Horizon* ⓉⒹⓉⒹⓉⒹ **Cité Corbeille, Avenue 7 Novembre. Road map** A5. 📞 (76) 430 328. **FAX** (76) 430 500. This restful, pleasant hotel has some imaginative decoration and a good swimming pool.	180		■	●	■
NEFTA: *La Rosa* ⓉⒹⓉⒹⓉⒹ **Road map** A5. 📞 (76) 430 696. **FAX** (76) 430 385. Beautifully located at the edge of a palm grove, La Rosa has comfortable, well-appointed rooms and flower-filled grounds.	190		■	●	■
NEFTA: *Caravanserail* ⓉⒹⓉⒹⓉⒹⓉⒹ **Tourist zone. Road map** A5. 📞 (76) 430 355. **FAX** (76) 430 344. This quiet hotel is situated in its own grounds, 20 minutes from Tozeur's airport. The outside pool and the hotel's rooms are both very pleasant. The hotel's nightclub is open only to guests. 🗎 📺	274	●	■		■
NEFTA: *Sahara Palace* ⓉⒹⓉⒹⓉⒹⓉⒹⓉⒹ **Tourist zone. Road map** A5. 📞 (76) 432 005. This beautiful hotel has large, stylishly furnished rooms, and is situated on the northern side of Nefta's scenic gorge. It has recently been refurbished to a high standard.	216	●	■	●	■
TAMERZA: *Les Cascades* ⓉⒹ **Road map** A5. 📞 (76) 485 332. Situated near a small waterfall, the chalets of this hotel stand in a palm grove and have a modest appearance and good furnishings.		●	■		
TAMERZA: *Tamerza Palace* ⓉⒹⓉⒹⓉⒹⓉⒹⓉⒹ **Road map** A5. 📞 & **FAX** (76) 485 322. @ tamerza.palace@planet.tn 🔳 www.tamerza-palace.com This is one of Tunisia's best "hôtels de charme" and has been tastefully furnished with traditional Tunisian furniture, carpets and rugs. The rooms overlook the valley and mountains. A swimming pool on the terrace overlooks the oasis. The building's stone construction is in keeping with the traditional Berber architecture of the area.	120	●	■	●	■
TATAOUINE: *Ksar Haddada* ⓉⒹ **Ksar el-Haddada, Ghomrassen. Road map** D6. 📞 (75) 860 605. **FAX** (75) 862 860. This romantic hotel has been converted from a *ksar* (fortified Berber stronghold). The rooms are modest, but the setting is memorable and resembles a scene from the film *Star Wars*.	38		■	●	
TATAOUINE: *La Gazelle* ⓉⒹⓉⒹ **Avenue Hedi Cheker. Road map** D6. 📞 (75) 860 009. **FAX** (75) 862 860. An attractive hotel situated in the town centre, La Gazelle has decent-sized rooms with en suite bathrooms. Breakfast is included in the price and it is possible to negotiate the rates.	45	●	■	●	

TATAOUINE: *Sangho Tatouine* ⓉⒹⓉⒹⓉⒹⓉⒹ 172
Route de Chenini el-Farch 186. **Road map** D6. 📞 *(75) 860 124.* 🅵🅰🆇 *(75) 862 177.*
Situated outside the village, the hotel is surrounded by a thick wall. Its style is reminiscent of traditional Berber houses. The interiors are very attractively furnished with antique bric-a-brac.

TOZEUR: *Aicha* ⓉⒹ 120
Road map B5. 📞 *(76) 452 788.* 🅵🅰🆇 *(76) 452 873.*
This quiet hotel has clean rooms but is a little way from the most interesting parts of Tozeur. Despite that, it represents value for money and serves as a good base for exploring the area.

TOZEUR: *Karim* ⓉⒹ 34
Avenue Abdul el-Kacem Chabbi. **Road map** B5. 📞 *(76) 454 547.*
This pleasant hotel has simply furnished rooms. All have en suite bathrooms. If possible, try to obtain a room away from the street, which can sometimes be noisy.

TOZEUR: *Niffer* ⓉⒹ 24
Place Bab el-Hawa. **Road map** B5. 📞 *(76) 460 610.* 🅵🅰🆇 *(76) 461 900.*
A simple but clean hotel, all the Niffer's rooms have en suite bathrooms. The hotel is conveniently located for the bus station.

TOZEUR: *Warda* ⓉⒹ 64
Avenue Abdul el-Kacem Chabbi. **Road map** B5. 📞 *(76) 452 597.*
🅵🅰🆇 *(76) 452 744.*
This inexpensive hotel has clean rooms, though bathrooms are shared. Breakfast is included in the price. It is convenient for the oasis and town.

TOZEUR: *Dar Ghaouar* ⓉⒹⓉⒹ 102
Road map B5. 📞 *(76) 452 782.* 🅵🅰🆇 *(76) 452 666.*
The spacious and clean rooms of this quiet town hotel are very pleasing.

TOZEUR: *Du Jardin* ⓉⒹⓉⒹ 40
Avenue de l'Environnement. **Road map** B5. 📞 *(76) 454 196.* 🅵🅰🆇 *(76) 454 199.*
Situated out of town on the road leading to Kebili, Du Jardin has an attractive garden.

TOZEUR: *Abou Nawas* ⓉⒹⓉⒹⓉⒹⓉⒹ 184
Road map B5. 📞 *(76) 452 700.* 🅵🅰🆇 *(76) 452 686.*
@ abounawastozeur@gnet.tn
This elegant and well-appointed hotel has beautiful rooms. The evening entertainment includes traditional shows. 🇹 📺

TOZEUR: *Dar Cheraït* ⓉⒹⓉⒹⓉⒹⓉⒹ 220
Tourist zone. **Road map** B5. 📞 *(76) 454 888.* 🅵🅰🆇 *(76) 452 399.*
@ darcherait@planet.tn
This luxurious hotel, situated in the Dar Cheraït museum building, resembles an Oriental palace. The rooms are magnificent and guests can enjoy evening performances of traditional *malouf* (folk) music. 🇹 📺

TOZEUR: *Ksar Rouge* ⓉⒹⓉⒹⓉⒹⓉⒹ 234
Road map B5. 📞 *(76) 454 933.* 🅵🅰🆇 *(76) 453 163.*
@ eldorado.ksar@planet.tn
This hotel boasts a fantastic location, with a view over the desert and the distant mountains. Its architecture is reminiscent of southern Tunisian palaces. The terrace affords a magnificent view of the surrounding area. 🇹 📺

TOZEUR: *Palmyre* ⓉⒹⓉⒹⓉⒹⓉⒹ 222
Road map B5. 📞 *(76) 452 041.* 🅵🅰🆇 *(76) 453 470.*
@ hotel.palmyre@gnet.tn
This hotel is situated in a traditional building. Evening folk shows are staged in the garden and the hotel has its own hammam (steam bath). 🇹 📺

TOZEUR: *Sofitel Palm Beach* ⓉⒹⓉⒹⓉⒹⓉⒹ 240
Road map B5. 📞 *(76) 453 111.* 🅵🅰🆇 *(76) 453 911.*
@ palmbeach.tozeur@gnet.tn
The interior design of this smart hotel has the flavour of an opulent eastern palace. It's the top hotel in Tozeur and the range of facilities, including a hammam and an excellent restaurant, reflects this. 🇹 📺 🍸 24 🏋

ZAAFRANE: *Zaafrane* ⓉⒹ 88
Road map C6. 📞 *(75) 491 720.* 🅵🅰🆇 *(75) 491 720.*
This pleasant hotel is located almost in the desert. It has clean rooms, some of which have a view of the oasis. 📺 🍸 24 🏋

For key to symbols see back flap

Price categories for a standard double room, with bath or shower, including service and tax. Prices are in Tunisian dinars.

- ⒯ below 30 TD
- ⒯⒯ 30–65 TD
- ⒯⒯⒯ 65–100 TD
- ⒯⒯⒯⒯ 100–150 TD
- ⒯⒯⒯⒯⒯ over 150 TD

RESTAURANT
This is also open to non-residents.

GARDEN OR TERRACE
Hotel has its own garden, a terrace or a courtyard with plants.

SWIMMING POOL
Hotel has a pool for the use of its guests.

AIR CONDITIONING
All rooms are air-conditioned.

Hotel	Price	Number of Beds	Restaurant	Garden or Terrace	Swimming Pool	Air Conditioning
ZAAFRANE: *Faouar*	⒯⒯⒯⒯	250	●	■	●	■

Road map C6. (75) 460 531. FAX (75) 460 576.
This simple hotel is close to the tourist office and has comfortable, clean rooms. Guests can stay in the hotel's Bedouin tents during peak season (Jul–Sep). TV Y 24 ♣

CENTRAL TUNISIA

Hotel	Price	Number of Beds	Restaurant	Garden or Terrace	Swimming Pool	Air Conditioning
GAFSA: *Ali Bacha*	⒯					

Road map B4. (76) 222 232.
This modest hotel is a good budget choice and has clean rooms, although none is en suite.

| **GAFSA:** *La République* | ⒯ | 43 | | | | |

Rue Ali Belhouane 28. **Road map** B4. (76) 221 807.
Close to the bus station, La République's rooms are modest but clean. Being close to the bus station it can be rather noisy.

| **GAFSA:** *Lune* | ⒯ | 18 | | | | |

Rue Jammal Abdenna Ceurcite Bayache. **Road map** B4. (76) 220 228.
This friendly little hotel, across the road from Hôtel Maamoun *(see below)*, is good value.

| **GAFSA:** *Gafsa* | ⒯⒯ | 93 | ● | | | ■ |

Rue Ahmed Snoussi 10. **Road map** B4. (76) 224 000. FAX (76) 224 747.
Catering mostly for tourist groups, the Gafsa attracts large numbers of visitors with its spacious clean rooms, spotless bathrooms, air conditioning and lower prices.

| **GAFSA:** *Maamoun* | ⒯⒯ | 138 | ● | ■ | ● | ■ |

Avenue Jamel Abdenaceur. **Road map** B4. (76) 220 470.
FAX (76) 226 440.
A well-appointed hotel, Maamoun is one of Gafsa's more upmarket establishments and has large rooms and a nice swimming pool. It is situated close to Gafsa's market square.

| **KAIROUAN:** *Sabra* | ⒯ | 70 | | | | |

Road map C3. (77) 230 269.
The hotel is situated in the town centre, opposite Bab ech-Chouhada. The simple rooms are all clean and of a reasonable size and the service is friendly and helpful.

| **KAIROUAN:** *Continental* | ⒯⒯ | 352 | ● | | ● | ■ |

Road map C3. (77) 231 135. FAX (77) 229 900.
Situated opposite the tourist office, the Continental has cosy rooms and its own swimming pool.

| **KAIROUAN:** *Splendid* | ⒯⒯ | 80 | ● | | | |

Rue 9 Avril. **Road map** C3. (77) 230 041. FAX (77) 230 829.
This upmarket hotel is in the town centre. The rooms are spacious, though somewhat lacking in character, but all are clean. There is a good bar downstairs. TV Y

| **KAIROUAN:** *Tunisia* | ⒯⒯ | 42 | ● | | | |

Avenue de la République. **Road map** C3. (77) 231 855. FAX (77) 231 597.
The hotel is situated in the town centre, a short way from the medina. It has large rooms with en suite showers or baths.

| **KAIROUAN:** *Amina* | ⒯⒯⒯ | 212 | ● | | | ■ |

Route de Tunis Gp, 3100 Kairouan. **Road map** C3. (77) 226 555.
FAX (77) 235 411.
Situated about 1 km (half a mile) from the tourist information bureau, the Amina is very popular with package holiday operators. All the comfortable rooms are en suite.

KAIROUAN: *Hôtel de la Kasbah* — 202
Avenue ibn al-Jazzar. **Road map** C3. (*(77) 237 301.* FAX *(77) 237 302.*
@ Kasbah.Kairouan@gnet.tn. W www.goldenyasmin.com
The best hotel in town is situated in the kasbah on the edge of Kairouan's medina. The communal areas are stylish and beautiful. The central courtyard has a wonderful pool and the former prison has been converted into a café. Some of the rooms are located in a modern part of the building and are a little disappointing.

KASSERINE: *De La Paix* — 29
Kasserine. **Road map** B3. (*(77) 471 465.*
Located in the main street, a short way from the town's central square, this hotel is in a busy district. All the rooms have an en suite bathroom. There is a restaurant downstairs.

KASSERINE: *Pinus* — 26
Road map B3. (*(77) 470 164.*
A short walk from Hôtel de la Paix *(see above)* and the main square on the road that leads to Sbeïtla, this hotel has attractively simple decor and represents good value for money.

LE KEF: *Ramzi* — 26
Road map B2. (*(78) 203 079.*
This modest but adequate hotel is in the town centre. Not all rooms are en suite. Breakfast is included in the price.

LE KEF: *Résidence Venus* — 39
Rue Mouldi Khanemessi. **Road map** B2. (*(78) 204 695.*
This hotel has a warm, family atmosphere and is situated just below the kasbah. Most rooms are en suite and are heated in the winter. The price includes breakfast.

LE KEF: *Les Pins* — 60
Avenue de L'Environnement. **Road map** B2. (*(78) 204 300/021.* FAX *(78) 202 411.*
Occupying a lovely spot at the edge of the town, Les Pins has bright modern furnishings. The hotel gets its name from its close proximity to the pine-clad mountain that it overlooks. All the en suite rooms are clean and comfortable.

LE KEF: *Sicca Veneria* — 64
Place de l'Indépendance. **Road map** B2. (*(78) 202 389.*
Situated in the town centre, the hotel's eclectic style is a combination of Oriental and European features. Its modest rooms are not particularly tastefully furnished, but compensate for this by being quite large. The windows look onto a busy square.

MAKTHAR: *Mactaris* — 9
Road map C3. (*(77) 876 465.*
The only hotel in town, this offers fairly simple accommodation. All the rooms are capable of triple occupancy.

METLAOUI: *Ennacim* — 16
Road map B5. (*(76) 241 920.*
The hotel is situated on the road leading out of Metlaoui towards Tozeur. The rooms are small but pleasant. There is a bar downstairs.

SBEÏTLA: *Bakini* — 78
Rue 2 Mars 1934, 1250 Sbeitla. **Road map** C3. (*(77) 465 244.*
A clean and comfortable hotel situated in the eastern part of the town near the mosque, the Bakini has reasonably-sized rooms.

SBEÏTLA: *Sufetula* — 92
Road map C3. (*(77) 465 074.* FAX *(77) 465 582.*
An attractive hotel, the Sufetula overlooks the Roman ruins. The hotel stands above the town, some 2 km (1 mile) from the ruins on the road to Kasserine.

SIDI BOUZID: *Chems* — 18
Road map C4. (*(77) 634 465.*
This friendly hotel is situated in the town centre. All rooms are en suite. The hotel's restaurant offers good value for money.

SIDI BOUZID: *El-Horchani* — 52
Road map C4. (*(76) 634 635.* FAX *(76) 633 775.*
El-Horchani has a wide choice of rooms – some fairly large and bright, others a little on the small side. All rooms are en suite.

WHERE TO EAT

ROM UPMARKET European-style restaurants to streetside vendors, Tunisia can cater for most tastes and budgets. Perhaps the best place to enjoy Tunisian food is in the local cafés. The spicy Tunisian cuisine served in many of these unassuming places often tastes better than in many expensive hotels. There is no need to be afraid of eating in small local eateries as they are almost uniformly

A display of Tunisian oranges

clean and offer good quality. Be aware that most Tunisian stews and sauces in traditional cafés are made with harissa, a fiery condiment that usually appears on the table without anyone asking for it. Alcohol is not generally available and those restaurants that do serve it tend to be pricier. Most major towns have good produce markets where a delicious picnic of baguettes, cheese and fruit can easily be bought.

Café with rugs by the medina wall in Hammamet

TYPES OF RESTAURANT

SIMPLE MEALS OF FISH, chicken, meat and vegetables are readily available in *gargottes* (small, inexpensive restaurants), which also serve soup. Bread and water are served at no extra charge.

Tourist restaurants, so called because they have been inspected and graded by the country's tourist authorities, offer a choice of Tunisian and European cuisine.

Hotels, especially those catering for package groups, offer "international cuisine" as well as tamer versions of Tunisia's spicy stews.

For those who do not wish to spend much time in restaurants, snack bars provide the best answer, offering, among others things, a slice of Tunisian pizza.

WHAT TO EAT

THE MOST POPULAR Tunisian dish is couscous – which is made from semolina and served with chunky stewed vegetables, meat or fish in a hot tomato sauce. Couscous appears in many varieties; the most popular is made with chunks of lamb that have been cooked with vegetables. The couscous is placed above the pot and cooks slowly in a *coucoussier* by absorbing all

Inside the popular Café M. Rabet in Souk et-Trouk, Tunis

of the steam and flavour from the stew bubbling below.

Another very tasty dish is *kamounia* – an aromatic meat dish made of beef or lamb that is cooked with plenty of cumin and other spices. The most popular dishes in the coastal region are grilled octopus and prawns, and *complet poisson* (a whole fish served with a salad made of tomatoes, lettuce and peppers).

The most common Tunisian snack is the *brik à l'oeuf* (an egg that has been fried inside a thin pastry envelope). For an authentic *brik*, the egg-yolk should be soft and the pastry envelope crescent-shaped. Sprinkled with lemon juice and eaten with the fingers, it makes a delicious lunch. Another very tasty snack is *Deglet Fatima* (Fatima's fingers), which are thin rolls of transparent pastry stuffed with meat or egg and then deep-fried. Tunisian pizza is usually made in large trays and often topped with chunks of tuna. Tuna is also

Floating restaurant in Port el-Kantaoui

the main ingredient of *salade tunisienne*, another favourite, which consists of crisp green lettuce, olives, tomatoes, cucumber and slices of hard-boiled egg.

Cheap and filling soups are part of the staple diet in Tunisia. Of all the varieties, *lablabi* is the most common and is made from chickpeas and served with bread and harissa. Sometimes it has a raw egg whisked into it. *Chorba* is a spicier soup. Usually prepared with chicken or lamb stock, it often includes pasta or grains of barley. A spicy fish version is popular in the Sfax region.

Bread is a staple of the Tunisian diet and is served with every meal.

OPENING HOURS

CAFÉS ARE USUALLY open from 8 or 9am until about 10pm. In small towns they close a little earlier. Local cafés, where men come to watch TV and smoke *chichas* (hookahs), usually stay open until about midnight. Some cafés remain open 24 hours a day. Restaurants are usually open from 10 or 11am. Lunch is served between noon and 3pm. Restaurants close about 10 or 11pm, though the kitchen normally stops serving an hour earlier.

PRICES

THERE IS A HUGE difference in the prices charged by hotels and tourist restaurants, and those charged in small establishments frequented by Tunisians. Meals in local restaurants are considerably cheaper. In a local restaurant or café a *brik à l'oeuf* will cost less than 1 TD, while in a tourist-zone restaurant it may cost 3 TD or more. A dish of couscous will cost about 4 TD in a local restaurant, while a hotel may charge 10 TD for virtually the same dish. A main course of grilled meat or a large portion of chicken

Restaurant in a converted medina palace

with chips and salad will cost about 3 TD in a local restaurant and up to 20 TD in an upmarket restaurant aimed exclusively at holidaymakers. A glass of mint tea served with sugar costs about 1 TD. English-style tea is less readily available and may well cost more than this. A puff on a hookah that can be shared by several people costs between 2 and 4 TD.

It is best to buy drinks from a shop. The lowest prices are found in supermarkets; in small shops the cost is normally 10 to 20 per cent more.

A pitta bread vendor in Kairouan

HYGIENE

TOURIST RESTAURANTS have stringent rules of hygiene. Local cafés and restaurants are also usually clean and tidy, as are the small pavement restaurants. For the first few days of your visit, however, it is best to avoid eating raw fruit and vegetables as these can cause stomach upsets.

RAMADAN

DURING RAMADAN, the ninth month of the Islamic calendar, Tunisians fast from sunrise until sunset. The fast is strictly observed and many local restaurants and cafés remain closed. Some restaurants do remain open but fewer options will be

available. Tunisians do not normally get indignant at the sight of a tourist eating and drinking during Ramadan, but it is good manners not to eat or drink in public places during the fast. Large towns usually have a few restaurants that cater for tourists.

Once the fast has been broken each evening, it is fairly easy to find a restaurant that serves a Ramadan dinner. Such restaurants stay open for a few hours after sunset and the streets became deserted while the locals sit down to a family meal. After dinner, many families attend concerts and parties. Some of the cafés in the medinas open their doors late in order to serve a final meal before the fast begins again at sunrise.

VEGETARIANS

TUNISIANS ARE FOND of meat and find it hard to understand people who are willingly vegetarian. In small local restaurants *(gargottes)* and fast-food stands or cafés it would be difficult to get a vegetarian meal. Salads are usually garnished with a piece of tuna fish, while soups are invariably prepared using meat or fish stock. Vegans will have an even harder time. However, vegetarian dishes can usually be ordered in tourist and hotel restaurants.

A restaurant garden in the centre of Sousse medina

What to Eat

Brik
A typical Tunisian snack consisting of a thin pastry with a savoury filling (the most common is egg).

DOMINATED BY MEAT AND FISH dishes eaten with large amounts of vegetables – cooked and raw – Tunisian cuisine is both tasty and inexpensive. It is also not a particularly spicy cuisine. Although meaty dishes such as couscous and hearty soups such as *chorba* often have plenty of harissa (red chilli sauce) added to them, this can always be left out if desired. The true power of harissa is best experienced at the start of a meal, when it is served with olive oil on a small plate as an appetizer and to enhance digestion.

Traditional almond pastry

Harissa
A very popular spicy condiment made of red chilli and garlic. Often served with olive oil, olives and fresh bread as a starter.

Mechouia
A kind of salad made of grilled aubergines, tomatoes, courgettes and onions. The vegetables are mashed with olive oil and garlic.

Chorba
A spicy soup with tiny pasta shapes or barley granules (chorba fric). Usually made with lamb or chicken stock.

Salade Tunisienne
A salad made of green lettuce, tomatoes, cucumbers, peppers and olives and often topped with slices of hard-boiled egg, pieces of tuna or prawns.

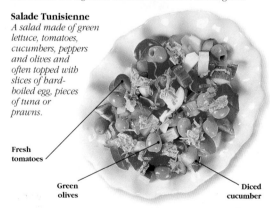

Fresh tomatoes

Green olives

Diced cucumber

Lablabi
Typical Tunisian soup, served for lunch, made of chickpeas with added bread and seasoned with harissa.

FRUIT

Locally-grown fruit is readily available. May is good for strawberries; the first grapes arrive in June; pomegranates ripen in October; dates are harvested in late autumn. The citrus fruit season lasts from December until March.

Melon

Orange

Strawberry

Fig

Prickly pear

Dates

Kamounia
A meat stew that is made with plenty of onions and liberally seasoned with cumin and other spices. It is delicious but is not as commonly served as couscous and may not always be on the menu.

Tunisian Couscous
Steamed grains of semolina, served with meat or fish and vegetables in a tomato sauce is Tunisia's most famous dish.

Grilled Fish
Just as anywhere else, grilled fish and seafood can be expensive in Tunisia and is best in the small seaside villages.

Stewed onion

Cuttlefish

Green peppers

Diced potatoes and carrots

Couscous flavoured with harissa

Tajine
This is a kind of baked omelette made with potatoes, cheese and meat (the ingredients depend on the chef's imagination). It may be served hot or cold.

Stuffed Cuttlefish with Couscous
One of many varieties of couscous. This one is spicy and made with cuttlefish, lots of vegetables and harissa.

DESSERTS
Both the French and Turks left behind them a legacy of delicious desserts for the Tunisians to enjoy. Numerous shops sell European cakes, as well as Eastern sweets. Alongside almond and chocolate cakes, croissants and gateaux, it is not unusual to see *loukoum* (Turkish delight), *baklava*, and dates filled with marzipan.

Oudnin el-Kadhi
These traditional cakes are made from nuts and honey, and fried in oil.

Baklava
Very sweet, baklava is a type of Eastern pastry made with filo pastry, nuts and almonds.

Makhroud
Date cakes are a speciality of the Kairouan region and a favourite Tunisian delicacy.

Zrir Tunisienne
This popular snack is a mixture of various types of nuts and raisins.

Samsa Delice
These resemble croissants and are filled with a variety of dried fruit and fried in oil.

What to Drink

THE MOST POPULAR TUNISIAN BEVERAGE is mint tea, which is drunk often and everywhere. Meals are usually accompanied by tap or mineral water as well as all kinds of fizzy drinks (known as *gazouz*), including the big-name brands as well as local products. Although a Muslim country, Tunisia produces good wines, both red and white, an interesting liqueur and one brand of home-brewed beer called Celtia. A range of brightly-coloured fruit syrups is also available that are diluted with water. Fruit juices are sold in many resorts in the summer.

A decorative coffee brewing set

A waiter pouring mint tea from a height to produce a froth

TEA

THE SLOW DRINKING OF MINT TEA is a ritual that is practised several times a day in Tunisia. Granulated black or green tea is stewed slowly, with a large amount of sugar and fresh mint (honey may be used in place of sugar), until it produces a dark infusion. This is poured from a pot into small glasses, from a height, so as to create a froth.

Fresh mint leaves or pine nuts are sometimes added to this. Tunisian tea is strong and aromatic and is not to everyone's taste though it is thought by Tunisians to assist the digestion. Tea is not often served with milk, apart from in the larger hotels or tourist centres and even these may use UHT in place of fresh milk.

A glass of mint tea

A packet of green tea

COFFEE

Strong, black coffee

TUNISIANS CAN SPEND A LONG TIME over a small cup of coffee as they contemplate the world passing by and every small café and even the most humble local bars can serve an excellent espresso. It is often served with small shortbread or date biscuits. The coffee is strong, but is not always offered with water, as it is in many countries. Coffee in Tunisia is normally served in small glasses. Anyone wanting a larger cup of slightly weaker coffee with milk can order a *café direct* (similar to a cappuccino) or a *café au lait* (a filter coffee with milk). Other popular types include coffee with condensed milk *(Capucin nouveau)*, not to be confused with cappuccino and Turkish coffee *(qahwa arbi)*. This strong, sweet brew is made by boiling the coffee and is served with the fine grounds still in it.

Coffee with milk

MINERAL WATER

UNLIKE MANY AFRICAN COUNTRIES, tap water is clean in Tunisia and can be safely drunk anywhere in larger towns. Its taste, however, leaves a lot to be desired and many people prefer to drink bottled water, which is cheap and readily available. The most popular mineral water – Safia – is produced in plain and sparkling versions (the latter is usually sold in glass bottles). They both taste good and should be considered indispensable when travelling around the country. In summer, a bottle of mineral water should always be taken on sightseeing tours of archaeological sites and open-air museums to avoid the risk of dehydration.

Water in large bottles

Safia bottled water

BEER

TUNISIA HAS ONLY ONE BRAND of home-brewed beer – Celtia – which is produced on licence from Stella Artois and Lowenbrau. It is slightly less potent than European beers, but it tastes good nevertheless. In shops, Celtia is sold only in red and white cans. However, not all shops sell beer. Some restaurants serve beer in bottles but prices tend to be higher than restaurants that do not serve alcohol. The more expensive restaurants and hotels offer foreign beers to their guests, but even here the choice is limited. The most easily available are the popular brands of German, Danish and Dutch beer.

Celtia in a bottle

Celtia in a can

WINE

TUNISIA HAS BEEN PRODUCING WINE for 2,000 years. New varieties of grape were introduced in the 1990s and in 2002 a new range of pricey wines was launched, including the Château Saint Augustin. Wine is produced in several regions. These include Cap Bon in the north, especially around Grombalia and Mornag, and in the vicinity of Jendouba in the west. The range of red wines is the safest choice and includes Château Feriani, Coteaux d'Utique and Lambolt. Noteworthy among the rosé varieties are Tyna and Koudiat. The white Coteaux de Carthage is also very good.

Red wine

Rosé wine

White wine

VODKAS AND LIQUEURS

THE ONLY STRONG ALCOHOLIC beverage produced in Tunisia is *boukha* – a clear spirit made from figs. It contains 40 per cent alcohol and resembles a dry fruit-flavoured vodka. It is often served with fizzy cola. *Laghmi* is a palm wine that is fermented for 24 hours. It is not sold in shops, but it can be obtained from one of the oases during the palm season. Another alternative is Thibarine, a liqueur derived from dates and herbs that is produced in the village of Thibar (near Dougga) according to a secret recipe handed down by French monks. Cedratine, a liqueur made from lemons, is also popular.

Boukha, made from figs

Thibarine, made from dates

Cedratine, made from lemons

LOCAL BEVERAGES

THE TUNISIANS PRODUCE their own kinds of fizzy drink which are sold alongside brand names such as Coca-Cola and Pepsi. The most popular of these is Boga, which comes in two varieties. The dark one is a cola-type drink; the orange one is more like orangeade. Also popular are syrups that must be diluted with water. Flavours include pomegranate and rose essence. Fresh fruit juices are available in some cafés and in the resorts.

Sparkling Boga

Sweet dark Boga

A glass of orange juice

Choosing a Restaurant

THE FOLLOWING RESTAURANTS have been chosen for their fine food, as well as for the quality of their decor and location. Establishments are listed by region starting with Tunis, and alphabetically within price categories. Colour-coded thumb tabs correspond to the regional chapter in the main section. Please note that few restaurants accept credit cards.

	LIVE MUSIC	OUTSIDE DINING	WINE OR BEER	EXCEPTIONAL DECOR
TUNIS				

TUNIS: *Abib* ⑪
Rue de Yougoslavie 98. **Road map** C1. ❰ *(71) 257 052.*
In the town centre and close to the medina, this inexpensive and unpretentious restaurant offers wholesome Tunisian food. ❙⑪❙ ⬤ *Sun.*

TUNIS: *Bella Italia* ⑪
Rue de Yougoslavie 114. **Road map** C1. ❰ *(71) 249 466.*
A modest-sized pasta restaurant in the centre of the Ville Nouvelle, in an attractive 19th-century palazzo-style building. This is a convenient place for a quick meal, although the clientele tends to be mostly men. ❙⑪❙

TUNIS: *Café Africa* ⑪
Avenue H. Bourguiba. **Road map** C1. ❰ *(71) 347 477.*
The café is part of the refurbished Hôtel Africa el-Mouradi *(see p249)*. Large, glazed and air-conditioned, it is a popular meeting place for Tunisians and serves good quality snacks and meals. Open late. 🗐▤ ❙⑪❙

TUNIS: *Café de Paris Restaurant* ⑪
Avenue H. Bourguiba. **Road map** C1. ❰ *(71) 240 583.*
This small restaurant has modern decor and is one of the few inexpensive places where it is possible to get a beer or glass of wine in Tunis. It is a congenial place for female visitors wishing to have a quiet meal. ▤ ❙⑪❙ ⬤ *Sun.*

TUNIS: *Café Girofle* ⑪
Close to Hôtel Africa el-Mouradi. **Road map** C1. ❰ *No telephone.*
A pleasant Moorish café that serves good espresso coffee, cappuccino and café crème. The Girofle is one of a handful of places close to Avenue Habib Bourguiba where a *chicha* (hookah) can be had. ▤ ❙⑪❙

TUNIS: *L'Astragale* ⑪
Rue Dauphine 17. **Road map** C1. ❰ *(71) 785 080.* **FAX** *(71) 785 270.*
Surrounded by a lush garden, L'Astragale is famous for its exquisite fish dishes and delicious beef tenderloin. The restaurant is close to the Belvedere Park and is one of the favourite haunts of Tunis's social elite. It can get busy, so book ahead. ⬤ *Aug & Sun.*

TUNIS: *Le Bleuet* ⑪
Rue de Marseille 23 bis. **Road map** C1. ❰ *(71) 349 280.*
This inexpensive and pleasant restaurant also serves wine and beer and plays music until late *(see p298)*.

TUNIS: *La Mamma* ⑪
Rue de Marseille 11 bis. **Road map** C1. ❰ *(71) 332 388, 240 109.* **FAX** *(71) 256 417.*
La Mamma's pasta dishes are popular with the locals. ❙⑪❙ ⬤ *Jul & Aug.*

TUNIS: *Restaurant du Caire* ⑪
Rue du Caire. **Road map** C1. ❰ *No telephone.*
This restaurant offers generous helpings of tasty fish and seafood and is a good choice if the Restaurant de Sfax, situated opposite, is full. ▤ ❙⑪❙

TUNIS: *Restaurant de Sfax* ⑪
Rue du Caire. **Road map** C1. ❰ *(71) 352 437.*
A pleasant and inexpensive restaurant, the dishes particularly worth recommending here include fish soup, *brik à l'oeuf* (a Tunisian snack), couscous and any of the grills. The restaurant is good value and can get busy, especially during the peak holiday season. ❙⑪❙

TUNIS: *Roi d'Espagne* ⑪
Rue de Lenin 34. **Road map** C1. ❰ *(71) 256 693.*
A modest restaurant, this is fairly popular with the locals and serves a good variety of Tunisian staples. ❙⑪❙

		LIVE MUSIC	OUTSIDE DINING	WINE OR BEER	EXCEPTIONAL DECOR

Price categories are for a three-course meal for one person, including cover charge, and service but not alcohol.
€ under 10 TD
€€ 10–15 TD
€€€ 15–20 TD
€€€€ 20–25 TD
€€€€€ over 30 TD

LIVE MUSIC
Live performances of traditional music or entertainment programmes.

OUTSIDE DINING
Meals can be served on a terrace, garden or courtyard.

WINE OR BEER
Wine or beer can be ordered with meals.

EXCEPTIONAL DECOR
Restaurant is situated in a beautiful building or inside a palace.

TUNIS: *Royal Self* €
Rue d'Alger 6. **Road map** C1. (*(71) 258 476.*
This clean and pleasant pizzeria/restaurant has the ambience of a fast-food bar. It is worth visiting during lunch hours, when it offers the largest choice of dishes. It's popular with local office workers. ▤ ¶❶¶ ● *Sun.*

TUNIS: *Sémaphaur* €
Rue de la Commission. **Road map** C1. (*No telephone.*
Situated by the entrance to the medina, adjacent to Bab el-Bahr, the traditional Tunisian cuisine served here makes this a busy place. ¶❶¶

TUNIS: *Almazara* €€
Rue de Marseille 11. **Road map** C1. (*(71) 355 077.*
The attractive decor and tasty food make this a good choice. On the menu are seafood and Tunisian dishes such as couscous. ▤ ¶❶¶ ● *Sun.*

TUNIS: *Carcassonne* €€
Avenue de Carthage 8. **Road map** C1. (*(71) 256 768.*
This long-established restaurant has reasonable prices and good service. The menu is a mix of Tunisian and French cuisine. ● *Sun.*

TUNIS: *Chez Nous* €€
Rue de Marseille 5. **Road map** C1. (*(71) 245 043.*
Situated in the centre of Ville Nouvelle, Chez Nous has a good set menu. It can get busy at lunch times. Open late. ● *Sun.*

TUNIS: *Dar Bel Hadj* €€
Rue des Tamis 17. **Road map** C1. (*(71) 339 549.* FAX *(71) 339 549.*
Situated north of the Great Mosque *(see pp70–71)* this upmarket eatery is in a beautiful 17th-century medina palace that once belonged to a wealthy Tunis family. The mix of Tunisian and French food is superb. ● *Sun & Jul.*

TUNIS: *Ghassen* €€
Rue de Palestine 57. **Road map** C1. (*(71) 892 962.*
The restaurant is situated in the Belvedere district of Tunis and serves good seafood and couscous. The prawns with garlic are wonderful. ▤ ¶❶¶

TUNIS: *Hollywood Dinner's* €€
Rue de Marseille 12–14. **Road map** C1. (*(71) 344 755.*
Situated in Oscar's Hotel *(see p249)*, the decor here has a cinematic theme. The menu is composed of international dishes. ▤ ¶❶¶

TUNIS: *L'Orient* €€
Rue Ali Bach Hamba 7. **Road map** C1. (*(71) 252 061, 335 970.* FAX *(71) 347 726.*
This typical Tunis brasserie has a pleasant atmosphere and serves a mix of French and Tunisian cuisine. A good place for a quick lunch. ¶❶¶ ● *Sun.*

TUNIS: *La Romanesca* €€
Avenue Mohamed Tilli 29. **Road map** C1. (*(71) 753 241.*
Famous for its excellent Italian cuisine La Romanesca has some mouthwatering dishes on the menu. Particularly worth recommending are the pasta with salmon and gnocchi with Gorgonzola. ▤ ¶❶¶

TUNIS: *Le Duc* €€
Rue Gandi 7 bis. **Road map** C1. (*(71) 350 020, 336 388.* FAX *(71) 339 020.*
Tasty fish and seafood coupled with a pleasant atmosphere and friendly service make this a popular place. There is music in the evenings. ▤ ¶❶¶

TUNIS: *Margaritas* €€
Rue de Hollande 6. **Road map** C1. (*(71) 240 632.*
A pleasant restaurant in the centre of town, Margaritas is on the ground floor of the Hôtel Maison Dorée *(see p248)*. It serves French cuisine including delicious salads and fish dishes. ¶❶¶ ● *Sun & Aug.*

Price categories are for a three-course meal for one person, including cover charge, and service but not alcohol.
- ⑩ under 10 TD
- ⑩⑩ 10–15 TD
- ⑩⑩⑩ 15–20 TD
- ⑩⑩⑩⑩ 20–25 TD
- ⑩⑩⑩⑩⑩ over 30 TD

LIVE MUSIC
Live performances of traditional music or entertainment programmes.

OUTSIDE DINING
Meals can be served on a terrace, garden or courtyard.

WINE OR BEER
Wine or beer can be ordered with meals.

EXCEPTIONAL DECOR
Restaurant is situated in a beautiful building or inside a palace.

	LIVE MUSIC	OUTSIDE DINING	WINE OR BEER	EXCEPTIONAL DECOR

TUNIS: *Mehdoui* ⑩⑩ — Outside Dining ●
Rue Jemaa Zitouna 79. **Road map** C1. [*No telephone.*
A local restaurant next to the Great Mosque, Mehdoui can be found at the end of the medina's main street. It is only open for lunch and closes in the afternoon, but the traditional couscous and grills are good value and very tasty. ❙⑩❙ ● *afternoons & Sun.*

TUNIS: *M. Rabet* ⑩⑩ — Live Music ■, Outside Dining ●, Wine or Beer ■, Exceptional Decor ●
Souk et-Trouk 27. **Road map** C1. [*(71) 263 681, 261 729.*
Overlooking a section of the Great Mosque *(see pp70–71)* M. Rabet derives its name from the three marabouts (holy men) who are buried nearby. The restaurant is pricey but you are paying for the location and the stylish interior. M. Rabet also has a café in the cellar. The more expensive restaurant is on the first floor. One of the medina's best-known venues for music, with plenty of authentic Tunisian atmosphere. ✿ 目 ❙⑩❙

TUNIS: *Oraz* ⑩⑩
Rue Jamal Abdennacer 16. **Road map** C1. [*(71) 321 714.*
This cheap and cheerful restaurant serves good pizza. ❙⑩❙

TUNIS: *Paradiso* ⑩⑩
Avenue des Etats Unis 16. **Road map** C1. [*(71) 786 863.*
Situated not far from Belvedere Park, the Paradiso is popular with diplomats, who drop in for lunch. The *plat du jour* is particularly good. 目 ❙⑩❙ ● *Aug & Sun.*

TUNIS: *Petite Hutte* ⑩⑩ — Wine or Beer ■
Rue de Yougoslavie 102. **Road map** C1. [*(71) 254 959.* FAX *(71) 734 026.*
This friendly restaurant serves mainly French cuisine. 目 ❙⑩❙ ● *Sun.*

TUNIS: *Savarin* ⑩⑩ — Wine or Beer ■
Rue du Lt Mohammed Aziz Taj 29. **Road map** C1. [*(71) 352 322.*
Serving mainly Tunisian cuisine, this restaurant has good beef dishes and a large selection of salads. Worth recommending are the *mechouia* (a mix of roasted vegetables served cold) and the *brik à l'oeuf* (egg inside an envelope of pastry). Open late. ❙⑩❙

TUNIS: *Verrière* ⑩⑩ — Outside Dining ●, Wine or Beer ■
Le Forum, Berges du Lac. **Road map** C1. [*(71) 860 352/994.* FAX *(71) 861 073.*
The restaurant is located a fair distance from the town centre, in an amusement park. It is a popular venue for Tunisian family outings. ❙⑩❙

TUNIS: *Dar el-Jeld* ⑩⑩⑩ — Live Music ■, Wine or Beer ■, Exceptional Decor ●
Rue Dar el-Jeld, La Kasbah 5. **Road map** C1. [*(71) 560 916.* FAX *(71) 567 845.*
One of the most interesting and the smartest of the medina's restaurants, Dar el-Jeld occupies a beautifully restored 19th-century aristocratic residence. The Tunisian cuisine includes delicious desserts. Live Arab music adds to the atmosphere. A large, grander sister restaurant is a few doors along at No. 10. ✿ 目

TUNIS: *Dar Hammouda Pasha* ⑩⑩⑩ — Live Music ■, Outside Dining ●, Wine or Beer ■, Exceptional Decor ●
Rue Sidi ben Arous 56. **Road map** C1. [*(71) 561 746, 566 584.*
Situated at the heart of the medina, close to Hammouda Pasha Mosque *(see p76)* and Place du Gouvernement, the restaurant occupies a beautifully restored palace. Most tables are in the monumental inner courtyard, covered with a glass roof. The traditional food, and frequent concerts, make it a popular place, especially at the weekend. 目 ❙⑩❙ ● *Sun & Aug.*

TUNIS: *Essaraya* ⑩⑩⑩ — Wine or Beer ■, Exceptional Decor ●
Rue B. Mahmoud 6. **Road map** C1. [*(71) 560 310, 563 091.* FAX *(71) 571 465.*
Visitors are greeted by a lantern-bearing doorman. The superior cuisine of this medina restaurant is matched by the beautiful, if somewhat cramped, interior of the historic house. ✿ ❙⑩❙ 目

TUNIS: *Chez Slah*
Rue Pierre de Coubertin 14 bis. **Road map** C1. (71) 258 588, 332 463.
This attractive restaurant has long maintained a high standard of service and cuisine. It specializes in fish dishes and also serves wonderful puddings. Booking is recommended. *Sun.*

TUNIS: *Diwan Dar el-Jeld*
Rue Dar el-Jeld 10. **Road map** C1. (71) 560 916. **FAX** (71) 567 845.
w www.dareljeld.tourism.tn
This restaurant occupies a converted medina palace. The decor is authentic and it makes a good choice for those who appreciate a fine meal in a formal atmosphere. Diwan Dar el-Jeld is also a venue for cultural events. *Sun, lunchtimes Jul & Aug, and Ramadan.*

TUNIS: *La Sofra*
Hôtel el-Hana International. **Road map** C1. (71) 331 144.
This hotel restaurant and nightclub is frequented mostly by wealthy Tunisians, hotel guests and business people.

TUNIS: *Le Carthage*
Rue Ali Bach Hamba 10. **Road map** C1. & **FAX** (71) 351 772.
The restaurant is opposite the Hôtel el-Hana and serves classic Mediterranean and Tunisian dishes. The street itself is not very prepossessing but the restaurant receives good reports.

TUNIS: *Club 2001*
Hôtel el-Mechtel. **Road map** C1. (71) 783 200.
Located in the Hôtel el-Mechtel *(see p249)*, this upmarket restaurant/club has good food and nightly entertainment.

GREATER TUNIS AND CAP BON PENINSULA

CARTHAGE: *L'Amphitrite*
Avenue de l'Union, Amilcar Plage. **Road map** C1. (71) 747 591.
Situated close to the beach, this restaurant specializes in seafood but also has a good selection of European dishes on its tourist menu, including grilled steak. The restaurant manages to maintain a good balance between the quality of the food served and the price charged.

CARTHAGE: *Le Neptune*
Rue ibn Chablat 1. **Road map** C1. (71) 731 456.
This attractively located restaurant features Mediterranean cuisine with Spanish and French dishes on the menu.

CARTHAGE: *Le Punique*
Rue Hannibal 16. **Road map** C1. (71) 731 799. **FAX** (71) 720 135.
Part of the Hôtel Residence Carthago, Le Punique is famous for its Moroccan cuisine. *Sun.*

EL-HAOUARIA: *Fruits de Mer*
Road map D1. (72) 297 017.
As its name implies, fish and other seafood are strongly represented on the menu here. The fish soup is especially good.

EL-HAOUARIA: *La Daurade*
Close to the Roman caves. **Road map** D1. (72) 269 080.
This highly-regarded seafood restaurant affords a magnificent view of Cap Bon. The menu includes a delicious couscous and freshly-caught lobster. Evening shows are staged during the peak season.

EL-HAOUARIA: *Les Grottes*
Road map D1. (72) 297 296.
A mix of Tunisian and European cuisine makes up the menu in this decent hotel restaurant. The restaurant can sometimes get busy.

GAMMARTH: *Le Lagon*
Chott el-Ghaba, Raoued Plage. **Road map** C1. (71) 743 500. **FAX** (71) 912 516.
As in most good Gammarth restaurants the menu is dominated by fish. There is also a good selection of Tunisian meat dishes.

GAMMARTH: *Les Ombrelles*
Gammarth Plage 107. **Road map** C1. (71) 742 964. **FAX** (71) 727 364.
The restaurant is situated not far from the Hôtel Megara *(see p251)* and has a superb location by the sea. It serves mostly French cuisine including some good fish dishes. Booking is necessary in the peak season.

<table>
<tr><td>

Price categories are for a three-course meal for one person, including cover charge, and service but not alcohol.
- ⓣⓓ under 10 TD
- ⓣⓓⓣⓓ 10–15 TD
- ⓣⓓⓣⓓⓣⓓ 15–20 TD
- ⓣⓓⓣⓓⓣⓓⓣⓓ 20–25 TD
- ⓣⓓⓣⓓⓣⓓⓣⓓⓣⓓ over 30 TD

</td><td>

LIVE MUSIC
Live performances of traditional music or entertainment programmes.

OUTSIDE DINING
Meals can be served on a terrace, garden or courtyard.

WINE OR BEER
Wine or beer can be ordered with meals.

EXCEPTIONAL DECOR
Restaurant is situated in a beautiful building or inside a palace.

</td></tr>
</table>

	LIVE MUSIC	OUTSIDE DINING	WINE OR BEER	EXCEPTIONAL DECOR
GAMMARTH: *Le Grand Bleu* — ⓣⓓⓣⓓⓣⓓ Avenue Taieb M'hiri. **Road map** C1. **(** (71) 746 900. **FAX** (71) 745 504. This restaurant specializes in seafood and fish dishes and is ideally situated on the seashore with a fine view. 🍽️		●	▪	
GAMMARTH: *Les Dunes* — ⓣⓓⓣⓓⓣⓓⓣⓓ Avenue Taieb M'Hiri 130. **Road map** C1. **(** (71) 743 379. **FAX** (71) 741 371. A scenic location and a beautiful interior make this smart restaurant a good choice. The seafood and fish dishes are excellent. 🍽️		●	▪	
HAMMAMET: *Barberousse* — ⓣⓓ Place 7 Novembre. **Road map** D2. **(** (72) 280 037. An open-air restaurant serving seafood and traditional Tunisian cuisine, Barberousse is located on top of the medina wall, with good views of the kasbah and the gulf. The seats are decorated with Berber designs. 🍽️		●	▪	
HAMMAMET: *Café des Mûriers* — ⓣⓓ **Road map** D2. **(** No telephone. This picturesque café is on a headland at the foot of the kasbah. Virtually no one knows its name, but it is still the most popular tea-house in Hammamet. Stools and seats covered with Berber designs and tea served with small, delicious date biscuits make it a memorable place to visit.			▪	
HAMMAMET: *Casa d'Oro* — ⓣⓓ Avenue Habib Bourguiba 60. **Road map** D2. **(** (72) 260 099. Situated a fair distance from the town centre; this restaurant is worth visiting for its tasty Italian food. 🍽️			▪	
HAMMAMET: *Belle Vue* — ⓣⓓⓣⓓ Centre Commercial. **Road map** D2. **(** (72) 280 825. Belle Vue serves inexpensive seafood. The grilled octopus is a treat. 🍽️		●	▪	
HAMMAMET: *Berbère* — ⓣⓓⓣⓓ Centre ville Hammamet. **Road map** D2. **(** (72) 280 082. **FAX** (72) 260 827. This pleasant restaurant specializes in Tunisian cuisine. The lovely terrace has a good view of the town and beach. The couscous is worth recommending. The restaurant is on the ground floor of a *brauhaus*, which makes and sells real German beer. 🍽️		●	▪	
HAMMAMET: *Fatma* — ⓣⓓⓣⓓ Centre Commercial. **Road map** D2. **(** (72) 280 756. This is one of several restaurants within the main shopping centre that serves decent food. 🍽️		●	▪	
HAMMAMET: *La Brise* — ⓣⓓ Avenue de la République 2. **Road map** D2. **(** (72) 278 910. The simple food, including delicious warm salads and traditional Tunisian dishes, makes this a safe choice. 🍽️			▪	
HAMMAMET: *Medina* — ⓣⓓⓣⓓ Medina. **Road map** D2. **(** (72) 281 728. Located on the fortified town walls, the Medina restaurant has wonderful views over the sea and puts on evening performances of folk music. 🍽️	▪	●	▪	●
HAMMAMET: *Pergola* — ⓣⓓⓣⓓ Centre Commercial. **Road map** D2. **(** (72) 280 993. Another restaurant in Hammamet's shopping centre, this serves a good mix of European and Tunisian cuisine.		●	▪	
HAMMAMET: *Restaurant Le Corail* — ⓣⓓⓣⓓ Avenue Habib Bourguiba 60. **Road map** D2. **(** (72) 261 866, 261 904. This town centre restaurant serves traditional Tunisian cuisine. The dish of the day is usually worth ordering.			▪	

HAMMAMET: *Dar Lella*
Rue Patrice Lumumba. **Road map** D2. (72) 280 871.
The traditional interior and beautiful, flower-filled terrace make this a pleasant place to dine. The food is good quality and is accompanied in the evenings by lively performances of traditional *malouf* (folk) music and belly-dancing.

HAMMAMET: *Les Trois Moutons*
Centre Commercial. **Road map** D2. (72) 280 981. **FAX** (72) 281 106.
The best restaurant in town is on the first floor of the Centre Commercial. The attractive restaurant specializes in fish and seafood and also serves an excellent *brik à l'oeuf* (egg inside an envelope of pastry). Another speciality worth trying is grouper served in a pepper sauce.

HAMMAMET: *Pomodoro*
Avenue Habib Bourguiba 6. **Road map** D2. (72) 281 254.
This smallish restaurant is situated between the harbour and the kasbah. The menu is a mixture of Tunisian and international cuisine. Music is performed in the evenings.

HAMMAMET: *Chez Achour*
Rue Ali Belhouane. **Road map** D2. (72) 280 140.
A very pleasant Moorish-style restaurant set in an attractive garden, Chez Achour offers a large selection of fish and seafood.

KELIBIA: *Anis*
Avenue Erriadh. **Road map** D1. (71) 295 777.
The Anis's restaurant serves tasty fish dishes and a nice selection of Franco-Tunisian cuisine.

KELIBIA: *El-Mansourah*
On the southern part of the Mansourah beach. **Road map** D1. (72) 295 169.
Situated on the headland by the Mansourah beach, this café-restaurant enjoys some magnificent views. The Muscat de Kelbia wine is especially good. Please note that it can get very busy.

KELIBIA: *La Jeunesse*
Road map D1. (72) 296 171.
The restaurant is located right in the centre of this small town and offers tasty snacks and generous helpings of seafood.

LA GOULETTE: *L'Avenir*
Avenue Franklin Roosevelt 18. **Road map** C1. (71) 735 758. **FAX** (71) 738 396.
La Goulette is known for its fish restaurants and this is one of the cheaper ones in town. In winter it has live music. Relaxed ambience.

LA GOULETTE: *Café Vert*
Avenue Franklin Roosevelt 68. **Road map** C1. (71) 736 156.
The town's favourite fish restaurant, Café Vert is very popular with Tunisians. In the summer some of the tables are placed outdoors, although the nearby road can get busy in the evenings. *Mon.*

LA GOULETTE: *Cordoue*
Avenue Franklin Roosevelt 13. **Road map** C1. (71) 735 476.
Excellent fish and seafood dishes are on the menu here.

LA GOULETTE: *El-Stambali*
Avenue Franklin Roosevelt. **Road map** C1. (71) 738 506.
El-Stambali's pleasant and unpretentious interior makes a good alternative to some of the smarter restaurants in town. As well as the fish and seafood it also offers a simple Tunisian menu. Fast service.

LA GOULETTE: *La Petite Fleur*
Avenue Franklin Roosevelt 30. **Road map** C1. & **FAX** (71) 738 271.
The grilled prawns are worth trying at this seafood restaurant.

LA GOULETTE: *Monte Carlo*
Avenue Franklin Roosevelt 4. **Road map** C1. (71) 735 338.
This inexpensive restaurant offers fresh fish and shellfish and has a good reputation. The choice varies depending on the day's catch.

LA GOULETTE: *Chalet*
Avenue Franklin Roosevelt 42. **Road map** C1. (71) 735 138, 736 452.
One of several restaurants in Avenue Franklin Roosevelt, this serves fish and other seafood. The prawns are delicious.

For key to symbols see back flap

			LIVE MUSIC	OUTSIDE DINING	WINE OR BEER	EXCEPTIONAL DECOR

Price categories are for a three-course meal for one person, including cover charge, and service but not alcohol.
- ⑩ under 10 TD
- ⑩⑩ 10–15 TD
- ⑩⑩⑩ 15–20 TD
- ⑩⑩⑩⑩ 20–25 TD
- ⑩⑩⑩⑩⑩ over 30 TD

LIVE MUSIC
Live performances of traditional music or entertainment programmes.

OUTSIDE DINING
Meals can be served on a terrace, garden or courtyard.

WINE OR BEER
Wine or beer can be ordered with meals.

EXCEPTIONAL DECOR
Restaurant is situated in a beautiful building or inside a palace.

LA GOULETTE: *La Belle Daurade*   ⑩⑩⑩   ●
Avenue Franklin Roosevelt 30. **Road map** C1. (71) 738 271.
This restaurant has one of the loveliest terraces in La Goulette. Fresh fish and seafood are a feature.

LA GOULETTE: *Lucullus*   ⑩⑩⑩   ● ■
Avenue Habib Bourguiba 1. **Road map** C1. (71) 737 310.
This modest restaurant serves some of the best seafood in town. Good meat dishes are also on the menu.

LA GOULETTE: *Restaurant Vénus*   ⑩⑩⑩⑩   ■
Avenue Habib Bourguiba 2. **Road map** C1. (71) 735 398.
One of the numerous fish restaurants along Avenue Franklin Roosevelt, this has a pleasant interior and excellent à la carte dishes on the menu. ⑩

LA MARSA: *Arthe*   ⑩   ●   ●
Rue Omar ben Ali Rabiaa 5. **Road map** C1. (71) 749 866.
Situated close to the TGM station, the villa housing this restaurant was built in 1935. It is typically Moorish in style and has a colonnaded inner courtyard. Essentially a patisserie and tea-house, slices of pizza or a delicious couscous with calamari can also be ordered. The establishment is renowned for its delicious desserts, however, and the chocolate cake is especially good. A large selection of teas is available. ⑩

LA MARSA: *Zephyr*   ⑩
Close to the TGM station. **Road map** C1. No telephone.
Located on the ground floor of the large Zephyr shopping centre are several fast-food restaurants. The sensational ice cream parlour is particularly recommended. ▤

LA MARSA: *Café Saf-Saf*   ⑩⑩   ● ■
Place du Saf-Saf. **Road map** C1. No telephone.
Located in a garden that overlooks the minaret of the nearby mosque, the restaurant is popular with the locals. It is also famous for its white camel that stands in the courtyard (usually during weekends) to draw water from an ancient well. The food includes a choice of excellent Tunisian snacks and a selection of delicious couscous dishes.

LA MARSA: *Bistro Garden*   ⑩⑩⑩   ● ■
22 Rue du Maroc. (71) 743 577. **FAX** (71) 742 554.
This smart restaurant is a good place for lunch. Wine is available. ▤ ⑩

LA MARSA: *Cap Farina*   ⑩⑩⑩   ● ■
Plage Sidi Ali el-Mekki. **Road map** C1. (71) 448 757.
Delicious grilled fish and seafood top the menu of this modest eatery. ⑩

LA MARSA: *La Falaise*   ⑩⑩⑩   ● ■
Rue Sidi Dhrif, La Marsa-Corniche. **Road map** C1. (71) 747 806. **FAX** (71) 742 575.
Situated a little way from the centre of La Marsa, this restaurant is worth visiting for its excellent meals served evenings and lunchtimes. ▦ ▤ ⑩

LA MARSA: *Renaissance Hotel Restaurant*   ⑩⑩⑩   ● ■
Les Cotes de Carthage. (71) 910 900. **Road map** C1.
This hotel has a beautiful position looking out over the sea. The restaurant specializes in Thai cuisine. The hot, green Thai curry is worth trying and makes a tasty alternative to the Tunisian staples. ▦ ▤ ⑩

LA MARSA: *Koubat el-Haoua*   ⑩⑩⑩⑩   ▪   ●   ■
1 Rue Mongi Slim, Marsa Plage. **Road map** C1. (71) 729 777.
@ koubat.elhoua@hexabyte.tn
This luxurious restaurant is situated right by the beach, in a domed former beys' bathing pavilion at the end of a pier. Its round dining rooms are arranged over two floors. ▦ ▤ ⑩

LA MARSA: *Au Bon Vieux Temps*   ⓉⒹⓉⒹⓉⒹⓉⒹⓉⒹ
Rue Aboul Kacem ech-Chebbi 1. **Road map** C1. [(71) 774 322.
Just a little way from the TGM station, this restaurant offers sophisticated
dishes, excellent French cuisine and a large selection of wines. It is also
good value for money considering the quality. In the peak season it is
necessary to book in advance. [ ] [ ] [ ] *Jul, Aug & lunchtimes.*

LA MARSA: *Le Golfe*   ⓉⒹⓉⒹⓉⒹⓉⒹⓉⒹ
Rue Arbi Zarrouk 5. **Road map** C1. [(71) 748 219. [& FAX (71) 747 185.
Housed in a beautiful villa that is set amid lush greenery and flowers, Le
Golfe benefits from cool sea breezes and magnificent views over the
beach. It has a deserved reputation for its fish and other seafood. The
restaurant is popular with prosperous Tunisians and booking is necessary
in the peak season. [ ] [ ] [ ]

NABEUL: *Café Errachidia*   ⓉⒹ
Avenue Habib Thameur. **Road map** D2. [No telephone.
This café serves delicious cakes and mint tea. Aromatic *chichas* (hookahs)
are available. [ ]

NABEUL: *Chamseddin*   ⓉⒹ
Close to the Pension Pasha. **Road map** D2. [No telephone.
Situated in the centre of town, this restaurant serves simple Tunisian dishes
and snacks such as *brik à l'oeuf* (egg inside an envelope of pastry). [ ]

NABEUL: *Moderne*   ⓉⒹ
Souk de l'Artisanat, Av. Farhat Hached 9. **Road map** D2. [No telephone.
This is one of a few inexpensive Tunisian restaurants where wine or beer
can be ordered with meals. Because it serves alcohol, this restaurant can
become a little "hearty" in the evenings. [ ]

NABEUL: *Rotonde*   ⓉⒹ
Road map D2. [(72) 285 782.
The typical Tunisian cuisine on the menu here includes a tasty *mechouia*
(a mix of roasted vegetables served cold) and snacks. [ ]

NABEUL: *L'Olivier*   ⓉⒹⓉⒹⓉⒹⓉⒹ
Avenue Hedi Chaker. **Road map** D2. [(72) 286 613.
Typical European and Tunisian dishes are on the menu here with the
emphasis being placed on fish and seafood.

NABEUL: *Au Bon Kif*   ⓉⒹⓉⒹⓉⒹⓉⒹⓉⒹ
Rue Marbella. **Road map** D2. [(72) 222 783.
This is the town's most expensive restaurant and the decor and menu are
both excellent. The seafood dishes are especially good. [ ] [ ] [ ]

SIDI BOU SAÏD: *Café Tamtam*   ⓉⒹ
Avenue du 7 Novembre. **Road map** C1. [(71) 728 535.
A pleasant café-restaurant offering light meals and snacks. Café Tamtam
has good service and a cheerful, elegant decor. Its terrace, though not
large, looks out onto the street leading into Sidi Bou Saïd. The restaurant is
situated a little way beyond the TGM station. [ ]

SIDI BOU SAÏD: *Le Chargui Restaurant*   ⓉⒹ
Avenue Habib Thameur 39. **Road map** C1. [(71) 740 987.
One of the town's less expensive restaurants, it occupies several roof-
covered terraces, though only one of them affords a view of the sea. A
large selection of traditional Tunisian dishes is on offer. [ ]

SIDI BOU SAÏD: *Pizza Bou Saïd*   ⓉⒹ
Rue Bechir Sfar. **Road map** C1. [No telephone.
This small pizzeria is close to the TGM station.

SIDI BOU SAÏD: *Sidi Chebanne*   ⓉⒹ
Rue Sidi Chebanne. **Road map** C1. [No telephone.
This unusual little café is arranged on several small terraces, each of which
is set at a slightly different level. The views over Sidi Bou Saïd yacht marina
and the town are wonderful. The café serves good pine-nut and mint teas
and has a welcoming atmosphere. [ ]

SIDI BOU SAÏD: *Le Pirate*   ⓉⒹⓉⒹ
Avenue du President Kennedy, Port Sidi Bou Saïd. **Road map** C1. [(71) 748 266.
This pleasant restaurant provides diners with a fine view of the yacht
marina. Tempting seafood and fish are on the menu and it is possible to
dine alfresco during the summer. [ ] [ ] [ ] *Sun.*

For key to symbols see back flap

	LIVE MUSIC	OUTSIDE DINING	WINE OR BEER	EXCEPTIONAL DECOR

Price categories are for a three-course meal for one person, including cover charge, and service but not alcohol.

ⓉⒹ under 10 TD
ⓉⒹⓉⒹ 10–15 TD
ⓉⒹⓉⒹⓉⒹ 15–20 TD
ⓉⒹⓉⒹⓉⒹⓉⒹ 20–25 TD
ⓉⒹⓉⒹⓉⒹⓉⒹⓉⒹ over 30 TD

LIVE MUSIC
Live performances of traditional music or entertainment programmes.

OUTSIDE DINING
Meals can be served on a terrace, garden or courtyard.

WINE OR BEER
Wine or beer can be ordered with meals.

EXCEPTIONAL DECOR
Restaurant is situated in a beautiful building or inside a palace.

SIDI BOU SAÏD: *Bon Vieux Temps* ⓉⒹⓉⒹⓉⒹ Rue Hedi Zarrouk. **Road map** C1. █ *(71) 744 733.* ⓕⓐⓧ *(71) 788 100.* The exquisite menu of this restaurant includes traditional Tunisian dishes and a large selection of fish. Close to the famous Café des Nattes *(below)*, the setting is picturesque with a garden and summer terrace overlooking the sea. Pleasant decor and old photographs and paintings add to the ambience. 🔲 🔳 ⫴ⓉⒹ⫴		●	■	
SIDI BOU SAÏD: *Café des Nattes* ⓉⒹⓉⒹⓉⒹ In the town's main square. **Road map** C1. █ *(71) 749 661.* This legendary café is located in Sidi Bou Saïd's main square. At one time it was the favourite haunt of an artistic avant-garde and a regular meeting place for artists such as Paul Klee and Auguste Macke. There are no tables inside (all are on the veranda) and many guests choose to sit on the spread rugs, adding to the Oriental ambience.		●		●
SIDI BOU SAÏD: *Dar Zarrouk* ⓉⒹⓉⒹⓉⒹⓉⒹⓉⒹ Rue Hedi Zarrouk. **Road map** C1. █ *(71) 740 591.* @ restaurantdarzarrouk@gnet.tn Opened in 2003, this upmarket courtyard restaurant enjoys superb views. At night the courtyard is lit by lanterns. The excellent menu includes a wide range of Mediterranean specialities with some good fish and seafood.				●

NORTHERN TUNISIA

BIZERTE: *Café Khamais Ternane* ⓉⒹ Place de Sadkaoui. **Road map** C1. █ *No telephone.* This café is situated at the far end of the old port. It has a good viewpoint from which to observe the daily goings on of Bizerte's residents. ⫴ⓉⒹ⫴		●		
BIZERTE: *La Mammina* ⓉⒹ Rue d'Espagne 1. **Road map** C1. █ *No telephone.* This pleasant and inexpensive Italian restaurant is a good place to go for tasty pizzas and pasta dishes. ⫴ⓉⒹ⫴ ⬤ *Sun.*			■	
BIZERTE: *Le Bosphore* ⓉⒹ Rue d'Alger. **Road map** C1. █ *No telephone.* Situated in the town centre, the pleasant interior and unfussy Tunisian cuisine make this a safe choice. ⫴ⓉⒹ⫴				
BIZERTE: *Patisserie la Paix* ⓉⒹ Rue 2 Mars. **Road map** C1. █ *No telephone.* A perfect place for a snack or some mouthwatering ice cream.				
BIZERTE: *Restaurant Eddalia* ⓉⒹ Avenue Habib Bourguiba 106. **Road map** C1. █ *(72) 346 490.* A large selection of traditional Tunisian dishes is on offer here, including salads, soups and meaty main courses. 🔳 ⫴ⓉⒹ⫴	■			
BIZERTE: *Du Bonheur* ⓉⒹⓉⒹ Rue Thaalbi. **Road map** C1. █ *(72) 431 047.* This smart restaurant has a good selection of Tunisian and international dishes on the menu. ⫴ⓉⒹ⫴			■	
BIZERTE: *L'Eden* ⓉⒹⓉⒹ La Corniche. **Road map** C1. █ *(72) 439 023.* Situated opposite Hôtel Corniche *(see p254)*, this upmarket restaurant serves tasty fish and seafood dishes.			■	
BIZERTE: *La Belle Plage* ⓉⒹⓉⒹⓉⒹ La Corniche. **Road map** C1. █ *(72) 431 817.* The varied menu here includes European and Tunisian dishes, fish and seafood. The interior decor is better than average. ⫴ⓉⒹ⫴			■	

BIZERTE: *Le Petit Mousse*   ⓣⓓⓣⓓ
La Corniche. **Road map** C1. 【 *(72) 432 185.* **FAX** *(72) 438 871.*
This hotel restaurant has delicious fish and sea food. It is popular with
Tunisian families for Sunday lunch. The crayfish is worth trying. 🗏 🍴ⓣⓓ🍴

JENDOUBA: *Atlas*   ⓣⓓ
Rue Juin 1955. **Road map** B2. 【 *(78) 602 217.*
A hotel restaurant, the Atlas has a good-value set menu and also serves
beer and wine. 🗐

RAF RAF: *Café Restaurant Andalous.*   ⓣⓓ
Road map C1. 【 *No telephone.*
This restaurant is located close to the coast and offers an inexpensive menu
with the emphasis on fresh fish.

TABARKA: *Café d'Andalous*   ⓣⓓ
Rue Hedi Chaker. **Road map** B1. 【 *No telephone.*
A highly popular Moorish café, this trendy meeting place is good for a cup
of tea, a game of cards and the chance to try a *chicha* (hookah). 🍴ⓣⓓ🍴

TABARKA: *La Perle du Nord*   ⓣⓓ
Avenue Habib Bourguiba 53. **Road map** B1. 【 *(78) 670 164.*
This very popular restaurant serves a good variety of Tunisian and
European cuisine. 🍴ⓣⓓ🍴

TABARKA: *Le Corail*   ⓣⓓ
Avenue Habib Bourguiba 70. **Road map** B1. 【 *No telephone.*
Tastefully prepared Tunisian dishes are on offer at this small eatery. 🍴ⓣⓓ🍴

TABARKA: *Sidi Moussa*   ⓣⓓ
Avenue 7 Novembre. **Road map** B1. 【 *No telephone.*
This unpretentious restaurant has plenty of delicious Tunisian dishes. 🍴ⓣⓓ🍴

TABARKA: *La Maisonnette*   ⓣⓓⓣⓓ
Route de Tunis. **Road map** B1. 【 *(78) 670 164.* **FAX** *(78) 670 651.*
As with the majority of Tabarka's restaurants. this one offers mainly fish
and seafood, though the meat dishes are also very good. 🍴ⓣⓓ🍴

TABARKA: *Le Mondial*   ⓣⓓⓣⓓ
Place Fréjus. **Road map** B1. 【 *(78) 670 709.*
Beautifully situated, with a terrace overlooking the marina, Le Mondial has
some mouthwatering fish and seafood dishes on the menu. 🍴ⓣⓓ🍴

TABARKA: *Le Pescadou*   ⓣⓓⓣⓓ
Place Fréjus. **Road map** B1. 【 *(78) 671 586.* **FAX** *(78) 673 873.*
Delicious crayfish and fish are the highlights of this restaurant's menu. The
restaurant has an outdoor terrace with a view of the marina. 🍴ⓣⓓ🍴

TABARKA: *Les Aiguilles Hotel Restaurant*   ⓣⓓⓣⓓ
Avenue Habib Bourguiba 18. **Road map** B1. 【 *(78) 673 789.* **FAX** *(78) 673 604.*
Some fine seafood and a good selection of Tunisian specialities can be
enjoyed on the pleasant terrace. 🗐 🍴ⓣⓓ🍴

TABARKA: *Le Pirate*   ⓣⓓⓣⓓⓣⓓ
Porto Corallo. **Road map** B1. 【 *(78) 670 061.*
Situated within the Corallo complex, next to the jetty, Le Pirate has some
very good fish and chicken dishes on the menu. 🍴ⓣⓓ🍴

TABARKA: *Mimosas Hotel Restaurant*   ⓣⓓⓣⓓⓣⓓ
Along the tourist route. **Road map** B1. 【 *(78) 673 018.* **FAX** *(78) 673 276.*
This hotel restaurant is situated on a hilltop, overlooking the town. Some
fine fish main courses are on offer, as well as Tunisian staples. The wild
boar and crayfish are particularly recommended. 🗐 🗏 🍴ⓣⓓ🍴

TABARKA: *Touta*   ⓣⓓⓣⓓⓣⓓ
Close to the marina. **Road map** B1. 【 *(78) 671 018.*
Within easy reach of the marina, this restaurant ranks as one of the better
in town with some good seafood and crayfish on the menu. 🗐 🗏 🍴ⓣⓓ🍴

TESTOUR: *Sidi Taib*   ⓣⓓ
In the main square. **Road map** C2. 【 *No telephone.*
This pleasant café is in the town's main square and is a welcoming place to
drop in for a cup of mint tea. The street leading to Sidi Taib square has a
number of inexpensive restaurants where an excellent meal and a cold
drink are available. 🍴ⓣⓓ🍴

For key to symbols see back flap

Price categories are for a three-course meal for one person, including cover charge, and service but not alcohol. ⓉⒹ under 10 TD ⓉⒹⓉⒹ 10–15 TD ⓉⒹⓉⒹⓉⒹ 15–20 TD ⓉⒹⓉⒹⓉⒹⓉⒹ 20–25 TD ⓉⒹⓉⒹⓉⒹⓉⒹⓉⒹ over 30 TD	**LIVE MUSIC** Live performances of traditional music or entertainment programmes. **OUTSIDE DINING** Meals can be served on a terrace, garden or courtyard. **WINE OR BEER** Wine or beer can be ordered with meals. **EXCEPTIONAL DECOR** Restaurant is situated in a beautiful building or inside a palace.	**LIVE MUSIC**	**OUTSIDE DINING**	**WINE OR BEER**	**EXCEPTIONAL DECOR**

THE SAHEL

GABÈS: *L'Oasis* ⓉⒹⓉⒹ
Avenue Farhat Hached 15–17. **Road map** D5. **(** *(75) 270 098.*
This restaurant is one of Gabès's top establishments and provides a successful combination of French and Tunisian cuisine. ❙ⓉⒹ❙ ● *Sun.*

	OUTSIDE DINING
	■

GABÈS: *Mazar* ⓉⒹⓉⒹ
Avenue Farhat Hached 39. **Road map** D5. **(** *(75) 272 065.*
An attractive interior, a roof terrace with a splendid view and some fine French-Tunisian cuisine make the Mazar a good option. ▤ ❙ⓉⒹ❙

● ■

KERKENNAH ISLANDS: *La Sirène* ⓉⒹⓉⒹ
Ar-Ramla. **Road map** E4. **(** *(73) 481 118.*
The best restaurant on the island, La Sirène is situated on the beach in Remla and has a pleasantly shaded terrace. The seafood is superb. ❙ⓉⒹ❙

● ■

MAHDIA: *Café Sidi Salem* ⓉⒹ
Rue du Borj. **Road map** D3. **(** *No telephone.*
Offers good value sandwiches, sea food and wonderful sea views.

MAHDIA: *L'Espado* ⓉⒹ
Route de la Corniche. **Road map** D3. **(** *(73) 681 476.*
Restaurant with a terrace and great view on the sea. ▤ ❙ⓉⒹ❙

● ■

MAHDIA: *Lido* ⓉⒹ
Avenue Farhat Hached. **Road map** D3. **(** *(71) 681 339, 681 476.*
One of several small restaurants clustered around the harbour, the Lido has a loyal local clientèle and serves fresh fish and Tunisian cuisine. ▤ ❙ⓉⒹ❙

● ■

MAHDIA: *Le Quai* ⓉⒹ
Avenue Farhat Hached. **Road map** D5. **(** *(73) 681 867, 626 973.*
This good-value restaurant has a similar menu to the Lido *(see above).* ❙ⓉⒹ❙

● ■

MAHDIA: *Neptune* ⓉⒹⓉⒹ
Avenue 7 Novembre. **Road map** D5. **(** *(73) 681 927.*
International and Tunisian cuisine, as well as excellent fish and seafood, are on the menu at this restaurant on Mahdia's north shore. ▤ ❙ⓉⒹ❙

● ■

MATMATA: *Chez Abdoul* ⓉⒹ
Road map D5. **(** *(73) 230 189.*
Chez Abdoul has a good selection of simple southern Tunisian dishes and is popular with the locals of Matmata. ❙ⓉⒹ❙

MATMATA: *Marhala* ⓉⒹ
Road map D5. **(** *No telephone.*
The set menus make this a good choice for a quick three-course meal. ❙ⓉⒹ❙

MATMATA: *Sidi Driss* ⓉⒹⓉⒹ
Road map D5. **(** *(75) 230 005.*
This hotel restaurant caters mainly for groups and serves good-value three-course meals. Fans of the film *Star Wars* will recognize the courtyard where Luke Skywalker sat down to eat with his aunt and uncle. ❙ⓉⒹ❙

■ ●

MONASTIR: *Calypso* ⓉⒹ
Cap Marina. **Road map** D3. **(** *(73) 462 305.*
This is one of the cheapest restaurants in the marina. The grilled fish is especially good value. ❙ⓉⒹ❙

MONASTIR: *Central* ⓉⒹ
Cap Marina. **Road map** D3. **(** & ℻ *(73) 461 597.*
This slightly cheaper version of the Captain and Le Grill *(see opposite)* has some good grilled fish, prawns and fish soup on the menu. ❙ⓉⒹ❙

■

MONASTIR: *El-Baraka*   ⑩
Souk Bab el-Karam. **Road map** D3. ⓒ *(73) 463 679.*
Though this restaurant is not easy to find it is worth the effort for the
excellent Tunisian dishes and snacks – including couscous, *tajine* (baked
omelette) and tasty *brik à l'oeuf.* Good value. 🍴⑩🍴

MONASTIR: *La Plage*   ⑩
Place 3 Août. **Road map** D3. ⓒ *(73) 461 124.*
This inexpensive restaurant serves large portions of fish including a
delicious grilled sea bream. 🍴⑩🍴

MONASTIR: *Le Medina*   ⑩
Medina. **Road map** D3. ⓒ *No telephone.*
A popular place, this restaurant is situated in the heart of the old quarter
and is perfect for a quick lunch. It is also very cheap. 🍴⑩🍴

MONASTIR: *Hannibal*   ⑩⑩
Medina. **Road map** D3. ⓒ *No telephone.*
Hannibal benefits from a terrace that overlooks the walls of the medina.
The food is good, too. 🍴⑩🍴

MONASTIR: *Le Chandelier*   ⑩⑩
Cap Monastir Marina. **Road map** D3. ⓒ *(73) 462 232.*
With tables offering views over the marina and some tasty fish dishes, Le
Chandelier is a good option. The grilled fish is well worth recommending,
as are the pizza and pasta dishes. 🍽 🍴⑩🍴

MONASTIR: *The Captain*   ⑩⑩
Cap Monastir Marina. **Road map** D3. ⓒ *(73) 461 449.* ғᴀx *(73) 473 820.*
This popular restaurant is aimed mainly at tourists but has a very
reasonable menu. 🍴⑩🍴

MONASTIR: *Le Grill*   ⑩⑩⑩⑩
Cap Monastir Marina. **Road map** D3. ⓒ & ғᴀx *(73) 462 136.*
Another of Monastir's good fish restaurants, Le Grill faces the quays and
has some fine octopus and prawns on the menu. 🍽 🍴⑩🍴

PORT EL-KANTAOUI: *L'Oliviers*   ⑩
Marina. **Road map** D2. ⓒ *No telephone.*
This pleasant restaurant is at the marina. The highly diversified menu
includes simple Tunisian dishes as well as pizza, hamburgers and chicken.
Cold beer is also available. 🍴⑩🍴

PORT EL-KANTAOUI: *Les Emirs*   ⑩⑩
Marina. **Road map** D2. ⓒ *(73) 348 700.* ғᴀx *(73) 348 750.*
Les Emirs is famous for its Tunisian cuisine and its attractive interior. Like
most local restaurants, it is situated at the marina. 🍽 🍴⑩🍴

PORT EL-KANTAOUI: *Misk Ellil*   ⑩⑩
Road map D2. ⓒ *(73) 348 952.* ғᴀx *(73) 348 950.*
A very pleasant restaurant, Misk Ellil has good food and a convivial
atmosphere. The main courses are the reason most people visit. 🍽 🍴⑩🍴

PORT EL-KANTAOUI: *Daurade*   ⑩⑩⑩⑩
Marina. **Road map** D2. ⓒ *(73) 348 893.* ғᴀx *(73) 348 892.*
A top-class fish restaurant by the marina, the Daurade has some excellent
dishes on the menu. The seafood bisque is superb. 🎫🍽 🍴⑩🍴

PORT EL-KANTAOUI: *Le Méditerranée*   ⑩⑩⑩⑩⑩
Marina. **Road map** D2. ⓒ *(73) 348 788.* ғᴀx *(73) 246 972.*
Situated by the harbourmaster's office, this is the best fish restaurant in the
marina. The first-floor dining room has a pleasant decor of navy blue and
white. The windows offer a lovely view over the quayside. The restaurant's
spicy prawns are well worth trying. 🍴⑩🍴 🌑 *Tue.*

SFAX: *Au Bec Fin*   ⑩
Place du 2 Mars. **Road map** D4. ⓒ *(74) 221 407.*
The high-standard Tunisian menu here includes tasty *briks* (snacks). Also
worth recommending are the *ojja* (vegetable stew) and a fantastic spaghetti
made with seafood. 🍴⑩🍴

SFAX: *Café Diwan*   ⑩⑩
Close to Bab Diwan. **Road map** D2. ⓒ *No telephone.*
This Moorish café, close to the medina's south gate, is popular with locals.
The roof terrace affords a panoramic view of the entire medina. 🍴⑩🍴

Price categories are for a three-course meal for one person, including cover charge, and service but not alcohol.

ⓉⒹ under 10 TD
ⓉⒹⓉⒹ 10–15 TD
ⓉⒹⓉⒹⓉⒹ 15–20 TD
ⓉⒹⓉⒹⓉⒹⓉⒹ 20–25 TD
ⓉⒹⓉⒹⓉⒹⓉⒹⓉⒹ over 30 TD

LIVE MUSIC
Live performances of traditional music or entertainment programmes.

OUTSIDE DINING
Meals can be served on a terrace, garden or courtyard.

WINE OR BEER
Wine or beer can be ordered with meals.

EXCEPTIONAL DECOR
Restaurant is situated in a beautiful building or inside a palace.

SFAX: *Chez Nous* ⓉⒹⓉⒹ
Rue Patrice Lumumba 28. **Road map** D4. ((74) 227 128.
Situated in Sfax's Ville Nouvelle (new town), Chez Nous specializes in fish and seafood dishes. The menu of the day is especially good value.
Wine or Beer

SFAX: *Le Baghdad Plus* ⓉⒹⓉⒹ
Avenue Farhat Hached. **Road map** D4. ((74) 298 173.
This newer version of Le Baghdad *(see below)* has a wider ranging menu and includes international cuisine as well as Tunisian favourites. *Wine or Beer*

SFAX: *Le Corail* ⓉⒹⓉⒹ
Avenue Habib Maazoun 39. **Road map** D4. ((74) 227 301.
This modern restaurant is next to Hôtel Thyna and serves a good selection of Tunisian dishes including some from the surrounding area. *Live Music, Outside Dining, Wine or Beer*

SFAX: *Le Monaco* ⓉⒹⓉⒹ
Rue Beyrouth 2. **Road map** D4. ((74) 236 330.
Le Monaco offers international cuisine as well as tasty fish dishes. *Wine or Beer*

SFAX: *Le Petit Navire* ⓉⒹⓉⒹ
Rue Haffouz 127. **Road map** D4. ((74) 212 890. FAX (74) 210 024.
This attractive Moorish-style restaurant is situated right next to the old port. It specializes in regional cuisine and the seafood and fish are prepared according to old recipies, which are given a modern twist. In addition, there is a choice of sophisticated French dishes including *foie gras*. *Outside Dining, Wine or Beer*

SFAX: *Le Printemps* ⓉⒹⓉⒹ
Avenue Habib Bourguiba 55. **Road map** D4. ((74) 226 973.
Situated in the centre of the new town, Le Printemps has good Tunisian and international cuisine and some excellent fish dishes. *Wine or Beer*

SFAX: *Le Baghdad* ⓉⒹⓉⒹⓉⒹ
Avenue Farhat Hached 63. **Road map** D4. ((74) 223 856.
Close to the medina, this little restaurant has a big reputation. There is a good selection of regional Tunisian dishes on the menu and most are reasonably priced for the quality on offer. *Wine or Beer*

SOUSSE: *Albatros* ⓉⒹ
Blvd. de la Corniche. **Road map** D3. ((73) 228 430.
This restaurant specializes in fish dishes including some sizzling grills. It is located along the road that leads to the tourist zone. *Wine or Beer*

SOUSSE: *Boule Rouge* ⓉⒹ
Blvd. Mongi Slim. **Road map** D3. ((73) 226 939.
A pleasant restaurant in the town centre, Boule Rouge's menu offers French and Tunisian dishes. The chef's *kamounia* (meat cooked in cumin) is particularly worth seeking out. *Wine or Beer*

SOUSSE: *Le Malouf* ⓉⒹ
Place Farhat Hached. **Road map** D3. ((73) 219 346.
French-Tunisian cuisine, friendly service and delicious tuna *briks* (snacks) are three good reasons to visit this centrally located restaurant. *Wine or Beer*

SOUSSE: *Les Trois Dauphins* ⓉⒹ
Blvd. 7 Novembre. **Road map** D3. ((73) 270 397.
This upmarket, yet friendly restaurant is in the hotel district and provides a wide choice of cuisine from Tunisian favourites to barbecues and even a Tunisian take on curry. *Wine or Beer*

SOUSSE: *Le Bonheur* ⓉⒹⓉⒹ
Place Farhat Hached. **Road map** D3. ((73) 225 742.
Situated on a busy square, international cuisine is on offer here with the accent firmly on French dishes. There is also a basic Tunisian menu. *Wine or Beer*

SOUSSE: *Le Gourmet*
Rue Amilcar. **Road map** D3. ((73) 224 751.
The chef's special is meaty lamb stews and grills. A large selection of other
Tunisian favourites is also on offer. 🍽 ▮🍴

SOUSSE: *La Marmite*
Rue Remada 15. **Road map** D3. ((73) 226 728.
This venue is reminiscent of a fishermen's tavern. Among the local dishes
are some fairly spicy stews that are flavoured with orange blossom to
produce a very interesting taste. There's a good wine list, too. 🍽 ▮🍴

SOUSSE: *Les Jasmins*
Avenue H. Bourguiba 22. **Road map** D3. ((73) 225 884.
Excellent couscous is probably the best choice at Les Jasmins. They have
also recently begun offering a vegetarian version. ▮🍴 ● *Mon.*

SOUSSE: *L'Escargot*
Blvd. de la Corniche 87. **Road map** D3. ((73) 224 779.
In this beach area restaurant diners enjoy the accompaniment of piano-bar
music. From the Franco-Tunisian menu, the duck and pâté are particularly
worth recommending. ▮🍴

SOUSSE: *Restaurant Dodo*
Rue el-Hajra. **Road map** D3. ((73) 212 326.
An attractive, traditional medina restaurant, the Dodo has a wide-ranging
menu that includes pizza, poultry, meat and fish. ▮🍴

SOUSSE: *Restaurant Libanais*
Route de la Corniche. **Road map** D3. ((73) 226 866.
The Lebanese cuisine on offer here includes freshly-made falafels (chickpea
balls) and succulent kebabs. ▮🍴 ◻ *until late at night.*

SOUSSE: *Le Baron*
Rue Taieb Mehiri. **Road map** D3. ((73) 227 682.
Le Baron specializes in fish and seafood. The crayfish, lobster and grilled
prawns are all superb. The decor is lovely, as is the *malouf* (folk) music
that is played here in the evenings. ▤ 🍽 ▮🍴

SOUSSE: *Le Viking*
Rue d'Algérie. **Road map** D3. ((73) 228 377.
Centrally located, the Scandinavian decor is very un-Tunisian but the tasty
food including pizza, fish and meat dishes is not at all bad. ▮🍴

SOUSSE: *Una Storia della Vita*
Blvd. 7 Novembre, Marhaba Beach Complex. **Road map** D3. ((73) 221 499.
This restaurant is part of the Marhaba beach complex, situated between
Sousse and Port el-Kantaoui. A good choice of international food is on
offer including some sophisticated fish and seafood dishes. ▤ 🍽 ▮🍴

JERBA AND THE MEDENINE AREA

AGHIR: *Le Capitaine*
Tourist zone. **Road map** E5. ((75) 600 894.
At the heart of the tourist zone, Le Capitaine specializes in Tunisian
seafood, though the menu also includes some European alternatives. ▮🍴

HOUMT SOUK: *La Mamma*
Rue Habib Bougatfa. **Road map** D5. (No telephone.
A simple, popular eatery, La Mamma offers unfussy and wholesome food
with a home-cooked taste. Its soups are particularly worth trying. This is a
convenient place for a quick meal. ▮🍴

HOUMT SOUK: *Les Palmiers*
Place d'Algérie. **Road map** D5. (No telephone.
Les Palmiers has a varied menu including a superb couscous. ▮🍴

HOUMT SOUK: *Restaurant du Sportif*
Avenue H. Bourguiba 147. **Road map** D5. (No telephone.
This cheap and cheerful restaurant serves meaty Tunisian cuisine. ▮🍴

HOUMT SOUK: *De l'Ile*
Place Hedi Chaker. **Road map** D5. ((75) 650 651.
One of several restaurants in Place Hedi Chaker, De l'Ile has some
excellent fish dishes. Out of the less expensive dishes is *ojja* – listed in the
menu under the starters – a vegetable stew with scrambled egg in it. ▮🍴

Price categories are for a three-course meal for one person, including cover charge, and service but not alcohol.
TD under 10 TD
TD TD 10–15 TD
TD TD TD 15–20 TD
TD TD TD TD 20–25 TD
TD TD TD TD TD over 30 TD

LIVE MUSIC
Live performances of traditional music or entertainment programmes.

OUTSIDE DINING
Meals can be served on a terrace, garden or courtyard.

WINE OR BEER
Wine or beer can be ordered with meals.

EXCEPTIONAL DECOR
Restaurant is situated in a beautiful building or inside a palace.

	LIVE MUSIC	OUTSIDE DINING	WINE OR BEER	EXCEPTIONAL DECOR
HOUMT SOUK: *Du Sud* TD TD Place Sidi Brahim. **Road map** D5. (75) 650 479. Often crowded, this good-quality tourist restaurant is in the town centre, close to Place Hedi Chaker.				
HOUMT SOUK: *Baccar* TD TD TD Place Hedi Chaker 16. **Road map** D5. (75) 650 708. This cosy restaurant is in the town centre and has a good reputation. There are some delicious fish dishes on the menu.			■	
HOUMT SOUK: *Blue Moon* TD TD TD Place Hedi Chaker. **Road map** D5. (75) 650 559. A pleasantly quiet restaurant, the Blue Moon offers Tunisian and Franco-Tunisian cuisine. Live music is played in the evenings.	■		■	
HOUMT SOUK: *La Princesse d'Haroun* TD TD TD TD Le Port. **Road map** D5. (75) 650 488. Probably the best restaurant in town, this has some tender calamari, octopus and lobster on the menu.			■	
MEDENINE: *Flore* TD TD Rue de Tunis. **Road map** D6. (77) 229 816. This is one of the few restaurants in Medenine to offer a mix of Tunisian and European dishes.			■	
MIDOUN: *Centre L'Oasis* TD TD Tourist zone. **Road map** D5. (75) 659 173. On Tuesdays, Fridays and Saturdays the Tunisian and European fare is enlivened by folk shows and music at this popular eatery.	■		■	
MIDOUN: *El-Guestile* TD TD Rue Marsa Ettoufah 21. **Road map** D5. (75) 657 724. The restaurant, just off the market square, is famous for its good food, particularly the seafood and fish dishes.			■	
MIDOUN: *Le Khalife* TD TD TD Route du Phare. **Road map** D5. (75) 657 860. A large selection of excellent seafood in various price ranges means that there is something for everyone at this restaurant.	■		■	
ZARZIS: *El-Borj* TD TD **Road map** E5. (75) 684 361, 683 360. Tunisian dishes and fish make up the menu at one of the few restaurants found outside Zarzis's tourist zone.			■	
ZARZIS: *La Vague* TD TD Tourist zone. **Road map** E5. (75) 706 630. Part of Hôtel Zeyn, La Vague specializes in Tunisian cuisine and has some excellent seafood on the menu.			■	
ZARZIS: *Abou Nawas* TD TD TD Tourist zone. **Road map** E5. (75) 684 583, 680 583. Many of Zarzis's best restaurants are based in hotels. This typical hotel restaurant offers high quality European and Tunisian cuisine.	■	●	■	
SOUTHERN TUNISIA				
DOUZ: *Ali Baba* TD Avenue du 7 Novembre. **Road map** C6. (75) 472 498. This pleasant little restaurant has a shadowy courtyard at the back where it is possible to dine in a Bedouin tent. It is cheap and clean and the chef's couscous is worth writing home about. The restaurant is a short distance from the roundabout, on the road to Kebili.		●		

Douz: *Café du Théâtre* ⓉⒹ ●
Road map C6. 🍴 *No telephone.*
This popular tiny Moorish café serves good teas and strong coffee. 🍴ⓉⒹ🍴

Douz: *La Rosa* ⓉⒹ
Place 7 Novembre 1987. Road map C6. 🍴 *No telephone.*
A small yet excellent restaurant, La Rosa offers a large selection of
inexpensive Tunisian favourites. 🍴ⓉⒹ🍴

Douz: *Kebili* ⓉⒹ
Khereddine. Road map C6. 🍴 *No telephone.*
This small restaurant in the town centre serves inexpensive but good
quality Tunisian dishes. 🍴ⓉⒹ🍴

Ksar Haddada: *Restaurant Ksar Haddada* ⓉⒹⓉⒹ ●
Road map D6. 🍴 *(75) 869 605.*
The restaurant is situated in an adapted *ksar* and often caters for large
groups of travellers who are exploring the south. There isn't much choice
but the couscous is usually excellent. 🍴ⓉⒹ🍴

Nefta: *Café de la Corbeille* ⓉⒹ ● ■
Route de la Corbeille, near the Hotel Mirage. Road map A5. 🍴 & 𝐅𝐀𝐗 *(76) 430 308.*
This café offers a magnificent panoramic view of the lower-down gulley
(corbeille) – a palm grove and a reservoir with a hot-water spring. It also
serves tea, coffee and cold drinks. 🍴ⓉⒹ🍴

Nefta: *Ferdaous/Zembretta* ⓉⒹ ●
Route de la Corbeille. Road map A5. 🍴 *No telephone.*
This restaurant is situated in a palm grove a short way into Nefta on the left
coming from the Tozeur direction. It offers a modest selection of dishes but
the food is good and the venue's location is magnificent. 🍴ⓉⒹ🍴

Nefta: *La Mamma* ⓉⒹ
Road map A5. 🍴 *No telephone.*
La Mamma is in the town centre, opposite the Mobil station. The *kamounia*
(meat cooked in cumin) is particularly good. 🍴ⓉⒹ🍴

Nefta: *La Source* ⓉⒹ ●
Avenue Habib Bourguiba. Road map A5. 🍴 *No telephone.*
The restaurant is at the far end of town, on the road to Tozeur. Diners can
eat indoors or out. The local dishes are well cooked and good value. 🍴ⓉⒹ🍴

Nefta: *Le Roi de Couscous* ⓉⒹ
Place de la République. Road map A5. 🍴 *No telephone.*
As its name suggests, this restaurant specializes in couscous. 🍴ⓉⒹ🍴

Tamerza: *Café-Restaurant Chedli* ⓉⒹ
Road map A5. 🍴 *No telephone.*
Any of the Tunisian dishes on the menu are worth a try. Make sure to
sample the homemade harissa (spicy sauce).

Tamerza: *Les Cascades* ⓉⒹ ●
Road map A5. 🍴 *(76) 485 322.*
This hotel restaurant set in a palm grove has a good-value menu. 🍴ⓉⒹ🍴

Tamerza: *Restaurant de Tamerza* ⓉⒹ
Road map A5. 🍴 *No telephone.*
This modest restaurant can be found on the road leading to the Hôtel les
Cascades *(see p262)* and serves an excellent couscous. 🍴ⓉⒹ🍴

Tamerza: *Tamerza Palace Restaurant* ⓉⒹⓉⒹⓉⒹⓉⒹ ● ■ ●
Road map A5. 🍴 *(76) 485 322.* @ tamerza.palace@planet.tn
Elegant and sophisticated, this hotel restaurant has a good view from the
terrace. Lunch is often in the form of a buffet on the terrace. 📇 ▤ 🍴ⓉⒹ🍴

Tataouine: *Chenini* ⓉⒹ ■
Relais Chenini. Road map D6. 🍴 *(75) 862 898.*
The restaurant resembles a canteen; it serves a very tasty, aromatic
couscous. Beer is available with meals. 🍴ⓉⒹ🍴

Tataouine: *Foum Tataouine* ⓉⒹⓉⒹ ● ■ ●
Hôtel Sangho Tataouine, on the road to Chenini. Road map D6. 🍴 *No telephone.*
This restaurant is part of the Sangho Tataouine hotel *(see p263)*, which is
outside the village on the road to Chenini. It serves Tunisian and French
cuisine, and also pizza. 🍴ⓉⒹ🍴

	LIVE MUSIC	OUTSIDE DINING	WINE OR BEER	EXCEPTIONAL DECOR

Price categories are for a three-course meal for one person, including cover charge, and service but not alcohol.
ⓉⒹ under 10 TD
ⓉⒹⓉⒹ 10–15 TD
ⓉⒹⓉⒹⓉⒹ 15–20 TD
ⓉⒹⓉⒹⓉⒹⓉⒹ 20–25 TD
ⓉⒹⓉⒹⓉⒹⓉⒹⓉⒹ over 30 TD

LIVE MUSIC
Live performances of traditional music or entertainment programmes.

OUTSIDE DINING
Meals can be served on a terrace, garden or courtyard.

WINE OR BEER
Wine or beer can be ordered with meals.

EXCEPTIONAL DECOR
Restaurant is situated in a beautiful building or inside a palace.

TATAOUINE: *Medina* ⓉⒹⓉⒹ
Hôtel Medina, Rue H. Mestaoui. **Road map** D6. **[** *(75) 860 999.*
Situated in the hotel of the same name, this restaurant is clean and has an attractive interior and friendly service. Modestly priced. ❚ⓉⒹ❙

TOZEUR: *Diamanta* ⓉⒹ
Avenue Abou el-Kacem Chabbi 74. **Road map** B5. **[** *(76) 453 867.*
The superb Tunisian cuisine available here includes some inexpensive meaty stews and delicious warm starters that are generous enough to be considered as main courses. ❚ⓉⒹ❙ — *Wine or Beer*

TOZEUR: *Du Paradis* ⓉⒹ
Avenue H. Bourguiba 17, close to Hôtel Essada. **Road map** B5. **[** *(76) 461 248.*
This small, budget-priced restaurant serves simple but well-cooked Tunisian dishes as well as some pasta alternatives. ❚ⓉⒹ❙ — *Outside Dining, Wine or Beer*

TOZEUR: *Restaurant du Soleil* ⓉⒹ
Avenue Abou el-Kacem Chabbi 58. **Road map** B5. **[** *(76) 452 445.*
One of a very few places in Tunisia, particularly in the south, where vegetarians could find something to their liking. The atmosphere is friendly and there's plenty of choice on the menu. ❚ⓉⒹ❙ — *Wine or Beer*

TOZEUR: *Les Andalous* ⓉⒹⓉⒹ
Route de Degache. **Road map** B5. **[** *(76) 454 196.* **FAX** *(76) 454 199.*
This restaurant is situated in the Hôtel du Jardin and is an excellent place to try some southern Tunisian dishes – including *bakesh* – a kind of spicy Tunisian pizza. *Malouf* (folk) music is played in the evenings. Booking is necessary in the peak season. ❚ⓉⒹ❙ — *Live Music, Wine or Beer*

TOZEUR: *Le Petit Prince* ⓉⒹⓉⒹⓉⒹⓉⒹ
Al-Berka. **Road map** B5. **[** *(76) 461 248.*
An upmarket restaurant, Le Petit Prince is in a little palm grove off Avenue Abou el-Kacem Chabbi. The chef specializes in southern Tunisian cuisine and is justly famous for his roast leg of lamb and a wide variety of couscous dishes. ❚ⓉⒹ❙ — *Outside Dining, Wine or Beer*

TOZEUR: *Dar Cheraït* ⓉⒹⓉⒹⓉⒹⓉⒹⓉⒹ
Tourist zone, situated in the hotel of the same name. **Road map** B5. **[** *(76) 454 888.*
The Tunisian and international cuisine and unusual decor of this hotel restaurant make it a popular spot. ✦ ☰ ❚ⓉⒹ❙ — *Live Music, Wine or Beer, Exceptional Decor*

CENTRAL TUNISIA

GAFSA: *Abid* ⓉⒹ
Rue Laadoub. **Road map** B4.
One of a handful of inexpensive restaurants situated near the bus station, the Abid offers some tasty Tunisian dishes. The *kamounia* (meat stew with cumin) is particularly good. ❚ⓉⒹ❙

GAFSA: *Bayech* ⓉⒹ
Avenue J. Abdennaceur 2. **Road map** B4. **[** *(76) 221 503.*
Though not always available, the Bayech's *kamounia* (meat stew cooked with cumin) is worth picking out from the menu. ❚ⓉⒹ❙

GAFSA: *Semiramis* ⓉⒹ
Avenue Ahmed Snoussi. **Road map** B4. **[** *(76) 221 009.*
Specializing in lamb dishes, this upmarket restaurant has some tasty hot starters which in themselves could constitute a main course. ❚ⓉⒹ❙ — *Wine or Beer*

GAFSA: *Tony Pizzeria* ⓉⒹ
Road map B4. **[** *(76) 229 913.*
As well as a variety of pizzas, there are some excellent Tunisian salads on offer. One pizza is usually enough for two people. — *Wine or Beer*

GAFSA: *Gafsa*   ⓉⒹⓉⒹ   ▪
Road map B4. 📞 *(76) 223 000.*
The lamb couscous is probably the best of the Tunisian and French cuisine
on offer here. 🍴ⓉⒹ🍴

KAIROUAN: *El-Karawan*   ⓉⒹ
Rue Souqeina bint el-Hussein. **Road map** C3. 📞 *(77) 232 566.*
This family-run restaurant is clean and friendly and has some well-cooked
Tunisian dishes on offer. All the dishes are reasonably priced. The
couscous is especially good. 🍴ⓉⒹ🍴

KAIROUAN: *Roi Du Couscous*   ⓉⒹ   ▪
Place 7 Novembre. **Road map** C3. 📞 *(77) 231 237.*
This is one of the few places in Kairouan that serves wine and beer. The
couscous is good, too. The inexpensive menu, which includes some good
starters makes this popular with tourists and locals alike.

KAIROUAN: *Sabra*   ⓉⒹ
Avenue de la République. **Road map** C3. 📞 *(77) 235 095.*
A pleasant restaurant situated next to Hôtel Tunisia *(see p264)*, this
restaurant's menu includes some good-value Tunisian dishes.

KASSERINE: *Olivier*   ⓉⒹ
Avenue de l'Environnement. **Road map** B3. 📞 *(77) 476 580.*
Olivier has only a limited choice of Tunisian dishes but the food is
flavoursome and well-cooked. 🍴ⓉⒹ🍴

LE KEF: *Venus*   ⓉⒹ
Rue F. Hached. **Road map** B2. 📞 *(78) 200 355.*
This popular restaurant has a good selection of Tunisian and European
cuisine on the menu including a good couscous and some starters that are
particularly worth trying. 🍴ⓉⒹ🍴

LE KEF: *Bou Maklouf*   ⓉⒹ
Rue Hèdi Chaker. **Road map** B2. 📞 *No telephone.*
Little more than a small, inexpensive café, this unassuming place offers
good food with some hot dishes including spicy soups and delicous
servings of couscous. 🍴ⓉⒹ🍴

METLAOUI: *Paris*   ⓉⒹ
Avenue H. Bourguiba. **Road map** B5. 📞 *No telephone.*
This popular and inexpensive restaurant serves tasty Tunisian salads
including a delicious *mechouia* (a mix of roasted vegetables served cold).
The restaurant is situated next to the Hôtel Essada. 🍴ⓉⒹ🍴

METLAOUI: *Ibis*   ⓉⒹⓉⒹ   ▪
In the hotel of the same name. **Road map** B5. 📞 *No telephone.*
Hôtel Ibis's restaurant serves a blend of Tunisian and European cuisine and
is one of the few places in Metlaoui where beer is available. 🍴ⓉⒹ🍴

METLAOUI: *Relais Thelja*   ⓉⒹⓉⒹ   ▪
In the hotel of the same name. **Road map** B5. 📞 *(76) 241 570.*
This better than average hotel restaurant offers Tunisian and French cuisine
at moderate prices. 🍴ⓉⒹ🍴

SBEÏTLA: *Capitol*   ⓉⒹⓉⒹ   ▪
Avenue de l'Environnement. **Road map** C3. 📞 *(77) 466 880.* 📠 *(77) 466 890.*
Located in a new complex in the modern part of Sbeïtla, this restaurant is
one of the few places to eat after looking at the Roman ruins.

SIDI BOUZID: *Anais*   ⓉⒹ
Oum Laadam. **Road map** C4. 📞 *(76) 634 222.*
This restaurant has a good selection of Tunisian and European dishes on its
reasonably-priced menu. 🍴ⓉⒹ🍴

SIDI BOUZID: *Shebrazeda*   ⓉⒹ
Avenue H. Bourguiba. **Road map** C4. 📞 *(76) 632 889.*
Like many of Sidi Bouzid's restaurants, Shehrazeda serves a basic repertoire
of Tunisian dishes and some good, hot starters.

TÉBOURSOUK: *Thugga*   ⓉⒹ   ▪
Hôtel Thugga (2 km/1 mile from the town centre). **Road map** C4. 📞 *(78) 466 647.*
📠 *(78) 466 721.*
This busy restaurant is popular with groups. During the hunting season
(Nov–Apr) it serves dishes made with wild boar. 🍴ⓉⒹ🍴

For key to symbols see back flap

SHOPPING IN TUNISIA

THROUGHOUT Tunisia there are colourful markets crammed with all sorts of Tunisian-made goods including rugs and carpets, ceramics, jewellery and perfumes. Tunisia also has large shopping centres, which have about as much charm as their European counterparts. Shops selling souvenirs can be found all over the country. Those aimed at tourists in

Cuddly stuffed camel

the big medinas often charge high prices and are stocked with poor quality goods. For this reason, it is worth stepping into one of the state-owned ONAT shops. These will give some idea of the prices of the most popular souvenirs. They may also help to spot poor quality items for sale in the souks that are sold as souvenirs of Tunisia but may well have been made elsewhere.

WHERE TO BUY

THE MOST INTERESTING places to shop in Tunisia are the souks, which can be found in most medinas of Tunisia's cities and towns. Prices charged at these market shops are not fixed in stone and are always open to haggling (see box). As well as the markets, visitors can also shop in large, state-owned department stores. These have fixed prices and opening hours. Small hotel shops usually sell high-quality goods, but charge top prices for them. In duty-free shops, often found at border crossings, goods must be paid for in convertible currencies and prices charged for Tunisian products are far higher than those paid in state-owned shops in souks.

The Bardo Museum (see pp88–9) sells good quality books on the art and history of Tunisia and North Africa, as well as in-depth guides to museums and archaeological sites all over the country.

Weekly market by the beach in Tabarka

OPENING HOURS

MOST TUNISIAN SHOPS close for lunch; they are also closed on Saturday afternoon and Sunday. Some shops close on Friday afternoons. Normally, the shops that sell food and household products are open from 8am until 12:30pm and 2:30pm to 6pm, Monday to Friday. Throughout the summer season the hours are 7:30am to 1:30pm.

Tunisia's state-run department stores are open from 8:30am until 9pm, Monday to Friday, and 8:30am to 10pm on Saturday. In tourist resorts souvenir shops stay open until late at night, and sometimes until the last shopper leaves.

During Ramadan, many shops open between 8 and 9am and close at about 1pm. They open again in the evening and often remain open until late at night.

HOW TO PAY

THE NATIONAL CURRENCY is the Tunisian dinar (TD). In privately owned shops, especially those that sell carpets, payment can often be made in US dollars or euros. When shopping for small items in souks, it is useful to have some one-dinar coins. In the state-owned department stores as well as in larger shops, shopping centres, ONAT shops and duty-free shops, credit cards are accepted. Credit cards are also accepted by some upmarket restaurants and hotels, from three-star upwards.

When settling a bill in a restaurant or a café it is customary to leave a tip. In cafés this need be no more than some small change. Waiters in more upmarket restaurants will expect about 10 per cent of the total bill.

Always be prepared to haggle in a souk. It is often possible to purchase an item for half the price that was originally quoted by the vendor.

A souvenir from Tunisia – colourful desert sands

Carpet and fabric shop in Tunis medina

SHOPPING CENTRES

THERE ARE shopping centres in most of Tunisia's larger towns. They are very popular with the locals, particularly the younger generation. Their boutiques stock many foreign-made goods, but prices are high and the quality can sometimes leave a lot to be desired.

A very popular shopping centre is the Palmarium, in Avenue Habib Bourguiba in Tunis. Situated on its ground floor (immediately by the entrance) is an ONAT shop. The large and popular Zephyr shopping centre can be found in La Marsa. This is not only a favourite shopping venue, but also a popular meeting place for young Tunisians. On the ground floor are restaurants and a number of stalls selling delicious ice creams. This is one of few places in Tunisia where low-fat ice cream can be obtained.

MARKETS

MARKETS were once the economic centre of Tunisian towns and were often given special privileges. Today, they still play an important economic role. Various parts of a market wake up at different times.

One of the few supermarkets to be found in Sousse

The first to open are the souks that sell meat and vegetables; the rest start trading a little later. Stalls and shops usually stay open until about 6 or 7pm, but the main tourist alleys, such as Rue Jemma Zitouna in Tunis's main souk, remain open much later.

Tunisia's markets are often covered with roofs that provide shelter from the sun. A few of the expensive shops, such as those selling carpets and gold, are air-conditioned.

Medinas also contain many small restaurants and cafés where it is a good plan to stop for a glass of tea and a sit down. One of the most charming and atmospheric of these is Café M. Rabet in the Souk et-Trouk, in Tunis medina (see p274). When planning a trip to one of Tunisia's markets, if looking for something specific, begin by finding out the location of the appropriate souk, as they are governed by a hierarchy (see pp294-5).

It is often worth venturing further than the main souks. In the souk situated near Tunis's Zaouia Sidi Mehrez (see p81), for instance, there are cheap, good quality ceramics, while in the Souk el-Grana it is easy to become caught up in crowds of women searching for shoes and clothes at bargain prices.

ADVICE ON HAGGLING

Although prices are not fixed in stone, haggling follows certain general rules. First of all, allow plenty of time and know roughly the value of the article required. Do not hurry. The conversation starts with general topics, later on an interest may be shown in some other object. Only after a while should one approach the article that is desired. Never mention a price before the vendor does. A rule of thumb is to begin negotiations from one third of the initial price. The seller puts on a show of indignation, but will lower the price. Smile and continue with the negotiations, saying that in this case you will have to think about it. Walking off will usually bring about a further reduction in price. However, stick to the rules of fair play and continue to haggle only if you really want to buy the product. If a compromise is not reached it is only necessary to smile and bid the vendor a pleasant goodbye. When buying several items at once, haggle over each of them separately, and then in the end ask for an overall discount. It can sometimes help to be the first or the last customer of the day.

Vegetable souk

ONAT Shops

Each large town and many smaller tourist resorts have state-owned outlets that sell a range of Tunisian handicrafts. The best of them are found in Sousse and Monastir. They are well worth visiting in order to see what products Tunisia as a whole has to offer.

ONAT (Organization Nationale de l'Artisanat) shops, sometimes referred to as SOCOPA, sell a wide range of good quality Tunisian handicrafts. Prices are fixed and ONAT shops give some idea of the prices to pay for many of the most popular souvenirs. Another benefit is that they provide an opportunity for people to distinguish the genuine Tunisian-made article from foreign imports.

Some shops, including the ONAT shop in Sousse, are vast, and spread over several floors. As there is so much to see, allow plenty of time when shopping for souvenirs in the large ONAT stores. The assistants are helpful and knowledgeable. They will take great care when wrapping up the articles, so that they will not get damaged during the journey home. Many of the ONAT shops are particularly good for top-quality leather goods. The ONAT shop in Monastir offers a good selection of attractive ceramics.

All of the ONAT shops can also provide information on carpets and tapestries, their patterns and weaving

ONAT shop selling the highest quality products

methods; but it is best to ask about them in Kairouan.

Another advantage of ONAT shops is that, having fixed prices, they present an opportunity for people who do not wish to haggle. Most ONAT shops will accept credit cards.

Art Galleries

Art galleries in Tunisia that deal only in paintings are few and far between and most establishments sell a range of artworks, from graphics and ceramics to books and sculpture. The influence of the École de Tunis *(see p16)* is evident in most of the contemporary paintings found in Tunisia's galleries. In the 1940s its pioneers introduced modern art to Tunisia and began to combine new trends such as Futurism with everyday scenes such as weddings, markets, and hammams (steam baths). Alongside these, there are more traditional paintings, executed in watercolours or oils, which attempt to capture the light and colour of Tunisian architecture and landscape. Also, traditional Islamic art, including calligraphy and arabesques, are combined with more modern techniques of abstract and figurative painting.

As well as paintings of this type, many galleries sell a variety of antiques and contemporary artifacts. These are not cheap, but every now and then a gallery has good quality works by less well-known Tunisian artists going

for very reasonable prices. One such shop is the gallery in Souk al-Caid, in Sousse. It sells attractive art works as well as beautiful fabrics. The Negrat gallery in Rue Sidi ben Arous, in Tunis, sells good quality lamps. Galleries selling contemporary Tunisian art, as well as work by foreign artists, can also be found in Sidi Bou Saïd and Port el-Kantaoui.

Antiques and old junk for sale in a souk in Houmt Souk

Antiques

There is a ban on exporting certain kinds of antiques from Tunisia. It is nevertheless worth looking at the shops that sell them, even if only to admire the beauty of the objects. Items such as old carpets, tapestries, fabrics, ceramics, traditional wedding costumes, antique mirrors and everyday items are not subject to an export ban. However, always make sure by asking the vendor if there are likely to be any problems with taking an item abroad.

One good Tunis antique shop is Ed-Dar, in Rue Sidi ben Arous; another can be found at No.7 in the Souk

One of the many art galleries in Sidi Bou Saïd

et-Trouk. The small shops in Rue des Glacières are excellent places for buying old bric-a-brac. With their shelves piled high with items, these shops can resemble the mythical cave discovered by Ali Baba. If seriously contemplating buying anything in an antique shop, allow at least one hour. The conversation usually starts with a glass of mint tea!

JEWELLERY

GOLD AND SILVER jewellery is popular in Arab countries. Common motifs include crescent pendants and the hand of Fatima, which is used in many different forms from earrings to necklaces.

Another frequent motif used in jewellery is the fish, which is a popular good luck charm against the "evil eye". Intricate pendants bearing a motif representing *basmala* (an important Islamic phrase meaning "In the name of God") proclaim membership of the Muslim community. According to Muslim tradition, this symbol figured on the wings of the Archangel Gabriel as witnessed by Mohammed.

Other popular items, beside pendants, include chunky bracelets. Coral and amber jewellery is popular in the Tabarka region. Items of jewellery sold in Houmt Souk, on Jerba, are produced by Jewish designers. This has

Golden pendant

long been a jewellery centre and is still a good place to purchase gold and silver.

Gold and silver hallmarks should be stamped on every item. This practice is regulated by the Standards Office. A scorpion means that the item is made of nine-carat gold, a goat stands for 14-carat gold while a horse's head, the Carthaginian symbol for money, denotes 18-carat gold.

Silver hallmarks include a bunch of grapes with the figure 1 (90 per cent silver) and an African head (80 per cent silver or less).

Gold and silver items that do not bear hallmarks are of dubious quality but visitors may wish to buy them solely for their attractive designs. Berber jewellery is also worth seeking out. Though Berber jewellery is usually made of low-grade silver it is nevertheless sought-after for the uniqueness of its ancient designs.

VAT REFUNDS

A REFUND ON VAT can be claimed when the value of goods exceeds 200 TD and the payment was made by credit card in a shop authorized to transact such deals. In order to apply for a refund, the shop must display an official sign saying "Credit Card Sales, Tax Back". A VAT refund applies only to foreign passport bearers who spend less than three months in Tunisia and purchase the articles here. Alcohol,

Pottery displayed in front of a shop in Nabeul

cigarettes and items of food are excluded. Ask the shop for a receipt and five copies of the purchase document. Present this on leaving the country, at the airport for example. Refunds are made by bank transfer.

DIRECTORY

ONAT/SOCOPA

Bizerte
Quai du Vieux Port.
((72) 439 684.

Hammamet
Avenue H. Bourguiba 72.
((72) 280 733.

Kairouan
Centre Kairouanais.
((77) 226 223.

Nabeul
Avenue H. Thameur.
((72) 285 007.

Sfax
Rue Hamadi Tej.
((74) 296 826.

Sousse
Avenue H. Bourguiba.
((73) 211 287.

Tunis
Avenue H. Bourguiba, Complex Palmarium.
((71) 348 860.

Jewellery shop in the centre of Sousse's medina

Souks

Tunisia's markets, which on the surface appear to be chaotic, are in reality well-ordered spaces. Every craft and every trade has its own allocated position and place in a hierarchy. The closer to the main mosque, the more numerous are the "noble" souks – those selling gold, scents, carpets and traditional Tunisian *chechias* (hats) worn by men. Away from the centre, the souks become less prestigious, producing and selling wrought-iron products, as well as trading in meat and vegetables.

Visitors can watch workmen decorating copper plates. This is supposed to guarantee its authenticity. For the best quality, try to find where the Tunisians buy such items.

A Tunisian souk is not only a place to shop and trade. For the Tunisians it is also a place of fun and recreation. Meetings with friends in a café to play a game of backgammon is a common sight in souks.

Perfume and jewellery can be bought in the most elegant souks, situated near the main mosque. They are easy to find as the intense fragrance of perfumes leads the way. Colourful and vibrant, these souks attract the most visitors.

COVERED BAZAARS

Since the 10th century the main streets and markets of towns were illuminated with lamps mounted on the walls of houses or on the roofs covering the streets. In the 11th century the main streets that run across the souks began to branch into smaller ones that form the present tangle of narrow alleyways. This labyrinth was ventilated by a system of roof openings.

Perfume-making and the production of essences have for years been traditional Tunisian crafts. Rose and jasmine oils are particularly highly valued.

The centre of the medina (old quarter) is the site of the most important souks, which remain open from morning until night with a break in the afternoon. It is busy at any time of day but gets particularly crowded during the summer, when the local shoppers are joined by visitors.

Weavers' workshops, as with the workshops that produce leather or wooden articles for sale, are often to be found in the souks, directly behind the shops that sell these goods.

The stone-paved street of a souk

Ventilation and illumination holes in the vault of a covered souk

Tunisians like to shop in souks where they can also buy clothes and household goods. The shopping ritual includes haggling and a thorough inspection of the goods.

Fruit and vegetable markets were often situated close to town gates to make trade easier for market gardeners. They give a glimpse of present-day Tunisian life.

What to Buy in Tunisia

THERE IS A WIDE RANGE OF PRODUCTS on sale in Tunisia. Much of what is available has been produced by local craftsmen and it pays to seek out items that have been made locally such as coral jewellery from Tabarka or a sea sponge from the Gulf of Gabès. Kairouan is famous for its carpets and leatherware; Nabeul and Jerba for their ceramics; Sidi Bou Saïd for its intricately made bird cages; Douz and Tozeur for footwear. If travelling in the south of the country it is worth looking out for Berber products including tapestries, beautiful ceramics and silver jewellery.

Ceramic vessel, Nabeul

Ceramics

The inhabitants of Guellala on Jerba have long been associated with pottery and employ Berber motifs in brown and beige. Nabeul craftsmen favour bright colourings dominated by blue and green. Berber ceramics from Sejnane are also famous (see p134).

Woollen tapestry

Carpets

The best places to buy carpets are in Tunis, Kairouan, Tozeur and Jerba. There are two basic types. Woven (Mergoum) carpets predate Islam and have Berber origins. They are distinguished by geometric patterns and sharply contrasting colours. Alloucha carpets are knotted and feature natural tones. These can be bought in Aïn Draham in northern Tunisia (see p129).

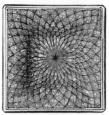

A cobalt-decorated plate

Bracelets

Tunisian jewellery is mostly made of silver or gold. The hedeyed is a wide bracelet that is worn on the wrist. Bracelets for the ankles are known as kholkal and are a symbol of fidelity. The largest jewellery centres are in Tunis, Sfax and Jerba.

Typical silver bracelet, with a fish motif

A headdress made of golden leaves

A richly embroidered waistcoat

Shoes

Leather shoes come in a wide variety of designs. It is worth looking out for the traditional balgha, which are worn mainly in the south of the country. In the north a more highly decorated version that is worn by women can be seen.

Necklace made of silver and precious stones

Perfumes

When visiting a souk that specializes in perfume look out for jasmine oil, as well as oil produced from the damask rose. White musk is also of a good quality. A small bottle costs about 5 TD.

Glass perfume bottle

Traditional shoes

Mosaics

Many of the products on sale in Tunisia stem from a variety of cultures and influences. Mosaics are a prime example of this, and most museums and souvenir shops sell ceramic tiles reminiscent of the mosaics from Carthage, Dougga and El-Jem.

Cinnamon

Pepper

Paprika

Rosemary

Saffron

Turmeric

Food and Drink

Tunisia produces good-quality wines and strong liqueurs such as boukha *(a clear spirit made from figs). When exploring a souk look out for spices and homemade* harissa *(a spicy sauce).*

Tunisian white wine

Chichas

Hookahs used for smoking tobacco, can be bought anywhere in Tunisia, but the best ones are produced in Tunis. Check that all the parts fit together and that the air flow is not obstructed. The mixture is readily available. Most Tunisians smoke an aromatic tobacco, flavoured with such things as apple or cherry.

Chicha from Tunis

Wooden Articles

The best wooden items are made of olive wood. Mostly produced in Sfax, these make good souvenirs, especially salad bowls and mortars.

Wooden mortar and pestle

A traditional ornamental coffee pot

A brass plate

Other Souvenirs

Probably the most typical Tunisian souvenir is a stuffed camel. Every souvenir shop has a large variety of them. Other popular souvenirs include woven mats, baskets, fans and the ubiquitous leather pouffes.

Metalwork

Very popular traditional copper and brass items for sale include trays, bowls, vases and jugs with distinctive narrow necks. Trays can be bought in several sizes, up to 65 cm (26 inches) in diameter, and in two types of finishes – shiny or matt.

A decorative brass plaque

A pouffe seat

Leather pouffe

ENTERTAINMENT IN TUNISIA

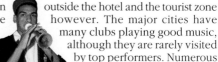

A fife-playing musician

TUNISIA HAS MORE to offer than beautiful beaches, and the lively programme of entertainment available to visitors is both rich and varied. Many of the most interesting events take place during the peak season. The big hotels provide their own nighly entertainment in the form of discos and performances of traditional dance. It is always worth venturing outside the hotel and the tourist zone however. The major cities have many clubs playing good music, although they are rarely visited by top performers. Numerous festivals take place throughout the year and these are also worth seeking out *(see pp38–42)*. These colourful events provide the best display of Tunisian culture and also a chance to meet some of the locals.

Evening performance of a jug-balancing act in a hotel

INFORMATION

INFORMATION ABOUT major cultural events and festivals can be found in French language newspapers, particularly *La Presse* which, although it does not have listings pages, has a good cultural section. The ONTT (Organization Nationale de Tourisme Tunisien), with its main office in Tunis, publishes a number of brochures containing information on annual festivals, which can be picked up in advance of a trip. The programme for the prestigious Carthage International Festival can be found in the local press or on the Internet. In June it is also available from ONTT information desks. The programme of the Medina Festival, held annually in Tunis during Ramadan, is published about three weeks in advance and is also available from the ONTT.

TRADITIONAL SHOWS

A VARIETY OF traditional performances can be seen in many places throughout Tunisia. Belly dancing is extremely popular, as are the Berber shows and dances. A good show can be seen in the M. Rabet café in Tunis medina *(see p274)*, which consists of a lively mix of traditional folk music, Berber dances and belly dancing. The show is an additional cost on top of the meal.

A novel alternative to belly dancing is a traditional dance with jugs *(left)*, which might be encountered on the island of Jerba.

MUSIC

SIDI BOU SAÏD'S **Centre of Arab and Mediterranean Music** puts on wonderful traditional concerts, which are held in the former palace of Baron d'Erlanger *(see p97)*. The varied programme includes not only classical Arab music, but frequent guest appearances of world-class artists performing various types of music – from flamenco to Chopin's mazurkas or modern music.

Any local festivals held in towns and villages are usually accompanied by music.

FESTIVALS

Horse riding display, the Sahara Festival

TUNISIA BOASTS A vast number of festivals, which are celebrated throughout the year *(see pp38–42)*. The reasons for celebrations range from marking the end of the harvests, to events of religious or cultural importance. Many festivals are of a local character. Most concerts and shows are staged during July, August and Ramadan.

The big event of the summer is the Carthage International Festival. Its programme is exceptionally

Evening concert in the El-Jem amphitheatre

rich, and includes top performances of symphony music, classical Arab music and pop music. In addition, the festival has theatre, ballet, musicals, operas, cinema and exhibitions. The main venue for the events is the Roman amphitheatre in Carthage *(see pp102–6)*. Another very interesting event is the Symphony Music Festival in El-Jem *(see p163)*. In the evenings the amphitheatre becomes a magnificent concert hall under the stars. Hammamet's Arab Music Festival, held in July and August, and the Jazz Festival held each year at the end of June in Tabarka are both very popular events, as is Testour's International Malouf Music Festival, which takes place in June.

CINEMA

GOING to the movies is a popular Tunisian activity and most large towns have at least one cinema. Tunis has a good selection including the **ABC** and **Le Palace**. The programme, however, is aimed mostly at young cinemagoers and consists mainly of action films shown in Arabic language versions. American and European blockbusters are usually dubbed into French. Information on programmes can be found in the cultural section of *La Presse*. Ticket prices start at around 3 TD for a seat in the stalls.

THEATRE

TUNISIA HAS only a handful of full-time theatre companies. The best-known and the most prestigious of the few that do exist is in Tunis, and performs in the **Théâtre Municipal** *(see p82)*. Its programme is dominated by plays of European playwrights, but it also puts on some Arab (mainly Egyptian) works. The splendid theatre building is also a frequent venue for concerts of both classical and Arabic music.

Casino in the Sousse tourist zone

NIGHTLIFE

THE BIG HOTELS usually run their own entertainment programmes which include nightly shows of belly dancing and performances of *malouf* (folk) music. Along with all this, many hotels have their own nightclubs, such as **The Blue Moon** attached to the Hôtel Hasdrubal in Yasmine Hammamet and Hôtel Topkapi's **Le Pacha Club** in Mahdia. These put on shows by artists from various Arab countries. Such places can be expensive and are frequented mainly by visitors.

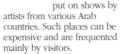
Ornate Théâtre Municipal in Tunis

The majority of Tunisia's clubs are in Tunis. The two most central are **Club 2001** and the **Joker Club**. Out in the suburbs, venues such as the **Cotton Club** and **Queen** tend to play more up-to-date dance music, and at greater volume. Outside of Tunis, clubs tend to be attached to major hotels such as **Abou Nawas Montazah** in Tabarka and **Club Le Rameau** in Sfax.

Similar to European clubs in music style and decor, Tunisia's clubs are popular with young Tunisians who can sometimes experience problems when trying to get in, either because they are under-age or do not meet with the door-staff's approval. Many clubs in Tunisia close at about 1am.

CASINOS

CASINOS IN TUNISIA are found only in large towns and tourist zones. They operate during the peak summer season and are open only to foreigners, though the staff consists entirely of Tunisians.

Two of the biggest are the **Cleopatra** in Hammamet and **Casino Caraibe** in Sousse. Both are glitzy affairs with a floor-full of blackjack, poker and roulette tables, bars, restaurants and live entertainment. A new casino, the **Casino de Jerba**, has recently opened.

In order to be allowed to play, visitors must show their passports or ID cards. Only convertible currencies are accepted. Men are expected to dress smartly in a suit and tie.

A live performance in a Tunisian club

CHILDREN'S ACTIVITIES

EXPLORING ANCIENT remains such as those at Dougga is fascinating but not to every child's taste. Fortunately, most hotels in the tourist zones have beach play areas for children. These are well organized and have trained supervisors to keep young guests entertained. Activities in these children's play areas range from beach volleyball and rounders to closely supervised paragliding taster sessions. Lessons in tennis and windsurfing for children can also usually be arranged.

If staying in the south of the country children will enjoy a visit to Tozeur's Dar Cheraït museum *(see below)*.

The north of the country has several funfairs. The best-known of these is **Parc des Loisirs Dah Dah** situated on the outskirts of Tunis, which has rides, merry-go-rounds and other amusements. **Parc des Loisirs Bah Bah** on Jerba is a more modest affair with a small fairground and bumper cars.

Park Friguia crocodiles

Another popular place for family outings is **Belvedere Park** in Tunis. This is Tunis's largest park and has plenty of room for children to let off steam. There is a small zoo in its southern section, and also a small but informative exhibition on the plants and wildlife of Tunisia *(see p87)*.

Many children may enjoy a trip to the **Oceanographic Museum** at Carthage where life beneath the waves can be discovered thanks to the numerous aquariums, scale models, educational boards and interactive displays.

Visitors exploring the ancient ruins in Dougga

AMUSEMENT PARKS

SITUATED CLOSE TO the town of Bou Ficha, 35 km (22 miles) from Hammamet and 58 km (36 miles) from Sousse is **Park Friguia**. This is a large recreation area, which combines a small, but well-run zoo with an amusement park. It is run by the Tunisian forestry commission and has a collection of African animals including crocodiles, giraffes and elephants. As well as the amusement area, which has all the usual rides, the park also includes a number of restaurants and a venue for performances of *malouf* (folk) music.

Tozeur has a private ethnography museum, **Dar Cheraït**, whose formula vastly exceeds that of a mere museum. It is devoted to the history and everyday life of southern Tunisia. A recently opened section carries visitors to the world of the *Thousand and One Nights*, where they will meet, amongst others, Ali Baba and the 40 Thieves, Sinbad the Sailor and Scheherazade. This display is popular with children and includes secret labyrinths, ghosts, fire-eaters and a hall of mirrors. The fairytale stories are accompanied by accounts of everyday life in Arabic countries. The museum is best visited in the evening when it is festooned with fairy-lights.

Planet Oasis was recently opened in the palm groves close to Tozeur. This vast cultural complex consists of a huge air-conditioned tent (used for concerts, occasional receptions and Ramadan dinners), a row of fountains and an amphitheatre seating 2,000 spectators. The stage is built on the Saharan sand, with the natural backdrop of palm trees. It makes the most of state-of-the-art laser effects to stage spectacular concerts and open-air events. Planet Oasis also has regular displays of handicrafts such as glass blowing, painting, leatherwork and pottery.

Tunisia's largest water park is undoubtedly **Acqua Palace** at Port el-Kantaoui. With water chutes, slides, drops, tunnels, whirlpools and every other kind of splashy fun, Acqua Palace provides an enjoyable way for children both big and small to find some cooling relief from the hot Tunisian sun.

The beach – a favourite place for children and adults alike

DIRECTORY

MUSIC

Centre of Arab and Mediterranean Music
Rue 2 Mars 8, Sidi Bou Said.
(76) 740 102.

CINEMAS

ABC
Rue ibn Khaldoun, Tunis.
(71) 336 360.

Le Palace
Av. Habib Bourguiba, Tunis.
(71) 256 989.

THEATRES

Théâtre fou – Mad'Art
Av. Habib Bourguiba, Carthage-Dermech.
(71) 734 877.

El-Hamra
Rue el-Jazira 28, Tunis.
(71) 320 734.
w www.theatrelhamra.com

El-Théâtre Complexe el-Mechtel
El-Omrane, Tunis.
(71) 791 795.

Etoile du Nord
Av. Farhat Hached, Tunis.
(71) 254 066.

Théâtre Municipal
Rue de Grèce 2, Tunis.
(71) 259 499.

NIGHTLIFE

Abou Nawas Montazah
Tabarka.
(78) 673 532.

Adonis
Hôtel Yadis Thalasso Golf, Midoun.

Ben's
Av. Moncef Bey, Hammamet.
(72) 227 053.

Club 2001
Hôtel el-Mechtel, Tunis.
(71) 783 200.

Club Le Rameau
Av. H. Bourguiba, Hôtel Abou Nawas, Sfax.
(74) 225 700.

Club Pin's
Hotel Mehari, Tabarka.
(78) 670 440.

Cotton Club
Hôtel Nova Park, Gammarth.
(72) 748 765.

Disco Marina Yasmine
Hôtel Marina Palace, Hammamet.

El-Barka
Hôtel Penelope, Houmt Souk.

Guitoun
Av. Moncef Bey, Hammamet.
(72) 248 820.

Hippocampe
Route Corniche, Hôtel Corniche, Bizerte.
(72) 421 222.

Hotel Morjene Dar Tabarka
Tabarka.
(78) 673 411.

Hotel Sfax Centre
Sfax.
(74) 225 700.

Joker Club
Hotel el-Hana, Tunis.
(71) 331 144.

La Baleine
Tourist zone, Hôtel Golf Beach, Tabarka.

La Bamba
Hôtel Alhambra, Port el-Kantaoui.

Las Vegas
Route Touristique Nord, Hôtel Nahrawess, Hammamet.

Le boeuf sur le toit
Av. Fatouma, La Soukra, Tunis.

Le Crocodile
Route Touristique Nord, Hôtel le Président, Hammamet.

Le Pacha
Hôtel Riu Royal Garden, Midoun.

Le Pacha Club
Route Corniche, Hôtel Topkapi, Mahdia.

Nirvana
Tourist zone, Hammamet.
(72) 278 408.

Queen
Hôtel Karim, Gammarth.

Rancho Club
Av. Moncef Bey, Hammamet.
(72) 226 462.

Sahara Club
Route Touristique, Hôtel Sahara Beach, Monastir.

Sirocco
Monastir.
(73) 462 305.

Sun Set City
Merezka, Hammamet.
(72) 282 976.

The Blue Moon
Hasdrubal Thalassa, Yasmine Hammamet.
(72) 248 800.

Tropicana
Route Touristique, Hammamet.
(72) 227 200.

Turquoise
Hôtel Abou Nawas Jerba, Sidi Mahares.
(75) 757 022.

Yamama
Corniche, Hôtel Abou Nawas Nejma, Sousse.
(73) 226 811.

CASINOS

Casino Caraibe
Av. 7 Novembre, Sousse.
(73) 211 777.
FAX (73) 211 798.

Cleopatra
Hotel Occidental, Hammamet.
(72) 226 935.
FAX (72) 226 315.

Grand Casino Hammamet
Route Touristique Nord, Hammamet.
(72) 261 777.

Casino de Jerba
Tourist zone, Sidi Mahares.
(75) 757 537.

CHILDREN'S ACTIVITIES

Belvedere Park
(71) 890 386.
@ ami.belvedere@planet.tn

Park de Loisirs Bah Bah
Rue 20 Mars, Houmt Souk, Jerba.

Park de Loisirs Dah Dah
Berges de Lac, Tunis.

Oceanograpic Museum
Rue 2 Mars 1934 28, Carthage.
(71) 730 420.

AMUSEMENT PARKS

Acqua Palace
Rue des Palmiers, Port el-Kantaoui.
(73) 348 855.
@ Contact@Acqua Palace.com
w www.acquapalace.com

Centre d'Animation Touristique les Grottes
Route des Grottes, El-Haouaria.
(72) 297 296.
FAX (72) 269 070.

Dar Cheraït
Route Touristique, Tozeur.
(76) 452 100.
FAX (76) 452 329.
@ darcherait@planet.tn

Park Friguia
On route GP1 between Enfida and Bou Ficha.
@ info@friguiapark.com

Planet Oasis
Tozeur.
w www.planet-oasis.com

SPORT IN TUNISIA

FOOTBALL IS Tunisia's favourite sport and men often gather in large groups to watch matches live on TV. Another popular sport is the annual Dakar Rally, which frequently passes through the Tunisian desert on its route from Europe to Senegal. Since the late 1960s, Tunisian athletes have often

A four-wheel-drive car in the Dakar Rally

done well in athletics and also in sports such as handball and volleyball, achieving world-class results. A little more recently, Tunisian swimmers have begun to win recognition. In 2003, Oussama Mellouli won a bronze medal in the 400-m medley at the World Championships in Barcelona.

Tunisia's national football team in action

FOOTBALL

AS ELSEWHERE IN Africa, football is a passion in Tunisia and it's not hard to find a game on television. Watching football matches is almost a ritual in many traditional Tunisian cafés. Viewers react with great passion during live transmissions and the outcome of a game is a matter of some importance to many Tunisian football fans. Demand for tickets is high, so anyone wishing to see a game should arrive at the ground well before kick-off.

Tunisia's national team ranks as one of the best on the African continent and won the African Nations Cup in 2004 when they beat Morocco 2–1. Tunisian league teams are also successful and usually reach the later stages of continental club competitions. Two particularly outstanding teams are Etoile Sportive du Sahel from Sousse and Tunis's Espérance Sportive, which plays at the El-Menzah ground at the Cité Olympique. Other teams that are also successful are Club Africain (which is also from Tunis and shares its ground

with Espérance Sportive), and Club Sfaxien, based in Sfax.

As in other countries, the Tunisian League championship is fiercely contested each year by the major clubs.

Tunisia's National Cup is held each year and provides the lower league clubs with an opportunity to play some of the top teams.

The undoubted star of Tunisian football is "the golden boy" Ali Zitouni, the talented young forward of Espérance Sportive who competed with the national team at the 2004 Olympics.

Tunisia have reached the finals of the World Cup three times (1978, 1998 and 2002) and, at the time of writing, are ranked 36th in the world by FIFA. Currently, the coach

of the Tunisian national team is Roger Lemerre, the former French national team coach.

Tunisia's match season starts in early October and finishes at the end of March. Most games are played on Saturdays and Sundays, with a 3pm kick-off. Information about matches can be found in the local press or via the Tunisian Football Federation's website at www.ftf.org.tn

HOT-AIR BALLOONING

TUNISIA PROVIDES favourable conditions for hot-air ballooning, although it is not as popular as it once was. The areas on the outskirts of the Sahara Desert are especially popular and are used as locations for many of the competitions that attract entries from all over the world. Hot-air balloons taking-off from this region can travel hundreds of kilometres.

Hot-air balloon race held around Douz

Rally car navigating northern Tunisia's rough terrain

RALLIES

THE FIRST PARIS–DAKAR Rally began on 26 November, 1978, with 170 entrants. Now the event is known as the Dakar Rally and traditionally starts on 1 January, in France. Each year the route of the rally, split into several sections, is changed, but it always leads through rough terrain and across the Saharan sands. The last time the rally passed through Tunisia was in 2003 when two of the legs took in Tunis, Tozeur and El-Borma. Vehicles participating in this punishing race include lorries, cross-country cars and motorcycles. Almost as popular as the Dakar Rally is the Tunisia Rally, which also attracts some of the world's top drivers.

ATHLETICS

TUNISIA HAS MANY talented athletes. In 2001 the country hosted the Mediterranean Games.

The most famous runner in Tunisia is Mohammed Gammoudi. Born in 1938, he became a national celebrity after winning medals in three consecutive Olympic Games. In 1964 he won a silver medal in Tokyo in the 10,000-m race. At the Olympic Games in Mexico City four years later, he picked up a gold medal for the 5,000 m, and then took a silver at the 1972 Munich Olympics for the same distance. Tunisian runners have also achieved numerous successes in world championships and excel in medium- and long-distance running.

HANDBALL

HANDBALL IS A game played on a court similar to that used in squash. It is popular in Tunisia and receives plenty of TV and press coverage. The men's team has participated several times in world championships and the Olympic Games, and Tunisia continually ranks among the world's leading teams. The country will host the Handball Championships in 2005.

Tunisian runner at the Mexico City Olympics

SAILING

TUNISIA IS A sailor's paradise, with its 1200-km (746-mile) long coastline, countless bays and coves, and an average air temperature of 18° C (64° F). Costs for sailing in Tunisia are very attractive, and lower than in other parts of the Mediterranean. The country has five large marinas. Port el-Kantaoui has 320 spaces for yachts. Sidi Bou Saïd's harbour can accommodate 380 vessels. Monastir's marina has space for 386 boats.

The most important sailing events include an annual race from Malta (Valletta) to Port el-Kantaoui and another from Marseille to Tabarka.

OTHER SPORTS

IN 2001, during the Judo World Championships held in Korea, Anisa Lounife became the first Muslim woman to win a gold medal at judo. In recent years swimming has been gaining popularity in Tunisia. Oussama Mellouli was voted Tunisia's Athlete of the Year in 2003 after winning a bronze medal in the 400-m medley at Barcelona's world championships. The 19-year-old was the first Tunisian to stand on the winners' podium for a world-ranking swimming event.

The Tunisian basketball team is one of the best in Africa. In 2001 the team managed to come fourth in Africa's Basketball Championship. Though the Tunisian team does not have many tall players (the tallest is just over 2 m (6 ft 6 in), Tunisian players have a world reputation and have competed in the Czech Republic and Poland.

Windsurfing is another sport that is becoming increasingly popular in Tunisia and the country was represented in the Athens Olympics for this event.

Volleyball has many followers and is particularly popular with Tunisian women. The high popularity of this sport is due to several spectacular victories, such as in the African Championships held in Lagos in 1997, when the Tunisian team defeated Cameroon 3–0.

Tunisian judo competitors at the Korean Olympics

ACTIVITIES FOR VISITORS

TUNISIA'S CLIMATE makes the country an exceptional place for all types of outdoor activity. Visitors naturally favour watersports, including diving and sailing. Tourist zones have excellent golf courses – the best ones are in Port el-Kantaoui, while the most scenic ones are located around Tabarka. More exotic sports,

Holidaymakers learning to windsurf

such as paragliding, surfing on the dunes and sand-yachting on the salt flats of Chott el-Jerid are specialities of the southern region. Horse riding on the beaches of Jerba and Zarzis is a popular activity, as is camel trekking across the desert. Tunisia's national parks and the mountains around Aïn Draham offer visitors plenty of opportunities for hiking.

Catamarans off the beach at Jerba

DIVING

SOME OF THE Mediterranean's best diving and snorkelling can be enjoyed in Tunisia. One of the most beautiful places to go is the coral reef off Tabarka where the clear, warm waters, coral and seawater beds are ideal for underwater exploration. Ten minutes by boat are enough to get to rocks surrounded by red coral. A little bit further on are magnificent tunnels, grottoes, underwater caves and caverns.

The warm sea and a vigorous and sustained programme of conservation mean that the reef is teeming with fish and other marine life. There are as many as six sites open to divers; each looks different and requires a different level of ability.

The yacht club in Tabarka and the International Diving Centre organize excursions to the reef for more experienced divers. The most popular site is Roche Merou – the Miller's Thumb Rock – where divers can swim amid rainbow-

coloured fish. La Tunelle, or Tunnels Reef, is less than 20 minutes from Tabarka and comprises a complex of tunnels, caves and caverns some 18 m (60 ft) below sea level. Club de Plongée, which is by the yacht jetty in Tabarka, also organizes taster excursions for total beginners as well as a 7-day course for less experienced divers. They also rent out boats and diving

equipment. Tabarka is not the only place where it it possible to go diving, however. The International Diving Centre in Port el-Kantaoui is open all year round and provides facilities for more experienced divers as well as running courses for beginners. Ideal conditions for exploring the beauty of the underwater world can also be found in Hergla, 15 km (9 miles) north of Port el-Kantaoui. Most diving clubs insist that divers are over 14 years old.

OTHER WATER SPORTS

TUNISIA IS A great place for windsurfing, which can be enjoyed all year round, although between December and April it is advisable to wear a wetsuit because the sea is so cool. One of the best windsurfing schools is situated in Sidi Bou Saïd. Favourable conditions for the sport are also found in Hammamet, Sousse and on Jerba. Seaside tourist resorts offer water skis for hire.

PARAGLIDING

ANOTHER popular sport in Tunisia is paragliding and lessons from qualified instructors can usually be arranged. Having the right equipment for this activity is essential and should always be supplied by the club or instructor.

Paragliding, a popular activity

HIKING

TUNISIA'S NATIONAL PARKS are splendid hiking grounds. An ideal place for this type of activity is Ichkeul National Park – one of the largest wintering sites for birds in the whole of the Mediterranean basin *(see pp136–7)*. Jebel Ichkeul, on the lake's south side, has a number of sandy footpaths leading through hills overgrown with wild olive trees. In the spring it can be carpeted with wild flowers.

Another great place is the Boukornine National Park. Situated near Tunis, it is full of Persian cyclamens that flower in the spring. Excellent conditions can also be found in the Khroumirie Mountains *(see p130)*, near Aïn Draham, where it is possible to climb to the top of Jebel Bir (1,041 m/ 3,415 ft) and the Col des Ruines overlooking the village.

**Wild boar hunting around
Aïn Draham**

HUNTING

THE FORESTS AROUND Aïn Draham are popular with hunters in search of wild boar. The season lasts from October until February. Hunting also takes place around El-Haouaria, Sbeïtla and Zaghouan. Special licences are required and can only be obtained by people who are part of an organized tour.

CAMEL TREKKING

THOSE DREAMING OF a real desert adventure should try a several day-, or several week-long trek across the sands of the Great Eastern Erg on a camel. The most popular

Caravan with tourists leaving Zaafrane

journey is a five-day trek from Douz to Ksar Ghilane. Shorter rides are also available and for a few dinars it is possible to enjoy an hour-long camel ride which, for some people, is quite enough.

The price per day (which includes all the necessary equipment and meals) is usually about 30–35 TD. An hour-long ride costs far less.

When embarking on a camel trek take a down-filled sleeping bag (nights are cold in the desert), a rolled-up sleeping mat, a pair of loose trousers and a large cotton scarf to protect the head and neck from the sun and wind. A flask containing water is, of course, indispensable. A tasty snack for the camel may also come in handy.

Another very important item when travelling in the desert is a well-stocked first-aid kit. As well as pain-killers, it is also advisable to carry a general antibiotic, a snake-bite serum, antihistamine and a remedy for gastric conditions. Also don't forget sunglasses, eye-drops, sun-block lip cream and large quantities of sun-cream.

Ideal months for such a trip are April, October and November as the temperature is then cooler. In December and January, however, night temperatures can drop to freezing. March brings sandstorms, while July and August are far too hot.

CYCLING AND MOTORBIKE TRIPS

MANY HOTELS OFFER bicycles for hire and tourist resorts also often run bike-hire services. Always check the condition of the hired bicycle before accepting it (usually it is far from perfect). Jerba and the coast of Sahel are ideal areas for cycling. If cycling around the country, take a set of spare parts such as inner tubes as there are practically no service and repair facilities outside the main towns.

A motorbike is an ideal vehicle for exploring the country. However, there is only one rental firm in Tunisia – Holiday Bikes on Jerba. Anyone wishing to hire a motorbike must be at least 21 years of age and hold a valid motorbike driving licence.

Driving a jeep across the desert – a taste of the Dakar Rally

Riders on a beach in Jerba

HORSE RIDING

HORSE RIDING is available in many seaside resorts in Tunisia as well as in the areas close to the hotels that run their own riding stables.

The most popular place for horse riding is Jerba. The island also has the greatest number of riding stables. Here, it is possible to gallop for hours along virtually deserted beaches. Horse riding at sunrise or sunset can be an unforgettable experience.

GOLF

ALTHOUGH TUNISIA does not have many golf courses, its climate is exceptionally favourable for the sport. Tunisia is firmly established on the international golf circuit and many people come to the country with the sole purpose of playing golf. There are a handful of top quality golf courses available. All of these offer a good range of facilities, including equipment hire, bars and restaurants. Friendly instructors are ready to assist those new to the sport.

Many hotels can arrange transfers to and from courses and also pre-set teeing-off times. Few of the clubs have stringent membership requirements though some of the larger ones may ask for a valid handicap certificate before they will allow a new player on the course. Failing that, a letter of introduction from a home club will often be sufficient.

The top golf course in Tunisia is the **El-Kantaoui**.

This 36-hole, professional course has a championship layout that winds through the olive groves opposite the marina. Twenty minutes from Tunis is the 18-hole **Carthage Golf Course**, which was founded in 1927. Two top-quality 18-hole courses are

Golfer on a course near Port el-Kantaoui

located in Monastir and Hammamet, while in Bir Bou Regba, near Hammamet, there is a 9-hole course. Jerba also has a golf club, which comprises three 9-hole courses. Tabarka's golf course is in the tourist zone and is set in a picturesque landscape of eucalyptus and olive trees overlooking the coast. The club features an 18-hole, 72-par course and a 9-hole practice course for less experienced players.

THALASSOTHERAPY

TUNISIA IS SECOND only to France in terms of its thalassotherapy facilities. This treatment uses hot seawater combined with seaweed or mud in order to alleviate such common ailments as stress, rheumatism and arthritis. Many people enjoy it for its own sake, however, and thalassotherapy centres tend to be attached to hotels that also run life-enhancing programmes such as quitting smoking. They usually also promote healthy eating in their restaurants. Three of the best are the **Abou Nawas**, Sousse, the **Residence Hotel,** Carthage and the **Hasdrubal Thalassa**, Hammamet.

OTHER ACTIVITIES

THERE ARE FEW facilities for extreme sports in Tunisia. Nevertheless, there are plenty of attractions for those who seek high-octane thrills. Most of them are associated with the southern regions of the country and with the Sahara.

Thrill-seekers should certainly try sand-skiing and sand-yachting. The latter is carried out on the dunes around Kelibia and Douz, while sand-skiing is practised in the El-Faour oasis, 30 km (19 miles) from Douz. The hard bottom of the dry Chott el-Jerid salt flat is perfect for the use of sand-yachts.

Any kind of flying is also very popular in Tunisia. The Sahara Desert offers good conditions for hang-gliding (although it is best to have your own equipment) and for flying light aircraft. These sports are, however, rather expensive and depend very much on the weather.

A microlight aircraft preparing for a flight over the Sahara

DIRECTORY

DIVING

HAMMAMET
Nabil Jegham
((72) 227 211.
FAX (72) 226 304.
@ nabil.jegham@
planet.tn

HERGLA
Hergla Scubadive
((73) 231 386.
FAX (73) 251 388.

JERBA
Merry Land Jerba
((75) 657 070.

MONASTIR
Cap Afrique
Mahdia
((73) 695 530.

Plongée et Loisirs
Cap Marina Monastir.
((73) 462 509.
FAX (73) 462 509.

TABARKA
Aquamarin
((78) 673 408.
FAX (78) 761 866.

Club Robinson
Tabarka
((78) 670 333.
FAX (78) 671 096

Loisirs de Tabarka
((78) 670 664.
FAX (78) 673 801.
@ diving.tunisie@planet.tn

Mehari Diving
Center "Le Crabe"
((78) 673 136.
FAX (78) 673 866.

YACHT MARINAS

HAMMAMET
Marina Yasmine
Sud
Rue Jaafar el-Barmaki 3.
((2161) 840 655.
FAX (2161) 842 417.
@ marina.yasmine
@planet.tn

MONASTIR
Marina Cap
Monastir
((73) 462 305.
FAX (73) 462 066.

TABARKA
Montazah Tabarka
((78) 670 599.
FAX (78) 643 595.

Yachting Club
de Tabarka
((78) 644 478.

BOAT CHARTER

PORT EL-
KANTAOUI
Tunisie Sailing
Quai Amilcar.
((73) 246 588.
FAX (73) 348 490.

SIDI BOU SAÏD
Tunis Nautic
Port de Sidi Bou Saïd.
((71) 748 564.

MOTOR RALLIES

Touring Club
de Tunisie
Rue d'Allemagne 15, Tunis.
((71) 323 114.
FAX (71) 324 834.

BICYCLE HIRE

JERBA
Holiday Bikes
((75) 657 169.

HORSE RIDING

JERBA
Hôtel Riu Royal
Garden Palace
((75) 745 777.

Hôtel Coralia Club
Palm Beach
((75) 757 404.

MAHDIA
Hôtel Cap Mahdia
((73) 680 300.

Hôtel Thapsus
((73) 694 495.
FAX (73) 694 476.

TUNIS
Club Hippique de
la Soukra
((71) 203 054.

Hippodrome
de Ksar Said
((71) 350 088.
FAX (71) 583 596.

GOLF

JERBA
Jerba Golf Club,
Tourist zone, Midoun.
((75) 745 055.
FAX (75) 745 051.

MONASTIR
Flamingo Golf
Course
B.P.168, Rte Ouerdanine.
((73) 500 284.

PORT EL-
KANTAOUI
El-Kantaoui Golf
Course
((73) 348 756.
FAX (73) 348 755.

TABARKA
Tabarka Golf
Course
Route touristique,
El-Morjane.
((78) 670 038.
FAX (78) 671 026.

TUNIS
Golf de Carthage
Choutrana 2, La Soukra.
((71) 765 700.

THALASSOTHERAPY

CARTHAGE
The Residence
B.P. 697, Les Côtes de
Carthage.
((71) 910 101.
FAX (71) 910 144.

HAMMAMET
Hasdrubal
Thalassa
Yasmine Hammamet.
((72) 248 800.
FAX (72) 248 923.

JERBA
Hasdrubal
((75) 730 650.

SOUSSE
Abou Nawas
Avenue Habib Bourguiba.
((73) 226 030.
FAX (73) 226 595.

TRIPS TO THE SAHARA

Afri Tours
Rue Jean Jaurès 61, Tunis.
((71) 254 799.

Au Coeur
du Désert
Rue Abou Kassem
el-Chabbi, Tozeur.
((76) 453 660/570.
FAX (76) 453 515.

Bel Travel
Services
Rue Amilcar, Midoun.
((75) 601 357.
FAX (75) 601 351.

Calypso Voyages
Avenue H. Bourgiba 69,
Houmt Souk.
((75) 620 561.
FAX (75) 620 558.
@ calypso.voyages
@planet.tn

Centrale de
Voyages (La)
Avenue Mohamed Badra,
Jerba.
((75) 652 815.
FAX (75) 623 704.

Comptoir de
la Tunisie
BP 162, Houmt Souk.
((75) 652 398.
FAX (75) 652 931.

Dream Travel
Route de l'Aéroport,
Houmt Souk.
((75) 673 451.
FAX (75) 673 504.

Hafsi Travel
Route de Nefta, Tozeur.
((76) 452 611.
FAX (76) 452 455.

Houria Voyages
Zone Touristique, Tozeur.
((76) 461 022.
FAX (76) 461 079.

Jerba Voyages
Rue ibn Khaldun 2, Tunis.
((71) 240 105.
FAX (71) 337 212.

Sable
d'Or Voyages
Avenue d'Afrique
26–Menzah, Tunis.
((71) 237 303.
FAX (71) 237 505.

Sud Tourisme
Residence Habib, Tunis.
((71) 724 184.

SURVIVAL
GUIDE

PRACTICAL INFORMATION 310–319
TRAVEL INFORMATION 320–327

PRACTICAL INFORMATION

TUNISIA IS A visitor-friendly place and, in its outlook, is probably one the the most "Western" of all Islamic countries. Within the tourist zones visitors may behave as they would at home. When venturing further afield, however, it is important to be aware of local attitudes and

A street name written in Arabic and French

customs. For instance exposed shoulders and the wearing of miniskirts by women are considered inappropriate. Mosques, particularly prayer halls, are not open to non-Muslims. Although Tunisia is a Muslim country, it follows the European calendar and has adopted Sunday as its day of rest.

Visitors resting on the steps of the Great Mosque, Tunis

WHEN TO VISIT

HOLIDAYS CAN BE taken in Tunisia at any time of the year. The hot summer season lasts from May until early October, although the heat is moderated by the sea breezes on the coast. Summer is the best time for sunbathing on the beach and swimming. If venturing inland or to the south of the country, however, then it can get unbearably hot during the summer months; the heat is particularly intense in the mountain valleys.

In autumn, cold currents coming from the northwest Atlantic can bring wind and rain. Then, the temperature drops to 20–24° C (68–74° F), though the sea remains warm. The most rainfall can be expected in the north.

During winter the days are warm and mostly sunny, with temperatures between 16 and 24° C (61 and 75° F), but be prepared for weather changes

as some of the most unpredictable weather occurs at this time. The daytime temperature may be 25° C (75° F) one day, and suddenly drop to just a few degrees above freezing the next. On windy days the cold can feel acute, particularly on the Cap Bon peninsula and in the northern regions of the country. These cold spells never last long, however.

In the main, the best seasons for visiting Tunisia are spring and autumn when sightseeing can be combined with sea-bathing. The best time to visit the south is from early September until May, but trips to the desert should ideally be undertaken in September, October or March, when the daytime temperature is 25–28° C (77–82° F). The main festival period is in summer. During Ramadan the shops stay open until late. Concerts and poetry evenings are held at numerous venues in the medinas of Tunis and Kairouan. On Jerba, the holiday season lasts most of the year, though the sea cools off towards the end of October.

PASSPORTS AND VISAS

CITIZENS OF THE European Union and nationals of the United States and Canada, Australia and New Zealand require a valid passport to visit Tunisia. It should be valid for at least six months after the date of arrival, and will allow visits of up to three months without a visa for citizens of the EU, USA and Canada. Australians and New Zealanders should apply for a visa in advance of their trip. For stays exceeding three months, most visitors will need to obtain a visa. If in doubt, contact the Tunisian Embassy, or seek advice from a travel agent.

CUSTOM REGULATIONS

THE LIMITS ON what can be taken in and out of the country are stated in detail in custom regulations. Duty-free allowances include 1 litre of spirits, 2 litres of wine, 400 cigarettes, 250 ml of perfume, two cameras, 20 rolls of film and one video camera. There are no limits on the amount

Transport for holidaymakers in Sousse

◁ **Avenue Habib Thameur – the main street of Nabeul**

Tourist information office in Houmt Souk on Jerba

in larger towns. Small information desks are also in some selected museums. Some of them hand out free pamphlets and detailed road maps, but there is not likely to be much detailed information from these small ONTT offices regarding sightseeing, transport or obtaining hotel accommodation. The ONTT also has an office in London, however, which can provide information on all aspects of Tunisia (see p247).

of foreign currency visitors may bring in. Tunisia has certain rules on the value of items brought into the country and it is advisable to declare items such as expensive cameras on arrival to save confusion when leaving the country.

Various products in duty-free shops can be purchased, using any convertible currency. Note that Tunisian duty-free shops do not take dinars. The prices of products bought in Tunisia's duty-free shops may be slightly higher than those in town.

phrases. In the main markets almost all languages can be heard. This is especially the case with shopkeepers and their assistants, who endeavour to encourage tourists to buy in as many languages as they can think of. Tunisia's Berber population has kept its own language, though they also usually speak Arabic. Tunisian children are generally able to speak French, as this is taught in school from primary level.

FACILITIES FOR THE DISABLED

THERE ARE NOT many facilities for wheelchair users in Tunisia. Wheelchair ramps are rarely seen and many of the major sights are inaccessible to wheelchair users for this reason. The Association Générale des Insuffisant Moteurs de Tunis can provide information for wheelchair users visiting Tunisia (see p247).

LANGUAGE

ARABIC IS THE official language of Tunisia, but French is also in common use and most educated Tunisians are practically bilingual. The staff working in tourist zones will usually also speak English, but in the hinterland English is virtually unknown, apart from a handful of basic

Road sign to the Dar Jellouli Museum in Sfax

TOURIST INFORMATION

ONTT TOURIST Information Bureaux (Organization Nationale de Tourisme Tunisien) can be found at all the major airports, as well as

STUDENTS

STUDENTS UP TO 32 years of age holding a valid International Student Identity Card (ISIC) are entitled to concessions in museums, historic buildings and archaeological sites. They are also entitled to reduced travel fares within the country. Tunisia also has a network of youth hostels that admits YHA card holders.

Health and Security

**Tunisian
Police badge**

MOST VISITORS TO TUNISIA will experience no serious problems with crime. The streets and hotels are discreetly patrolled by security guards and plain-clothes policemen. This high level of safety is due to untiring official vigilance, especially in the tourist zones. Crimes, such as groping, against women do happen, but are rare. Even so, a woman travelling alone risks a degree of unwanted attention. The greatest danger is posed by the sun; ignoring basic safety precautions may lead to severe burns and sunstroke.

**Policemen talking to young
people on the street in Sfax**

POLICE

WHEN STAYING IN Tunisia, even on a brief visit, visitors soon become aware of the large numbers of police. The National Guard are responsible for national security and its officers wear military khaki uniforms. The Sûreté, or state police, wear light and dark blue uniforms and mainly operate in the towns. Crimes and thefts should be reported to the state police. Police personnel speak French, but very few are likely to speak much English. The National Guard have

Patrol car of the Gendarmerie

responsibility for rural areas and the country's borders. They may set up road blocks, stop cars, check documents and the contents of the car. Tourist cars and coaches are usually not checked, but a hired car may be stopped. Visitors must then present their documents and explain the purpose of their journey. Although this may seem excessive, it has to be remembered that Tunisia shares borders with Algeria and Libya. The police are mainly on the lookout for smugglers, arms dealers and terrorists.

With tourists' safety in mind, police stations have been built in virtually every tourist zone. If visitors are a victim of a crime, they should request a police certificate (a copy of the police report) in order to claim compensation from their insurance company.

PERSONAL PROPERTY

THEFTS IN HOTELS are rare but it is recommended that any valuables be stored in a safe or at least kept out of sight. Every hotel employs security staff; the porter not only opens the doors, but also stops any stranger from entering the premises.

Beaches are patrolled around the clock to make sure that no unauthorized persons use this means to enter the hotel compound. Thefts are usually committed by outsiders, arriving from other parts of the country.

A lost or stolen passport should be reported to the Sûreté. In markets, trams and other crowded places be especially vigilant about pickpockets. In some of the larger resorts, such as Sousse, Jerba and Hammamet, it also pays to keep personal property out of sight. In places such as the narrow, crowded alleys of the medinas (old quarters) avoid carrying valuables in a handbag or backpack. It is better to keep wallets or purses under a shirt. The safest method is to use an inside pocket in a shirt or jacket that is fastened with a separate button or zip. Be aware, also, when on the beach – sleeping tourists can sometimes fall victim to pickpockets or bag-snatchers.

**Sign of a private ambulance
service in Jendouba**

HEALTH AND HYGIENE

TUNISIA IS A COUNTRY where restaurants maintain high standards of hygiene. This applies not only to the big hotel restaurants, but every small café that offers a quick meal will have a washbasin. Tunisians wash their hands before and after eating. Food poisoning is rare.

Despite this, visitors may experience stomach problems a few days after arriving in Tunisia. The usual symptoms are fever, shivering, general weakness, and diarrhoea. Usually this is not a case of food poisoning, but the body's reaction to the sun and the different diet and climate. This type of problem may be avoided by keeping out of the sun and reducing the consumption of raw vegetables and salads, particularly during the first few days of a visit. Prior to leaving home be sure to provide yourself with remedies for diarrhoea. The most important thing when suffering from an upset of this kind is to replace the fluid that is lost. In the course of such an illness drink plenty of bottled water.

There are not many public toilets in Tunisia. Most are usually at petrol stations. In an emergency look for a restaurant or a hotel. It is worth carrying a roll of toilet paper for such an eventuality.

The greatest health hazard in Tunisia is the sun. In summer always keep the head covered and avoid long exposure. Another danger is heatstroke, which is particularly likely in the desert, and in the mountain valleys. Among the signs of heatstroke are disorientation, headaches and a high body temperature without the other signs of fever. When out in the sun, drink plenty of water. In larger towns the tap water is fit for drinking. Try to avoid drinks that have been chilled too much as these can also upset your stomach.

During desert trips wear ankle-length boots to protect against scorpion bites.

MEDICAL CARE

EVERY HOTEL HAS a list of doctors who will come at any time of day or night, when called by the reception. Medical advice is not expensive in Tunisia; doctors

A fire engine from Bizerte

Neon sign of a pharmacy in Tunis

charge about 25-30 TD for a visit. Nevertheless, it is worth taking out insurance.

Tunisian hospitals have well-trained medical staff and good quality equipment; they also have their own ambulances. Dental services are also of a high standard. If there is a minor medical problem ask for advice in a pharmacy *(see below)*. In more remote and sparsely populated areas (particularly in southern Tunisia) emergency treatment and transport are provided by the police and army. Many of the big tourist hotels have doctors and nurses on call round the clock.

PHARMACIES

TUNISIAN PHARMACIES are clean, well stocked and can be found in many small towns and some villages. Their staff are well trained and likely to speak fluent French, although they may not be able to speak more than a few words of English. They will be able to offer simple medical advice and prescribe a wider range of drugs than are available without prescription in

Europe. Most towns will have a pharmacy that remains open all night – a list of pharmacies open round the clock is printed in the French language newspapers such as *La Presse* or *Le Temps*. The symbol for a pharmacy in Tunisia is a serpent on a green background.

FIRE BRIGADE

IF A FIRE breaks out within the hotel compound, contact the reception or call the number of the fire brigade *(Protection Civile)*. The operator will speak French, but only rarely be able to communicate in English. The fire engines in Tunisia are painted red.

The fire service is also called out during heavy rainfall, to pump water out of flooded cellars and apartments and to unblock the main drainage systems.

DIRECTORY

EMERGENCY NUMBERS

Police
📞 197.

Protection Civile (Fire)
📞 198.

Ambulance
📞 341 250 or 341 280.

Emergency Ambulance
📞 (71) 599 900.

**Medical Help
Allo Docteur**
📞 (71) 780 000

SOS (Medical)
📞 (71) 599 900

Poisons Centre
📞 (71) 245 075.

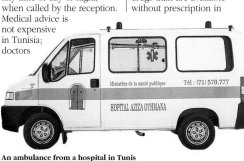

An ambulance from a hospital in Tunis

Banking and Currency

T HE NATIONAL CURRENCY is the Tunisian dinar (TD). The exchange rate is fixed on a daily basis. This can be looked up in the local paper but at the time of publication 2 TD is roughly equivalent to £1. The TD cannot be traded, like the US dollar or UK pound, and it is illegal to either import or export it, so Tunisian currency cannot be purchased before arriving. All of Tunisia's larger towns, provincial capitals and tourist resorts have banks and bureaux de change.

Cash dispensers can be found in large towns and tourist zones

BANKS

T HE COUNTRY'S MAIN bank is the Central Bank of Tunisia – Banque Centrale de Tunisie. There are also a number of state-owned banks. The first private bank – Amen Bank – was established in 1995. Branches of Tunisian banks can be found all over the country. There are a number of foreign banks, which also offer a full range of services.

Banks are usually open Monday to Thursday, from 8 to 11:30am and from 2 to 5pm; between July and August they are open from 8 to 11am. Opening times are shorter during Ramadan. In larger towns, during Ramadan the longest opening hours are offered by small branches of the Amen Bank – some even stay open until 4pm. Banks remain closed during Muslim holidays as well as during state and national holidays. In the tourist areas banks are often open longer for visitors to exchange money.

EXCHANGING MONEY

B ANKS AND MOST large hotels in Tunisia can exchange the main world currencies, including sterling, euros and US dollars, into Tunisian dinars (TD). The exchange rate is determined on a daily basis by the Central Bank of Tunisia. Differences in the exchange rate between banks are negligible, and involve only the commission. The private Amen Bank usually offers a slightly better rate. Hotels give less favourable rates, but even here, the difference is never very large.

In addition to the banks there is also a network of bureaux de change, which are usually more convenient than a bank. They can be found in many parts of the main towns and tourist zones and are often open longer than banks. There are a number of automatic exchange machines (though these are still few and far between) which change foreign currencies into dinars. Money can also be changed at some post offices. If venturing away from the main tourist areas, however, it can be harder to find facilities

Distinctive automatic currency exchange machine

for exchanging money, especially in rural areas.

It is illegal to take Tunisian currency out of the country, or to bring it in. Visitors who have not used all their dinars by the time they are ready to leave may change back 30 per cent of the total sum, but not more than 100 TD, on presenting the original proof of exchange. It is therefore worth changing only small sums of money at one time and keeping all the exchange receipts, including the ones issued by ATMs. Foreign currencies in excess of 500 TD should be declared on arrival.

It is worth remembering that even luxury hotels that quote their prices in euros or US dollars on their websites or in brochures can only accept cash payments in Tunisian dinars.

Readily identifiable sign of cash dispenser in Tunisia

CREDIT CARDS AND TRAVELLER'S CHEQUES

B ESIDES CASH, most large shops and hotels, as well as the tourist-orientated restaurants, will accept payment by the major credit cards including Visa, MasterCard and Eurocard. Some of the more upmarket restaurants also accept Diners Club cards. Cards are not accepted at petrol stations. Cards can also be used to draw cash from a bank. Most banks will want to see a passport before they do this. Please note that credit cards are often required when checking in at some of the more upmarket hotels.

Another form of payment is traveller's cheques, such as those issued by American Express or Thomas Cook. These are accepted at most banks and many hotels. If traveller's cheques are lost or stolen this should be reported to the issuing company's Tunisian office. Most companies should be able to replace lost traveller's cheques within 24 hours.

CURRENCY

THE TUNISIAN dinar is divided into 1,000 millimes. Banknotes are issued in denominations of 1, 5, 10, 20 and 30 TD; the face values of coins are 0.5 TD (often expressed as 500 millimes), 1 TD and also 5, 10, 20, 50 and 100 millimes. Prices are sometimes quoted in millimes, which can be confusing – if a sign says 1,800 it means 1 dinar, 800 millimes. The smallest denomination is the 5 millime coin. It is always worth having some low denomination coins to hand particularly when going shopping in the medinas.

When leaving Tunisia remember that at airports dinars are accepted only up to the border crossing point. In duty-free zones visitors are expected to pay in convertible currencies.

CASH DISPENSERS

CASH DISPENSERS (ATMs) can be found on the main streets of big towns and in the larger medinas. They are also in all the major holiday resorts. Only those displaying the sign of Visa, MasterCard or Eurocard will dispense money on cards issued by foreign banks. Cash dispensers display instructions in Arabic, French and English.

Banknotes
Banknotes differ in colour and (slightly) in size. The highest denomination – 30 TD – is a distinctive orange colour. Banknotes bear images of prominent figures from Tunisia's history, and Arab lettering.

5 dinars

10 dinars

20 dinars

30 dinars

5 dinars

1 dinar

1/2 dinar

100 millimes

50 millimes

20 millimes

10 millimes

5 millimes

Coins
Coins are issued in denominations of 1 dinar and 5 dinars, as well as 5, 10, 20, 50 and 100 millimes. Coins from 10 to 100 millimes are golden in colour, and are worth very little. Half-dinar and one-dinar coins are silver in colour.

Communications

POST OFFICES IN TUNISIA offer the whole range of postal services and can also be used to send a fax or make a telephone call. More convenient, however, is the system of public phones, known as taxiphones, which can be found all over the country – these can be used to phone abroad.

Tunisia's public phone sign

Foreign newspapers and magazines are sold in Tunis, Tabarka and Bizerte, as well as tourist areas of the Sahel. The French language version of *La Presse*, the national daily paper, is available everywhere.

The most frequently-seen type of coin-operated telephone

TELEPHONE AND FAX

MAKING A LOCAL CALL is fairly straightforward in Tunisia as only the subscriber's number need be dialled. When making a long-distance call within the country, precede the number with 7, followed by the appropriate area code, e.g. 1 for Tunis, 2 for Bizerte. When calling a Tunis number from Bizerte, for example, dial 71, followed by the number. Telephone boxes can usually be found near post offices. Some shops have public phones (identifiable by their blue signs). Calls made from hotels are expensive (this applies to telephones installed in guest rooms and reception areas). A telephone call made from a post office is cheaper than one made from a hotel, which charges a higher rate for the first three minutes.

The most practical solution is provided by taxiphones. These are small telephone exchanges found in almost every town and village. Identifiable by their yellow signs, there are several booths and attendants who can supply change. They can be used to make a call (from a coin-operated phone) or to send a fax. Taxiphones are very popular and have an extensive network. Calls made from taxiphones are much cheaper than ones made from hotels. Most Tunisian public telephones are coin-operated. Telephone calls are cheaper between 8pm and 6am.

Making an international call from Tunisia is also fairly straightforward, although it can be costly. To dial abroad from most public phones, first dial the international code 00, followed by the country code, then the local code and finally the number. The country code to dial Tunisia from abroad is 216.

Mobile phones can be used in most of Tunisia apart from the desert areas. Visitors may need to notify their provider before going abroad in order to have their international access switched on.

INTERNET

ALTHOUGH THE INTERNET has been in operation in Tunisia since the late 1990s, it is still not widespread, though its use is steadily growing. Access to the net is provided primarily by the state-owned Publinet company. It now has over 280 branches throughout the country (including the southern regions), where Internet terminals are available for use by the locals and visitors to the country. Internet terminals can be found in the larger towns and are usually open between 8am and 8pm, daily. They are expensive, however, and do not offer discounts for frequent use or long connections. Schoolchildren, students, disabled persons and journalists are entitled to a 25 per cent discount.

An alternative to the Publinet branches is to visit one of the European-style Internet cafés. These are still rare but can be found in larger towns, particularly in Tunis (one is located close to the railway station at Rue de Grèce 4, near Place Barcelone). Their opening hours are longer (often 8am–midnight), and their prices are comparable with those of Publinet.

Telephone booths inside a taxiphone exchange

Post office in Monastir

RADIO AND TV

Tunisia has only one national public TV channel, Channel 7, which is broadcast to a number of other countries via satellite. Channel 7 transmits exclusively in Arabic, except for a daily news broadcast in French at 8pm. For the rest of the time, the schedule includes frequent studio productions, game shows and Friday night films. Though the output of Channel 7 is not going to appeal to everyone, it does give an insight into Arab customs.

It is also worth watching the frequent transmissions of contemporary music concerts, recorded at the Carthage Festival of the Medina, for instance, or live studio performances of *malouf* (folk) music. These broadcasts not only provide some good quality Arab music, but also demonstrate how deeply such music is rooted in Tunisian culture.

Rai Uno and France 2 are two additional TV channels received throughout much of Tunisia. Such terrestrial channels are now under threat from the increase in privately owned satellite dishes, which provide access to a huge number of international channels. Tourist zone hotels normally offer a number of international TV channels via satellite. News channels generally include

BBC, CNN, Euro News and Al-Jazeera (in Arabic). Eurosport is also generally available in English. Some Tunisian TV can be seen before visiting on the Internet at www. tunisiatv.com

A French-language radio station (broadcasting on about 98 FM) also transmits in English from 2–3pm; in German from 3–4pm and in Italian from 4–5pm. Radio Tunis is a French language station that is good for music and is available at 93.1 FM. In addition, a number of European stations are available, including Voice of America and the BBC's World Service, which can be picked up on short wave at 15,070 and 12,095 MHz.

Sign displaying post office logo

THE PRESS

European magazines and newspapers are readily available in Tunis from large hotels and at various newsagents throughout the city centre. They usually arrive one day late. There are three French-language newspapers published in Tunisia (*La Presse*, *Le Renouveau* and *Le Temps*) and one weekly English-language magazine, *Tunisia News*. *La Presse*, in particular, is a valuable source of information. Its weekend edition has a large cultural section, which contains the programmes of cinemas, shows and other current cultural events. Alongside these, it also publishes reviews and announcements for all major forthcoming attractions. *Le Temps* puts more of an emphasis on international events; *La Presse* is good for coverage of sporting events.

POSTAL SERVICES

Tunisian post offices are easy to recognize by their yellow boards inscribed with the letters PTT. Postboxes are usually yellow too. There are post offices in all sizeable towns. Stamps can be bought from them and letters, parcels, telegrams or cash can be sent abroad. Overseas telephone calls can also be made from a Tunisian post office.

The Tunisian postal system is reliable. Letters to Europe take seven to 10 days. Letters take about two weeks to the USA and Australia. Post offices also provide an express mail delivery service *(Rapide Poste)* which guarantees delivery anywhere in Europe within two working days.

Some hotels have a system whereby they collect their guests' mail in decorative cages situated in the reception areas. Hotel staff then take them to the post office.

Stamps can be obtained from newspaper kiosks and from the larger souvenir shops. Stamps are also often available from taxiphone offices. During the summer, post offices are open Monday to Saturday, from 7:30am until 1pm. Throughout the rest of the year they are open from 8am until noon, and again from 3 to 6pm. On Saturdays post offices are only open from 8am until noon. During Ramadan, post offices are open from 8am to 3pm, though these opening hours can be subject to change.

Light yellow postbox, as seen everywhere in Tunisia

TRAVEL INFORMATION

THE MOST convenient way of getting to Tunisia is by air; there are frequent scheduled services year-round from the UK, France and other European countries. Tour operator services, often using charter flights, and usually including accommodation and airport transfers, are competitively priced and can represent excellent value when compared with scheduled airfares. If planning to take a car, travelling by ferry from France or Italy, book tickets well in advance as ferries can be very busy, especially in summer. Overland travel via Algeria or Libya, which can be difficult to arrange, is not recommended.

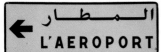

Road sign to an airport

AIR TRAVEL

FLIGHTS TO TUNISIA from the UK take about three hours. Tunisia's national airline is **Tunisair**, which operates direct scheduled flights from London Heathrow to Tunis four times a week. **British Airways/GB Airways** also has four services a week, from London Gatwick Airport. Alternatively, it is possible to fly indirectly via Paris or Amsterdam, with connections from several UK regional airports. Tunisair and Tuninter have connecting flights from Tunis to Monastir, Sfax, Jerba and Tozeur. There is also a new direct service, weekly on Sundays, operated by **Nouvelair** between London Gatwick and Monastir. There are no direct services between the Republic of Ireland and Tunisia; it is best to travel via London or Paris. Likewise, from North America and Australasia, the fastest routings are likely to be via London or Paris.

Apart from scheduled flights, a wide range of charter flights is offered by tour operators direct to Monastir from London and selected UK regional airports. These include Luton, Birmingham, Manchester, Newcastle and Glasgow; travel agents can provide details.

Prices vary according to season and are highest in July and August. Short-notice spring and autumn bookings can prove excellent value, and it is possible to save money by booking online via an airline or one of the discount travel websites. On all airlines weekend flights usually cost more.

INTERNATIONAL AIRPORTS

TUNISIA HAS SIX international airports. The three main ones are: Tunis Carthage Airport (6 km/4 miles from Tunis); Monastir Habib Bourguiba Airport (12 km/7 miles from Monastir, Sousse and Port el-Kantaoui); and Jerba (9 km/6 miles from the island's capital Houmt Souk). All three are able to handle large numbers of flights and passengers. Tunisia's other airports are at Sfax, 112 km (70 miles) south of Monastir; Tabarka, on the coast close to the border with Algeria; and Tozeur, in Tunisia's western desert region.

Sign for a taxi rank at one of Tunisia's airports

TRAVELLING FROM THE AIRPORT

TUNIS CARTHAGE AIRPORT is a short drive from the centre of Tunis. A taxi ride to Avenue Habib Bourguiba should take about 15 minutes (depending on the traffic) and cost not more than 5 TD. Taxis are plentiful and the competition is fierce. The price of a taxi ride is likely to go up at night or during the rush hour. Negotiate the cost before getting into the taxi. An alternative means of getting from the airport to the town centre is by bus. The No. 35 bus leaves twice an hour. It takes about 30 minutes and terminates at Tunis Marine station on Avenue Habib Bourguiba. The bus also makes drop-off stops at Avenue Habib

Tunisair aircraft at Tunis airport

Tunisair's logo

Thameur and Place Palestine.
It costs about 1 TD. Tunis
airport also has a direct bus
link with Bizerte and Sousse.
Just a short walk from the air
terminal is a train that
connects Monastir's airport to
Monastir, Mahdia and Sousse.

Road sign for La Goulette harbour

From Jerba's airport take a
taxi (about 5 TD), although
many hotels on Jerba are
happy to arrange transport
for their guests.

TOUR OPERATORS

OVER 60 TOUR operators offer
packages to Tunisia from
the UK and Ireland; many are
specialists while others offer
only flight and beachside
hotel packages. In addition to
hotel, apartment and self-
catering accommodation, tour
operators can arrange car
rental, golf packages and
private transfers. Holiday
durations can vary from
weekend breaks to month-
long winter sunshine
vacations. Special interest
holidays range from golf,
hiking, deep-sea diving and
desert adventures on a camel
to archaeology, gastronomy
and thalassotherapy.

For those people interested
in a particular activity,
booking through a specialist
operator can work out
cheaper than organizing
something once in the
country. The Tunisian Tourist
Office in London can provide
a comprehensive list of tour
operators (see p247).

FERRIES

ANOTHER WAY OF getting to
Tunisia is by ferry.
Between July and the end of
September there is a regular
car ferry service from
Marseille to La Goulette –
Tunisia's main passenger
port. Two companies,
CTN and **SNCM**, handle
most of the crossings. In
July there is also a
weekly service to Bizerte.
Throughout the rest of
the year there are two to
three services a week. The
journey from Marseille takes
24 hours. It is also possible to
sail to La Goulette from Italy.
The ferries sail from Trápani
(Sicily), and also from Genoa,
Naples and La Spezia. The
weekly service from La Spezia
(100 km/62 miles southeast of
Genoa) to La Goulette is
much cheaper than sailing
from either Genoa or Naples.

OVERLAND TRAVEL

IT IS POSSIBLE to travel to
Tunisia overland, from
Algeria or Libya, though it
requires a special visa, which
must be translated into Arabic
if travelling through Libya.

There is a daily bus service
from Tripoli to Tunis that
takes about 16 hours. A daily
bus service from Tripoli to
Sfax takes about 10 hours.
There is also a *louage* (shared
taxi) that runs from Annaba in
Algeria to Tunis's medina.

Although people do travel
to Tunisia via Libya or
Algeria, the border regions
of these two countries can be
dangerous. Furthermore,
since the outbreak of the
civil war in 1993 Algeria has
been practically out of
bounds to tourists.

A small ferry sailing to Jerba

DIRECTORY

AIRLINES

GB Airways
Beehive Ringroad, Gatwick
Airport, W. Sussex, RH6 0PB.
(0845) 773 3377 (UK).
(70) 963 120 (Tunis).
www.gbairways.com

Nouvelair
GSA in UK – Tunisia First.
(01276) 600 100 (UK).
(73) 500 600 (Tunis).
www.tunisiafirst.co.uk

Tunisair
24 Sackville St, London, W1S 3DS.
(020) 7734 7644.
(71) 700 100 (Tunis).
www.tunisair.com.tn

AIRPORTS

Tunis Carthage
(71) 754 000 or 755 000.

Monastir Habib Bourguiba
(73) 460 300.

UK TOUR OPERATORS

Aspects of Tunisia
(020) 7836 4999.

Cadogan Holidays
(023) 8082 8313.

First Choice Holidays
(0870) 750 0001.

Panorama Holidays
(0870) 759 5595.

Sunway Holidays
(01628) 660 001.

FERRY COMPANIES

Compagnie Tunisienne de Navigation (CTN)
Av. Dag Hammarskjoeld 5, Tunis.
(71) 341 777.
FAX (71) 345 736.
www.ctn.com.tn

SNCM
(+33) 0891 701 801.
www.sncm.fr

Tirrenia Navigazione
(+39) 923 21898 (Trápani).
(+39) 10 275 8041 (Genoa).
www.tirrenia.it

Travelling Around Tunisia

Tunisia has a well-developed road network. Air-conditioned buses provide transport links between most major towns. A more convenient way of travelling is by *louage* (shared taxi). These travel between many of the small towns and villages and operate more frequently than buses. On shorter routes to villages, visitors will need to take a taxi (only yellow ones). Much of the rail network (SNCFT) is devoted to freight. The passenger trains that do run, however, are comfortable and punctual. The main routes run south from Tunis to Sfax and Gabès. Tunisia has a number of internal flights, run by Tuninter. The most popular routes are those that connect Tunis with the south of the country.

Train crossing the main square in Sousse

Travelling by Train

The Société nationale des Chemins de Fer Tunisiens (SNCFT) has over 2,000 km (1,250 miles) of track, and was built by the French during the Colonial period. The main routes run from Tunis: north to Bizerte (about 2 hours); west towards the Algerian border (about 6 hours); southwest to the Tell region (about 6 hours), and south to Sfax and Gabès, via Hammamet and Sousse. The most popular line is the one that links Tunis with Sfax and Gabès (via Sousse). There are six trains a day to Sfax and three to Gabès. The journey time is 5 hours and costs about 14 TD. One train a day runs to Metlaoui and Gafsa. About eight services a day run to Sousse; the journey takes 2 hours and the ticket costs about 6 TD. A journey to Hammamet takes one hour and costs about 4 TD.

There is a narrow gauge train that runs between Nabeul and Hammamet and stops in several places within the tourist zone. A ticket from Hammamet to Nabeul costs

Sfax railway station

about 400 millimes. Metro Sahel is another convenient service and runs between Sousse, Monastir and Mahdia.

A local service, called the TGM, runs from Tunis to many of its suburbs including Carthage, La Goulette and Sidi Bou Saïd.

Most Tunisian trains have two classes. First class is about 40 per cent more expensive than second class and is air-conditioned. Second class is usually very crowded and in order to be sure of a seat it is best to board the train at the first stop. Even the suburban trains include first class carriages, which are generally less crowded and have soft, padded seats. Long-

distance trains usually have an additional *Grand Confort* class. This is more expensive than first class and offers travellers slightly more exclusive compartments.

Long distance trains usually include a restaurant car, where a hot meal, sandwiches and drinks are available. When planning several train journeys, consider buying the Blue Card that gives unlimited travel within the country. These are valid for one, two or three weeks and can represent good value. Costs are: one week – 19.50 TD (second class), 27.50 TD (first class); two weeks – 39 TD (second class), 54.60 TD (first class); three weeks – 58.50 TD (second class), 81.90 TD (first class).

There is also a ticket that gives unlimited train travel within the country and free entry to the major museums. This Rail-Museum Card costs 28 TD (second class) or 35 TD (first class) and is valid for one week.

Timetable details are available in the daily press, although it is always best to check at the station. It is essential to reserve a seat on mainline trains at holiday periods otherwise passengers may end up standing.

Sousse bus station

Colourful "Intercity" bus run by the SNTRI company

DIRECTORY

RAILWAY STATIONS

BIZERTE
Avenue Habib Bourguiba.
(72) 285 054.

MONASTIR
Avenue Habib Bourguiba.
(73) 460 755.

NABEUL
Avenue Habib Bourguiba.
(72) 285 054.

SOUSSE
Blvd. Hassouna Ayach.
(73 224 955
FAX (73) 226 955.

TUNIS
Place Barcelone, Tunis
SNCFT 67 Avenue Farhat Hachet.
(71) 259 977 or 334 444.

BUS STATIONS

TUNIS
North Bus Station
Bab Saadoun
Rue Nord de Bab Saadoun, Tunis.
(71) 562 299 or 490 358.

South Bus Station
Bab Alleoua
Rue Sud de Bab el-Fellah, Tunis.
(71) 495 255.

BUSES

THE SOCIETE NATIONALE de Transport Rural et Interurbain (SNTRI) is the state-owned bus company, and runs services between most of Tunisia's towns. Services to the smaller towns run once a day. There are about 10 daily services from Tunis to Sousse, Hammamet and Sfax. The price of a bus ticket is comparable to a second-class train ticket. In the summer, due to the hot weather, long-distance buses sometimes travel at night. Buses are more comfortable than *louages* and offer plenty of space for passengers and their luggage. They are also air-conditioned. In addition to SNTRI, there are also a number of suburban carriers, serving various local villages and small towns. There are quite a number of these smaller companies and it can be difficult to obtain information about their schedules. Quite often one town is served by a number of carriers and the staff of one will not always know about the timetable of another carrier, even if they operate from the same bus station.

Tunis has two main bus stations. Bab Saadoun serves the north of the country and is at the bottom of Rue Sidi el-Bechir and Avenue 9 Avril. Bab Alleoua, sometimes also referred to as Bab el-Fellah, connects Tunis to the centre and south of the country and is just south of Place Barcelone. A transport link between the two stations is provided by the Nos. 50, 72 and 74 buses.

AIR TRAVEL

THERE ARE AIRPORTS in Tunis, Monastir, Sfax, Tozeur, Gabès, Gafsa, Tabarka and Jerba. The most popular routes are between Tunis and Jerba (several flights a day), Tunis and Sfax and Tunis and Tozeur. In the summer there are also flights to Gabès and Gafsa. A one-way ticket costs about 50 TD. There is also an air-taxi service, Tunisavia. This is often used by VIPs and businessmen and lands not only at the major airports, but also at a number of small regional ones.

LOUAGES

SHARED TAXIS ARE A popular form of transport in Tunisia, covering the whole of the country. *Louages* do not run to any particular schedule and depart only when they have a full complement of passengers (in practice one never need wait long). Though they are less comfortable than buses, they offer greater convenience. The price of a ride is only fractionally higher than that of a bus ticket. *Louage* stops are usually situated near the bus and railway stations.

There are two types of *louage* – the ones marked with a red stripe are allowed to travel all over Tunisia; the ones with blue stripes are permitted to travel only on local routes.

Tunis has three main *louage* stops. *Louages* departing from the square in front of the south station (Bab Alleoua) go to Cap Bon; the ones leaving from the stop at the east end of Rue Aid el-Jebbari travel south. From Place Sidi Bou Mendil yellow *louages* marked with a white stripe go to Libya and Algeria.

Louage with a red stripe, licensed to travel anywhere in the country

Travelling by Car in Tunisia

T UNISIA'S ROAD NETWORK IS EXCELLENT, with clear signs and well-maintained surfaces for most of the country. The traffic regulations are almost the same as in Europe. The standard of driving is good, too, as Tunisian drivers do not tend to travel too fast. They are usually ready to offer help in case of a breakdown. There are numerous police patrols on the roads. Generally they do not stop tourists, but visitors should nevertheless carry their passports with them at all times. Hiring a rental car is an excellent way of exploring Tunisia, though it can be fairly expensive.

Winding narrow roads around Toujane

A frequently-seen sign in Tunisia – Warning! Camels!

HIGHWAY CODE

T UNISIA'S HIGHWAY CODE does not differ significantly from mainland Europe. Vehicles drive on the right, and overtake on the left. The road signs are clear and mostly bilingual (French and Arabic). The speed limit is 90 km/h (55 mph) on open roads; 50 km/h (30 mph) in towns and built-up areas. The only stretch of road where it is permitted to travel at 110 km/h (70 mph) is the toll motorway running between Tunis and Sousse.

Seatbelts are supposed to be worn at all times in Tunisia. Frequent patrols and heavy fines ensure that Tunisians rarely exceed speed limits or break the rules of the road. In fact, the main hazards on the roads come from straying animals, motorcycles and pedestrians.

ROAD SIGNS

I N ADDITION TO THE commonly seen road signs there are warning signs with a picture of a camel. These are seen mostly in the south and warn about the possibility of encountering one of these animals on the road. Take heed, too, of the signs warning about the danger of wet surfaces during or after a period of heavy rainfall.

ROADS

M OST OF THE country's roads are well surfaced and reasonably straight. There are two motorways: one runs from Tunis to Sousse, the other from Tunis to Bizerte.

Warning sign – Stop!

A-roads are known as *Routes Nationales* (RN), and B-roads are referred to as *Routes Regionales* (RR). Surface damage on RN roads is rare. Even on the RR roads, potholes are few and far between. Outside the summer season, however, some of the roads may become impassable due to rainfall. Roads in the south are not so good, but are still passable.

Driving on desert roads requires a four-wheel-drive vehicle. Whilst driving in the desert, always travel in a group of at least two cars (to assist each other in case of breakdown). Also bear in mind that desert roads can suddenly disappear if they get buried in the sand. When this happens it can be difficult to see in which direction to drive. Because of the dangers, trips to the desert are best undertaken with a Tunisian driver who knows the area.

TOWN DRIVING

A LTHOUGH TUNISIAN drivers are generally careful, pay particular attention to motorcycles and pedestrians when driving in towns. This is especially true during the rush hours, between 5 and 8pm and at night. Pedestrians can be disconcerting in towns, giving the impression that they have not seen oncoming vehicles. Drivers should use their horn if in doubt as to whether other road users are aware of their presence.

The crowded centre of Sousse

The situation can be worse when there is heavy rainfall. At these times it can be better to resort to walking instead.

MAPS

ROAD MAPS CAN be purchased from hotel shops and bookstores. Generally, however, the maps published by the ONTT (Tunisian Tourist Bureau) are clear and, for the most part, accurate and include additional information in English and French relating to historic sites. The range published by the ONTT includes maps of Carthage and Tunis's medina. The ONTT offices can also provide street maps of a number of the other most popular towns. When travelling by car around Tunisia purchase a more detailed road map before leaving. Michelin produces a good one (No. 956), as do Freytag and Berndt. Both are on a scale of 1:800,000 and provide information on Tunisia's major and minor roads.

BUYING PETROL

THE PRICE OF FUEL in Tunisia is cheap by European standards. One litre of super (high octane) fuel costs about 650 millimes; lead-free petrol costs 690 millimes and is now available throughout Tunisia; diesel is 395 millimes a litre. Generally, there are no problems with finding somewhere to fill up with petrol in Tunisia, even on Sunday or late at night.

Information on parking in the centre of Tunis

CAR RENTAL

CAR HIRE FIRMS are in all of the major towns and tourist resorts. Their services are rather expensive, but hiring a car enables you to visit many interesting and less accessible parts of the country.

There should be no problem with finding a major rental firm; Avis, Azur, Europcar and Hertz all have offices in Tunis and elsewhere. The best option, however, is provided by local firms – these are cheaper and are often more willing to strike a deal. Prices start from about 60 TD per day for a small car, plus 250 millimes for each kilometre travelled. Though it may mean having to pay a higher daily rate, it can work out far cheaper to hire a car from a company that does not charge extra for the distance travelled, especially if intending to use the car for long journeys.

Rental companies will require that the driver be over 21 years old and hold a licence that has been valid for at least a year.

When hiring a car it is imperative to check that the vehicle documents include an accident report form. In case

of an accident both parties are required to complete such a report. Visitors who do not fill out the form may be liable for the costs, even if the accident was not their fault.

BREAKDOWNS AND ACCIDENTS

TUNISIA HAS NO roadside telephones or road emergency services. In case of a breakdown ask another driver for a tow to the nearest town or village where there is a garage able to repair the car. Alternatively, it may be necessary to wait for a passing police patrol. Repair services are cheap in Tunisia, but parts can be expensive.

In the case of a serious accident, such as one involving injury to a pedestrian, the driver should endeavour to contact the police. The driver may be detained and should contact his or her Embassy in Tunis as soon as possible.

Petrol on sale in southern Tunisia

Getting Around Tunis

TRANSPORT WITHIN TUNIS includes a variety of options. The furthest corners of the city should be accessible without any problem, if not by public transport, then by taking a taxi, which is cheap by European standards. Tunis's medina is partly pedestrianized and can easily be explored on foot. Travelling to seaside resorts close to the capital is also quite easy. The best way of getting to them is by using the fast TGM train that stops near the town centre.

A tram – one of the best means of getting about in Tunis

TRAMS

TRAMS ARE probably the most convenient way of moving around Tunis. This network, known as *métro leger*, runs down the middle of the street and has green paintwork with distinctive white and blue stripes. The city's trams are efficient and not particularly expensive, though they can be crowded, especially at peak times.

Five main lines run to various parts of Tunis. All except No. 5 pass through the centre. Since many streets in central Tunis are one-way, the tram often returns by a different route (usually along a parallel street). Tickets must be purchased before boarding the tram and are available from the kiosks at the entrance to each station. The standard fare is 380 millimes.

Line No. 1 runs from Tunis, Marine via Place Barcelone, to Bab Alleoua, at the south end of the town. Bab Alleoua is the best stop for the southern bus station.

Line No. 2 runs from Place de la République and heads north towards Ariana.

Line No. 3 runs from Place Barcelone, via Place de la République, to Ibn Khaldoun.

Line No. 4 starts by Tunis Marine and runs westwards, through Place de la République. This line is particularly convenient for the Bardo Museum (Bardo) and the north station – Saadoun; alight at Bouchoucha.

Line No. 5 is an extension of line No. 3, and runs from Ibn Khaldoun to El-Intilaka.

BUSES

ALTHOUGH TUNIS'S BUSES are modern and in better condition than those in other major towns of the country, travelling by them is not a particularly pleasurable experience, particularly since they are often even more crowded than the trams.

The bus number and the direction in which it is heading are usually written in Arabic and placed at the rear of the bus by the entry door. The Latin alphabet is used only on those buses serving the most popular tourist destinations, such as the Bardo Museum or the airport. On these buses the Latin number is displayed at the front.

There are three main stops in Tunis. These are Tunis Marine, situated close to the TGM train stop at the end of Avenue Habib Bourguiba; the stop at Place Barcelone near the railway station and the stop in Jardin Thameur, near Avenue de France. Bus No. 3 begins at Tunis Marine and runs to the Bardo Museum. Transport to the airport is provided by the No. 35 bus, which also departs from the Tunis Marine stop.

Tickets are fairly cheap, costing about 380 millimes and are purchased on the bus. Alternatively, a book of tickets is available from Tunis Marine bus station.

TAXIS

TUNIS'S YELLOW TAXIS are a cheap and efficient means of getting about. Many locals use them and it can sometimes be hard to find a free cab for this reason. All taxis are fitted with meters. In general, the drivers stick to the meter, apart from journeys to the airport that start from bus stations or the railway station. A trip from the town centre to the airport will cost about 5 TD; a taxi to the Bardo Museum will cost about 3 TD. At night (from 9pm–5am) the prices can be slightly more. Always check that the meter has been activated, though it is rare that a taxi driver will attempt to swindle his fare.

Taxis can be hailed from the side of the road, just as they can in other major cities. It is worth paying attention to the condition of the car, however. Some of Tunis's taxis are old and rather dilapidated. Most, however, are new and well maintained. It is worthwhile holding out for a new model, particularly if intending to travel a bit further, to Sidi Bou Saïd or Carthage for instance.

As well as hailing a taxi, it is possible to book one by phone. This is especially useful for trips to the airport when carrying a lot of luggage. Hotels are usually able to arrange this.

A typical Tunisian yellow taxi

A sign prohibiting entry to a mosque for non-Muslim drivers

DRIVING

D RIVING IN TUNIS is not a good idea. Unless there is no alternative, don't even consider it. Despite being wide, all the main streets of town get congested. Tunis's drivers show little respect for marked traffic lanes and it often happens that a three-lane road suddenly becomes an impromptu five-lane one. Police help or understanding cannot be counted on either. Policemen only try to ease the traffic flow at the most congested junctions. If stuck in traffic, pay particular attention to motorcycles and pedestrians that often weave in and out of the stationary cars with little apparent concern for their own safety.

Although Tunis's drivers undoubtedly break many regulations, it is very rare for them to break the speed limit. If attempting to drive in town, remember that many streets are one-way, and getting to a destination may not be as simple as it appears from the map. There may also be serious problems when parking. Pay close attention to the paid parking zones, as there are severe fines for not paying the required amount.

WALKING

T HE CENTRE OF TUNIS, like most towns in Tunisia, is fairly compact. At its heart is the medina, much of which is closed to traffic. A stroll around the medina can be a real pleasure and enables visitors to soak up the ancient atmosphere at a leisurely pace. In parts of the medina where the streets are relatively wide, visitors should be on the alert for scooters or delivery vans, which can arrive at speed. Tunis's Ville Nouvelle is also suitable for exploring on foot. The only problem with this area is the heat in summer. To avoid heat exhaustion, walk on the shady side of the street and carry a bottle of mineral water. Anyone who feels tired should sit down in a café and have a drink.

Outside Tunis, there is no sense in walking the large distances that separate the towns from the tourist zones, unless it is to walk along the seashore.

"Pay Here" sign for a public car park

GUIDES

T HE QUALITY OF service provided by Tunisian guides varies tremendously. When somebody offers to act as a guide for free, it is practically certain that the person works for a carpet shop or a store selling some other kind of merchandise. The trip will therefore end very quickly in one of the medina's markets. However, employing guides who work at archaeological sites, such as Dougga or Bulla Regis, can be particularly useful if the details of the site and its history are of interest.

TGM TRAINS

A N EXCELLENT WAY of exploring Tunis's environs and the coast of Carthage is by taking the TGM train that links the centre of Tunis with Carthage, Sidi Bou Saïd and the main beaches. The train leaves from the end of Avenue Bourguiba (Tunis Marine station). The journey to the final station (La Marsa) takes about 35 minutes. The first station after crossing the causeway is Le Bac. Confusingly, Aeroport, the sixth stop, has nothing to do with the airport as TGM trains do not run there. Salammbô has a nice beach, while Carthage Byrsa is the main stop for Carthage's Museum and Byrsa Hill. Sidi Bou Saïd (see pp96–7) is an excellent stopping-off point, as is La Marsa, which has the best beach in the vicinity of Tunis.

The ticket costs about 600–800 millimes. Many people opt for the first-class ticket, which is only slightly more expensive. The first train on a weekday leaves before 4am, and the last runs about half past midnight (slightly later at weekends). The departure times of the last trains should, however, be checked at the station – in Tunis, Sidi Bou Saïd or La Marsa.

Station on the suburban TGM line

Beaches (cont.)
  Northern Tunisia 143
  The Sahel 149
  Sidi Mechrig 134
  Tabarka 126
  Zarzis 186
Beauvoir, Simone de 96
Bechri 207, 208
Bedouin tribes 198, 201
Beer 271
Béja 123, **131**
  Wheat Festival 41
Belisarius 49
Belly dancing
  in hotels 247
  M. Rabet Café (Tunis)
  298
Belvedere Park (Tunis)
  87
Ben Abdallah 78
Ben Ali Zine el-Abidine
  16–17, 59, 86
Ben Guerdane 186, 188
Beni Metir 128
Berbers **30–31**, 194
  abandoned village
  (Midès) 211
  architecture **22**, 31
  Festival of *Ksour* (Ksar
  Ouled Soltane) 41
  Festival of the
  Mountain Oases 38
  language 311
  origins 45
  pottery 36, 134
  tattoos 221
  under Byzantine rule
  49
  under Roman rule 48
  see also Ksour; Ksour
  Festivals
Berlin Congress 55
Bertolucci, Bernardo 200
Bey, Mohammed 226,
  236
Beys, hereditary 54–5
Bicycle hire 305
Bin Ali, Husayn 54–5,
  226, 237
Bin Kairouan el-Maafri,
  Mohammed 235
Bir Barouta (Kairouan)
  234–5

Bir Bou Regba 120
Birdcages 97
Birds, Tunisian **135**,
  136–7
Birdwatching
  Gulf of Gabès 172
  Jebel Zaghouan 231
  Kebilia 111
  Lake Ichkeul 124, 135,
  136–7
  see also National parks;
  Nature reserves
Birth rate 14
Bizerte 123, **140–41**
  Festival d'Evacuation
  de Bizerte 41
  hotels 254
  Jasmin Road 40
  restaurants 280–81
  World War II 58
Blidet 157, 207
Boat charter 307
Bordier, Captain 224
Borj Bourguiba 195
Borj el-Hissar (Chergui
  Island) 172
Borj el-Kebir (Houmt
  Souk) 178, **179**
Borj el-Kebir (Mahdia)
  162
Borj Ennar (Sfax) 165
Borj Jillij 181
Bou Ficha 153
Bou Grara 188
  Gulf of 188–9
Bou Hedma National
  Park 227
Bou Salem 129
Boukha 271
Boukornine National
  Park **227**, 305
Bourguiba, Habib 16,
  154
  Borj Bourguiba 195
  Bourguiba Mosque
  (Monastir) 24, **155**
  Hammam Bourguiba
  128
  imprisoned 172
  independence
  movement 38, 57–9
  Mausoleum (Monastir)
  154, 158–9

Bourguiba, Habib (cont.)
  monument (Sfax) 165
  and position of
  women 17
  schoolboy statue
  (Monastir) 155
Bouzguend, Taieb 155
Brahem, Anur 33
Brass products 36
Bread 267
  Bedouin 198
Breakdowns and
  accidents 325
Brik à l'oeuf 266, 268
British Airways 320
British 8th Army 217
Bulla Regia 124–5, 128,
  132–3
Bureaux de change 316
Burkina Faso 41
Buses 323
  airport 320–21
  Tunis 326
Byrsa Hill (Carthage)
  102–3
Byzantium 49

C

Cadogan Holidays 321
Caesar Augustus,
  Emperor 103, 113
Caesar, Julius 112, 154
Cafés 313
  Café des Nattes (Sidi
  Bou Saïd) 96
  Café Ez-Zitouna
  (Tunis) 77
  Café Le Pasha (Bizerte)
  141
  Café M. Rabet (Tunis)
  72, 298
  Café Saf-Saf (La Marsa)
  94
  Café Sidi Chabaane
  (Sidi Bou Saïd) 97
  opening hours 267
  see also Food and
  drink; Restaurants;
  Where to eat
Calligraphy, Arabic **167**,
  292
  Dar Jellouli Museum
  (Sfax) 169

Camels 203
  Bir Barouta (Kairouan) 234–5
  caravans **199**, 204–5
  treks 38, 63, 305
Camp Sites 246
Cap Blanc 141, **142**
Cap Bon 110
Cap Bon peninsula 91–3, **108–20**
  climate 43
  getting there 93
  map 92–3
  sights at a glance 93
  where to eat 275–80
  where to stay 250–53
Cap Negro 134
Cap Serrat **134**
Cap Zarzis 189
Capellianus 49
Capitol (Dougga) 23, **228**
Capitol (Sbeïtla) 218
Capsian people 45
Car rental 325
Caravans 199
Carpets 36
  Kairouan 241, 292
  ONAT Museum (Kairouan) 237
  shopping for 296
Carthage 102–7
  architectural influence 22
  fall of 47, 48, 224
  history of 46–7, 102
  hotels 250
  International Festival 298–9
  International Film Festival 41
  map 103
  restaurants 275
Cash dispensers 316, 317
Casinos 299, 301
Castles and fortifications
  arsenal (La Goulette) 99
  Borj el-Kebir (Houmt Souk) 178, **179**
  Borj el-Kebir (Mahdia) 162
  Borj Ennar (Sfax) 165

Castles (cont.)
  Borj Jillij (Jerba) 181
  Byzantine fort
  Bulla Regis 132
  Haïdra 221
  Kebilia 111
  Byzantine fortress
  Jugurtha's Table 221
  Kasserine 220
  defensive walls and towers 170–71
  Fort Sidi el-Hanni (Bizerte) 141
  Genoese fort (Tabarka) 54, **126**
  kasbah forts (Le Kef) 226
  Ksar Lemsa 240
  Osta Murad Dey fortress (Ghar el-Melh) 143
  Roman fort (Ksar Ghilane) 198
  Spanish Fort (Bizerte) 141
  see also Kasbahs; Ksour; Ribats
Catacombs, Sousse 51, **153**
Cathedrals
  St Louis (Carthage) 102
  St Vincent de Paul and St Olive (Tunis) 23, **82**
Causeway, Douz to Tozeur route 206, 208
Caves
  El-Haouaria 109
  see also Troglodyte homes
Cedouikech 182
Cedratine 271
Cemeteries
  Jellaz Cemetery (Tunis) 87
  Muslim soldiers' (Haffouz) 240
  Phoenician 107
  Sidi el-Mezeri (Monastir) 154
  see also Marabouts; Necropolis; Tombs and mausoleums; Zaouias
Censorship 58

Central Tunisia 212–41
  character 213
  climate 43, 213
  getting there 214–15
  map 214–15
  sights at a glance 214–15
  where to eat 288–9
  where to stay 264–5
Centre of Arab and Mediterranean Music (Sidi Bou Saïd) 96, 298
Ceramics 15, **36**
  Berber 30, 134
  Nabeul 112, **114–15**
  Phoenician 104–5
  Sejnane 134
  shopping for 296
  tiles 26, 115
Chafaar 147
Chambi 220
Charles V, King of Spain 99, 161
Chauves-Souris cave (El-Haouaria) 109
Chebika 35, **210**
Chechias **29**, 37, 312
Chemtou 126, 128, **130**
Chenini 194
Chergui Island 172
Chichas 29, 297, 313
Children 247
  activities for 300, 301
  in hotels 247
  see also Amusement parks; Water parks; Zoos
Chorba 267, 268
Chott el-Gharsa 21
Chott el-Jerid 20–21, 63, **208**
  crossing 206
  mirages 200, 208
  in The English Patient 35
Christianity 50–51
  Catacombs (Sousse) 153
Chryses visiting Agamemnon (mosaic) 116–17
Churches 50–51
  Basilica (Carthage) 106

Churches (cont.)
  Basilica (Henchir Khira) 82
  Basilica of the Martyrs (Haïdra) 220–21
  Bellator Basilica (Sbeïtla) 218
  Byzantine church (Bulla Regia) 132
  Church of St Peter (Le Kef) 226
  Mellus Basilica (Haïdra) 221
  St Cyprian Basilica (Carthage) 105
  St Servus (Sbeïtla) 219
  St Vitalis Basilica (Sbeïtla) 218
  Thuburbo Majus 230
Churchill, Sir Winston 120
Cillium see Kasserine
Cinema 34–5, 299, 301
Cippi 107
Circumcision 29, 208, 313
Cisterns
  Aghlabid Basins (Kairouan) 236
  Great Mosque (Kairouan) 238
Climate 43, 310
Clothes
  etiquette 312
  in the Sahara 200
  in tourist zones 246
Club Africain 302
Club Méditerranée 245
Club Sfaxien 302
Coastline 21
  see also Beaches
Coffee 270
Coins, Phoenician 105
Colonial architecture 23
Communications 318–19
Communist Party 16
Constantine the Great 49
Constitution 16, 59
Copper products 36
Coral **126**, 293, 296
Coral Reef (Tabarka) **127**, 304

Coralis festival (Tabarka) 41
Cork harvesting 130
Cork Museum (Tabarka) 126
Corsairs see Piracy
Costumes
  Dar Jellouli Museum (Sfax) 168
  Museum of Traditional Costume (Monastir) 155
Couscous 266, 269, 312
Crafts see Handicrafts
Cranes, common 135
Credit cards 316
  at petrol stations 316
  booking hotels by 245
  in shops 290, 292
  VAT refunds 293
Crime 314
Cruises, Port el-Kantaoui 148
Culture 14–15
Currency 290, 316–17
Custom regulations 310–11
Customs see Traditions
Cycling and motorbike trips 305, 307
  Kerkennah Islands 172

D
Dakar Rally 42, **217**, 303
Dar ben Abdallah (Tunis) 78
Dar Cheraït Museum (Tozeur) 208, 300
Dar el-Achab (Dougga) 228
Dar el-Annabi (Sidi Bou Saïd) 97
Dar el-Bey (Tunis) 68, **72–3**
Dar el-Haddad (Tunis) 79
Dar el-Shariff (Gafsa) 216
Dar Ennejma Ezzahra (Sidi Bou Saïd) 97
Dar Essid (Sousse) 153
Dar Hammamet 118
Dar Hussein (Tunis) 77, **79**

Dar Jellouli Museum (Sfax) 63, **168–9**
Dar Lasram (Tunis) 74–5, **80–81**
Dar Lounga (Gafsa) 216
Dar Othman (Tunis) 78
Dars 171
Date Harvest Festival (Kebili) 41
Dates 18, 202
Degache 206
Deglet Fatima 266
Democratic Constitutional Assembly (RCD) 16
Democratic-Socialist Movement (MDS) 16
Department stores 290
Desert, types of 191, 200
  see also Sahara Desert
Desert rose 206
Desserts 269
Destour Party 57, 154
Dhahak, Brahim 98
Dialling codes 318
Dido, Princess of Tyre 46, 106
Disabled travellers 246, 247, 311
Discounts
  child 247
  student 311
Diving and snorkelling 304, 307
  festivals of diving 40, 41
  Kerkennah Islands 172
  La Galite archipelago 134
  Port el-Kantaoui 148
  Tabarka 126, 127
Dolls, Tunisian 153
Donatists 50, 230
Donatus, Bishop of Carthage 50
Door handles 208, 209
Doors, Tunisian 121
  Sidi Bou Saïd 93, **96**
Dougga 228–9
  International Festival of Classical Theatre 40
  Numidian mausoleum 46

Dougga (cont.)
  site map 228–9
  Temple of Caelestis
    215
  Ulysses and the Sirens
    (mosaic) 225
Douz **198**, 207
  driving tour 206–7
  hotels 261
  International Festival
    of the Sahara 30, **42**,
    198
  restaurants 286–7
  Sahara excursions from
    201
Dragut 162, 179
Drama *see* Theatre
Drinks *see* Food and
  drink
Driving 324–5
  in towns 324–5
  in Tunis 327
Driving tours
  around the Gulf of
    Bou Grara 188
  around Tabarka 128–9
  Douz to Tozeur 206–7
Dunes, sand 200
Duty-free
  allowances 310–11
  shops 290, 311

E
Eco-museum (Ichkeul
  National Park) 137
École de Tunis 15, 98,
  292
Economy 18–19
Education 14
El-Attaia 172
El-Azifet 33
El-bijazi script 167
El-Djadid 234
El-Faouar 207
El-Ghriba Synagogue
  (Jerba) 38, **180**, 183
El-Hadi Beness el-
  Mekhnessi 226
El-Haouaria 109
  falconry festival 40
  hotels 250
  restaurants 275
El-Jem 48, 145, **163**

El-Jem (cont.)
  hotels 255
  International Festival
    of Symphonic Music
    40, 299
El-Kadima 154
El-Kantara 188
El-Katib Mosque
    (Mahboubine) 181
El-Mansour, Caliph 240
El-May 180
El-Mouradi hotel chain
    245
El-Sadiq Bey,
    Mohammed 55
El-Sheikh Mosque
    (Houmt Souk) 178
Embassies 311
Emergency numbers 315
Enfida 153
English Patient, The 34,
  35
  Midès 211
  Sfax 165, 166
  Tamerza 211
Entertainment 298–301
  amusement parks 300,
    301
  casinos 299, 301
  children's activities
    300, 301
  cinema 299, 301
  festivals 298–9
  information 298
  music 298, 301
  nightlife 299, 301
  theatre 299, 301
  traditional shows 298
Erlanger, Baron
    Rodolphe d' 96, **97**
Erlanger, Elizabeth d' 97
Eros (bronze statuette)
    88
Esparto grass 200, 220
Espérance Sportive 302
Etiquette 310
  alcohol 313
  clothing 312
  during Ramadan 267
  photography 313
  in tourist zones 246
Etoile Sportive du Sahel
    302

European Union 18
Evacuation Day 41
Events, calendar of
    38–42
Extreme sports 306

F
Falconry 109
  festival (El-Haouaria)
    40, 109
Fantasia (Midoun) 182
Fantasia (Sidi Ali ben
    Nasrallach) 240
Farhat, Ammar 98
Fatima, daughter of
    Prophet Mohammed
    53, 77
Fatima, Hand of **77**, 209,
    293
Fatimid dynasty 53
  ceramics 114
  coins 240
Fatimid Port (Mahdia)
    162
Fax services 318
Feija National Park 227
Fennec fox 20
Fernana 129
Ferries 321
  Jerba 177, 181, 188
  Kerkennah Islands 172
Festivals 15, 38–42,
    298–9
Film festivals 41
Film-makers in Tunisia
    19, **34–5**
Fire brigade 315
First Choice Holidays 321
Fish, coral reef (Tabarka)
    127
Fishing industry 18
  La Goulette 99
  Tuna fishing (Sidi
    Daoud) 109
Five Pillars, of Islam 27
Fizzy drinks 270, 271
Flamingo Island 181
Flamingoes 135, 181
Flavian dynasty 48
  Mausoleum 220
Flying, light aircraft 306
Folk art festival
    (Tataouine) 38

Folk Tales, Dar Cheraït
(Tozeur) 208
Fondouks 244
Food and drink
Bedouin bread 198
shopping for 297
Tunisian condiments
198
what to drink 270–71
what to eat 266, **268–9**
see also Cafés;
Restaurants; Where to
eat
Football 302
Foreign affairs 17
Fortresses *see* Castles and
fortifications
Forum, Roman
Bulla Regis 133
Dougga 228
Makthar 224
Sbeïtla 219
Thuburbo Majus 230
France
colonial rule 55, 56–8
ferries to/from 321
independence from 16,
58–9
Funfairs 300

G

Gabès 58, **172**
Gulf of 135, **172**
hotels 255–6
restaurants 282
Gabriel, Archangel 293
Gafsa **216**, 217
hotels 264
restaurants 288–9
Galite archipelago 126
Galleries *see* Museums
and galleries
Games 29, 294
Gammarth 94
beaches 95
hotels 250–51
restaurants 275–6
Gammoudi, Mohammed
303
Gargottes 266
Gateways 171
Bab Diwan (Sfax) 164
Bab Djedid (Kairouan)

Gateways (cont.)
234, 237
Bab ech-Chouhada
(Kairouan) 234
Bab el-Aïn (Makthar)
224
Bab el-Bahr (Tunis) 77
Bab el-Khoukha
(Kairouan) 234
Bab Tunis (Kairouan)
234
Skifa el-Kahla
(Mahdia) 160
GB Airways 320, 321
Genets 136
Genoese fort (Tabarka)
54, **126**
Genseric 49
Getting there and around
320–27
Central Tunisia 214–15
Greater Tunis and Cap
Bon Peninsula 93
Jerba and the
Medenine Area 177
Northern Tunisia 125
The Sahel 146
Ghar el-Melh 122, 143
Gharbi Island 172
Ghardimaou 128
Ghorfas 196–7
Ksar Haddada 193
Ksar Ouled Soltane
192, 194
Medenine 186
Gide, André 63, 96, 120
Gightis 188
Golden Tulip hotel chain
245
Golf 306, 307
Port el-Kantaoui 148
Good Shepherd
Catacombs (Sousse) 153
Gordian I 48–9, II 49
Granaries, fortified *see*
Ksour
Grand Erg Oriental *see*
Sahara Desert
Great Eastern Erg *see*
Sahara Desert
Greater Tunis 91–108
getting there 93
map 92–3

Greater Tunis (cont.)
sights at a glance 93
where to eat 275–80
where to stay 250–53
Green Tunisia 134
Grombalia 120
wine festival 41, 120
Guellala 114, 177, **182**
ceramics 36, 182
Guettar 217
Guides 327
Gulf of Bou Grara *see*
Bou Grara, Gulf of
Gulf of Gabès *see* Gabès,
Gulf of
Gulf War (1990) 17

H

Habib Bourguiba
Mausoleum (Monastir)
154, 158–9
Haddada tribe 193
Hadiths 33
Hadrian, Emperor 230,
231
Haffouz 240
Hafsid dynasty 53, 54
ceramics 114
Tunis under 65
Haggling 290, **291**
Haïdra 220–21
Hamdoun tribe 193
Hammam *see* Baths
Hammam Bourguiba 128
hotels 254
Hammam Sousse
beaches 149
festivals 153
Hammam Sultan (Sfax)
166
Hammamet 118–20
Arab Music Festival
299
beaches **119**, 120
hotels 250–53
map 119
orange blossom
festival 38
restaurants 276–7
Hammouda Bey (Pasha)
55
Hammouda ibn Ali Bey
99

Hammouda Pasha 69, 87, 236
Hammouda Pasha Mosque (Tunis) 69, **76**
Hand of Fatima talisman **77**, 209, 293
Handball 303
Handicrafts 36–7
  dolls 153
  and the economy 18
  see also ONAT shops; Shopping
Hanefite School 178
Hang-gliding 306
Hanifa, Imam ibn 120
Hannibal 44, 47, **102**
  exiled on Kerkennah Islands 172
Hannibal Park (Port el-Kantaoui) 148
Hara Kebira 180
Hara Sghira 175, **180**
Harissa 111, 198, 268
Hassan ibn Ali Bey 96
Hathor Miskar Temple (Makthar) 224
Hats, traditional Tunisian see Chechias
Hauli 30
Health 314–15
Heatstroke 315
Hela 30, **31**
Henchir el-Fouar 131
Henchir Khira 82
Henna **28**, 30, 172
Henson, John and Violet 120
Hergla 146, **148**
  beaches 149
Hermes Catacombs (Sousse) 153
Herodotus 46
Highway code 324
Hijab 15, 28, 312
  attempt to ban 17
Hiking 305
Hilalian invasions 224, 234
Hiram I, King of Tyre 46
Historic houses
  Dar ben Abdallah (Tunis) 78
  Dar Cheraït Museum

Historic houses (cont.)
  (Tozeur) 208, 300
  Dar el-Achab (Dougga) 228
  Dar el-Annabi (Sidi Bou Saïd) 97
  Dar el-Bey (Tunis) 68, **72–3**
  Dar el-Haddad (Tunis) **79**
  Dar el-Shariff (Gafsa) 216
  Dar Ennejma Ezzahra (Sidi Bou Saïd) 97
  Dar Essid (Sousse) 153
  Dar Hammamet 118
  Dar Hussein (Tunis) 77, **79**
  Dar Jellouli Museum (Sfax) 68, **168–9**
  Dar Lasram (Tunis) 74–5, **80–81**
  Dar Loungu (Gafsa) 216
  Dar Othman (Tunis) 78
  House of Amphitrite (Bulla Regis) 132
  House of the Cascades (Utica) 142
  House of the Historic Capitals (Utica) 142
  House of the Hunt (Bulla Regis) 132
  House of the Hunt (Utica) 142
  see also Dars; Palaces
History 45–59
  Arab rule 52–5
  Byzantine rule 49
  early settlers 45
  French colonial rule 55, 56–8
  Independence Movement 56–7, 58–9
  Ottoman rule 53–4
  Phoenician period 46–7
  Post-war period 58–9
  Roman period 48–9
  Vandal empire 49
  World War II 58
Hookahs see Chichas

Horse riding 306, 307
Hospitality 312
Hospitals 315
Hot springs
  Korbous 108–9
  Ksar Ghilane 198
Hot-air ballooning 302
  Douz 198
Hotels 244–65
  air conditioning 244
  booking 245
  children in 247, 300
  choosing 248–65
  entertainment 247, 298
  excursions 247
  hotel categories 244–5
  hotel chains 245, 247
  hôtels de charme 244, 245
  nightlife 299
  prices 245
  shops 290
  swimming pools 244
  in tourist zones 246
  types of 244
Houbara bustards 135
Houmt Souk 178–9
  hotels 259
  jewellery 293
  map
  restaurants 285–6
  Ulysses Festival 40
House of Amphitrite (Bulla Regis) 132
House of the Cascades (Utica) 142
House of the Historic Capitals (Utica) 142
House of the Hunt (Bulla Regis) 132
House of the Hunt (Utica) 142
Hunting 130, 305
Husaynid dynasty 54–5
  Ali Turki Mausoleum (Le Kef) 226
  Tourbet el-Bey (Tunis) 78–9
Hussein, Bey 78, 118
Hussein, Saddam 17
Hygiene 314–15
  restaurants 267, 314

I

Ibadites 175, 180
Ibd Mahmud 78
Ibn al-Aghlab, Ibrahim
    52
Ibn Khaldoun 33
Ibn Nooman, Hassan 52,
    65
Ibn Nusair, Musa 52
Ichkeul National Park
    135, **136–7**, 305
Ifriqiyya 45, 52
Imru'al-qays 32
Independence Day 38
Independence Movement
    56–7, 58–9
Ingram, Rex 34
Ingres, Dominique 173
International Cultural
    Centre (Hammamet)
    120
International Festival
    (Carthage) 298–9
International Film
    Festival (Carthage) 41
International *Malouf*
    Music Festival
    (Testour) 40, 131, 299
International Oases
    Festival (Tozeur) 41
Internet
    access 318
    booking hotels on 245,
    247
Irrigation systems 210
    Aghlabid Basins
    (Kairouan) 236
Islam 26–7, 313
    architectural influence
    24–5
    calligraphy 167
    festivals calendar 39
    in Tunisia 26–7
    see also Sufism
Islamic art *see* Art,
    Islamic
Israeli-Palestinian conflict
    17
Italy
    World War II 58
    ferries to/from 321

J

Jallouli, Taieb 34, 35
Jama'a el-Baldawi
    Mosque (near Ajim)
    180
Jasmine 148
Jasmine Road (Bizerte)
    40
Jazz festival (Tabarka)
    40, 299
Jebel Biada hills 217
Jebel Bir 129, 305
Jebel Chambi 213, **220**,
    227
Jebel Dyr 226
Jebel Ichkeul 136, 305
Jebel Zaghouan 213, **231**
Jellaz Cemetery (Tunis)
    87
Jemaa el-Zitouna *see*
    Mosques, Great
    Mosque (Tunis)
Jendouba 129
    hotels 254–5
    restaurants 281
Jerba 63, **175–85**
    auberge de jeunesse
    246
    beaches 187
    ceramics 114, **182**,
    184–5
    character 175
    climate 43, 176
    getting there and
    around 177
    map 176–7
    olive festival 42
    Passover festival 38
    sights at a glance
    176–7
    where to eat 285–6
    where to stay 259–60
Jerid region 211
    carpets 36
    Jerid festival 38
Jewellery 37
    coral 126
    Dar Jellouli Museum
    (Sfax) 169
    Phoenician 107
    shopping for **293**, 294,
    296

Jews, Jerba 175, 180,
    183
Jihad 180
Jorf 177, 181, 188
Judaism *see* Jews
Judo 302, 303
Jugurtha, King of
    Numidia 47, 221
Jugurtha's Table 214, **221**
Julia Carthage 48
Julius Mosaic (Bardo
    Museum, Tunis) 89
Jupiter, statue of (Bardo
    Museum, Tunis) 230
Justinian, Emperor 49,
    131, 221

K

Kaalim, Mustapha 58
Kab el-ghazal 194
Kabadu, Sheikh
    Mohammed 56
Kahia el-Hanafi, Slimane
    78
Kairouan 170, **234–41**
    carpets 36, 232–3, **241**
    excavations 107
    Great Mosque 53, 212,
    238–9
    history 52
    hotels 264–5
    map of medina 235
    olive festival 42
    restaurants 289
Kalaa Kebira, olive
    festival 42
Kalaat es-Senam 221
Kamoun Mosque (Sfax)
    165
Kamounia 266, 269
Kasbah Mosque (Tunis)
    80
Kasbahs 25
    Béja 131
    Bizerte 141
    Hammamet 118
    Kairouan 240
    La Goulette 99
    Le Kef 170, 226
    Sfax 166
    Sousse **152**, 170
    Toujane 186
    Tunis 73, **80**, 170

Kasserine 213, **220**
  battle of 220
  hotels 265
Kasyda 33
Kebili 207
  date harvest festival 41
  hotels 261–2
Kelibia 111
  hotels 253
  restaurants 277
Ken 153
Kerkennah Islands 146,
  172
  beaches 149
  festivals 38, 40
  hotels 256
  restaurants 282
Kerkouane **110–11**, 113
Khair ed-Din Barbarossa
  see Barbarossa
Khalaout el-Koubba
  (Sousse) 146, **152**
Kharijism 180
Kharja Festival (Sidi Bou
  Saïd) 40
Kheiredine Pasha 56
Khnis 157
Khroumirie Mountains
  124, 128, **130**
  hiking 305
Khroumirie tribesmen 55,
  129, 130
Klee, Paul **94**, 96, 98
Knotted carpets *see*
  Alloucha carpets
Koran, the 26–7, 167
Korba 111
  Amateur Theatre
  Festival 40
Korbous 108–9
Kriz 208
Ksar see also Ksour
Ksar Ghilane 198
  hotels 256
Ksar Haddada 34, **194**
  restaurants 287
Ksar Lemsa 240
Ksar Ouled Soltane 192,
  195, 196
Ksour 22, 31, **196–7**
  map 197
  Medenine 186
  Nabeul 112

Ksour Essaf 162
Ksour festivals 38, 41
  Ksar Ouled Soltane
  195
  Tataouine 194
Kufic script 167, 235

L

La Corbeille (Nefta) 209
La Galite archipelago 134
La Goulette 99
  beaches 95
  hotels 253
  restaurants 277–8
La Kesra 240
La Marsa 94
  beaches
  festivals 40
  restaurants 278–9
Lablabi 267, 268
Labus (chieftain) 46
Laforcade, Josepha de 87
Lag Ba'omer 183
Laghmi 271
Lakes
  Bizerte 140
  Ichkeul 111, 124–5,
  135
  Tunis **99**
Lalla 217
Lalla Ma (goddess) 226
Lamta 157
Landscape 20–21
Language 311
Lasram, Hammoud 80
Lavigerie, Cardinal 102
Le Kef 226
  French take control of
  55, 126, 226
  hotels 265
  restaurants 289
Leatherware 37, 295, 296
Legal system 16
Lemerre, Roger 302
Leptis Minor *see* Lamta
Les Mimosas (Tabarka)
  126
Lézard Rouge *see* Red
  Lizard Train
Life of Brian 34, 35, 156
Life of Christ 156
Lighthouses
  Borj Jillij 181

Lighthouses (cont.)
  Ras Taguerness 182
Liqueurs 271
Literacy 14
Literature 14–15, **32–3**
Lluria, Roger de, King of
  Sicily 179
Louage see Taxis
Louis IX, King of France
  102
Lounifie, Anisa 302, 303
Lucas, George **34–5**, 172
  194–5
Lycinian Baths (Dougga)
  229

M

Macke, Auguste 98
Madame Butterfly (film)
  35
Maghreb, the 54, 56
Maghribi calligraphy 167
Mahalli, Bey 55
Mahboubine 181
Mahdia 145, **160–62**, 170
  hotels 256–7
  map 161
  olive festival 42
  restaurants 282
Mahdia shipwreck 88, 89
Mahmoud Bey 96
Mahrès, Plastic Arts
  Festival 40
Maisons des jeunes 246
Makhroud 269
Makhtar 222–3, **224**
  hotels 265
Malekite School 175, 178
Malouf 16, **33**
  Centre of Arab and
  Mediterranean Music
  (Sidi Bou Saïd) 97
  in hotels 247
  International *Malouf*
  Music Festival
  (Testour)
  40, 131, 299
Man on a Donkey
  (Dhahak) 98
Mansourah beach 111
Maps
  around Tabarka 128–9
  buying 325

Maps (cont.)
Carthage 103
Central Tunisia 214–15
Dougga site map
228–9
Douz to Tozeur 206–7
Greater Tunis and Cap
Bon Peninsula 92–3
Gulf of Bou Grara
188–9
Hammamet 119
Houmt Souk 179
Jerba and the
Medenine Area 176–7
Kairouan Medina 235
Mahdia 161
Monastir 155
Nabeul 113
The Sahel 146–7
Sbeïtla site map 218
Sfax Medina 165
Sousse Medina 151
Southern Tunisia
192–3
Tunis town centre
66–7
Tunisia 10–11, 62–3
visiting a *Ksar* 197
Marabouts 157
see also Cemeteries;
Tombs and
mausoleums; *Zaouias*
Marble quarries
(Chemtou) 130
Marcus Aurelius,
Emperor 224
Marhalas 246
Marinas 307
Hammamet Jasmine
146, 149
Monastir 154, **157**, 303
Port el-Kantaoui 146,
148, 303
Sidi Bou Saïd 97, 303
Marius (Roman
commander) 216
Markets 291
Béja 131
Ben Guerdane 186,
188
Enfida 153
Fernana 129
fish market (Sfax)

Markets (cont.)
165
Main Market (Tunis)
86
Menzel Temime 111
Midoun 182
Nabeul 112
Sfax 164, **166**
Tataouine 194
see also Shopping;
Souks
Martyrs' Monument
(Bizerte) 141
Masjid see Mosques
Massinissa (Numidian
king) 221, 228
Matanza 109
Mateur Plain 227
Matmata 34, **172**
hotels 257
restaurants 282
troglodyte pit houses
22, 172
Mausoleums *see* Tombs
and mausoleums
Meals 312
Mecca
Kairouan connections
with 234, 235
pilgrimage to 27, 238
Mechouia 268
Medenine 175, **186**
hotels 260
restaurants 286
Medenine Area
character 175
climate 43
getting there and
around 177
map 176–7
sights at a glance
176–7
where to eat 286
where to stay 260–61
Medersas 25
Medersa of Husayn
(Kairouan) 237
Medersa Mouradia
(Tunis) 79
the Three Medersas
(Tunis) 69, **72**
Zaouia of Sidi Brahim
(Houmt Souk) 178

Medical care 315
Medina Conservation
Society 81
Medina Festival (Tunis)
41, 298
Medinas 25, 170–71
Béja 131
Bizerte 141
Gafsa 216
Hammamet 118
Kairouan 234–5
Mahdia 160–61
Midoun 182
Monastir 154–5
Sfax 164–6, 170
Sousse 150–53
Tebourba 131
Tunis **68–81**, 84–5
Medjerda Valley 20, 48,
123
Mehrez ibn Chalaf *see*
Sidi Mehrez
Mellouli, Oussama 302,
303
Mellus Basilica (Haïdra)
221
Mellus, Bishop 221
Memmi, Albert 33
Memmian Baths (Bulla
Regis) 133
Mendès-France, Pierre 58
Menzel Bou Zelfa 110
orange blossom
festival 38
Menzel Bourguiba 140
Menzel Temime 111
Menzels 181
Jerba 175
Mergoum carpets 36,
241, 296
Mermaid Festival
(Kerkennah Islands) 40
Metalwork 36, 297
Metameur 186
Metlaoui 211, **216**
restaurants 289
Micipsa (Numidian
leader) 221
Midès 211
festival of the
mountain oases 38
Midoun 181, **182**
restaurants 286

Military Academy
(Bizerte) 141
Minarets 24
    Great Mosque (Gafsa)
    216
    Great Mosque
    (Kairouan) 24, 238
    Great Mosque (Sfax)
    164
    Great Mosque
    (Testour) 131
    Great Mosque (Tunis)
    70
    Mosque of the
    Strangers (Houmt
    Souk)
    178
    Mustapha Hamza
    Mosque (Mahdia) 160
    Ottoman period 161
    Zaghouan 231
    Zaouia of Sidi Bou
    Makhlouf (Le Kef)
    226
    Zaouia of Sidi Sahib
    (Kairouan) 236
    Zaouia Zakkak
    (Sousse) 151
    Zitouna Mosque
    (Kairouan) 237
Minghella, Anthony 35,
    165
Mining 18
Mirages 200
Mitterand, Frédéric 35
Modernism 23
Mohammed, the Prophet
    and the Archangel
Gabriel 293
    and cicumcision 29
    hairs from his beard
    236
    and Islamic
    architecture 24
    Islamic calendar 39
    Koran revealed to 26
Mohammed V, Sultan 99
Mohammedia 108
Moillet, Louis 98
Monastir 145, **154–9**
    airport 146
    beaches 149, 157
    hotels 257

Monastir (cont.)
    map 155
    port 157
    restaurants 282–3
Money 316–17
Montgomery, General
    Bernard Law 58, 217
Monty Python 34, 35,
    156
Monument of Skulls
    (Houmt Souk) 179
Mosaics 15, 37, 50–51
    Archaeology Museum
    (Nabeul) **113**, 116–17
    Bardo Museum (Tunis)
    63, **88–9**
    Bulla Regis 132
    Carthage Museum 104
    Kasbah Museum
    (Sousse) 152
    National Museum of
    Gafsa 216
    Roman 225
    shopping for 297
    Thuburbo Majus 230
Mosques
    Abdellatif Mosque
    (Testour) 131
    Ali el-Mezeri Mosque
    (Monastir) 154
    architecture **24**, 171
    Bourguiba Mosque
    (Monastir) 24, **155**
    El-Katib Mosque
    (Mahboubine) 181
    El-Sheikh Mosque
    (Houmt Souk) 178
    fortified 180
    Great Mosque,
    Bizerte 141
    Gafsa 216
    Hammamet 118
    Kairouan 53, 212,
    238–9
    Le Kef 24, **226**
    Mahdia 161
    Monastir 154, **155**
    Nabeul 112
    Sfax 164
    Sousse 150
    Great Mosque,
    Tebourba 131
    Testour 131

Mosques (cont.)
    Tunis 65, 69, **70–71**
    Hammouda Pasha
    Mosque (Tunis) 69, **76**
    Jama'a el-Baldawi
    (near Ajim) 180
    Kamoun Mosque
    (Sfax) 165
    Kasbah Mosque
    (Tunis) **80**
    Le Kef 24
    Menzel Bourguiba 140
    Mosque of the Barber
    (Kairouan) 236
    Mosque el-Bey
    (Kairouan) 234
    Mosque el-Maalek
    (Kairouan) 234
    Mosque of Sidi Bou
    Makhlouf (Le Kef) 226
    Mosque of the
    Strangers (Houmt
    Souk) 178
    Mosque of the Three
    Doors (Kairouan) 235
    Mosque of the Turks
    (Houmt Souk) 178
    and Muslim worship
    27
    Mustapha Hamza
    Mosque (Mahdia) 160
    Nefta 209
    Sidi Abdel Kader
    (Hammamet) 118
    Sidi Driss Mosque
    (Gabès) 172
    Sidi Mehrez Mosque
    (Tunis) 67, **81**
    Sidi Sahab Mosque
    (Kairouan) 214
    Sidi Youssef Mosque
    (Tunis) 68, **72**
    Slimen Hamza Mosque
    (Mahdia) 161
    Umm et-Turkia (El-
    May) 180
    Zitouna Mosque
    (Kairouan) 237
Motor rallies 42, 217,
    303, 307
Motorbikes 305
Mouashabat dawa 33
Mouloud 39

Mountain Oases, Festival of the 38
Muezzins 24, 237
Murad Bey 141
Murad II 79
Muradid dynasty 54
Museums and galleries
  Archaeological Museum (Sfax) 166
  Archaeology Museum (Nabeul) **113**, 116–17
  Bardo Museum (Tunis) 63, **88–9**
  Carthage Museum 104–5
  Centre of Arab and Mediterranean Music (Sidi Bou Saïd) 96
  Chemtou site museum 130
  Cork Museum (Tabarka) 126
  Dar Cheraït (Tozeur) 208, 300
  Dar Essid (Sousse) 153
  Dar Jellouli Museum (Sfax) 168–9
  Eco-museum (Ichkeul National Park) 137
  El-Jem 163
  Enfida 153
  Guellala Museum of Popular Traditions 177, **182**
  International Cultural Centre (Hammamet) 120
  Islamic Art Centre (Ribat, Monastir) 156
  Kasbah Museum (Sousse) 152
  Makthar 224
  Modern Art and Cinema Museum (Tunis) 87
  Municipal Museum (Mahdia) 160
  Museum of Arts and Popular Traditions (Houmt Souk) 179
  Museum of Popular Arts and Traditions (Gabès) 172

Museums and galleries (cont.)
  Museum of Popular Arts and Traditions (Sousse) 152
  Museum of Popular Arts and Traditions (Tozeur) 208
  Museum of Traditional Architecture (Sfax) 166
  Museum of Traditional Costume (Monastir) 155
  National Museum of Gafsa 216
  National Museum of Islamic Art (Reqqada) 240
  Oceanographic Museum (Carthage) 106
  Oceanography Museum (Bizerte) 141
  ONAT Museum (Kairouan) 237
  Regional Museum of Popular Arts and Traditions (Le Kef) 226
  Roman and Paleo-Christian Museum (Carthage) 105, **106**
  Sbeïtla site museum 219
  Utica 142
Music **33**, 298, 301
  Aissaouia 226
  Centre of Arab and Mediterranean Music (Sidi Bou Saïd) 96, **97**
  festivals 38, 40, 120
  influences on 14, 16
  instruments 194
  International Cultural Centre (Hammamet) 120
  malouf 16, **33**
Muslims 24–5, **26–7**, 313
  see also Islam
Mustapha Hamza Mosque (Mahdia) 160

N
Nabeul **112–17**, 308–9
  ceramics 36, **114–15**,

Nabeul (cont.)
  242–3
  hotels 253
  map 113
  orange blossom festival 38
  restaurants 279
Nador 142
Nador (Ribat, Sousse) 150
National Assembly 16
National Library 69, **76–7**
National Museum of Islamic Art (Reqqada) 240
National Palace (Monastir) 154
National parks 227
  Bou Hedma National Park 227
  Boukornine National Park 227
  Chambi 220, 227
  Feija National Park 227
  Ichkeul National Park 135, **136–7**, 227
  Zembra **109**, 227
Neapolis (Nabeul) **113**, 116–17
Nechon 46
Necropolis
  Mahdia 162
  Utica 142
Nefta 13, **209**
  hotels 262
  Jerid festival 38
  restaurants 287
Neo-Destour Party 57, 59, 154
Neolithic period 226
Neptune's Triumph (mosaic) 225
New Era Day 41
New Year 42
Newspapers 319
Night Scene, The 98
Nightlife 299, 301
Northern Tunisia 122–43
  climate 43
  getting there 125
  history 123
  map 124–5
  sights at a glance 124

Northern Tunisia (cont.)
  where to eat 280–81
  where to stay 254–5
Nouvelair 320, 321
Numidia 47, 216, 224
  Chemtou 130
  Jugurtha's Table 221
  Numidian tombs (Le
  Kef) 226

O

Oases 21, 199, **202–3**
  International Oases
  Festival (Tozeur) 41
  see also Chebika;
  Degache; Douz; El-
  Faouar; Gabès; Gafsa;
  Guettar; Ksar Ghilane;
  Lalla; Midès; Nefta;
  Remada; Tamerza;
  Tozeur
Obeid Allah el-Mahdi
  160, 161, 162
Oceanographic Museum
  (Carthage) **106**, 300
Oceanography Museum
  (Bizerte) 141
Octavian Augustus,
  Emperor 48, 108
Octopus Festival
  (Kerkennah Islands) 38
Odysseus 175
Old Port (Bizerte) 140
Olive festivals 42
Olive oil 18, 145, 153
ONAT Museum
  (Kairouan) 237
ONAT shops 37, 290,
  292–3
  Artisanat, Monastir
  155, 292
  Artisanat, Sousse 150,
  292
  Artisanat, Tunis 86
Opening hours
  banks 316
  restaurants and cafés
  267
  shops 290
Oqba ibn Nafi 52, 152,
  234, 235
Orange blossom festival
  38

Orchids 227
Order of the White
  Fathers 102
Organization Nationale
  de l'Artisanat see
  ONAT
Osta Murad Dey fortress
  (Ghar el-Melh) 143
Othman, Bey 69, 76, 78
Othmana, Aziza 69, 76
Otters 136
Ottoman rule 53–4
Oudna **108**
Oudnin el-Kadhi 269
Oued 20
Oued Cherichera 240
Oued el-Habeb 220
Oued Meliane 231
Oued Seldja 211
Ouled Chehida tribe 194,
  196
Ouled ech-Cherif (Nefta)
  209
Ouled el-Hadef (Tozeur)
  208
Ouled Kacem 172
Overland travel 321

P

Package holidays 244,
  321
Painting **15–16**, 292
Palaces
  Abdallia Palace (La
  Marsa) 94
  Dar ben Abdallah
  (Tunis) 78
  Dar el-Annabi (Sidi
  Bou Saïd) 97
  Dar el-Bey (Tunis) 68,
  72–3
  Dar el-Haddad (Tunis)
  79
  Dar Ennejma Ezzahra
  (Sidi Bou Saïd) 97
  Dar Hussein (Tunis)
  77, **79**
  Dar Lasram (Tunis)
  74–5, **80–81**
  Dar Othman (Tunis)
  78
Palaces (cont.)
  National Palace

  (Monastir) 154
  Palace of Ahmed Bey
  (Mohammedia) 108
  Presidential Palace
  (Carthage) 105
  Qasr el-Fath (Reqqada)
  240
  Sabra (near Kairouan)
  240
  see also Historic
  houses
Palaeolithic era 45
Palaestra of the Petronii
  (Thuburbo Majus) 230
Palm Tree, Medersa of
  the (Tunis) **72**
Panorama Holidays 321
Paper production 167,
  213, 220
Paragliding 304
Parks and gardens
  Belvedere Park (Tunis)
  87, 300
  botanical garden
  (Tozeur) 208
  Hannibal Park (Port el-
  Kantaoui) 148
  Park Friguia (Bou
  Ficha) **153**, 300
  see also Amusement
  parks; Water parks
Parti Socialiste
  Destourien (PSD) 59
Passover festival (El-
  Ghriba Synagogue,
  Jerba) 38, 180
Passports 310, 314
Patton, General George
  58
Perfumes 37
  shopping for 294, 296
  Souk el-Attarine
  (Tunis) 76
Personal property 314
Petro-chemicals 18
Petrol 325
Phantom Menace, The
  34, 194, 195
Pharmacies 315
Phoenicians 45, **46–7**
  art 104, 107
  culture 107
  introduce alphabet 32,

Phoenicians (cont.)
107
   shrines 107
   see also Carthage;
   Kerkouane; Sousse;
   Utica.
Phosphates 18, 210, 216
Photography 105, 313
Pilgrimages 24–5
   El-Ghriba (Jerba) 183
   Kairouan Great
   Mosque 234, 238
   to Mecca 27
   Zaouia of Sidi Amor
   Abbada (Kairouan) 236
Piracy 54, 55, **81**
   La Goulette 99
   Mahdia 162
   replica pirate ship
   (Port el-Kantaoui) 35,
   148
Pirates (Polanski's film)
34, 35
Place du Caire (Mahdia)
160–61
Place Farhat Hached
   (Sousse) 150
Place du Gouvernement
   (Tunis) 68, **73**
Place du Gouvernorat
   (Monastir) 155
Place Hedi Chaker
   (Houmt Souk) 178
Place de l'Indépendence
   (Le Kef) 226
Place de la Kasbah
   (Tunis) 65
Place Lahedine
   Bouchoucha (Bizerte)
   141
Place des Martyrs
   (Sousse) 150
Place de la République
   (Sfax) 165
Planet Oasis (Tozeur)
   208, 300
Plastic Arts Festival
   (Mahrès) 40
Poetry 32–3
Polanski, Roman 34, 35
Police 314, 315
Politics 16–17
Polygamy 17, 28

Pony-trekking, Belvedere
   Park (Tunis) 87
Population 14
Port el-Kantaoui 35, **148**
   beaches 148, 149
   diving and snorkelling
   304
   hotels 257
   marina 146, 148
   restaurants 283
Porto Farina 143
*Portrait of an Old
   Woman* (Turki) 98
Postal services 319
Pottery *see* Ceramics
Pottery workshop (Itica)
   142
Prayer Hall (Great
   Mosque, Kairouan) 239
President, role of the 16
Presidential Palace
   (Carthage) 105
Press, the 319
Prices
   hotels 245
   restaurants 267
   youth hostels 246
Public holidays 42
Punic architecture **22**,
   110
Punic mausoleum
   (Makthar) 224
Punic period *see*
   Phoenicians
Punic Ports (Carthage)
   105, **106**
Punic Wars **47**, 102
   First 226
   Second 221
   Third 142, 163
Pupput 120

Q

Qadiriyya group 240
Qasr el-Fath (Reqqada)
   240
Quarries (Chemtou) 130
Quo Vadis 35
Quran *see* Koran

R

Radio 319
Raf Raf 123, **143**

Raf Raf (cont.)
   hotels 255
   restaurants 281
Rahmania Brotherhood
   226
Raiders of the Lost Ark
   (film) 34, 35
Rail travel 322, 323
   Central Tunisia 215
   Greater Tunis and Cap
   Bon peninsula 93
   Red Lizard Train 216
   The Sahel 146
   TGM trains 86, 93, **327**
Rainfall 43
Ramadan 15, **39**, 202
   restaurants during 267
   shopping during 290
   visiting during 310
Ras ben Sekka 142
Ras Jebel peninsula 141,
   143
Ras Remel **181**, 187
Ras Taguerness **182**, 187
Rass el-Aïn (Le Kef) 226
Rhab 33
Red Lizard Train 216
Religion 26–7, 313
Religious buildings *see*
   Cathedrals; Churches;
   Mosques; Tombs and
   mausoleums
Remada **195**
Republic Day 40
Reqqada 240
Restaurants 266–89
   choosing 272–89
   hygiene 267
   meals 312
   opening hours 267
   prices 267
   Ramadan 267
   types of 266
   vegetarian 267
   what to eat 266, **268–9**
   see also Cafés; Food
   and drink; Where to eat
Ribats 145
   Monastir 154, **156–7**
   Sousse 150–51
Riu hotel chain 245
Road travel 324–5
   breakdowns and

Road travel (cont.)
accidents 325
Greater Tunis and Cap
Bon peninsula 93
highway code 324
maps 325
Northern Tunisia 125
petrol 325
road signs 324
roads, state of 324
The Sahel 146
town driving 325
Roman period 47–9
architecture 23
Bardo museum, Tunis
88–9
colonial system 111
literature 32
Roman and Paleo-
Christian Museum
(Carthage) 105, **106**
see also Bulla Regia;
Carthage; Chemtou;
Dougga; El-Jem; Gafsa;
Haïdra; Kasserine;
Makthar; Nabeul;
Oudna; Pupput;
Sbeïtla; Thuburbo
Majus; Utica; Zaghouan
Rommel, Field-Marshal
Erwin 58, 217
Rue el-Aghlaba (Sousse)
151
Rue des Aghlabites
(Sfax) 164, 166
Rue Borj Ennar (Sfax)
164–5
Rue de la Grande
Mosquée (Sfax) 164
Rue de la Hafsia (Tunis)
80
Rue Jemaa Zitouna
(Tunis) **77**
Rue Mongi Slim (Sfax)
164, 166
Rue Obeid Allah el-
Mahdi 160
Rue du Pasha (Tunis) 80
Ruspina 155

S

Sabine, Thierry 217
Sabra 240

Sacrifices 106
Sadiki College 57
Sahara Desert 20, 191,
200–1
climate 200
International Festival
of the Sahara (Douz)
30, **42**
in prehistoric times 45
safety in 200, 305, 315
trips to 307
see also Douz; Ksar
Ghilane; Tataouine
Sahel, the 144–72
climate 43
getting there 146
history 145
map 146–7
sights at a glance 147
where to eat 282–5
where to stay 255–9
Sahnoun ibn Sa'id 33
Sailing 303, 307
Port el-Kantaoui 148
St Augustine **32**, 50
St Cyprian 105, 221
St Cyprian Basilica
(Carthage) 105
St Louis Cathedral
(Carthage) 102
St Perpetua 50, 103, 230
St Servus Church
(Sbeïtla) 219
St Vincent de Paul and St
Olive Cathedral (Tunis)
23, **82**
St Vitalis Basilica
(Sbeïtla) 218
Salade tunisienne 267,
268
Salakta 162
Salambo, beaches 95
Salt lakes 208
Sand regattas 208, 306
Sand-skiing 306
Sand-yachts 306
Sartre, Jean-Paul 96
Sbeïtla 49, 62, **218–19**
hotels 265
restaurants 289
Schola Juvenus
(Makthar) 224
Scorpions 200, 315

Sea travel 321
Seasons 38, 40–42
Seatbelts 324
Sebastian, George 118,
120
Villa (Hammamet) 23,
120
Sebkha Kelbia 135
Sebkhet el-Mellah 189
Security 314–15
Sejnane 124, **134**, 296
Seldja Gorge 35, 216
Sened 217
Septimius Severus,
Emperor 48
Sfax 25, **164–9**, 170
airport 146, 215, 320
hotels 258
medina map 165
music festival 38
restaurants 283–4
World War II 58, 165
Sheltering Sky, The (film)
200
Shoes 296
Shopping 290–97
antiques 292–3
art galleries 292
carpets 237, 241,
292, 296
department stores 290
handicrafts 36–7,
292
how to pay 290
jewellery 293
ONAT shops 290, **292**
opening hours 290
perfume 294
shopping centres 291
state-owned shops
290, 292
what to buy 296–7
where to buy 290
see also Markets; Souks
Shrines, Phoenician 107
Sicca Venera *see* Le Kef
Sidi Abd el-Juada, tomb
(Jugurtha's Table) 221
Sidi Abdel Kader Mosque
(Hammamet) 118
Sidi Abdel Qadir el-
Djilani, tomb
(Kairouan) 240

Sidi Abou Zammaa el-Balaoui, tomb (Kairouan) 236

Sidi Abu el-Hasan, mausoleum (Sfax) 165

Sidi Ahmed ben Adjel 186

Sidi Ali ben Aissa 226

Sidi Ali ben Nasrallach 240

Sidi Ali Bey 56

Sidi Ali Mahjub, tomb (Ksour Essaf) 162

Sidi Amor Abbada, tomb (Kairouan) 236–7

Sidi ben Arous, tomb (Tunis) 76

Sidi Bou Ali, mausoleum (Nefta) 209

Sidi Bou Makhlouf, tomb (Le Kef) 214, 226

Sidi Bou Mendil, tomb (Hergla) 148

Sidi Bou Saïd 90, **96–7**, 100–1
  artists in 63, **98**
  beaches 95
  festivals 40
  hotels 253
  restaurants 279–80

Sidi Bou Saïd, tomb (Sidi Bou Saïd) 96

Sidi Bouzid **217**
  hotels 265
  restaurants 289

Sidi Brahim, tomb (Houmt Souk) 178

Sidi Daoud 109

Sidi Dar ben Dhahara, mausoleum (Tamerza) 211

Sidi Driss Hotel (Matmata) 34, 195

Sidi Driss Mosque (Gabès) 172

Sidi el-Ghariani, tomb (Kairouan) 234

Sidi el-Hanni Fort (Bizerte) 141

Sidi el-Kantaoui Festival (Hammam Sousse) 153

Sidi el-Mekki 143

Sidi el-Mezeri cemetery (Monastir) 154

Sidi Frej 172

Sidi Mechrig beach 134

Sidi Mehrez Mosque (Tunis) 67, **81**

Sidi Mehrez (patron of Tunis) 81, 157

Sidi Mostari, tomb (Bizerte) 141

Sidi Rais 108

Sidi Sahab Mosque (Kairouan) 214

Sidi Sheb'an, tomb (Sidi Bou Saïd) 97

Sidi Thabet, tomb (Tebourba) 131

Sidi Tuati, mausoleum (Tamerza) 211

Sidi Youssef 172

Sidi Youssef Mosque (Tunis) 68, **72**

Sienkiewicz, Henryk 35

Silences of the Palace, The (film) 34

Silk 160

Silver jewellery 293

Sirocco wind 43

Sisfari 28

Skanès 157
  beaches 149
  hotels 258

Skifa el-Kahla (Mahdia) 160

Slavery
  on Jerba 181, 182
  slave market, Kebili 206

Slimania Medersa (Tunis) **72**

Slimen Hamza Mosque (Mahdia) 161

Snack bars 266

Snorkelling see Diving and snorkelling

Society 14

SOCOPA see ONAT shops

Soft drinks 270, 271

Soliman 110

Souk Ahras 32

Souks **28**, 171, 291, **294–5**

Souks (cont.)
  Great Souk (Tunis) 68, **73**
  Kairouan 235
  Souk ar-Rab (Houmt Souk) 178
  Souk ar-Rabi (Sfax) 166
  Souk des Etoffes (Sfax) 166
  Souk el-Attarine (Tunis) 69, **76**
  Souk el-Berka (Tunis) 72
  Souk et-Trouk (Tunis) 68, **72**
  see also Markets; Shopping

Soups 267, 268

Sousse 145, **150–53**
  beaches 149
  catacombs 51
  hotels 258–9
  kasbah 25
  medina map 151
  restaurants 284–5
  spring festival 38
  World War II 58, 150

Southern Tunisia 190–211
  architecture 22
  character 191
  climate 43
  getting there 193
  map 192–3
  sights at a glance 192–3
  where to eat 286–8
  where to stay 261–4

Souvenirs
  birdcages 97
  dolls 153
  what to buy 296–7
  see also Handicrafts; Shopping

Spanish Fort (Bizerte) 141

Spas
  Jebel Oust 231
  Korbous 108–9

Special interest holidays 321

Speed limits 324

Spices 111, 198, 297
Spielberg, Steven 34, 35
Sponge Festival
    (Zarzis) 40
Sponges 172, 181, 296
Sport 302–3
    athletics 303
    basketball 303
    football 302
    handball 303
    hot-air ballooning 302
    judo 302, 303
    rallies 42, 217, 303,
    307
    sailing 303, 307
    swimming 302, 303
    volleyball 303
    windsurfing 303
    see also Activities for
    visitors.
Spring Festival (Sousse)
    38
Square of the Winds
    (Dougga) 229
Star Wars (film) 19,
    34–5, **195**
    Ksar Haddada 194, 195
    Matmata 172, 195
    Obiwan Kenobi's
    house 181
    Tataouine 194
State-owned shops 290
Steles 167
    Makthar 224
Still Life With Fish
    (Dhahak) 98
Stomach upsets 314–15
Storks 134
Student travellers 311
Sufetula *see* Sbeïtla
Sufism 96, 120, **209**
    in Le Kef 226
    marabouts 157
    in Nefta 192, 209
    Qadiriyya group 240
    zaouias 25
Suleyman the
    Magnificent 54
Summer Baths
    (Thuburbo Majus) 230
Sunni Islam 25, 26
Sunshine 43
Sunstroke 315

Sunway Holidays 321
Swimming 302, 303
    hotel pools 244
Symphony Music Festival
    (El-Jem) 299
Synagogues
    El-Ghriba (Jerba) 38,
    180, 183
Syracuse 111

T
Tabarka 54, 62, **126**
    coastline 21
    diving and snorkelling
    304
    festivals 40, 41
    hotels 255
    jazz festival 40, 299
    restaurants 281
Tajine 269
Tamerza 35, 62, **210–11**
    festival of the
    mountain oases 38
    hotels 210–11, **262**
    restaurants 287
Tanit and Baal Hammon
    sanctuary (Carthage)
    105, **106**
Tanit, goddess 110, 113,
    120
Tapestries 296
Tarafah 32
Tataouine 194
    festivals 38
    hotels 262–3
    restaurants 287–8
Tattoos, Berber 221
Taxis 323
    Central Tunisia 215
    The Sahel 146
    to/from airports
    320–21
    Tunis 326
Tea 270
Tebourba 131
Téboursouk 125, 129
    restaurants 289
Telephone services 318
Television 319
Tell region 21, 216
Temperatures 43
Temples, Roman
    Dougga 229

Temples, Roman (cont.)
    Makthar 224
    Temple of Apollo
    (Bulla Regis) 133
    Temple of Caelestis
    (Dougga) 215
    Temple des Eaux
    fountain (Zaghouan)
    231
    Temple of Jupiter,
    Juno and Minerva
    (Thuburbo Majus) 230
    Temple of Mercury
    (Thuburbo Majus) 230
    Temple to Aesculapius
    and Hygiei (Jebel
    Oust) 231
Tents, Bedouin 198, 201,
    202
    staying in 244, 246
Terracotta figures,
    Phoenician 107
Tertullian 32
Testour 123, **131**
    International *Malouf*
    Music Festival 40, 131,
    299
    restaurants 281
Textiles 18, 295
    Berber 30
    see also Carpets
TGM trains 86, 93, **327**
Thalassotherapy 306, 307
Thapsus, battle of 154
Theatre 299, 301
    festivals 40
Theatres
    Planet Oasis (Tozeur)
    208
    Roman 23
    Roman theatre
    (Haïdra) 221
    Roman theatre
    (Kasserine) 220
    Roman theatres (Utica)
    142
    Théâtre Municipal
    (Tunis) 82, 299
Theft 314
Thibarine 271
Thomas, Philippe 216
Three Medersas (Tunis)
    69, **72**

Thuburbo Majus **230**
Thysdrus *see* El-Jem
Tidjani 211
Tiles, ceramic 26
Tipping 290
Tlatli, Moufida 34
Toilets 315
Tolerance Edict 50
Tombs and mausoleums
　Aziza Othmana (Tunis) 69, **76**
　Habib Bourguiba Mausoleum (Monastir) **154**, 158–9
　Hammouda Pasha (Tunis) 76
　Mausoleum of the Flavii (Kasserine) 220
　Punic mausoleum (Makthar) 224
　Sidi Abd el-Juada (Jugurtha's Table) 221
　Sidi Abou Zammaa el-Balaoui (Kairouan) 236
　Sidi Abu el-Hasan (Sfax) 165
　Sidi Ali Mahjub (Ksour Essaf) 162
　Sidi Amor Abbada (Kairouan) 236–7
　Sidi Bou Ali (Nefta) 209
　Sidi Bou Makhlouf (Le Kef) 214, 226
　Sidi Bou Mendil (Hergla) 148
　Sidi Bou Saïd (Sidi Bou Saïd) 96
　Sidi Brahim (Houmt Souk) 178
　Sidi Dar ben Dhahara (Tamerza) 211
　Sidi el-Ghariani (Kairouan) 234
　Sidi Mostari (Bizerte) 141
　Sidi Sheb'an (Sidi Bou Saïd) 97
　Sidi Tuati (Tamerza) 211
　Tomb of the Unknown Soldier (Monastir) 154
　Tourbet el-Bey (Tunis)

Tombs and Mausoleums (cont.)
　78–9
　see also Cemeteries; Marabouts; Necropolis; Tophets, *Tourbets*; *Zaouias*
Tophets
　Carthage 105, **106**
　Makthar 224
Topless sunbathing 246
Toujane 174, 186
Toulon-Bizerte yacht race 40
Tour operators 321
Tourbets
　Tourbet of Aziza Othmana (Tunis) 69, **76**
　Tourbet el-Bey (Tunis) 78–9
　Tourbet of Hammouda Pasha (Tunis) 76
Tourism 19
Tourist information 247, 298, 311
Tourist zones 19, **246**
Towers *see* Castles and fortifications
Town Hall (Sfax) 166
Towns, traditional Arab 170–71
Tozeur 206, **208**
　driving tour 206–7
　film production 34, 206
　hotels 263
　International Oases Festival 41
　restaurants 288
Trade routes, ancient 130, 220, 224
Traditional shows 298
Traditions 14–15, **28–9**, 312–13
　Dar Jellouli Museum (Sfax) 168–9
　Guellala Museum of Popular Traditions 177, **182**
　Museum of Arts and Popular Traditions (Houmt Souk) 179

Traditions (cont.)
　Museum of Popular Arts and Traditions (Gabès) 172
　Museum of Popular Arts and Traditions (Sousse) 152
　Museum of Popular Arts and Traditions (Tozeur) 208
　Regional Museum of Popular Arts and Traditions (Le Kef) 226
Trains *see* Rail travel
Trajan, Emperor 216, 224
Trajan's Arch (Makthar) 224
Trajan's Bridge (near Béja) 131
Trams 326
Transport 320–27
　air travel 320–21, 323
　around Tunis 326–7
　buses 323
　overland travel 321
　rail travel 322, 323
　road travel 324–5
　sea travel 321
　taxis 323
Traveller's cheques 316
Treasury Building (Utica) 142
Tribes, Saharan 201
Troglodyte homes
　Jugurtha's Table 221
　pit houses 22, 34, **172**
　Sened 217
　staying in 244
Tuna fishing 109
Tunis 64–89
　airport 93
　beaches 95
　cinema 299
　climate 43
　history 55, 58, 65
　hotels 248–50
　map: the Medina street-by-street 68–9
　map: town centre 66–7
　Medina Festival 41, 298
　nightlife 299
　restaurants 272–5

Tunis (cont.)
  sights at a glance 67
  travelling around
    326–7
  Ville Nouvelle
    architecture 83
  see also Greater Tunis
Tunisair 320, 321
Tunisia
  architecture 22–5
  area 10
  arts 15–16
  calendar of events
    38–42
  character of 13
  Christian Tunisia 50–51
  climate 43
  culture 14–15
  economy 18
  film-makers in 19,
    34–5
  foreign affairs 17
  handicrafts 36–7
  history 45–59
  independence 16
  Islam in 26–7
  landscape and wildlife
    20–21
  literature and music
    32–3
  map 10–11
  politics 16–17
  population 14
  society 14
  tourism 19
  traditions 14–15, **28–9**
  women in 17–18
Tunisia Rally 303
Tunisian Constitutional
  Party see Destour
Turki, Yahia 15–16, 98
Turks, Ottoman 53–4
Tyre 46, 111

U

Ulysses Festival (Houmt
  Souk) 40
Ulysses and the Sirens
  (mosaic) 225
Umm et-Turkia Mosque
  (El-May) 180
Ummayad rule 32
Upenna 153

Uthina see Oudna
Utica 123, **142**
  Roman capital 47, 48

V

Valerian, Emperor 105
Vandals, the **49**, 102
VAT refunds 293
Vegetarians 267
Veils see Hijab
Venus, Temple of
  (Makthar) 224
Villa de la Volière
  (Carthage) 103
Villas, Roman
  Bulla Regis 132–3
  Carthage 103
Ville Nouvelle (Tunis)
  77, 82, 86–9
  architecture 22, **83**
  development of 56
Virgil 106, 225
Virgil and the Muses
  (mosaic) 225
Visas 310
Volleyball 303

W

Wahbis 180
Walking 327
Walking tours, Tunis
  72–3
Walls
  defensive (Ribat,
    Monastir) 156
  Ksour 196
  medina walls
    (Kairouan) 234
  medina walls (Sousse)
    152
  in traditional Arab
    towns 170
Water 270
Water buffalo 137
Water parks 300
  Acqua Palace (Port el-
    Kantaoui) 148
Water-skiing 304
Waterfalls, Tamerza 210,
  211
Waxworks, Guellala
  Museum of Popular
  Traditions 177, **182**

Weaving 295
  Kairouan carpets 241
Weddings 28–9
Wells 203
  Bir Barouta (Kairouan)
    234–5
Wheat Festival (Béja) 41
When to visit 310
Where to eat 266–89
  Central Tunisia 288–9
  Greater Tunis and Cap
    Bon peninsula 275–80
  Jerba and the
    Medenine Area 285–6
  Northern Tunisia
    280–81
  The Sahel 282–5
  Southern Tunisia
    286–8
  Tunis 272–5
  see also Cafés; Food
    and drink; Restaurants
Where to stay 244–65
  Central Tunisia 264–5
  Greater Tunis and Cap
    Bon peninsula 250–53
  Jerba and the
    Medenine Area 259–61
  Northern Tunisia
    254–5
  The Sahel 255–9
  Southern Tunisia
    261–4
  Tunis 248–50
Whirling dervishes 209
Wildlife 20–21
  coral reef **127**, 304
  Ichkeul National Park
    136–7
  Saharan 200
  Tunisian birds 136
  see also Birdwatching;
    National parks; Zoos
Windsurfing 303, 304
Wine
  festivals 41
  production 120, 123
  what to drink 271
Winter Baths (Thuburbo
  Majus) 230
Women
  Bedouin 201
  Berber 30–31

Women (cont.)
position of 17–18
segregation of 169
Women's Day 40
Women at the Baths
(painting) 173
Women travellers 314
Woodwork 37, 297
World War I 56
World War II 57, **58**, 140
Battle of Kasserine 220
cemetery, Haffouz 240
Le Kef 226
monument, Place des
Martyrs (Sousse) 150
Sidi Bouzid 217
Wright, Frank Lloyd 120

Y

Yachting *see* Sailing
Yasmine Hammamet 119,
120
hotels 251–3
marina 146, 149
Youssef, Sidi 72
Youth hostels 246, 247

Z

Zaafrane 207
hotels 263–4

Zaghouan **231**
Zaouias 24, **25**
Bizerte 141
The Sahel 145
Sidi Abdel Qadir el-
Djilani (Kairouan) 240
Sidi Abou Zammaa el-
Balaoui (Kairouan) 236
Sidi Ali Mahjub (Ksour
Essaf) 162
Sidi Amor Abbada
(Kairouan) 236–7
Sidi ben Arous (Tunis)
76
Sidi Bou Makhlouf (Le
Kef) 226
Sidi Brahim (Houmt
Souk) 178
Sidi el-Ghariani
(Kairouan) 234
Sidi Sahab (Kairouan)
236
Sidi Sheb'an (Sidi Bou
Saïd) 97
Tebourba 131
Zaouia Zakkak
(Sousse) 151
see also Cemeteries;
Marabouts; Tombs and
mausoleums

Zarbia carpets 36
Zarziha Rock (Korbous)
108
Zarzis **186**, 189
hotels 261
restaurants 286
Sponge Festival 40
tourism in 176, 186
Zarzis peninsula 176, 177
Zeffirelli, Franco 35, 156
Zembra, island of **109**,
227
Zembretta, island of 109,
227
Zirid dynasty 53
ceramics 114
coins 240
Zitouna Mosque
(Kairouan) 237
Zitouna theological
university 56–7
Zitouni, Ali 302
Zoos
Belvedere Park (Tunis)
87, 300
Park Friguia (Bou
Ficha) **153**, 300
Tozeur 208
Zrir tunisienne 269

Acknowledgments

DORLING KINDERSLEY would like to thank the following people whose contribution and assistance have made the preparation of this book possible.

PUBLISHER
Douglas Amrine

PUBLISHING MANAGER
Kate Poole

MANAGING EDITOR
Vicki Ingle

SENIOR EDITOR
Jacky Jackson

CARTOGRAPHY
Caspar Morris

DTP DESIGNER
Conrad Van Dyke

CONSULTANT
Mike Gerrard

FACTCHECKER
David Bond

PROOFREADER
Stewart Wild

INDEXER
Helen Peters

Special Assistance
WIEDZA AND ŻYCIE would like to thank the following persons and organizations for their help in the preparation of this guide:
Faical Aouni
Zbigniew Dybowski, Biuro Podróży Kredytowa 2, Warszawa
Abdelfettach Gaida
Raouf Ghazzai, Odyssée Resort, Zarzis
Pawel Kulesza, ONTT in Warsaw
Joanna Nowowiejska-Moskal, ONTT in Warsaw
Startours, Hammam-Sousse
Katarzyna Wierzba, ONTT in Warsaw

The Publisher would also like to thank all persons and organizations for their permission to reproduce photographs of their property and for allowing the use of photographs from their archives.
Bijouterie Bel Hadj Younes Frères, Midoun
Bijouterie du Musée el-Kobba, Sousse
Corbis/Agencja Free in Warsaw (Maciej Sztyk, Łukasz Wyrzykowski, Aleksandra Żymełka)
Centre Culturel d'Animation Touristique Dar Houidi, Nefta
La Grotte, Souk Erebaa, Sousse
Military Museum of the Mareth Line, Mareth
Musée Dar Essid, Sousse
Musée Guellala, Jerba
Ocean-Photos (Carlos Minguell)
Scoop Organisation (Mourad Mathari)
Tunisair in Warsaw
ZOOM s.c.

PICTURE CREDITS
t=top; tl=top left; tc=top centre; tr=top right; c=centre; cl=centre left; cr=centre right; cb=centre below; ca=centre above; clb=centre left below; crb=centre right below; cla=centre left above; cra=centre right above; b=bottom; bl=bottom left; br=bottom right, bla=bottom left above; bra=bottom right above; blb=bottom left below; bcb=bottom centre below; brb=bottom right below; bcl=bottom centre left; bcr=bottom centre right; ra=right above; la=left above.
CORBIS: 26-27, 34c, 35t, 39ca, 39cr, 39cb, 46t, 47t, 48t, 49dp, 50cla, 53t, 53c, 55t, 55c, 55b, 56t, 53c, 56cb, 56bl, 56br, 57c, 57b, 58t, 58c, 59ca, 81c, 102b, 106bl, 143br, 173t, 173b, 199bl, 209c, 220b, 303c, 303b; Shean Adey 137cb; Theo Allofs 137ca; Dave Bartruff 33b; Philip de Bay 27br; Nial Benvie 135clb; Yann Arthus-Bertrand 10, 11t, 11b, 196t, 204-205, 229t; Michael de Boys 39b; Margareth Courtney-Clarke 30t, 30b, 31b; Nigel J. Dennis 135cla, 135clb; Bernard and Catherine Desjeux 42t, 114-115, 219b; Rick Ergenbright 38c, 40b, 270; D. Robert Franz 135bl, 137t, 227b; Stephen Frink 127bl; Lowell Georgia 18b; Richard Hamilton Smith 60-61; Klaus Honal 21ca; Erick Hosking 135br; Peter Johnson 136cb; Wolfgang Kaehler 181c; Steve Kaufman 227t; 227clb; Douglas Kirkland 35b; David Lees 46c; Michael S. Lewis 199cr; Peter Lillie 227clb; Araldo de Luca 44; Francis G. Mayer 32t; Francoise de Mulder 39t; Christine Osborne 110t; Fulvio Roiter 31ca; Hans Georg Roth 26b, 41b, 173clb, 173crb, 221t; Kevin Schafer 20c; Michael T. Sedman 306t; Jonathan Selkowitz 95b; Michael Setboun 183cla, 183clb, 183cr, 183br; Sean Sexton 56ca; Monika Smith 26lw; William Thompson 199ca; Roger Tidman 136ca, 227ca; Ruggero Vanni 25c; Tim De Waele 302c; Patrick Ward 30c, 30-31; John Watkins 135cra, 136t; Kurt-Michael Westermann 173cra; Nik Wheeler 149b, 183bl; Martin B. Withers 135t; Roger Wood 13t, 27bl, 31t, 46b, 54cl, 220c, 231c; Inge Yspeert 38b, 191, 203br;
PIOTR KIEDROWSKI: 77b, 97c, 266b
ANDRZEJ LISOWSKI: 27tr, 35c, 41t, 42b, 78b, 98cra, 98br, 142t, 143t, 143ca, 203bl, 209b, 292c, 298ca, 298cb
GRZEGORZ MICUŁA: 5cl, 14c, 17c, 20cl, 148br, 179b, 193, 198b, 199t, 206b, 247t, 270cla, 324ca; CARLOS MINGUELL: 127cl, 127tr, 127cl, 127cr, 127br; IZABELLA MOŚCICKA: 93b, 115c, 154t, 154cb, 158-159, 244t, 304b, 318c, 319t, 320cb, 323t; ROBERT G. PASIECZNY: 17b; SOCOPA: 299b
TUNISAIR: 320b; ZOOM S.C.: 268 bra, 268 bcl, 268dc, 268dc, 268dcr, 268brb; ANDRZEJ ZYGMUNTOWICZ AND IRENEUSZ WINNICKI: 268tl, 268tr, 268cla, 268cra, 268clb, 268crb, 268bl, 269tl, 269tc, 269tr, 269, 269cr, 269bla, 269bra, 269blb, 269bcb, 269brb.
JACKET: FRONT: ROBERT HARDING.COM: D.Beatty bl.
All other images Dorling Kindersley
For further information see:
www.dkimages.com

Glossary

Abbasids: Rulers of the Arab Empire from AD 749–1258.

Aghlabids: Ninth-century Arab dynasty that ruled Tunisia from Kairouan.

Aisha: the third and favourite wife of the Prophet Mohammed, who unsuccessfully opposed the fourth caliph, Ali.

Al-Hasan and Al-Husayn: sons of Ali, revered as Shia martyrs.

Ali: Ali ibn Abi Talib, the fourth orthodox caliph, cousin and son-in-law of the Prophet Mohammed, husband of his daughter Fatima. He originated the greatest split in the history of Islam – into Sunni and Shia Muslims. According to the Shia tradition he was endowed with spiritual gifts and the power to perform miracles. To Shias he is virtually god incarnate.

Allah: the highest and the only god in the Muslim pantheon, the creator of the world and its people. He is believed to be omnipotent, omnipresent and merciful. He has 99 names by which he may be addressed.

alloucha: carpets produced in beige and brown, or black and white colours with a medallion pattern in a shape of a stylized octagon with floral design.

Almoravids: Berber dynasty from Morocco that invaded Tunisia in the 12th century.

aysha: the first tattoo given to a child soon after birth. It is usually placed on the cheeks or on the forehead.

Baal Hammon: the most important god in the Phoenician (later Punic) pantheon, often identified with Saturn.

bab: gate.

balgha: traditional slippers with flattened toe-ends.

baraka: divine blessing passed down from parent to child; the power to work miracles, may be obtained by pilgrimage.

basilica: Roman administration building, early Christian church.

basmala: a popular Muslim expression – "Bismi Allah ar-rahmani ar-rahim" (In the name of Allah the Beneficient, the Merciful). Every *sura* or chapter of the Koran begins with it. Uttered by Muslims prior to any activity such as meals or travel. It is also the most popular ornamental motif used on ceramics and in architecture, etc.

Berbers: non-Arab, indigenous inhabitants of Tunisia with their own distinctive language, culture and customs.

bey: title of a provincial governor in the Ottoman Empire. During the Ottoman era it was used by the Tunisian rulers.

bir: well.

borj: turret or tower that is set in the walls of fortified houses and castles.

boukha: a clear alcoholic spirit made from figs.

brik: Tunisian snack, a kind of pastry.

burnous: hooded cloak made of thick wool, worn by Arab men.

caliph: Muslim chief, title designating Mohammed's successor.

capitol: Roman town's principal temple.

caravanserai: see *fondouk*.

chamsa: hand of Fatima – a talisman that symbolizes five pillars of faith, five daily prayers, five holy nights, etc.

chechia: red cap with silk tassle.

chicha: hookah or hubble-bubble pipe used for smoking tobacco.

chorba: delicious soup with noodles, normally made of chicken stock.

chott: salt lake or marshland.

corsairs: pirates, active on the North African coast from the 16th to the 19th century.

couscous: a dish made of steamed semolina that is served as the main course with boiled mutton, vegetables and spices.

dar: house, palace or residence.

dawwar: a circle of tents with which tribesmen surrounded their chieftain's abode, creating a mini-state. It was sovereign and autonomous.

deglet ennour: a variety of dates.

diwan: sultan's privy council in the former Turkish state, alternatively spelled divan.

djellaba: wide, spacious cloak worn by men in Arab countries.

driba: an outer entrance room in a *dar*, used for receiving callers.

emir: governor or military leader.

erg: expanse of desert sand.

Fatima: Mohammed's only daughter and the wife of Ali. In the Muslim tradition she originated the Fatimid dynasty. Fatima is the subject of many legends and, with time, this has given rise to a belief in her protective powers.

Fatimids: Muslim dynasty founded by Fatima that replaced the Aghlabids and ruled Tunisia from AD 909 to 1171.

fondouk: a type of inn, also known as a *caravanserai*, that was used as a hotel by journeying merchant caravans.

fouta: cotton towel provided in a hammam.

fula: a triangular tattoo placed on a Berber woman's chin.

gargotte: small, inexpensive restaurant serving basic food.

garum: fish sauce.

ghorfa: originally a *ksar*'s granary. The cells, built cylindrically around a courtyard, later began to serve as dwellings.

guetiffa: thick-pile carpets used by Berber tribes.

hadith: tale of deeds and teachings of the Prophet Mohammed as reported by his companions; source of religious knowledge for Muslims.

hadj: pilgrimage to Mecca, one of the five pillars of Islam.

hamada: rocky desert.

hammam: public steam bath.

Hanefite: one of four schools of orthodox Sunni Islam.

harissa: spicy sauce made of peppers, tomatoes, olive oil and salt.

hauli: an attire worn by Berber women, consisting of a draped length of cloth held by a belt and fastened at the shoulder.

hela: a Berber pin made of silver; often believed to have magic properties.

henna: a dye obtained from privet leaves which is used by the Berbers for marking the skin.

hijab: veil or headscarf worn by Muslim women in the presence of strangers.

hijra: emigration of Mohammed and his early followers from Mecca to Medina in AD 622. It is also the name of the Muslim calendar.

houch: courtyard of a troglodyte house carved in soft rock.

Husaynids: dynasty that ruled Tunisia from 1705 to 1957.

Ibadites: Offshoot of Kharajite sect found on Jerba and also in parts of Algeria.

Ifriqiyya: term used to describe Africa by the Romans.

imam: a learned Muslim cleric, prophet and religious leader of the Shia, caliph, spiritual and lay leader of Islam.

Isa: Islamic name for Jesus Christ, who is regarded by Muslims as a noble and honourable messenger who was sent to reveal to the world the coming of the Prophet Mohammed.

jami mosque: from the Arabic "jam", meaning to "gather things". Usually the Great Mosque, it was initially the only mosque with a *minbar*.

kamounia: an aromatic meat stew.

kasbah: castle, fortress.

Khadija: the first wife of the Prophet Mohammed.

Kharijites: early sect of Islam which won Berber support.

khutba: traditional sermon preached on Fridays by the *imam*.

Koran: the holy book of Islam.

koubba: a dome that often covers the tomb of a marabout.

ksar: fortified Berber village.

louage: shared taxi.

Maghreb: term used to describe northwestern section of Africa that includes Morocco, Algeria and Tunisia.

mahari: camelback expedition to the desert lasting several days. Those taking part often sleep in Bedouin tents or *ghorfas*.

mahdi: in the Arab tradition "the One who is led by God" – a spiritual leader endowed with power to bring about religious revival, and restore order.

Malekite: school of orthodox Sunni Islam founded in the 8th century.

malouf: Tunisian folk music.

marabout: Islamic holy man and also his place of burial.

mashrabiyya: wooden latticework panel used in the windows of mosques and houses.

nedersa: residential Islamic school. A type of Muslim college that is often built around a courtyard and attached to a mosque.

medina: traditional Arab town or a town's oldest part.

Medina: also known as Madinat an-Nabi (Town of the Prophet), or Madinat el-Munawwara (City of Light). It is situated 300 km (186 miles) north of Mecca. The Prophet and his followers found refuge there after fleeing Mecca.

menzel: a traditional fortified farm compound.

mergoum: lightweight carpets of Berber origin with vivid colours and geometric patterns.

mihrab: niche found in a mosque that points in the direction of Mecca, and therefore prayer.

minaret: tower of a mosque from which the muezzin calls the faithful to prayer.

minbar: pulpit in a mosque, from which the *imam* delivers his homily during Friday prayers.

Mohammed: (*c*.570–632), founder of Islam and creator of the Arab state. He experienced his first revelations at the age of about 40 (AD 610). These are collected together in the Koran.

mosque: Arab place of worship and a house of prayer. It usually consists of a courtyard, a minaret and a prayer-hall.

muezzin: person who calls the faithful to prayer from the minaret. In the early days of Islam the calls were made from the roofs of mosques.

mukarnas: a distinctive ornamental element of the interior design in Muslim architecture (in the shape of a stalactite).

mullah: a Muslim theologian and scholar. Also a teacher, and an interpreter of religious law and Islamic doctrines.

Muradids: hereditary line of beys that ruled Tunisia during the 17th century.

Musa: The Arabic name for Moses. The Koran presents him as one of many predecessors of Mohammed.

oued: river that is often dry.

Phoenicians: seafaring and trading nation that dominated the Mediterranean in the 1st century BC; the founders of Carthage.

Protectorate: period of French control over Tunisia from 1881–1957.

Punic: Phoenician culture.

qibla: the direction (towards the Al-Kaaba temple in Mecca) in which Muslims turn when saying their prayers; in mosques it is usually indicated by the *mihrab*.

Ramadan: the ninth month of the Muslim lunar calendar (numbering 354 days and eight hours). It is also a period of fast.

reg: stony desert.

ribat: fortified Muslim monastery that is surrounded by defensive walls including watchtowers. Inside is the prayer hall (and sometimes a mosque).

salat: obligatory prayer said five times a day. It is one of the five pillars of Islam.

sa'alik: knight errant of the desert, an exile expelled by the tribes. They congregated into groups in order to survive.

sawm: fast during Ramadan, one of the five pillars of Islam.

sebkha: salt flat.

serir: stony desert.

shahada: a proclamation of faith, one of the five pillars of Islam.

shashi: warm or hot sirocco wind.

Shia: the smaller branch of Islam. Its followers regard Ali as the true *imam*.

sidi: Muslim leader, sir. This title is accorded to a Muslim of noble birth or outstanding merits.

sirat: in Arab literature a knightly episode recounting historic events, fantasy or legendary tales and romances.

souk: market place or covered bazaar that is organized into areas according to the goods on sale.

Sufi: ascetic sect of Islam which places an emphasis on spiritual development rather than on a study of the Koran.

Suleyman: in Muslim tradition Suleyman is endowed with magic powers; he knows the language of birds, is able to control the wind, and rules over the earth and air spirits.

Sunni: the main branch of Islam, created by followers of the Ummayyad caliphate.

sura: verse of the Koran.

Tanit: goddess in the Punic pantheon associated with the cult of Baal Hammon. She is also the patron of Carthage.

tesserae: small pieces of brick, glass or marble smoothed round the edges and used for laying mosaics.

tourbet: mausoleum.

vikala: a stately *caravanserai* for wealthy merchants.

zakat: the giving of alms to the poor, one of the five pillars of Islam.

zarbia: knotted carpets with geometric patterns, produced in a mixture of red, green and blue colours.

zaouia: building – a dwelling place of people who devote their lives to spiritual practices, a sanctuary of Sufi mystics.

zhirak: a strong tobacco mix smoked in a *chicha*.

Phrase Book

IN EMERGENCY

Help!	Au secours!	oh se**koor**
Stop!	Arrêtez!	aret-**ay**
Call a doctor!	Appelez un médecin!	apuh-**lay** uñ med**sañ**
Call an ambulance!	Appelez une ambulance!	apuh-**lay** oon oñboo-**loñs**
Call the police!	Appelez la police!	apuh-**lay** lah poh-**lees**
Call the fire department!	Appelez les pompiers!	apuh-**lay** leh poñ-**peeyay**
Where is the nearest telephone?	Où est le téléphone le plus proche?	oo ay luh tehlehfon luh ploo prosh
Where is the nearest hospital?	Où est l'hôpital le plus proche?	oo ay l'**opee**tal luh ploo prosh

COMMUNICATION ESSENTIALS

Yes	Oui	wee
No	Non	noñ
Please	S'il vous plaît	seel voo **play**
Thank you	Merci	mer-**see**
Excuse me	Excusez-moi	exkoo-**zay** mwah
Hello	Bonjour	boñ**zhoor**
Goodbye	Au revoir	oh ruh-**vwar**
Good night	Bonsoir	boñ-**swar**
Morning	Le matin	matañ
Afternoon	L'après-midi	l'apreh-**meedee**
Evening	Le soir	swar
Yesterday	Hier	eeyehr
Today	Aujourd'hui	oh-zhoor-**dwee**
Tomorrow	Demain	duh**mañ**
Here	Ici	ee-**see**
There	Là	lah
What?	Quel, quelle?	kel, kel
When?	Quand?	koñ
Why?	Pourquoi?	poor-**kwah**
Where?	Où?	oo

USEFUL PHRASES

How are you?	Comment allez-vous?	kom-moñ tal**ay voo**
Very well, thank you.	Très bien, merci.	treh byañ, mer-**see**
Pleased to meet you.	Enchanté de faire votre connaissance.	oñshoñ-**tay** duh fehr votr kon-ay-**sans**
See you soon.	A bientôt.	byañ-**toh**
That's fine	Voilà qui est parfait	vwalah kee ay par**fay**
Where is/are...?	Où est/sont...?	oo ay/soñ
How far is it to...?	Combien de kilomètres d'ici à...?	kom-**byañ** duh keelo-metr d'ee-see ah
Which way to...?	Quelle est la direction pour...?	kel ay lah deer-ek-**syoñ** poor
Do you speak English?	Parlez-vous anglais?	par-**lay** voo oñg-**lay**
I don't understand.	Je ne comprends pas.	zhuh nuh kom-**proñ** pah
Could you speak slowly please?	Pouvez-vous parler moins vite s'il vous plaît?	poo-**vay** voo par-**lay** mwañ veet seel voo play
I'm sorry.	Excusez-moi.	exkoo-**zay** mwah

USEFUL WORDS

big	grand	groñ
small	petit	puh-**tee**
hot	chaud	show
cold	froid	frwah
good	bon	boñ
bad	mauvais	moh-**veh**
enough	assez	assay
well	bien	byañ
open	ouvert	oo-**ver**
closed	fermé	fer-**meh**
left	gauche	gohsh
right	droit	drwah
straight ahead	tout droit	too drwah
near	près	preh
far	loin	lwañ
up	en haut	oñ oh
down	en bas	oñ bah
early	de bonne heure	duh bon **urr**
late	en retard	oñ ruh-**tar**
entrance	l'entrée	l'on-**tray**
exit	la sortie	sor-**tee**
toilet	les toilettes, les WC	twah-**let**, vay-**see**
free, unoccupied	libre	leebr
free, no charge	gratuit	grah-**twee**

MAKING A TELEPHONE CALL

I'd like to place a long-distance call.	Je voudrais faire un interurbain.	zhuh voo-dreh fehr uñ añter-oorbañ
I'll try again later.	Je rappelerai plus tard.	zhuh rapel-**eray** ploo tar
Can I leave a message?	Est-ce que je peux laisser un message?	es-**keh** zhuh puh leh-**say** uñ mehsa**z'**
Hold on.	Ne quittez pas, s'il vous plaît.	nuh kee-**tay** pah seel voo play
Could you speak up a little please?	Pouvez-vous parler un peu plus fort?	poo-**vay** voo par-**lay** uñ puh ploo fo.
local call	la communication locale	komoonikah-**syoñ** low-**kal**

SHOPPING

How much does this cost?	C'est combien s'il vous plaît?	say kom-**byañ** seel voo play
I would like ...	je voudrais...	zhuh voo-**dray**
Do you have?	Est-ce que vous avez?	es-kuh voo zavay
I'm just looking.	Je regarde seulement.	zhuh ruh**gar**, suhl**moñ**
Do you take credit cards?	Est-ce que vous acceptez les cartes de crédit?	es-**kuh** voo zaksept-**ay** leh kart duh kreh-**dee**
Do you take travellers' checks?	Est-ce que vous acceptez les chèques de voyage?	es-**kuh** voo zaksept-**ay** leh shek duh vway**azh**
What time do you open/close?	A quelle heure vous êtes ouvert/fermé?	ah kel urr voo zet oo-**ver**/fer-**may**
This one.	Celui-ci.	suhl-wee-**see**
That one.	Celui-là.	suhl-wee-**lah**
expensive	cher	shehr
cheap	pas cher, bon marché	pah shehr, boñ mar-**shay**
size, clothes	la taille	tye

TYPES OF SHOPS

bakery	la boulangerie	booloñ-**zhuree**
bank	la banque	boñk
chemist	la pharmacie	farmah-**see**
grocery	l'alimentation	alee-moñta-**syoñ**
hairdresser	le coiffeur	kwa**fuhr**
market	le marché	marsh-**ay**
newsstand	le magasin de journaux	maga-**zañ** duh zhoor-**no**
post office	la poste	pohst
supermarket	le supermarché	soo pehr-**marshay**
tobacconist	le tabac	tabah

SIGHTSEEING

bus station	la gare routière	gahr roo-tee-**yehr**
library	la bibliothèque	beeb**leeo**-tek
museum	le musée	moo-**zay**
tourist information office	les renseignements touristiques, le syndicat d'initiative	roñsayn-**moñ** too-rees-**teek**, sandee-ka d'eenee-syat**eev**
train station	la gare (SNCF)	gahr (es-en-say-**ef**)
public holiday	jour férié	zhoor fehree-**ay**

STAYING IN A HOTEL

Do you have a vacant room?	Est-ce que vous avez une chambre?	es-kuh voo-**zavay** oon shambr
double room, with double bed	la chambre à deux personnes, avec un grand lit	shambr ah duh pehr-**son** avek un gronñ lee
twin room	la chambre à deux lits	shambr ah duh lee
single room	la chambre à une personne	shambr ah oon pehr-**son**
room with a bath, shower	la chambre avec salle de bains, une douche	shambr avek sal duh bañ, oon doosh
I have a reservation.	J'ai fait une réservation.	zhay fay oon rayzehrva-**syoñ**

EATING OUT

Have you got a table?	Avez-vous une table libre?	avay-**voo** oon tahbl leebr
I want to reserve a table.	Je voudrais réserver une table.	zhuh voo-**dray** rayzehr-**vay** oon tahbl
The bill please.	L'addition s'il vous plaît.	l'adee-**syoñ** seel voo play